NO SEA TOO ROUGH

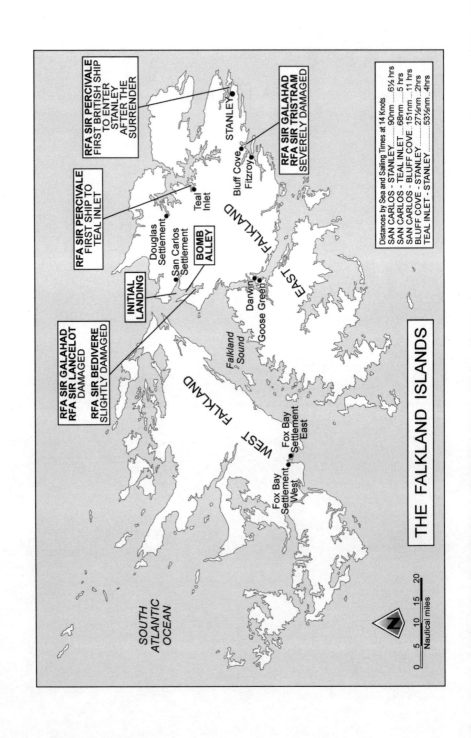

THE FALKLAND ISLANDS

RFA SIR PERCIVALE
FIRST BRITISH SHIP
TO ENTER
STANLEY
AFTER THE
SURRENDER

RFA SIR GALAHAD
RFA SIR TRISTRAM
SEVERELY DAMAGED

RFA SIR PERCIVALE
FIRST SHIP TO
TEAL INLET

RFA SIR GALAHAD
RFA SIR LANCELOT
DAMAGED
RFA SIR BEDIVERE
SLIGHTLY DAMAGED

INITIAL
LANDING

BOMB
ALLEY

STANLEY

Bluff Cove
Fitzroy

Teal
Inlet

Douglas
Settlement

San Carlos
Settlement

Darwin
Goose Green

Falkland
Sound

EAST
FALKLAND

WEST FALKLAND

Fox Bay
Settlement
East

Fox Bay
Settlement
West

SOUTH
ATLANTIC
OCEAN

Distances by Sea and Sailing Times at 14 Knots
SAN CARLOS - STANLEY ....90nm ....6½ hrs
SAN CARLOS - TEAL INLET ....68nm ....5 hrs
SAN CARLOS - BLUFF COVE ....151nm ......11 hrs
BLUFF COVE - STANLEY ....27½nm 2hrs
TEAL INLET - STANLEY ....53½nm 4hrs

N

0   5   10   15   20
Nautical miles

NO SEA TOO ROUGH

The Royal Fleet Auxiliary in the Falklands War
The Untold Story

GEOFF PUDDEFOOT

Foreword by HRH The Earl of Wessex

Today's Royal Navy moves, courtesy RFA.
RFA motto (strictly unofficial)

CHATHAM PUBLISHING
LONDON

Dedication

To the men of the Royal Fleet Auxiliary and especially those who never came home again, this book is respectfully dedicated.

Comment is free, but facts are sacred
C P Scott, *Manchester Guardian*, 5 May 1921

Copyright © Geoff Puddefoot 2007

First published in Great Britain in 2007 by
Chatham Publishing
Lionel Leventhal Ltd,
Park House, 1 Russell Gardens,
London NW11 9NN

Distributed in the United States of America by
MBI Publishing Company
Galtier Plaza, Suite 200, 380 Jackson Street,
St Paul, MN 55101-3885, USA

A CIP record for this book
is available from the British Library

ISBN 978-1-86176-314-3

Designed and Typeset by MATS Typesetters, Leigh-on-Sea, Essex
Printed and bound in Great Britain by CPD (Wales) Ebbw Vale

Contents

BAGSHOT PARK

April 2007 marks the 25th Anniversary of the Falklands Conflict, when the men of the Royal Fleet Auxiliary Service engaged in their greatest logistical operation of the post-war era.

There have been many books written about the conflict, but this book tells the remarkable story of the ships and men of the Royal Fleet Auxiliary, and their service in the South Atlantic, of which they can be justifiably proud.

Of the twenty three ships of the Royal Fleet Auxiliary at the time, twenty were part of the Task Force in the South Atlantic. These were the tankers, store and ammunition ships, and the LSL's (Landing Ship Logistic) including the ill-fated Sir Galahad and Sir Tristram, which tragically became casualties at Bluff Cove.

In addition the Service took under its wing the *ships taken up from trade*, the tankers, the ferries and a variety of vessels all of which had officers and men of the Royal Fleet Auxiliary onboard to enable fleet communications, replenishment at sea and helicopter operations.

Congratulations and thanks must go to Geoffrey Puddefoot, the author, for taking so much time and trouble to ensure that the vital role the Royal Fleet Auxiliary played in the Falklands Conflict has now been properly recorded. Equally thanks must go to Rex Cooper and the Royal Fleet Auxiliary Association for making this publication possible and thereby remembering the part played by so many of its members.

HRH The Earl of Wessex KG, KCVO, ADC
Patron, Royal Fleet Auxiliary Association

PREFACE: RFA FALKLANDS 25

THERE CAN BE no doubt that the Falklands conflict was a defining moment in the history of the RFA Service. The events of 1982 triggered many questions about our equipment, training, capability and status, and while some of these questions will rumble on, I have only to look around me to see that the majority of the hard-won lessons have been learned and that the results are clearly visible in the ships and people of today.

While I have no doubt that the RFA is a better service for the experiences of 25 years ago, I also have no doubt that we owe a great deal to the men who delivered and transported the vital material of war in the face of extreme weather and violence. Their devotion to duty, their determination, their toil and their sacrifice are remembered with great respect and when you read their personal recollections in this book, you might bear in mind that many have served, and continue to serve, with distinction in the many operations and conflicts since then.

The men and women of the RFA have risen to the challenges of war and peace in the demanding and unforgiving environment of the sea. Their story is not often told, but it is a good one and this book tells part of that story in the words of those who were there in the South Atlantic in 1982. I am immensely proud of our contribution and our achievements.

Commodore R C Thornton RFA

ACKNOWLEDGEMENTS

I WOULD LIKE to take this opportunity to thank the following people for their help, advice and personal recollections. I would also like to express a special thank you to Lesley Frampton, who drew the maps that illustrate this book; without them part of the story would be missing.

Captain R Allen DACOS, RFA
Mr M Andrews, ex Royal Marines
Mr J Blamey
Mr D Bolton CPO (C), RFA (retd)
Colonel M Bowles MBE, 20 Port and Maritime Regiment, RCT
Dr K Bunten
1st Officer (X) N Colvill, RFA Fleet Media
Captain R A Cooper OBE, RFA (retd)
Chief Officer (X) Mike Day RFA (retd)
Lt Col R Dickey RA
Captain J B Dickinson OBE, RFA (retd)
Captain M Farley RFA (retd)
Mr R Fearnley
1st Officer (X) G Ferguson RFA (retd)
Chief Officer (X) D Gerrard RFA (retd)
Captain G R Green DSC, RFA (retd)
Mr G Haines
Dr E J Harrison RFA (retd)
Captain J Hobbs RFA (retd)
Mr M Hobbs RFA (retd)
Mr A Jones SAMA (Wales)
Captain S Jones RFA

CPO (D) M Jordan RFA
1st Officer (SE) J Keller RFA
Chief Officer (X) J Kelly RFA
Chief Officer (X) J Kilner RFA (retd)
Mr K Lawrence RNSTS
SGIA B Lester RFA (retd)
Rev P J McCarthy RFA (retd)
Commodore J Miller RN
Chief Officer (X) I Moores RFA
Chief Officer (X) G Mortimore RFA (retd)
Chief Officer (X) P Nelson RFA (retd)
1st Officer (SE) D Palin RFA
Captain A Pitt DSO, RFA (retd)
Captain S Redmond OBE, RFA (retd)
Captain P J G Roberts DSO, RFA (retd)
Mr R Robins PSTO(N)
Mr P Robinson
Commodore R Thorn CBE, RFA (retd)
Lt Mike Tidd, A Flight Commander, 845 NAS (retd)
Mr T Tomkins
Chief Officer (SE) M Troman RFA
Captain B Waters OBE, RFA (retd)
Mr G Wilson DGST (N) (retd)

CHAPTER ONE

INTRODUCTION

T HIS IS A BOOK about a war, the Falklands War, and some of the men and ships that helped the British to win it. It is not about the political ramifications or motivations behind what happened in the South Atlantic, nor is it about the battles fought and won by the servicemen who sailed and yomped and, in some cases, died on those barren islands, thousands of miles from home and family.

No, this is a book about the forgotten men, the officers and ratings of the Royal Fleet Auxiliary, the service whose back the Royal Navy rides on. They're used to being forgotten because, that, I suppose, goes with the job.

They supply the fuel and lubricating oil, the bombs and bullets, the beans and bacon, the mail and toilet rolls that keep the Royal Navy afloat and its usual efficient self.

Everything a Royal Navy vessel uses comes to it courtesy of the RFA, especially if that vessel is in the middle of a shooting war. And during that southern hemisphere autumn of 1982, it was the RFA's duty to keep the Fleet at sea.

They refuelled and resupplied the destroyers, frigates, aircraft carriers and landing ships of the Task Force, under the minute-to-minute threat of bombs and missiles from an Argentine Air Force whose professional capabilities have long been underestimated by many commentators on this war, watching from the safety of their armchairs.

As well as supplying the ships around the Falklands, they forged a supply chain 8,000 miles long. Its links were the ships and men of the RFA and Merchant Navy, and it says something about the material of which it was made that the chain was never broken during those months of conflict and its long-drawn-out aftermath.

Having met some of the men who had served in the South Atlantic, I found that the RFA have a motto, which also serves as their job description. It's just about the shortest of any service and it sums up completely the character of the men who serve aboard the ships. It reads simply: 'No sea too rough, no job too tough.'

So that's why the title of this book is:

'No Sea Too Rough: the Royal Fleet Auxiliary in the Falklands War.'

And that is the story between the covers.

CHAPTER TWO

PREPARATIONS

O
N 2 APRIL 1982, Argentina invaded the Falkland Islands. The military
government (Junta) had eventually lost patience with the endless rounds of
diplomacy and political negotiation which had lasted almost from the time of the
initial British occupation in 1833.

When the Argentine invasion, 'Operation Rosario', finally came, at 04.30 local
time, it was a reasonably well-organised affair. Strict criteria had been laid down
from the first plans in early March: there was to be complete surprise, there
should be no casualties among civilians or British troops and it had to be completed quickly. The reasoning behind this, confirmed later by separate Argentine
sources, was simple. If there were no casualties then the invasion could reasonably
be presented as a simple police action, and, the Junta assumed misguidedly, could
be used as a starting point for further negotiation. The one flaw in this scenario
lay in their assessment of the character of the British Government and in
particular, its leader, Margaret Thatcher, the so-called 'Iron Lady'.

Owing to bad weather, the Argentine fleet was delayed north of the islands
and by the time it was in position, intelligence had reached the Falklands about
the invasion plans. The reinforced garrison of seventy Royal Marines, under
Major M J Norman, were ready and waiting. It did not really do them much
good, because, in the end, the Argentines landed such an enormous amount of
men and equipment (some estimates suggesting as many as 2,000 men came
ashore) that the Marines were quickly overwhelmed. Moody Brook, the
Marines' barracks, came under attack first, by amphibious commandos using
automatic weapons and phosphorus grenades.

A second group surrounded Government House, where most of the Royal
Marines had taken up defensive positions. Some Marines had managed to
disable an Argentine Amtrak personnel carrier with light anti-tank weapons on
the road between the airport and Port Stanley. But even Royal Marines did not
have a chance against the sort of odds they were facing, so after an attempt at
negotiation, Governor Hunt ordered Major Norman's men to lay down their
arms at 09.30, the Royal Marines having, fortunately, not sustained a single
casualty. Argentine casualties were five killed and seventeen wounded.

On South Georgia, Lieutenant Keith Mills RM and his men were also eventually forced to surrender, a day later, but not before they'd shot down an Argentine troop helicopter and badly damaged an anti-submarine frigate, the *Guerrico*.

The British Government hadn't been taken entirely by surprise, however. The first intimation that the normal diplomatic stand-off might be taking a more serious turn was on 26 March, when British intelligence reported suspect preparations in and around the main Argentine naval ports, although their considered assessment was that this was in line with a joint exercise taking place with the Uruguayan Navy. It appears that the decision to invade was actually taken by the Junta early on the 26th. In response to this increase in Argentine naval activity, RFA *Fort Austin* (Commodore S C Dunlop OBE, CBE), then in Gibraltar after a gruelling six months on the Armilla Patrol, was ordered to immediately re-store and sail for the South Atlantic, where she was to replenish HMS *Endurance* with dry stores. Her Chief Officer, John Kilner, remembers:

Fort Austin sailed from the UK in October 1981 for a five and a half month deployment in the Gulf, on the Armilla Patrol, and was due to return to the UK after the 1982 Exercise Springtrain in early April 1982. It had been an eventful deployment, not least because of the grounding of HMS *Glamorgan* on the first day of the patrol, and her subsequent return home. We spent six weeks in Mombassa over Christmas and New Year, and needless to say everybody had enjoyed that part of the trip. We were joined by HMS *Sheffield* in January 1982, and had a very good visit to Diego Garcia in her company. We eventually got back to Gibraltar late in March 1982 to prepare for the preparatory get-together of the Springtrain participants.

During this period it was obvious to most, if one read the papers, that things were not going too well in the South Atlantic, and despite great secrecy on board, it became obvious to some that we were not going to join Springtrain but were going elsewhere. But the word was, keep it under your hat. I well remember going to one social function on the Saturday lunchtime at RAF Gibraltar, along with others and seeing *Fort Austin* being brought into the harbour from her usual position outside the breakwater and being put alongside the detached mole for essential repairs to the engine. Also during that weekend we disembarked the Flight we had embarked the day before! We had also to do a lot of storing of the essentials, just in case we ran out of food etc. I am told that some of the shops in Gibraltar did run dry of such things as tonic water during that weekend, but that is only hearsay.

When the Springtrain fleet sailed on the Monday morning, we stayed put, eventually sailing later the same day and meeting up with a tanker for an essential top-up of fuel, then immediately afterwards turning to the south.

We had apparently been ordered to go and top-up HMS *Endurance* with supplies as she was running extremely low on provisions etc. We proceeded at best speed towards Ascension, listening to the news as we went.

Fort Austin was a fairly new addition to the RFA Fleet, only being commissioned in 1978. Commodore S C Dunlop was Master, the RFA's senior sea-going officer, who immediately set his men to work. There were a few grumbles, to be sure, particularly since the impending trip meant the cancellation of at least one wedding, but by 29 March, *Fort Austin* had weighed anchor and was headed south. Dr E T Harrison remembered clearly what happened:

Usually during my deployment with the *Fort Austin*, on the way out from the UK and on the way back, we would, if able, always call at Gibraltar for a ship's party.

Out to cheer us up after leaving our wives etc, on the way back to have to face them again!

This particular weekend was immediately after the end of our usual party at Gibraltar. The next morning, after leaving the Straits, we turned left instead of right to the Bay of Biscay. I thought that our helmsman had perhaps a little too much the night before.

The Captain (Commodore Dunlop) then called us to a conference and told us not to worry but that we had to sort out a little bother in South Georgia but that we would still be home for Easter. I particularly did not worry as I thought that Georgia was somewhere in Canada.

It was another three months before we got home. We were on our way to Ascension Island at the start of the Falklands Conflict.

On 27 March, further reports had been received, indicating intense activity in and around Puerto Belgrano, although one bright spot on the horizon was confirmation by *Endurance* that the *Bahia Paraiso*, an Argentine supply ship that had called at Leith, in South Georgia, to illegally land men and supplies, had sailed, unfortunately leaving all the disputed personnel behind.

There was no significant improvement in the situation by next day, the 28th, and, in the evening, Mrs Thatcher telephoned her Foreign Secretary, Lord Carrington, expressing her concern. She was informed that Carrington was seeking the intervention of General Alexander Haig, the American Secretary of State. On their way to Brussels next morning, the British Prime Minister and Lord Carrington decided to send a nuclear submarine to the area, as reinforcement for *Endurance*. Later, the Ministry of Defence confirmed that the submarine would be sent, along with *Fort Austin*, which, having replenished *Endurance*'s rapidly dwindling supplies, would then remain on station to service any other ships sent to the area.

That evening, in Gibraltar, Admiral Sir John Fieldhouse ordered Rear Admiral John (Sandy) Woodward to make contingency plans to detach a group of ships from the annual Springtrain exercises in Gibraltar for duty in the South Atlantic. Amongst the warships, RFA *Tidespring* (Capt S C Redmond OBE) and RFA *Appleleaf* (Capt G P A McDougal), the latter having been diverted to Gibraltar from her planned fuel run between Curacao and the UK, were also ordered to begin preparations.

Captain Shane Redmond, Master of *Tidespring*, remembers vividly the Sunday before the order came:

We'd been to church in Gib, as usual, and in the evening, many of us, RFA and Naval officers, attended a concert in St Michael's Cavern.

Earlier that week, on the 26th, Commodore Dunlop visited me, at which time we discussed the situation in the South Atlantic at some length. We were both of the opinion that there was a very strong possibility ships would be sent south and that *Tidespring* and *Fort Austin* would also deploy for obvious reasons. We both agreed that, *Tidespring* being alongside, the way ahead was to load everything I could get my hands on and, departing a day after everyone else, we did just that. (The delay was due to a minor incident resulting in a six-foot gash on my starboard side – somebody had moved the South Breakwater knuckle which got in my way as I was leaving harbour.) *Tidespring* subsequently sailed at 100% plus capacity, our inventory including AS 12 missiles in the swimming pool, hundreds of drums of lub-oil over our normal operational load lashed down on the upper decks and enough food and general stores for six months at normal consumption rates.

Unfortunately not all our RN colleagues were in the same well-found position!

Following a general signal to report holdings of essential stores, it became apparent that some units were in fact well under-provisioned. An averaging out then took place which left *Tidespring* below her normal stock level, a situation we were to find particularly discomforting, post South Georgia, with nearly three times our normal numbers to feed and take care of!

And aboard RFA *Engadine*, things began to be done in a rush, despite an important anniversary. One of her crew, Dave Bolton, remembered it very well:

Engadine was a nice ship, plying between Plymouth, Falmouth and Portland with various flying groups doing their training and the permanent RN acting as if it was their private yacht. When the Falklands War came up we sort of knew that we would have to go at some point.

We were in Falmouth for a changeover session between flying groups and celebrating the 25,000th deck landing, for which a brilliant cake had been made, a replica of the ship scaled down and given correct colours etc.

When it came to the actual celebration and publicity bit for the local papers, the Captain did try and get me out of the picture, but I was staying with my cake! A Wren cut it and the crews all dutifully toasted the milepost that we had achieved. The cake was thirty-five inches long and weighed thirty-five pounds, took approximately ten hours in the oven and had to be cooked in a wooden box as there was no tin big enough to take something that size.

Later that month, we were on an exercise, probably Springtrain, with the carrier group and quite a large number of warships and RFAs. Gibraltar was rather full of ships and crews, as we all wanted a break from the exercise. As usual, the ammo ships had to anchor out and rely on a liberty boat to get ashore and back.

During the day, there had been news of the Falklands invasion or troubles, not sure now.

Then, while we were ashore the local radio broadcast a message for the crew of the RFA *Fort Austin* to return to their ship as soon as they could: we knew things were afoot then.

That evening, the 'Fort' went alongside on the detached mole, unheard of, and proceeded to load cargo well into the night. They set off the next day with some of the ships from the exercise.

The exercise carried on, and suddenly a message went out to all ships, to get all stores ready to be moved to the carrier who would then allocate them to the ships that made up the first part of the task force. Enough food and stores to get back to the UK was all that was to be left on board: everything that could be offloaded was to be moved, this included engine stores, cleaning gear, food, just everything. A busy day for everyone, with helicopters coming backwards and forwards to all the ships, emptying them out for the Task Force.

During this time, an Algerian ship had been lost at sea and the group found the survivors, rescued them and transferred them to us as we had a doctor and hospital. There were seven live ones and we had to empty out the deep freeze, which was almost empty anyway because of the fleet, and put the eight dead crewmen into that for transport back to the UK, where the live ones would be repatriated and the dead would be taken care of by their embassy officials.

Once back in the UK and the fridge cleaned out, we restocked and then went down to Falmouth to pick up another training group.

The training took us to Plymouth and while there we heard of the sinking of the *Sheffield* and, of course, we all knew that it would not be long before we went off to the war.

At the end of the training session, we went to Falmouth and offloaded the squadron, and also did the celebration for the 25,000 deck landings.

Then the Captain briefed us that we would be going to war and any that could not face this prospect were allowed to leave. One of the catering staff POs [Petty Officers] decided that he was too ill to do this trip and paid off. Also at this time we got a new PO steward, who managed during the war to get quite a black market going in alcohol as the bars were closed once we got near to the war zone and we all had to 'dry out'. Many of us put our valuables ashore, 'just in case' and then got on with the task of storing the ship and getting ready for the conflict, a job that we had been 'sort of' trained for and were designed to operate in.

Larry Wrigley (Mr Mince) was the Chief Cook and between us, we built up a truly amazing store of food and goodies to keep things going for an indefinite stay down there.

We did think quite well on what we would need, using our experience and training, so stocked up well over-the-odds on sausages, milk, frozen bread and eggs, as we figured that these were the items that would be in short supply.

We did well, lasting the trip and having some to trade as well. While in the war, we were used by the missile crews around Stanley as a rest and recuperation point, so we were always full up with new mouths to feed; our reputation as a good feeder must have got around.

On 31 March, the British Naval Attaché in Buenos Aires signalled the

Ministry of Defence (MOD) that most of the Argentine fleet was at sea, destination unknown, and that this seemed very much in advance of the planned Easter exercises. In the early evening of the same day, the British Secretary of State for Defence, John Nott, was informed by MOD officials that intelligence strongly indicated that the Falkland Islands would be invaded by Argentine armed forces on 2 April. Almost immediately, he was able to meet with the Prime Minister, together with Foreign Office and MOD officials, the latter including the then First Sea Lord, Sir Henry Leach.

It may perhaps be useful, at this point, to re-examine the Naval and MOD background against which these decisions were being made. John Nott's 1981 Defence White Paper had ordered sweeping cuts to be made to the Royal Navy's surface vessel establishment, particularly the sale or scrapping of its two remaining aircraft carriers. The RFA were also to be hit hard by the cuts. Both *Tidespring* and *Tidepool*, the two fast fleet tankers, were to be disposed of, as well as *Stromness*, the last of the excellent Ness–class store ships. *Tidepool*, in fact, had already been sold to the Chilean Navy and was on her way to her new home when the war broke out.

In addition to the ship losses, over 1,000 RFA men were to be made redundant and it is a little ironic, to say the least, that the first of these redundancy notices began to drop through letter boxes on 2 April, just as desperate telephone calls were being made from Empress State Building in London (Royal Naval Supply and Transport Service [RNSTS] and RFA headquarters), summoning those very men back to their ships. It says something for the quality of the men who belong to the service that not only did every man report to his ship, but the switchboard at Empress State Building was deluged with calls from men on leave and even some who were retired, many demanding to be sent to sea at once.

Admiral Leach, as First Sea Lord, had been mightily opposed to Nott's defence cuts, arguing fluently that such an approach, relying solely, as it did, on a submarine-based Trident deterrent, lacked the inherent flexibility, particularly for amphibious operations, which is an essential prerequisite for a modern navy.

So, when during the course of this House of Commons meeting, Mrs Thatcher asked him, in nearly so many words, what he could do, Leach replied succinctly that he could sail a task force south, with sufficient ships and personnel, to withstand the worst of the Argentine Air Force, and land the requisite number of troops to reoccupy the islands and dispossess the incumbent Argentine garrison. Mrs Thatcher gave permission immediately for the assembly and preparation of such a task force.

This was clearly seen in many quarters as complete vindication of what Leach had been maintaining all along and Admiral Woodward claims that Mr Nott, perhaps not surprisingly, 'went white' when Sir Henry stated, with characteristic bluntness, what could be done. Woodward has further stated that that Sir Henry had seized this opportunity to 'expose the folly of immense cuts in the strength of the Royal Navy' (Woodward 1992, page 73).

If that is so, one has cause to wonder if the First Sea Lord had taken time to reflect on the dangerous nature of the gamble which the government was about to embark upon, principally at his suggestion, and starkly revealed, one month later, in the freezing waters of the South Atlantic.

By the afternoon of 1 April, the decision to send this task force had been confirmed and wheels were beginning to turn. 'Operation Corporate', Britain's bid to recapture the Falklands, was in full swing.

In the UK, HMS *Hermes* and *Invincible*, the Royal Navy's only remaining carriers, were ordered to 24-hour readiness for sea, despite the fact that *Invincible* had just been put back together after a major refit. RFA *Stromness* (Captain J B Dickinson), having been almost completely de-stored and prepared for sale, was hastily prepared for sea. The old 'Super Sampan', as *Stromness* was affectionately known, was not designed for use as a trooper. She had no accommodation, washing or cooking facilities to handle a large group of Marines, let alone sufficient space to allow for the training necessary to keep them at peak fitness. Portsmouth Dockyard set out to remedy this situation.

Within four days, No 4 Hold upper deck level had been turned into a dormitory for 303 troops and it is ironic to think that most of the men who laboured so hard and well turning *Stromness* into a troop transport did so literally with their redundancy notices 'in their back pockets' as Barrie Dickinson, Master of *Stromness*, so succinctly put it. So bare and inhospitable did the dormitory look that the dockyard men had a whip round, raising ninety pounds, which they used to buy, amongst other things, a dart board, which was installed in the dormitory's central recreation area.

Cooking facilities for 500 men were installed, including a giant microwave and two banks of electric tea urns, six each side, these latter erected at the after end of the clearway in an area which soon became known as 'Tea Urn Square'. *Stromness* also loaded 15,000 man-months of food, twice her normal operational cargo, and all the equipment required to build what eventually became known as HMS *Sheathbill*, the San Carlos airstrip.

With 429 Royal Marines of 45 Commando embarked she sailed on the morning of Wednesday 7 April, when just five days before, she had been a de-stored hulk.

Off Gibraltar, RFA *Tidespring* and *Appleleaf*, as ordered, joined TG (Task Group) 317.8, which consisted of: HMS *Antrim* and *Glamorgan* (County-class destroyers), HMS *Coventry*, *Glasgow* and *Sheffield* (Type 42 destroyers), HMS *Arrow* (Type 21 frigate) and HMS *Brilliant* (Type 22 frigate). This group spent the day re-storing, off Gibraltar, from those RN ships which had also been attached to Exercise Springtrain but which, for a variety of reasons, had been ordered back to the UK. RFA *Tidespring*, of course, eventually sailed with her swimming pool full of AS 12 missiles, and enough general stores and food for three months.

At Empress State Building, the London headquarters of the Royal Naval Supply and Transport Service (RNSTS), who were responsible for supplying the Navy with everything, from an Olympus turbine to the Captain's paper clips, the order to send the Fleet to sea came as a complete surprise. In fact, many of the senior staff were at a party to celebrate the appointment of Mr Gordon Wilson as the RFA's new Fleet Manager (Personnel & Operations). He recalls:

My last day as Assistant Director (Industrial Relations) for the Royal Naval Supply & Transport Service was Friday 2 April, 1982. The invitation list for my farewell drinks was long, and included many colleagues from naval circles in Whitehall. As the morning wore on, the trickle of apologies swelled to a flood as we realised something big was afoot. I saw a copy of a signal ordering many warships to sea, and bringing an impressive list of others to immediate notice. The word 'Exercise' did not appear in the signal: this was for real. My new appointment as RFA Fleet Manager for Personnel & Operations had started with a bang.

Almost immediately, daily meetings were being held of the National Maritime Board (on which I now represented the RFA, one of its largest members). The burning issue was to reach agreement on the boundaries of a War Zone to enable *Canberra* and *Uganda* to be taken up from the trade to sail for the Falkland Is. [British Merchant Navy rules required all members of the crew to be told of the potential danger and given the option to leave their ship prior to sailing. Once in the Zone, very substantial bonus payments were earned.] I argued that the RFA differed from other shipping companies in that its primary task – its whole reason for being – was to support the Royal Navy anywhere in the world. Bonus payments for doing this were either unnecessary or should be kept to an absolute minimum. Under terrific pressure from ship owners and naval operational staff to reach agreement and get the first ships away, a deal was finally struck. For all British merchant ships except the RFA the War Zone would be the (huge) sea area south of Ascension Is. For the RFA it would be limited to the Naval Exclusion Zone, 200 miles around the Falkland Is.

Whilst these negotiations were ongoing the whole RFA fleet (twenty-seven vessels) was gearing up for war. Refits were being hurriedly completed, crews were augmented, full (and often rather unusual) loads were embarked and extra equipment fitted, and the roles of some were changed (e.g. to help carry large numbers of troops south) – all in record time. In all, twenty-two ships joined the operation, with the remaining five deployed on other essential tasks – the first time ever, I believe, that the whole fleet was at sea at the same time.

The initial shock having quickly passed, every RNSTS depot, situated at the major naval dockyards, now began a massive stores, fuel and clothing deployment to ships going south, desperately trying to second-guess the requirements of the sailors and Marines whose job it would be to make Operation Corporate succeed.

CHAPTER THREE

SUPPLYING THE FLEET

THE ROYAL NAVAL SUPPLY AND TRANSPORT SERVICE (RNSTS)

FORMED IN 1965, by an amalgamation of the four original Admiralty Supply Departments, at the time of the Falklands the RNSTS was responsible for the provision and delivery of everything a Royal Navy ship required to remain operational. As well as this immense task, the Service also organised the food supply for the whole of Britain's armed forces.

The origins of the RNSTS go back to 1550, when the Victualling Service was formed to improve supply of food and clothing to Henry VIII's fleet. Over time further Supply Departments were established by the Admiralty to provide: guns; ammunition and missiles; engines and auxiliary machinery (including a vast array of spares and components); navigation and communications equipment; and fuel and transport. By the early 1960s the need for rationalisation across the departments, and the integration of Afloat Support, was becoming clear, and so the new amalgamated service came into being. It was headed by a senior Civil Servant, the Director-General of Supply and Transport (Naval), who was directly responsible to the Chief of Fleet Support, a member of the Admiralty Board.

The organisation carried an inventory of over a million items to support the Royal Navy worldwide and had its main headquarters in Bath but with Fuel and Afloat Support located at Empress State Building in London. The RNSTS discharged its role through some forty bases and depots in the UK, Gibraltar, Hong Kong and Singapore in a manner roughly analogous to the outlets of a major international supermarket chain, albeit one with twenty-four-hour capabilities. These outlets fell into four main groups:

1. A stores organisation in each of the main dockyards, controlled by a Principal Supply and Transport Officer (Naval) who was responsible to the Port Admiral for Royal Navy support and to the Director-General for all RNSTS business.
2. Specialist depots for the supply of things like ammunition, electronic and

mechanical equipment, and all manner of spares formed a second, significantly smaller, group.
3. The third group was the RFA, which functioned then as the RNSTS afloat delivery service.
4. The fourth group were the NATO supply depots – stores of fuel and ammunition run for NATO by the RNSTS.

When the invasion came, the RNSTS response was immediate and wholehearted. The dockyard depots switched, more or less smoothly, to twenty-four-hour operation, and by 7 April, the main body of RN and RFA vessels had been stored and sent on their way. The depots were then able to concentrate on the more involved task of converting, loading and allocating RFA and RN personnel to the fifty-two chartered or requisitioned STUFT (Ships Taken Up From Trade) merchant vessels which were needed to supplement the activities of the specialised RFAs. RNSTS personnel also organised and ran the Ascension Island stores distribution operation.

Throughout the rest of the war, the RNSTS worked tirelessly behind the scenes, running, amongst other things, a STUFT cell, which organised ship charter or requisition, a Casualty cell, responsible for dealing with enquiries from families about their men (and women) who were on the ships and believed possibly injured or dead, and a Personal Enquiry cell. Kevin Lawrence, a senior RNSTS manager, recalls:

The Officers and Ratings in the RFA reacted magnificently to the challenge of putting the entire RFA Fleet to sea during Corporate and also to manning the STUFTs – but the role of the entirely civilian Appointers, Managers and general support staff, mostly very young and junior in rank, is not so well recognised.

This team sustained 24/7 operations during the entire period of the South Atlantic campaign, often turning up for work at their normal time in the morning, doing a full day's work, then a full night shift in the Ops Cell followed by another day's work before going home to snatch a night's sleep before starting the process again.

A complete generation had passed since the Department had faced the problems of support to large-scale combat operations and their commitment and professionalism in facing challenges and difficulties completely outside their experience was extraordinary.

Supplying the Task Force

Supplying the Task Force with all it required was of necessity an immensely complex logistics operation, which, although controlled and organised by the RNSTS, relied on the RFAs and STUFT for its smooth delivery.

The RFA was usually responsible for transporting and supplying two sorts of commodity, liquid and dry goods.

Liquid supplies included fuel, lubricating oil and water. Fuel was of three types: furnace fuel oil (FFO), used by older vessels such as HMS *Hermes*; diesel (Dieso), used by newer ships such as the Type 42; and aviation fuel (AVCAT) for jet aircraft and helicopters. Some ships even had to land their 'summer' fuel, which would be no use in the South Atlantic.

Dry goods consisted mainly of food, ammunition and clothing, along with a range of general store items needed keep the fleet at sea.

To begin with, the concern was to get ships to sea and so be seen to be reacting positively to Argentine aggression, although this laudable aim was slowed somewhat by the need to modify many of the STUFT ships. After the formal Order in Council had been issued on 4 April, decisions were made about which merchant ships to charter or requisition at TUFT (Taking Up From Trade) meetings, usually in consultation with the Government Broker. The Shipping Policy Division of the Department of Trade also set up a 'Call Up Merchant Ships' operation in support of the Royal Navy. This entailed the largest call-up of ships since the Suez Crisis of 1956.

Dealing with the Baltic Exchange through both the Government Ship Broker and the General Council of British Shipping, this latter representing ship owners, they were responsible, under the powers of the Order in Council, for the actual chartering or requisitioning of all the merchant ships taken up during the period of hostilities and for many months afterwards, once the decision that a ship was needed had been made by TUFT.

After chartering or requisitioning, the selected ships were then examined by a team consisting of an RFA Technical Superintendent, a representative of the Chief Marine Superintendent and the RFA's Assistant Oil Fuel Technical Advisor, who specified any modifications or other requirements necessary after reflagging. These could include refuelling at-sea facilities, additional water tanks or provision of a helicopter flight deck. Communications equipment requirements were assessed by the RFA Electronics Superintendent.

Individual ships were then moved to one of a number of UK dockyards, where the necessary work was carried out, before the STUFT was stored and sent south, with a separate contingent of RFA personnel aboard to organise operations such as fire-fighting and replenishment drills. Every STUFT had RFA personnel aboard, often including a radio officer, a deck officer, a petty officer and one or two deck ratings (three STUFT also embarked an RFA engineer officer), while some ships also carried RN communications ratings and Naval liaison officers.

Forty RFA Radio Officers were embarked on STUFT and this drastic re-assignment of ROs meant that, at one point, with ninety per cent of the RFA's RO complement at sea, there were no RFA sparks available for duty in the UK, except the two at the headquarters building!

One RFA officer seconded to *British Wye* recalls:

I joined the *British Wye* on 20 April having been called off leave. I joined Peter Breeze (First Officer) and an RFA Bosun's Mate. The *Wye* was undergoing A&As in Portsmouth dockyard; most importantly being modified to receive a NATO fuelling rig on her starboard side. It was fairly evident that she had been built with modifications in mind and that the installation kits were ex-stock. The *Wye* was undergoing a crew change at the time, the new crew being a little wary of just where we were going and for how long. There were some tense negotiations regarding wives at sea! We were fortunate in that the new Captain David Rundle realised the importance of what was happening.

Goods kept arriving from Naval Stores without being ordered, RAS hoses, connectors, clothing, ration packs, torch batteries, sound-powered phones, gunline, etc. I was given two bags of confidential books, two coding machines and a portable UHF set. Having no safe on board I took them home every night for safekeeping.

We left Portsmouth and proceeded to Devonport to load a full cargo at Yonderberry; this included over 200 drums of lub-oil. Space was so tight that we used the bridge wings and swimming pool to store the drums. Once loaded we were sailed south to Ascension.

One of the problems we faced was trying to change the mind-set of the BP crew from being a freighting tanker running a standard routine to having to face the certainty of some fleetwork, station keeping and RAS [Replenishment at Sea]. The BP manning scale was minimalist, and the ship, apart from the bridge, ran a nine to five routine, the engine room being unmanned at night. The major occupation was carrying out the planned maintenance routines.

Between Peter Breeze and myself we laid down the basics for fleetwork and RAS reception although what FOST would have made of it is debatable and the BP Health & Safety Manager would certainly have had to rewrite his manuals. However it all worked. Looking back it now seems rather strange that although the Ministry of whatever were involved with the designs of the ships, it seems nobody thought to give some basic, regular training to the officers and crew. Most of them had no idea of how the Navy was controlled, or how a task force operated. Fortunately, you could learn the basics in a couple of days . . . and everyone did!

Initially, to facilitate their quick response, RFAs were loaded as rapidly as possible in the UK, without too much thought being given to the invasion force's offload requirements, while each of the individual groups of the task force went south with their own RFA tanker. Added to their loading difficulties, however, some of the RFAs were certainly showing their age. For example, *Tidespring*, commissioned in 1963, had a number of worrying defects, as the Master, Shane Redmond, listed:

Shortly after departure from Gibraltar and while in transit to Ascension Island, an assessment of *Tidespring*'s operational capabilities in a hostile environment was made. The results were to say the least worrying if not annoying and formed a substantial part of my Report of Proceedings (ROP).

a. A positive pressure could not be achieved in either the forward or after Citadels due to a failure to carry out proper repairs and tests after other work had been completed during refit. Ships' engineers were successful in plugging air leaks and recovering the forward Citadel. (Defence against airborne contaminants – gas etc – a possible threat in the S. Atlantic)

b. The dimmer switches associated with the navigation lights were inoperative having been removed from the refit list of defects. Repairs could not be carried out by ship's staff as no spares were held. (Safety)

c. The Type 182 Sonar was inoperative despite efforts by the Communications and Engineering branches. Again, a failure to carry out maintenance at refit. (Anti-torpedo defence – poor but better than nothing)

d. De Gaussing was inoperative. Thought to be due to being disconnected and later, damp penetration (mine counter measures – not relevant in SA)

e. No ECM [Electronic Countermeasures] systems were in place though 3-inch rocket launchers (chaff) were later provided and fitted by ship's staff with the assistance of naval personnel.

f. There is no doubt that the ship's company lacked formal training for operating in a hostile environment. This is hardly surprising given that forty per cent of the Rating element was drawn from the Merchant Navy Pool and were not RFA personnel. An appropriate internal organisation covering all aspects of threat and defence had not at this stage been developed for the RFA and countermeasures had largely been directed towards the peacetime emergencies of fire and damage control. However, with a nucleus of ex-service ratings and a small number of RFA personnel who had attended formal training courses it was possible to bring the ship's company to a passable level by the time South Georgia was reached. Similarly, a functional, though somewhat sketchy, defensive organisation was cobbled together that seemed to work surprisingly well!

The above list represents a snapshot of a more comprehensive report on defects and other items relating to RFA operations in the South Atlantic contained in my ROP and subsequent papers.

Engineering remained a considerable concern throughout the campaign based on the experience of the previous three months in the Caribbean during which breakdowns were fairly commonplace. It is worth noting that throughout the period in question there were no such occurrences, due entirely to the effort of George Norcott the Chief Engineer, his deputy Bob Kirk and the Engineering Department as a whole, a group of men for whom I had the highest regard. Without their sterling efforts there is no doubt that *Tidespring* would have been at considerable risk.

According to Captain Redmond's draft ROP, most of these faults were present after the 1981 refit. Added to this, on a previous trip to the West Indies, engine breakdowns had, in fact, averaged one per fortnight. In the South Atlantic, as he says, due to the unceasing work of the engine room staff, there was not a single breakdown. Unfortunately, no other list is available but given the general age and work rate of the RFA's fleet, some of the other vessels must have been suffering at least as many faults, if not more.

Major rearrangement, taking several weeks, of the first wave of both store and troop ships, particularly the LSLs (Landing Ship Logistics) and tankers, was made at Ascension Island, before the individual components of the Task Force then once again proceeded south accompanied by their own RFA tanker. HMS *Antrim*'s group, TG (Task Group) 317.8/ Group I, for example, which was responsible for retaking South Georgia, had RFA *Tidespring*, while HMS *Fearless* and the LSLs were accompanied by RFA *Pearleaf*.

Later, with the TEZ (Total Exclusion Zone) established and the component parts of the Task Force collected together, distribution, in both the UK and South Atlantic, of necessity became more organised.

Station tankers were designated for Ascension Island and Cumberland Bay in South Georgia, these ships being changed on a regular basis. As well as station tankers, there were what came to be known as the 'motorway service stations'. These were tankers, either RFA or STUFT ships, which simply sailed a box course on a designated position in order to replenish any task force ship either sailing south, or back to Ascension or the UK. Typically, they were stationed between 1,000 and 2,000 miles south of Ascension. This was referred to by the ships involved as 'motorway tanking'.

Nearer the TEZ was the Tug, Repair and Logistics area (TRALA), originally known as the Logistics and Loitering Area (LOLA), and the Red Cross Box, this latter being designated strictly for the hospital ship, MV *Uganda*, and the ambulance ships, HMS *Hecla* and *Hecate*, although on several occasions, *Uganda* anchored in the calmer waters of San Carlos to allow more delicate procedures to be carried out.

RFAs, including tankers, store ships, LSLs, STUFT troopships like *Canberra*, and tugs and repair ships, like the 'Stenas', were temporarily marshalled in the TRALA, under the command of a Royal Navy frigate. This vessel, designated the TRALA manager, organised the dispatch of vessels and escorts to where they were needed, usually either to Ascension or South Georgia for replenishment or south to San Carlos once the invasion was in full swing.

As well as the ships in the TRALA, some RFAs remained in company with the Task Force. Their replenishment activities and distribution to San Carlos, Ascension or Cumberland Bay, when required, were controlled from there.

Both RFA and STUFT tankers were used to replenish warships with fuel, although most operations of this sort were carried out by the RFAs. All fuel replenishment in San Carlos and the other immediate war zones was conducted by RFAs.

Newer STUFT tankers could be used to replenish Royal Navy vessels with fuel but this wasn't the case with dry stores like food and ammunition. STUFT ships were fitted with derricks, effectively ship-borne cranes, for moving cargo out of the holds and onto the deck. These are fine in the calm conditions of a harbour or quayside, but in the open sea with any sort of wind or swell they are impossibly difficult and dangerous. RFAs like *Resource* did not have this problem, being fitted with five- or ten-ton lifts for the movement of cargo from hold to deck. Their cargo was also arranged in waterproof, single-pallet loads suitable for VERTREP, ie transport by helicopter. Clearly, only the RFAs like *Fort Austin* or *Resource* could replenish a warship safely with dry stores in a seaway but there weren't enough of this type of auxiliary to make the round trip to Ascension every time they needed to re-store.

To get round this problem, STUFTs like *Elk* and *Avalona Star*, amongst others, were used to carry ammunition and food respectively from Ascension Island to Cumberland Bay, South Georgia, where a makeshift harbour was established under the supervision of Capt Nick Barker, commanding officer of HMS *Endurance*. The RFA store ships could then replenish from these vessels in the relatively calm waters of the bay before heading north to the main body of the task force or San Carlos Water.

Later, when the San Carlos anchorage was relatively safe, STUFT such as *Elk* made a number of escorted trips to unload their ammunition direct to the Brigade Holding area which had been established there.

Once the Task Force was established in the vicinity of the TEZ, the system for replenishment, in general terms, was that STUFT ships moved fuel or dry goods (these latter waterproofed and palleted to normal RNSTS specifications) from the UK or Ascension to either the TRALA or Cumberland Bay, where they were transferred to RFAs who replenished the warships, either in the war zones, like San Carlos water, or at sea with the Carrier Battle Group. A number of fuel replenishments to RN vessels were also carried out by STUFT tankers, notably vessels belonging to the BP River-class, which, some years earlier, had been successfully trialled as convoy escort oilers for North Atlantic work.

Troopships were slightly exceptional, in that they usually anchored in Cumberland Bay before moving briefly to the TRALA or Carrier Battle Group, where they picked up an escort, frequently being joined by other vessels inbound to San Carlos; the major concern here being to make the passage from South Georgia to San Carlos in the shortest possible time, thus keeping the troops on board vessels like *Canberra* or *Stromness* in peak condition.

In all, twenty-two ships of the RFA fleet were involved in the recovery of the Falklands.

Replenishment at Sea (RAS)

Replenishment at Sea or RAS, as it is more commonly known in the RFA, can be broadly divided into two types: RAS (L), during which fuel or water is transferred and RAS (S), where solids such as food or ammunition are passed across. Capt Shane Redmond, Master of *Tidespring* during the war, describes the strategic process:

RAS (L) is usually scheduled in two ways: single-ship demand where no other units are involved; and the commander of a group or formation where multi-ship requirements and overall co-ordination is essential. Superimposed on this are tactical/strategic requirements prevalent at any given time. So broadly speaking replenishment operations fall into three main groups:

1. Non-operational: a vessel on passage without time constraints.
2. Peacetime operational: a unit or number of units proceeding to meet a peacetime commitment or during exercises.
3. War or hostile intent exists together with the constraints associated with this:

In 1. or 2. above, the overriding consideration is one of safety for the participating units and their personnel, the mission in general being relegated to one of secondary importance. This can lead to the postponement or cancellation of a serial, for example, owing to prevailing weather conditions or density of commercial shipping. Condition 3, on the other hand presents an almost complete reversal in the scheduling process where the overriding priority is the achievement of the operational plan and, where possible the preservation of units involved. Safety of the individual must by the nature of hostilities take a lower priority. In all cases the urgency of a need to replenish may also have a major bearing on the time and the area in which a RAS takes place, for example persistent bad weather, or units critically low on fuel, ammunition or other items of stores held in the RFA. Preservation of the unit(s) and the safety of her (their) crew(s) takes priority over all else. Assuming that the material state of the ship is satisfactory for normal peacetime operations, and those involved are properly trained, safety is then largely dependent on a combination of selecting a course and speed to minimise the effect of weather and provide as much protection as possible to personnel on the RAS decks. Consideration must also be given to ship movement and the detrimental effect this can have on running gear and equipment in general – a torn out rig does not get repaired at sea! Ship routines also weigh heavily in peacetime – RAS during meal times is not popular with our Naval colleagues and therefore avoided. Unfortunately, our mealtimes rarely co-incide!

Weather, of course, played a major part not only in RAS but also in the daily lives of all concerned, ranging from delightful in the Ascension Island area to unpleasant or downright awful in the operational areas in and around South

Georgia and the Falklands, where maintaining an effective RAS capability was of paramount importance. Skill, experience, conceptual thinking and a great deal of common sense were the factors that got things done that would at any other time have been impossible to achieve. Damage to RAS rigs, though frequent at the outset, did nevertheless decline as experience was gained throughout the Task Force. Even so, the need to overhaul and make good often under the most arduous conditions continued to be a threat to the safety of personnel through-out the major part of the campaign.

Once in area, the Carrier Battle Group spent most of its time in a holding area to the northeast of the Falkland Islands, loitering at speeds often as low as eight knots. Given that the optimum speeds for RAS range from ten to fourteen knots, moving outside the protected zone was a serious possibility. Add to this a unit's urgent need to replenish during a period of particularly bad weather where the only course option with any hope of achieving success often led to a com-pounding of the protection problem. The solution was to top-up whenever the opportunity presented itself. While no specific instructions were ever issued to this effect sensible commanders either asked or simply informed the CTG (Commander Task Group) of their intentions to fuel or store their vessels, called the RFA, then got on with it.

Morale was never in question aboard *Tidespring*. As in any group faced with a similar situation there were one or two members of the ship's company who experienced acute difficulty but they in no way impinged on the willingness and dedication of those onboard. Examples which illustrate the general feeling throughout the ship at that time were that of a boy rating, who thinking that he would be repatriated on account of his age, pleaded to be allowed to stay, and the Number One Chinese laundryman who during RAS provided reassurance to his fellow countrymen onboard.

The level of morale enabled the ship to increase overall operational availability and deliver a 'without notice' facility throughout the period. Normally under such conditions an RFA would expect to be placed at thirty minutes' notice during the day and sixty minutes' at night.

Further thought was given to fuel grade availability at the RAS points and also the vexed question of fuel onboard versus that which could actually be issued. The answer was simply to declare that the main grades, Dieso, FFO and AVCAT, were available at virtually any RAS point (certain grades were not available on both sides of the ship or at every RAS point). This had the distinct advantage of enabling frigates, destroyers and landing ships to use leeward side rigs and take some protection from the elements provided by the bulk of *Tidespring*. A spin-off of this was that those RAS points which had FFO and Dieso, or Dieso and AVCAT 6-inch hose, could double their output by providing each grade through both hoses.

Alternatively, when supplying through two rigs, for example to *Hermes* or *Invincible*, the quantity issued (and therefore the time alongside) could be reduced by utilising an otherwise redundant 6-inch hose. A similar logic was also applied to pumpovers where a STUFT tanker taking a *Tidespring* rig could connect both hoses to their discharge manifolds thereby dramatically increasing the supply rate of a single high-usage grade such as Dieso. The advantage of operating in this manner proved most useful when loading from a STUFT or RFA Leaf-class support tanker, where two or more rigs could be engaged simultaneously thus providing an extra hose for the main commodity required. This had the net effect of reducing the time alongside by up to one third.

The weight of fuel in a ship's tanks makes an important contribution to stability, and a tanker normally needed to retain anything up to thirty per cent of her operational load, resulting in a serious but not always understood reduction in a force commander's available fuel stock. *Tidespring's* crew worked out a method whereby they could refill her tanks with seawater ballast in a controlled manner which allowed them to issue her full stock of fuel.

None of this could have been achieved without careful planning and a high level of morale. The effort involved in cleaning hoses to prevent cross-contamination after use, coupled with the washing of main cargo tanks for ballasting and the need to keep personnel at immediate readiness for long periods under poor weather states, is self evident.

Tidespring introduced and led the way in these moves to enhance the service the RFA provided in the South Atlantic in 1982.

Some practical details of what a pumpover involves for the crew are provided by a long-time RFA Petty Officer (E), Peter Robinson:

Replenishment at Sea or RAS for short is what the RFA does better than anyone else, and even though I might be biased, I defy anyone to say otherwise: the RFA is a highly trained and highly professional body of men (and women too now).

What is a RAS and what happens? A good question, first off let me set the scene for you.

A warship at sea can only expend a certain amount of fuel from its tanks before it has to replenish, and then it either has to find the nearest port or nearest replenishment ship.

A RAS is a highly-complex and dangerous operation that is performed in normal operations in anything up to a force 7 sea state, but during the Falklands we regularly RAS'd in weather up to force 9, which resulted in some definitely underwear-enhancing moments. And decidedly wet and cold to boot.

In normal operations the issuing ship, let's say the RFA Fleet Tanker *Tidespring*, is stationed within a specified RAS box, a designated area of sea that it must conduct the operation within. The receiving ship will signal that she needs fuel and a rendezvous will be arranged – that is in an ideal world. What happened in the Falklands is that most ships just turned up and wanted fuel there and then, day and night, a bit like a twenty-four-hour Esso garage at sea but without the Mars bars.

Tidespring will call her crew to RAS stations and the deck crew will prepare one or two of the rigs (*Tidespring* had five rigs for abeam fuelling and two stern rigs which trail the hose behind for the receiving ship to pick up). Once the rigs are ready and *Tidespring* is settled on the replenishment course and speed the ship then hoists flag 'R' or Romeo, as it is known, to the top of the signal mast. The receiving ship will also raise the same flag to the same position when she is ready and commencing her final approach.

Right, now let's get to the exciting bits. With the receiving ship alongside, the deck crew of *Tidespring* warns them that the 'gunline' is about to be fired. Three short blasts on a whistle and a signal with a red hand-held bat tell them to prepare to receive the gunline and take cover. The business end of the gunline, which is a foot-long yellow plastic tube, with an orange rubber top, a bit like something one would see in an adult shop, is then fired across using a normal military rifle with a special adaptor on the muzzle and using blank ammunition. At the base of this object is attached a thin line made of polypropylene, and at the end of this line is a series of bigger lines. First comes the messenger, and clipped to this is the distance and tele-phone lines. This in turn leads into the hose line or the jackstay messenger depend-ing on the type of rig being used. The distance line is taken forward to a position where it can be easily seen from the receiving ship's bridge, which then uses it to maintain a safe distance (usually between thirty and sixty metres) between ships. On some occasions the supplying ship may in fact take on this responsibility. The telephone cables are connected into the receiving ship's system and provide direct communication between both ships' bridges and the respective RAS points.

The two standard liquid replenishment systems used in the South Atlantic were the derrick and heavy jackstay rigs. The former consisted of three troughs or saddles over which the hose ran: these were suspended by heavy wire cable from a large latticework derrick swung out over the ship's side at an angle of around forty-five degrees. The height of the troughs were controlled by hand driven winches, this governed the length of hose suspended between ships. The engine room crew, usually a Petty Officer and two ratings manned the ATW, or Automatic Tensioning Winch which fed the heavy wire cable out, set the tension during a RAS, and brought it back at the end. It was along the cable on this winch that the troughs would travel.

With the derrick rig the hose line is used to haul in the hose end in unison with the lowering of the troughs. Once it is on deck, the hose is then secured by a 'senhouse' slip, the quick release coupling (QRC) at the hose end is connected to the ship's refuelling point and the shut off valve opened, then the signal is given to start pumping and the fuel is delivered.

When the heavy jackstay is in use, the jackstay messenger is used to haul in the wire jackstay as it is veered by the ship. Once it has been secured, the hose trough wires are veered and the hose moves down the tensioned wire. Two options were available for connecting the rig, first the probe which looks a bit like a giant phallus, which is designed to slide down the wire and engage in a female receiving cup (yes I know, sex preoccupies all sailors) where the delivery valve opens automatically and fuelling commences. The alternative to this was to use a quick-release coupling instead of the probe and connect up as above.

With the severe weather that we nearly always had and the need to replenish ships (on what seemed like an assembly line) outside the normal operating limits for rigs, we often used the QRC as it proved to be far superior to the probe, which at that time had a habit of failing to engage in heavy weather.

When everything is coupled up the receiving ship will then signal to *Tidespring* to commence pumping: she may be taking a number of liquids as well as fuel – she could be taking lub-oil, fresh water and AVCAT (aviation fuel).

The pump room on *Tidespring* then opens up the pumps and the fuel and other liquids start to flow, if I remember correctly we could pump Dieso (diesel fuel) at around 400+ tons per hour, and if we had two hoses going, which was what the carriers required, then we could easily pump 800 tons per hour. If you work that out at roughly 200 gallons to the ton then that is 80,000–160,000 gallons per hour, and the ships may be coupled together for anything up to eight hours.

It has to be remembered that in the South Atlantic the weather and sea were none too kind and we frequently replenished in winds up to a force 9; that means we could have thirty-foot waves with forty-five-foot troughs, as well as a wind and heavy ice-cold spray, and seas breaking over the bow and slopping down the sides. The selection of a course to minimise these effects was not always possible for tactical reasons, and as the ships plough along the designated RAS course they are both fighting through these seas, as well as rolling alarmingly. The hoses on the jackstay wire will be dancing around all over the place and a careful eye must be kept out to ensure that the rig does not pull out, or worse still that the hose does not spring a leak. Rig damage often became the order of the day in these conditions and the deck crew spent long hours carrying out repairs so that we could stay in business. It has also to be remembered that the RAS crew had to wear full foul-weather gear and hard hat, as well as a life jacket, survival suit, gas mask, and anti-flash gear (the latter items were carried by all crew day and night, even when you went to the bathroom).

Tidespring has now been pumping for four hours and the receiving ship signals that she is nearly full, so the receiving ship hoists the 'prep' flag at the dip (halfway up the mast) to signal that there are fifteen minutes to the end of the RAS. When pumping is complete the 'prep' flag is raised to the top of the signal mast on the receiving ship to signify that she is ready to disengage, and both these signals are answered by *Tidespring* to show she acknowledges. The hose is detached and hauled back in board to the *Tidespring*, the jackstay cable and the other lines are all tied together again and are sent back over. When this is done, both ships haul down the 'prep' flag and the receiving ship then steams away to make room for the next customer (there always was one!) and it all begins again.

One interesting note here, *Tidespring* was capable of refuelling three ships at once, one on either beam (side) and one at the stern. As well as that she could also use her two helicopters to lift stores from the flight deck to other ships, this is known as a VERTREP or Vertical Replenishment.

On stores and ammunition ships the RAS operation is similar up to a point, except that the stuff going over to the receiving ship is usually solid and in some cases a lot more dangerous, and the RAS rigs are designed for different use. There were two basic types of RAS rig on these ships, the heavy jackstay rig and the GEC Mk1a, affectionately known as the 'Noddy' or nodding donkey.

Food, spares, ammunition and other solid stores are usually palletised: these rigs have hooks on the end of their travelling blocks and the loads are hooked on to these. Now in the waters of the South Atlantic the loads usually became very lively when they were being sent across and it is a truly laxative moment to see a pallet-load of bombs swinging wildly in the air. Even worse is the pallet of beer that is halfway across when the cable goes slack – the result is that the top of a swell catches the load and the fish are having a very unexpected party.

The RFA pumped thousands of tons of fuel to warships and STUFT vessels during the Falklands, as well as receiving thousands of tons of fuel. We also issued and received thousands of tons of ammunition, food, drink and other stores and the RAS and flight decks were in constant operation, usually in appalling weather and at all times of the day and night. We operated in times of extreme danger and there was more than one RAS that had to be hurriedly curtailed because of the Argentinean Air Force, or in the case of *Tidespring* whilst undergoing a much needed pumpover from RFA *Brambleleaf*, because the captain of the Argentinean submarine *Santa Fe* was lining us both up for a full spread of torpedoes. Thankfully he was deterred by our friends in the Royal Navy.

The Fleet Air Arm

The RFA's working relationship with the Fleet Air Arm began in 1951 when the first helicopter trials involving a deck landing on an RFA were conducted with one of the early Fort-class vessels, RFA *Fort Duquesne*. Westland Dragonflies of Naval Air Squadron (NAS) 705 were used for the trials and they were so successful that many of the older RFAs were fitted with helicopter decks and hangars to allow these aircraft to land.

1966 saw two new specialist store ships in commission, RFAs *Regent* and *Resource*, both of which were fitted with helicopter pads as part of their standard build. As well as having the landing pads, the ships were also allocated permanent helicopter flights, these aircraft being Wessex HU 5s from NAS 829, originally based at Yeovilton.

Usually, RFAs transfer dry goods by heavy jackstay, which involves a steel rope being passed between ships so that palleted loads of about a ton can be literally swung across. Sometimes, for a variety of reasons, such as time, tactical considerations or delicacy of the load, this method cannot be used for dry goods, and the pallets are then transferred by helicopter in a process termed Vertical Replenishment or VERTREP. VERTREP has a number of advantages over the jackstay, the main one being the possibility of transferring material between vessels which are actually out of visual range of each other.

RFAs usually carry either Wessex or Sea King helicopters, with RN aircrews and maintenance staff embarked as part of the ship's complement.

Mike Tidd, CO of *Tidespring*'s flight, explains the procedure for VERTREP:

Whilst many of the heavy stores that need to be transferred between ships at sea are transferred by good old 'seaman-like' jackstay transfers, if deck space and helicopters are available and/or the weather is rough, VERTREP is quicker and safer.

During the Falklands campaign large amounts of stores needed to be cross-decked between ships on the way south to get them in the right place ready for the landings. Once the shooting war started resupply of ammunition of one sort or another became a high priority as ships returned from the gunline after carrying out shore bombardment, and as the Harrier force expended bombs, bullets and missiles.

The Task Force could rarely afford to accept the manoeuvring constraints required for jackstay transfers and the sea state often made this difficult and dangerous. For these reasons VERTREP was often the best way of meeting these requirements quickly and efficiently.

VERTREP was co-ordinated by the CTG's [Commander Task Group's] Ops staff based in HMS *Hermes*, who would issue a flying tasking signal (Opgen Foxtrot) each evening, detailing which units should supply aircraft for which tasks the next day. For VERTREP tasks the maximum load weight would normally be specified, though most crews would tend to treat this with a healthy degree of scepticism as netted loads tended to turn out heavier than advertised.

The aim once airborne on a VERTREP sortie was to keep the loads moving as quickly and efficiently as possible. To make pickup and drop-offs slick, aircraft would usually fit an eight-foot strop to the load-lifting hook. This gave better clearance from obstructions, allowing more rapid manoeuvring above the deck, as well as keeping the underslung load clear of the airframe in transit.

If the load had to be lifted from amongst higher obstructions then a twenty-foot strop could be used, though this made station-keeping more difficult as the aircrewman conned the pilot into position over a pitching, rolling deck.

The deck crew would be equipped with a 'shepherds crook' with which to catch the hook and earth it to get rid of the static build-up before handling it (something that could give you a kick like a mule in the cold South Atlantic air!).

Due to operational necessity we were often forced to carry out these VERTREPs in conditions that were well outside of peacetime limits, which led to some 'interesting' and often amusing moments, such as when one crew released a container of two 500-pound bombs over the deck of *Hermes* just as the deck dropped away from under them. The container hit the deck with a crash and there was a mass 'Oooooooh' from the aircrew and deck crew alike, and the FDO expressed his displeasure in enlightening terms over the RT.

The wind was so high on that particular lift that when I got back to *Tidespring* the weather was a long way outside of normal limits. Shane Redmond, *Tidespring*'s captain, manoeuvred his ship until he found the best combination of deck movement and relative wind that was obtainable, which meant approaching and landing on facing Red 90 into a howling wind and onto a deck that was heeling about ten degrees to starboard. The landing went OK despite the huge updraught coming over the port side of the deck and once lashed down, we proceeded to shut the aircraft down. To our astonishment the rotor RPM dropped to about sixty per cent and then stabilised, even though the engines were now stopped. After a bit of head scratching we realised that the updraught from the side of the ship was causing the rotor to autorotate and so, at the risk of burning out the rotor brake, I had to apply the brake at well above normal limits in order to stop the rotor. Luckily it didn't catch fire and no damage was done.

On another occasion, Ian Georgesson and I were tasked to move ship repair materials in the form of long pipes from *Stena Seaspread*, the battle-damage repair ship. This lift was made more challenging by the fact that she had high superstructure on three sides of her well deck so, as she pitched and rolled, we had to fly our aircraft with its underslung load into the well deck, avoiding being 'swatted' by the moving superstructure.

The one VERTREP task that normally brought you a warm welcome was the mail HDS (Helicopter Delivery Service). On one occasion I turned up at one of the STUFT (Ships Taken Up From Trade) to find the flight deck deserted and no interest being shown by the team on the bridge. After hovering alongside the bridge windows and making a lot of self-explanatory hand signals we finally got an irate call over the RT from the ship's RN Liaison Officer, telling us to go away as we were not scheduled to visit them. Amazingly though, when I innocently transmitted back 'So I take it that you don't want your mail then?' there was a hasty retraction and the flight deck was manned in double quick time!

We often ended up VERTREPing in conditions of appalling visibility where, apart from the difficulty of avoiding other aircraft, one faced the additional problem of trying to find particular ships from amongst a large formation, spread out over an awful lot of sea. One of the easier ships to find was our 'mother' *Tidespring*. She produced a very white sulphurous smoke from her funnel and so we would aim to pass astern of her reported position, leaving the cockpit window open. Once you smelled sulphur you turned along the ship's course until you found her wake, and followed the smoke trail through the fog and mist to the ship! Unorthodox but effective.

During the Falklands War, Fleet Air Arm helicopters were used for a number of jobs outside of the usual RFA remit, such as the landing on South Georgia's Fortuna Glacier and all of the transport and logistics work they were called upon to do in moving men and material from San Carlos to Stanley for the final push, although because of the loss of so many helicopters with *Atlantic Conveyor*, especially the three giant Chinooks, much of this fell to the lot of the RFA's overworked LSLs, working in close conjunction with the helicopters.

The crews' workrate was really extraordinary. For example, in NAS 820, a Sea King squadron, the squadron logged 1,560 flying hours during May, which is the equivalent of two aircraft, flying twenty-four hours a day, every day for the whole month.

ABOVE: A lighter moment: the traditional indignities of a 'Crossing the Line' ceremony in RFA *Sir Tristram*.

LEFT: The ironies of war: Steward Chen Kwok Leung with an Argentinean contribution to the kitchen.

ABOVE: Assembling at Ascension Island: the assault ship HMS *Fearless*, RFAs *Stromness* and *Plumleaf*, three landing ships, and the tug *Typhoon*.

RIGHT: South Atlantic winter: RFA *Sir Lancelot*, oldest of the Landing Ships Logistics (LSLs).

BELOW: RFA *Regent* replenishing the carrier HMS *Invincible*, South Atlantic, 1982.

LOW: Refuelling at sea requires both skill and nerve: HMS *Argonaut*, closing to refuel from RFA *Plumleaf*.

RIGHT & BELOW: Warships are well practised in conducting refuelling at sea, but during the campaign the STUFT merchant ships also had to learn the techniques. Here the ferry *Elk* demonstrates how close ships need to be, during a stern refuelling with RFA *Plumleaf*.

ABOVE: Even giant liners like RMS *Canberra*, seen here off Ascension, refuelled at sea.

LEFT: South Georgia: RFA *Regent* amongst the ice floes.

ABOVE: A Mexeflote raft operating in the San Carlos anchorage.

RIGHT: RFA *Sir Lancelot* at action stations in San Carlos Water on the first day of the landings.

BELOW: An O-class diesel-electric submarine approaching the *Stena Seaspread*.

ABOVE: The anchorage at San Carlos.

TOP: The bomb that could have won the war, landing fifty yards from RFA *Fort Austin*. Photograph taken from RFA *Stromness*.

ABOVE: A Type 22 frigate seen through a hole in the side of RFA *Sir Lancelot* caused by a 20mm cannon shell.

LEFT: San Carlos, 24 May: RMS *Canberra*, RFA *Stromness*, RFA *Blue Rover*, a Landing Ship Logistic (LSL) and MV *Europic Ferry*.

LEFT: The final view of RFAs *Sir Galahad* and *Sir Tristram*.

RIGHT: RFA *Sir Tristram*, showing the result of the 1,000 pound bomb.

BELOW: RFA *Sir Galahad*, still burning on 11 June.

Neil Barclay   Dave Tooze   John Irvine   CEO Jim

Dave Palin   Tony Stainton-Ellis   Mark Hurley   Capt Robin Green   Barry Hayes

Robin Bailey   Robin Hookh

LEFT: Survivors from RFA *Sir Tristram* on board MV *British Trent*.

BELOW LEFT: Members of the Task Force mourn the lost Landing Ships Logistics and their crew members.

BELOW: Dedication of the RFA Memorial: Hong Kong Chinese crew members from RFA *Sir Geraint* make their offerings, Fitzroy, 8 June 1985.

RENT

ary Wilson

Alan Roach

Andy Wills

Chris Forrest

The repair ship RFA *Diligence* and the frigate HMS *Penelope*: even after the surrender, the RFA's job wasn't finished.

RFA *Sir Tristram* on board the heavy lift ship
MV *Dan Lifter* on her way home to be
repaired and returned to service.

Service helicopters, however, were uncomfortable places. They had no internal heating and much of their seating and equipment was stripped out to maximise carrying capacity. This, added to the huge amount of flying they did, meant crews were often without food and sleep for dangerously long periods.

In an effort to ease the burden of the helicopter crews with whom they had always had a close working relationship, the RFAs operated an 'open house' policy, supplying hot meals, AVCAT and often a bunk to the overworked men and aircraft. RFAs *Sir Lancelot* and *Sir Percivale*, for example, both acted as helicopter refuelling points while anchored in Teal inlet.

And when *Sir Galahad* and *Sir Tristram* were hit at Fitzroy, it was the helicopter pilots of the Fleet Air Arm who risked their lives and their aircraft to winch the wounded off the LSLs' burning, white-hot decks, disregarding the exploding shells and rockets which had formed so much of their cargo.

With the cease-fire, it was still business as usual, the helicopters carrying out their normal VERTREP activities as well as numerous other jobs, such as ferrying VIPs, for which it appeared only a helicopter would do.

Arming the RFAs

The arming of RFAs is an issue that has always been fraught with problems. In wartime, an auxiliary which is capable of defending itself, and therefore does not always require the services of a naval escort, has obvious advantages, but set against that is the difficult question of at what point an armed RFA ceases to be an auxiliary and legally become a warship, with all the attached problems which RN vessels have in entering even a friendly harbour. Manning, including extensive training, is also a significant issue, together with those relating to command and control within the ship.

A civilian-registered RFA, of course, can literally sail where she will, collect cargo, be it fuel oil or dry stores, and then leave to replenish a warship or group of warships without any legal complications and it is this major advantage which weighed against including weapons in an RFA's standard fit.

During WWII, over 9,500 allied merchant ships had some sort of armament and they used those weapons very effectively, destroying scores of U-Boats and over 300 aircraft.

The RFA kept its weapons when peace was declared, but 1950 saw a change of policy with a general order that all guns and mountings were to be landed at the ship's home port. Deck stiffening and other structural features were to be retained, presumably so the weapons could be repositioned in case of need. By April 1982, however, few RFAs had any weapons fitted, in line with the comments made in 1955 by the then Director of Gunnery Division, Naval Staff:

'Guns mounted in afloat support ships have been more for morale purposes than with a view to contributing to any effective anti-aircraft defence.' This despite a total of 330 aircraft shot down by merchant vessels during WWII.

Upon arrival at Ascension Island, all the LSLs, at least, were fitted with 40mm Bofors guns, mounted in their original positions on the fore deck, except *Sir Percivale* and *Sir Galahad*, which had only a single Bofors fitted.

Despite Naval misgivings however, most of the RFAs managed to procure some sort of defensive armament, albeit from a variety of sources. On *Tidespring*, the only ship for which there is any record of crew training, gun crews were trained by the embarked Royal Marines, a Marine serving initially as No 1 on the weapon and the RFA crewman serving as No 2, ie the loader. Once the RFA man had gained sufficient experience, he took over as No 1, initially under the guidance of a Marine, and a second crewmen was appointed as No 2, so that by the time the Royal Marines disembarked, the ship had fully-trained gun crews at their weapons.

She also had her own 'home-made' missile launcher, as Lt Mike Tidd describes:

Later on, PO John Humphries, my Scottish armourer, was to display great initiative when, with the help of the ship's engineers, he set about making suitable mountings so that our GPMGs could provide anti-aircraft fire from the ship's upper deck and also created a steerable trolley with two 2-inch RP half rocket pods strapped to it, which was intended to take on any aircraft attacking us from astern. Whilst the mechanics of this looked feasible in theory I think everybody except PO Humphries was very glad that we were never called upon to use it in anger!

Interestingly, *Tidespring*'s training regime mirrored in some ways the WWII situation where courses like 'Merchant Seaman Gunner' and 'Mercantile machine gunner' were offered to RFA ratings, with the added incentive of an allowance of 6d and 3d being added to the seaman's pay once he had passed the course. As far as their effectiveness goes, *Fort Austin* claimed at least one Argentine Dagger shot down with her miscellaneous collection of rifles and machine guns, which must have done the crew's morale no end of good. Although as one of her crew recalled, it wasn't the RFA who turned out to be a danger to their own side:

On the first day in San Carlos, it was a beautiful morning . . . we couldn't believe it . . . *Glamorgan* was behind us and when the Argies came over, she let off a Sea Slug that missed us by a few feet . . . that's a great start, I thought.

Lessons were learned from the Falklands War, however, and RFAs now carry a substantial number of weapons, including 20mm and 30mm BMARC Oerlikons, chaff rockets and GPMGs (General Purpose Machine Guns).

Nuclear Deployment in the Task Force

Amongst its many other tasks, the RFA was also responsible for the transport of what the Navy coyly call 'special weapons'. This is navyspeak for nuclear devices and, contrary to popular belief, aided by the then Government's determined policy of non-information, certain ships in Britain's Task Force did go south with nuclear weapons aboard.

Weapons were of the nuclear depth charge type, a variant of the WE 177 freefall bomb then in service with the RAF, and were intended for use in an anti-submarine role. HMS *Invincible, Hermes, Brilliant* and *Broadsword* had weapons of this type embarked during their involvement in the initial stages of Operation Corporate.

Concerns at the Ministry of Defence were initially centred on the removal of these weapons from the Task Force, without destroying the momentum gained in those first weeks. Although the Ministry envisaged problems associated with RN vessels containing these rounds operating in or near waters governed by British territorial obligations under the Treaty of Tlateloco, opposed to this was their very real concern that, if a 'state of tension' should develop with the Soviet Union, redeployment of RN warships in their designated NATO role would be delayed until nuclear weapons could be re-embarked.

The terms of the Treaty of Tlateloco are such that British warships were prohibited from carrying nuclear weapons in the territorial waters around the Falklands, South Georgia or the South Sandwich Islands, although there could be no objection to the carriage of such material in the waters outside those limits, nor, of course, their storage in a secure military establishment outside the UK.

Ascension was clearly first choice for the offload but an MOD review of the facilities soon showed up a number of problems. Firstly, transfer could only take place either by Landing Craft (LCT), operating from the Landing Platform Dock (LPD) HMS *Fearless*, or by helicopter. Heavy swell and lack of a suitable quayside reception point rendered the LCT option impractical. Helicopter transfer was safe enough, as long as such transfers were conducted at low level, but would have been highly visible and might easily have led to the load being identified as nuclear material. Added to this was an unacceptable delay to the ships involved and security difficulties associated with either storage at Ascension or transport to the UK.

Incidentally, MOD sources stated at the time that the possibility of an 'atomic bomb-type explosion' was non-existent, although a high explosive detonation was a greater risk and this might result in contamination of the surrounding area with radioactive material.

Given these constraints, the decision was taken to allow the nuclear rounds to remain with the Task Force but to effect heavy jackstay transfer of *Brilliant*'s and *Broadsword*'s weapons, initially to *Hermes* and *Invincible*, where they could be more safely stored in the dedicated, armoured magazines deep in these ships. Risk of damage to these facilities from an Exocet strike was considered to be minimal with only moderate risk of damage from a torpedo or mine.

RFAs *Fort Austin, Fort Grange, Regent* and *Resource* had similar dedicated deep magazines and so could also be used to store special weapons while at sea, with similar minimal risks of damage. Transfer to the unarmed and unarmoured RFAs was, however, considered to be less desirable as these ships were absolutely essential to the RFA's logistics effort, particularly for ammunition supply and helicopter support, as well as being more vulnerable to attack. Those Task Force ships carrying nuclear rounds would have to remain outside the relevant territorial waters, transferring their weapons as and when required for supply duties.

The chronology in the appendices at the end of this book shows the distribution of nuclear weapons and training and surveillance rounds during Corporate, as well as the heavy jackstay transfers it was found necessary to effect.

For much of the period of hostilities, the RFAs remained in company with the Task Force and thus benefited from the protection of its accompanying warships. For several periods, however, RFAs carrying nuclear rounds were exposed to a significantly greater risk. For one period from 16 April to 3 May, RFA *Fort Austin*, after receiving *Brilliant*'s nuclear round and *Sheffield*'s surveillance round then proceeded to Ascension Island, unaccompanied, where she re-stored, before returning south again, not rendezvousing with the Task Group until 3 May. During this period, elements of the Argentine Navy (Task Groups 79.1, 79.2, 79.3 and 79.4) were continually at sea in the region of Puerto Deseado, some 400 miles from Stanley. Although, in reality, they probably presented very little danger to *Fort Austin* during Corporate, if the Argentines had chosen, more logically, to concentrate their activities on the Navy's supply line rather than attacking the warships, things might have been very different.

More worryingly, between 1 and 11 May, an Argentine submarine, the *San Luis*, was on patrol in the waters to the north of East Falklands, where she claimed to have attacked HMS *Alacrity* and *Arrow* on 11 May, with a wire-guided torpedo. Neither warship was hit, although the captain of the *San Luis* claimed to have detected a 'small, metallic explosion' on sonar, which may have been a hit on *Arrow*'s towed target decoy, which was found to be damaged upon later recovery. Needless to say, *San Luis* would have been ideally placed to sink or even capture the 'Fort', had the sub encountered the RFA on her way back to the Task Force.

These nuclear deployments also put the potential attack by the *Belgrano* in a new light, since RFA *Resource* and *Fort Austin* were both carrying nuclear rounds in company with or close to the Task Force during 1–2 May, when the *Belgrano* threat was at its greatest.

MOD claims minimising the effect of Exocet, mines or torpedoes on the dedicated deep magazines of these vessels had not mentioned the possible effects of a 6-inch shell, weighing 105 pounds, impacting on an unarmoured RFA. While it is true the nuclear weapon would not have exploded, there seems at least the theoretical potential for serious contamination.

Another potentially dangerous situation also developed on 25 May, when *Atlantic Conveyor* was sunk by Exocet, RFA *Regent* being then in company with the Task Force, carrying a nuclear round and a training round.

Final deployment of nuclear weapons was effected to Fort Austin on 2–3 June, the RFA finally transporting three live, two surveillance and six training rounds back to Devonport in an unescorted trip from South Georgia. *Resource* took the remaining weapons, one live and two training rounds, back to the UK on her return, departing 20 July.

No Royal Navy ships were sunk or even damaged while carrying nuclear rounds during Corporate, although HMS *Brilliant* did suffer minor damage on 21 May while carrying a training round. Such rounds do not contain nuclear material. Compromises are reached in war based on the assessment of acceptable risk, and the procedures adopted for the deployment of nuclear weapons during Corporate seem, in the main, to have kept the level of risk within acceptable limits.

Without the specialist store ships of the RFA, however, it would have been a very different story. With only *Hermes* and *Invincible* capable of storing such weapons safely while at sea, the task force would have been unable to push these essential vessels close enough inshore in the later stages of the war to allow the Harriers to play their vital role with maximum effectiveness.

And, of course, transport back to the UK would have had to be effected by the carriers, with all the concomitant publicity.

The RFA's role in this, as in all other areas of logistics support, proved a vital element, once again making a crucial difference between success and failure of the Royal Navy's operations.

CHAPTER FOUR

GOING SOUTH

O N 2 APRIL, the same day as Argentine forces began to land near Stanley, Task Group (TG) 317.8a, accompanied by *Tidespring* and *Appleleaf*, left Gibraltar for Ascension.

And as Sir Anthony Parsons (British Ambassador to the UN) called for an emergency session of the UN Security Council, RFA *Sir Tristram* (Capt R Green DSC) sailed from Belize and RFA *Brambleleaf* (Capt M Farley) was detached from the Indian Ocean to join the Task Group by way of Cape of Good Hope. Her Master remembers:

RFA *Brambleleaf*, prior to Paraquat [the operation to recapture South Georgia], was engaged freighting between Bahrain to Singapore. We had completed shipping our first cargo to Singapore, and had loaded our second cargo at Bahrain. On leaving the Gulf we were ordered to relieve RFA *Olna* which was suffering from MBC [Microbiological Contamination] in her fuel. RFA *Olna* at the time was escorting three warships. We rendezvoused with *Olna* and transferred various stores and equipment. The group with RFA *Brambleleaf* as consort was enroute to Mombassa.

A few days before we arrived in Mombassa, I was having lunch aboard one of the warships with the other Captains, when scrap-iron merchants in South Georgia came into the conversation; no particular interest was shown by anyone on this matter. The next day, of course, we received a signal detaching us from the group and ordering us to proceed to the vicinity of the Cape of Good Hope and await further orders. Wives were landed at Mombassa and all mail was stopped.

Meanwhile, back in Britain, 3 Commando Brigade were preparing to go to war. The Brigade consisted of three separate units: 40 and 42 Commando, both based at Plymouth, and 45 Commando, based at Arbroath. They were supported by a number of specialist elements, including artillery, helicopter and logistic units.

42 and 45 Commando were Arctic- and mountain-warfare trained; 40 Commando were not Arctic-trained to the same degree, although all the Royal Marines had a high level of fitness and military expertise. There was also an Arctic and Mountain Warfare training Cadre, all specialist, highly trained mountain warfare experts, which was eventually used in the Falklands as a reconnaissance unit. More importantly, each Commando had seen service in

Northern Ireland, which was as close to real battle conditions as any troops of that era had experienced.

As well as the three infantry units, the Brigade's specialist units were also mobilised. These included: 29 Commando Regiment, Royal Artillery, a specialised, Arctic-trained artillery unit equipped with helicopter-transportable 105mm guns; the Air Squadron, flying Gazelle and Scout helicopters; and the 1st Raiding Squadron equipped with light boats and inflatables and trained for covert work. Her Majesty's Sappers were represented by 59 Commando Squadron, Royal Engineers, while the Commando Logistics Regiment, the Blowpipe-equipped Air Defence Troop and the Electronic Countermeasures Unit also began preparation for the trip south. All members of these support units had passed the arduous commando selection test and so were trained in commando techniques as well as being expert in their own specialities.

Usually, once the Brigade was mobilised and all its kit packed ready for shipping the troops were moved by air. For a number of very good reasons, conditions in the Falklands made this impossible, so the men and their equipment went south by ship.

In New York, the UN session called for by Parsons convened on 3 April, and after a fairly stormy interlude the UN demanded immediate Argentine withdrawal and negotiation. Panama, interestingly in light of Belaúnde Terry's later intervention over the *Belgrano*, tried, unsuccessfully, to veto the motion.

Part of the Argentinean response to British claims of illegal invasion included a claim that they were simply '. . . recovering lost territory and bringing an end to imperialism.'

Later in the day, General Galtieri also addressed the crowds from the balcony of the Casa Rosada, claiming: '. . . there would be no disruption to the lives of the islanders', and that Argentina still wanted good relations with Britain.

In Britain, a Saturday session of Parliament was called for the first time since the Second World War and, with what might charitably be described as much flag-waving, it was decided that Britain's honour demanded that a Task Force be sent. Moderate voices, like MP Tam Dayell, who were calling for at least an attempt at negotiation before the military option was put in place, were shouted down.

It was, however, decided, that the Task Force's role was merely to bring diplomatic pressure to bear on the Argentineans and that force would be a last resort. Some political observers have suggested that it was the strength of the Labour Opposition's responses, in particular a speech made by their leader, Michael Foot, which endowed the military option with so much popular support. Of course, news of the invasion of South Georgia and the capture of the Marine garrison only added to the fury many were feeling.

Next day (4 April), things began to move again in Buenos Aires, when the Junta learned that the Americans had permitted the British to use Ascension Island as a military base. In direct response, General Galtieri decided to reinforce the Argentine military presence on the Falklands to try and force a negotiated settlement.

The stakes, however, were rising.

In the UK, one of Britain's nuclear-powered submarines, HMS *Conqueror*, slipped her moorings and crept quietly out of Faslane naval base, Falklands bound. While in London, an Order in Council, known as the Requisition of Ships Order, allowing the Government to requisition any British merchant ship or anything on board that ship for Her Majesty's service, was submitted and approved by Queen Elizabeth II.

Meanwhile the logistics effort was increasing. The RAF airlift to Ascension gathered pace, deliveries including Lynx and Wessex helicopters and crews, the former intended for deployment with Sea Skua on RFA *Fort Austin* while the latter were marked for embarkation on RFA *Tidespring*.

Ships were moving too – including some of those that were being disposed of in John Nott's defence cuts. While RFA *Stromness* was being hastily modified and re-stored at Portsmouth, RFA *Tidepool* received her recall signal while she was in Chile, being prepared for handover to the Chilean Navy. Within hours, she was on her way back, having, with a certain amount of difficulty, refused the kind offers of a number of Chilean servicemen who wanted to come back with her and shoot at their Argentinean neighbours. *Tidepool*'s Chief Officer recalls:

During 1981 I was Chief Officer on RFA *Olwen*. For the latter part of that year, together with HMS *Euryalus* and HMS *Charybdis* we formed the Armilla patrol. *Olwen* had embarked the flight from HMS *Ardent* commanded by Lt Cdr John Sefton. During the period of the patrol he became a good shipmate as did the rest of the flight. In December 1981 we returned to the UK and went our separate ways.

At this time the *Tidepool* was about to be sold to the Chilean Navy and I was asked if I would take a short leave, join *Tidepool*, take it to Chile and stay on there for a couple of months showing them the 'ropes'. The carrot for this was, at last, a summer leave and being able to watch the World Cup live.

I joined *Tidepool* in February 1982 and from the outset there was a lot to be done. We had only an RFA 'running crew' plus a team of Chilean Naval Officers and POs. The ship had to be prepared for the run, practically de-stored with just enough left to get us to Chile. No rigs, no stores, only enough paint to 'make it pretty when you get there'! There was an awful lot of tank cleaning and digging out. The Chileans spent the day tracing pipes, looking and measuring lockers and sticking DYMO labels in Spanish on everything. I remember one, 'Medico' (Doctor) stuck on a Junior Engineer's cabin door. When I queried this with the Chilean Commander, he said that the Doctor's cabin was too good for their 'Medico'.

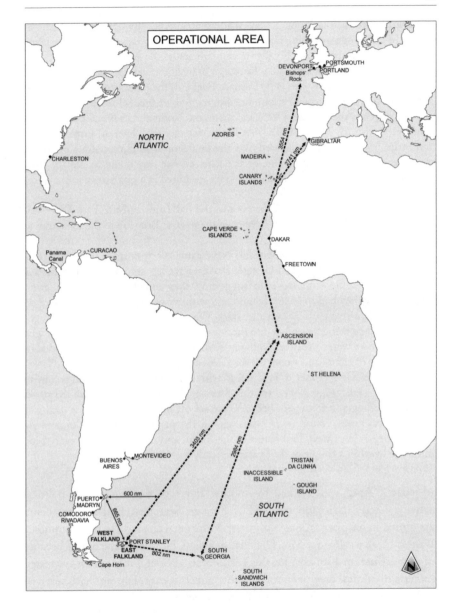

It was then decided that we needed a mini-workup at Portland. We, the RFA crew, thought this would be an instructional period for the Chilean Navy to accustom themselves to the ship. No way: the RFA crew were 'put through the wringer' as normal whilst the Portland team commented and the Chilean Navy looked on in amusement.

After this we spent a couple of days loading up goodies the Chileans had bought to take home: fridges, washing machines, dishwashers, TV's etc, and a car to be taken out for British Embassy use. Finally we were off across the Atlantic.

First stop was Curacao to load a full cargo of aviation fuel and diesel. But as you can imagine after so long with FFO [Furnace Fuel Oil] the tanks were not acceptable. After a lot more cleaning and a lot more digging out we finally loaded.

Next stop was the Panama Canal and a break at Rodman US Naval Base where I conformed with Mr Ron Robin's [RFA Fleet Manager for Material] instructions to 'tart it up'. Whilst there we handed over the final stores, all but one folio of charts, radios 'except a crystal set' to one of the LSLs on her way home to the UK from Canada. It was then downhill to Chile and we anchored in a small town in the north called Arica.

By this time hostilities had broken out in the Falklands and the Task Force was being assembled. I think we must have been the nearest Brit ship to the Falklands at that time.

Anyway both the Chilean Army and Navy came out to inspect their new ship. Meanwhile Mrs T had phoned General P asking for her ship back. The Chileans were eager to come with us, even suggesting they mount and man the guns. Unfortunately they had to be left behind and within twenty-four hours we were on our way north, arriving off Balboa after dark. We entered the Canal about midnight and really rushed through, sailing into the Atlantic about 6.30 the next morning. The idea was that we weren't seen transiting in daylight. The British Consul provided us with a couple of charts and we set off for Curacao again.

Captain Rex Cooper met us in Curacao with a mountain of stores and a crew to bring us up to full strength. The aviation fuel was changed for AVCAT, all the stores loaded including a 'few' cans of beer and we set off for Ascension. More gear was loaded there, hoses, connections, wires and all the paraphernalia for RAS, and rig building began in earnest. Full marks to the Bosun and crew who threw everything into it and within a couple of days we were ready for the job.

Monday 5 April was marked by another flurry of diplomatic and political activity. Lord Carrington resigned as Foreign Secretary, Francis Pym being appointed in his place. Along with these Ministerial changes, in the Commons, Dennis Healey called for Mrs Thatcher to resign. Nothing came of this because of popular national support for the Task Force, although it has been suggested by certain political commentators that her government might not have survived if the Task Force hadn't been mobilised so quickly.

In South America, Señor Costa Mendez, Argentina's Foreign Minister, made a speech to the Organisation of American States, in which he said, amongst many other things, that: '. . . Argentina will attack if British forces come within 200 miles of the Islands'.

The build-up continued as both the aircraft carriers left Portsmouth. With the ships now designated the Carrier Battle Group, HMS *Hermes* was carrying 11 Sea

Harriers (SHARs) from 800 Naval Air Squadron (NAS) and 18 Sea King helicopters, while *Invincible* had 9 SHARs from 801 NAS. *Hermes* had only lost the last of the scaffolding around her 'island' a bare twenty-four hours before setting sail. RFA *Olmeda* sailed from Devonport, to join the Carrier Battle Group, while the big freighting tanker RFA *Pearleaf* left Portsmouth to join HMS *Alacrity* and *Antelope*. *Olmeda* was carrying FFO, which was required to replenish the older *Hermes*, as well as two anti-submarine Sea Kings of 824 NAS.

It wasn't just the large warships and supply vessels that responded to the call. Along with her more glamorous and larger colleagues, the Royal Maritime Auxiliary Service tug RMAS *Typhoon* also set off on the long trek south.

Getting to the operational zone was only one part of the task. As they sailed, RFA crews also began to prepare themselves and their ships for wartime conditions. In the Gulf of Oman, on board RFA *Brambleleaf*, things began to get a little fraught. Her Master explains:

During the passage to the Cape of Good Hope, we prepared for entering an area of conflict. The reasoning behind a lot of the preparations was pure survival. *Brambleleaf* had no weapons or defensive equipment. We were maintaining HF [High Frequency radio] silence, and the ship was blackened out. The wheelhouse deck head was painted black because the light reflected from the bridge instruments was quite phenomenal. It also seemed to have an effect of deadening all noise. All white paintwork was greyed out including the ship's name and numbers. All fire lines were greyed out as well, lifeboats were stocked with extra rations, emergency routes were marked with fluorescent tubes, and a wooden stowage was constructed on the poop deck for dangerous stores which could be jettisoned in emergency. Fire and emergency drills were practised frequently. The main object was to save the ship if possible, hence one of our actions was to cover the lifeboats so that the orange interiors could not be seen. However, if we had to use them, then we certainly wanted to be seen.

The next phase began when we were ordered to rendezvous at Ascension; then two days later we were ordered to a position further south in the Atlantic, but not to close within 1,350 miles of the Argentinean coast! A succession of positions followed, leading us ever southwards. At one point we were hove to in heavy weather, when we suffered damage. Several pieces of equipment were washed away: gangway, rails, catwalk gratings, our wooden dangerous stores stowage on the poop. The bow plates were 'dished in' but no damage was sustained to the tanks. None of the damage affected the operational capability of the ship.

It wasn't just the military and RFA who were making a significant contribution, though, as Martin Hobbs, an ex-RFA man who was then working for a UK marine electronics company, remembers:

As soon as the news broke of the invasion in the South Atlantic I realised that communications with ships in remote southern latitudes would be difficult and

Satcoms [Satellite Communications] would be invaluable. I telephoned Ken Henderson, RFA Electronics Superintendent, to offer assistance and tell him that my company was in a position to supply terminals from current production and was willing to divert units from existing orders to RFAs if required.

The response from Empress State Building was almost immediate and enthusiastic – a contract number was issued and an initial order placed for a small number of units which later increased to over twenty. By this time the first elements of the task force had sailed and it became clear that we would have to organise 'flying' teams of installation engineers to travel with tools and equipment wherever ships needed fitting out.

The first installation was on *Stromness* and led to a much more personal involvement for me than I had expected. She had been in the process of sale to the US Military Sealift Command and was being de-stored and stripped of MOD equipment including the MOD Radio Station. The process was rapidly reversed and we were instructed to supply and fit the first of the Saturns from the contract. At the same time as the delivery instructions were received from RFA HQ, my wife and I learned that our son, who was nearing the end of his Deck Cadetship, had been appointed to *Stromness* and was to join her immediately in Portsmouth – she was sailing within twenty-four hours! The only unit immediately available was one that had been ordered for stock well before these events and it was being delivered by ordinary sea and road freight from the factory in Norway. It was 'in transit' somewhere between Oslo and Croydon and after a number of increasingly urgent telephone calls was traced to a truck on the road from Felixstowe to Croydon. We asked the truck company to get hold of the driver and redirect him to Portsmouth with all speed.

Meanwhile I arranged for John Temperley from our associate service company to pack a bag of tools and fly down from Newcastle to sail with the ship and complete the installation and commissioning of the Saturn on passage to who knows where!

At the same time my wife loaded son and kit into her car and set off for Portsmouth. Husbands Shiprepairers were instructed to fabricate and supply a steel stumpmast for the Saturn Antenna unit (this was the first of many such masts that they made for us), while a 'commissioning application' was sent to Inmarsat headquarters in London with equipment, ship and shipowner details and asking for priority allocation of the ship's Inmarsat number and registration.

The truck driver phoned in to his office during his lunch break and was sent off down the A3 complete with a police 'blue light' escort (arranged by MOD Portsmouth) to hasten his progress all the way in to the dockyard and alongside the ship.

Remarkably everything happened in the right order: son was delivered and found himself supervising the loading and fitting of the stumpmast; the truck with its police escort arrived under the crane and the Saturn antenna unit was hoisted on to the stumpmast; the rest of the equipment went up to the radio room and finally a somewhat out of breath John Temperley came aboard to start running cables and connecting up.

All this happened in the midst of taking on stores, loading cargo and embarking 45 Royal Marine Commando! *Stromness* sailed the following day for Ascension Island to join up with the rest of the task force.

Britain made its first demand that the EU impose sanctions on Argentina on Tuesday 6 April, and while Alexander Haig, the US peace envoy, was talking separately to the British and Argentine ambassadors in Washington DC, the US quietly stopped all arms sales to Argentina. But this did not stop Galtieri's planned reinforcement of the islands, and Argentina's 8th Regt was moved by air to Stanley, supplementing the already sizeable, mainly conscript, garrison. The next day, Brigadier-General M B Menendez, the new Argentine Governor, also arrived in Stanley.

It wasn't only military preparations that occupied the higher echelons of the RFA. More mundane issues such as pay and conditions for their workforce and for the Merchant Navy needed to be thrashed out. One such was the definition of the war zone and the size of special hazard payments due to seamen operating in the zone. The organisation for deciding this was the UK National Maritime Board (NMB), which convened in London. After some discussion the Board agreed to create two zones. The first was within 200 miles of the Falklands and would be where all serving Merchant Navy (MN) and RFA personnel would be covered by the NMB death and injuries agreement and would be paid a 150 per cent bonus while in the zone. A second zone was created west and south of Ascension and south to Antarctica, but here the bonus payments were for MN personnel only. This agreement was to spark a certain amount of ill feeling amongst the RFA, especially the Hong Kong Chinese crews of the LSLs.

Most of the RFAs that had been in the UK since the beginning of April sailed on 6 April. RFA *Sir Geraint* (Capt D E Lawrence DSC) and RFA *Sir Galahad* (Capt P J Roberts DSO) left from Devonport, while RFAs *Sir Percivale* (Capt A F Pitt DSC) and *Sir Lancelot* (Capt C A Purcher-Wydenbruck OBE) sailed from Marchwood. These LSLs (Landing Ship Logistics) were carrying anything up to 400 personnel over complement, including Marines, Naval or RAF, as well as stores, weapons, ammunition and the helicopters of 3 Commando Brigade Air Squadron.

Known as the 'Round Table' class, these ships weren't renowned as good sea boats, as one RO (Radio Operator) who sailed in them explains:

Sir Lancelot, L3029 was, like all her class, a very bad sea boat, and she rolled as easily as a donkey on wet grass. She did actually move in dry dock once, which only promoted the stories about her sea keeping qualities. Being virtually flat-bottomed to enable them to conduct beach landings, the LSLs rode high in the water and were 'lively' to sail in!

The flat bottom made stability a problem, so the hull was steel with an aluminium superstructure, a totally new concept at that time, thus reducing the 'top heavy' weight of the vessel considerably; otherwise they would have been even worse in a seaway.

On one occasion on passage to Hong Kong from Singapore, *Sir Lancelot* hit some very heavy weather in the South China Sea, and not only did we lose some paint, but the bridge and superstructure went one way and the hull went another! A huge gap rose between the base of the superstructure and the deck, where the steel and aluminium met!

The ship went into dry dock at Hong Kong for immediate repairs, which proved difficult, as aluminium cannot be welded to steel. 'L' plates were made and welded to the steel and on the other side the 'L' was clamped and riveted to the superstructure. Once repaired, we continued on our way.

Another problem encountered in bad weather was when the 'bottle screws' holding the bow doors together used to give way. The *Herald of Free Enterprise* disaster was the result of bow doors opening and, whilst at sea, if our bow doors had gone then we would have been one of the largest submarines in the Navy! I can remember the Bosun and the Bosun's Mate standing by to replace these door bolts whilst actually under way.

Loading was no picnic, either, because there wasn't time to distribute the equipment tactically, such that their load could be accessed as required in the war zone. Redistribution had to be done, if at all, at Ascension. The Masters of *Sir Percivale* and *Sir Galahad* describe the problems:

Sir Percivale was loading cargo at Zeebrugge when the orders were received to expedite the operation and proceed to Marchwood to prepare for Operation Corporate. At this time certain officers, including the Commanding Officer, were playing golf at Ostende and, although a driver was despatched, he did not carry out his instructions and the message was not passed until the round was completed. Meanwhile, as the weather was becoming foggy, the Chief Officer decided, with the local pilot, that it would be prudent to sail the vessel and await the arrival of the errant officers clear of the harbour confines. A very worrying time for the CO to find his command had sailed. A short boat ride later and the two were reunited and the vessel proceeded to Marchwood Military Port (MMP).

The ship berthed, bows in, on the north side of MMP jetty at 030445Z April 1982, which was a Saturday. At this time it was known that a Mexeflote would be side-carried to the area of operations and it had been hoped it could be carried on the port side. However, due to tidal constraints, the ship was unable to berth the opposite way as required to achieve this.

Because the ship was shortly due to commence refit she had to be completely restocked with fuel bunkers, lubricating oil, fresh water, provisions, bonded stores and medical stores. Signals were hastily compiled and sent. All that could be done then was to sit back and wait to see what happened.

The ship was discharged on the Saturday and ready for loading by early evening. The main loading did not start until Sunday morning and consisted mainly of War Maintenance Reserve (WMR). During Sunday the CO and Navigator attended the Op Corporate Mounting Meeting in Plymouth which, although useful, also wasted valuable time as it entailed seven hours travelling time. Although it did give the opportunity for the 'old man' to say goodbye to his family.

Throughout Sunday and Monday the loading of cargo and stores continued as and when they became available. A lot was accomplished in a short time. The passengers commenced arriving late Monday morning and continued throughout the afternoon. Three Gazelle helicopters of 'M' Flt, Brigade Air Squadron (BAS), were also embarked in the early afternoon.

After consultation with Heads of Departments (HODs) it was decided to sail as soon as all passengers, stores and cargo were embarked and secured. This would enable the ship to 'shakedown' the next day, Tuesday, away from the confines of MMP, which was becoming more like a madhouse by the minute.

The ship finally sailed from the jetty on Monday 5 April at 1820Z, fourteen inches over-loaded and in possession of a quite lethal deck cargo. That night the ship anchored in Lyme Bay, well clear of prying eyes.

The situation aboard *Sir Galahad* was similar:

On 2 April 1982 I received the signal with the magic words Operation Corporate. At first I thought it was some paper exercise that the Radio Officer and I had forgotten about, but no, it was for real (and how).

The Falklands war had begun. We proceeded at best speed to Plymouth, arriving on 3 April. Our cargo, ex-Norwegian exercises, was quickly off-loaded and fantastic efforts were made by the Dockyard to back-load with ammunition, rations, rigid raider boats, petrol, land rovers, waterproofing kits and a whole host of ancillary stores. This was completed by the evening of 4 April.

On the morning of 5 April we embarked some 350 Royal Marines of 40 Commando, HQ and Signals, 59 Commando, No 1 Raiding Squadron plus three Gazelle helicopters and their crews from 3 Commando Brigade Air Squadron. Ten Royal Corps of Transport soldiers were embarked as part of the ship's company to act as stevedores. Three Royal Navy signalmen were also embarked.

My ship's officers were frantically storing up with every conceivable item that we thought we might need over the next ninety days. Every available space was crammed to capacity, as were the main fridges.

Sir Galahad proudly set sail from Plymouth at 15.00 on 6 April with the Royal Marines lining the ship's side, Gazelles ranged on the flight deck, battle ensign flying. We all felt very honoured to be setting off to do our utmost for Queen and country.

The LSLs, which were to be a major component of the Amphibious Landing Group, rendezvoused with HMS *Alacrity*, *Antelope* and RFA *Pearleaf* (Capt J McCulloch) at sea, then waited for the rest of their group. They were soon joined by the core of the group, HMS *Fearless*, the Landing Platform Deck (LPD) assault ship. As well as troops she carried Brigade HQ with Brigadier Julian Thompson and Commodore Michael Clapp, and three 846 NAS Sea King helicopters. The whole group, transport, support and escorts, then proceeded in company to Ascension.

At the same time RFA *Resource* (Capt B A Seymour) left Rosyth, sailing down the east coast at nearly her top speed of seventeen knots, loaded with troops and equipped with a Sea King for VERTREP [replenishment from the air]. She cleared her decks of the remaining cargo piled there as she went, which was just as well because the next day she began a massive VERTREP, receiving some twenty-three loads of essential stores from a total of nine aircraft. Some of these helicopters relayed their loads distances of up to eighty-five miles from both Portland and Culdrose, while *Resource* chased the *Fearless* group down the Channel. During this VERTREP, Chinooks from Culdrose were used to supply the RFA for the first time, being able to carry much greater underslung loads than their smaller brethren.

Further south, RFA *Fort Austin* arrived at Ascension and embarked her three Lynx helicopters, complete with the untried Sea Skua missile system. Without weapons of her own, these helicopters now gave her a formidable offensive or defensive capacity.

Elsewhere, things weren't going quite so smoothly, HMS *Invincible* having developed a problem with her starboard main gearbox coupling. Luckily, the equipment to replace the gearbox could be flown to Culdrose and then brought on board by Chinook, allowing the problem to be fixed mid-channel.

Now that the main body of RN and RFA vessels had left the UK, the dockyards would be concerned with re-storing RN and RFA vessels for the next wave and the conversion of the fifty-two Ships Taken Up From Trade (STUFT). Many of these needed RN communications equipment, extra accommodation, more fuel tanks, helicopter decks and equipment for replenishment at sea (RAS). Private firms were also involved in conversions, such as Vosper Ship Repairers, in Southampton, who took delivery of RMS *Canberra* and by 9 April had her ready to go south, complete with two helicopter decks, RAS and communications gear to turn her into a 'Landing Platform Luxury (Large)'.

Captain Richard Thorn, appointed STUFT 1 by Captain Gordon Butterworth, the RFA's Marine Superintendent, describes his own view of the situation:

For three months prior to the start of the Falklands Conflict, I was seconded to the Staff of the RN Tactical School at HMS *Dryad* – awaiting the time and opportunity to relieve Commodore Sam Dunlop CBE DSO of command of RFA *Fort Austin*. At the start of the conflict, the RN Tactical School Staff went to their war post in JHQ [Joint Headquarters] Northwood, *Fort Austin* turned south from Gibraltar, and I was called to RFA HQ, where the Director Tony Kemp asked me primarily to liaise with AD73 [Assistant Director, Fuel] over the charter of suitable commercial tankers, then to assist in the management interface between commercial ship owners and the MOD. I had recently been the project officer from the RFA HQ to assist in the oversight of the installation of an Astern Replenishment at Sea facility in two BP

River-class tankers – a NATO funded project, but with an in-house add-on that enabled the BP Tankers to receive an RFA's abeam refuelling or solid stores rig during a RAS. A number of BP River-class tankers were chartered by AD73 very early on, and the STUFT 1 (Ships Taken Up From Trade) task and acronym were born. With troop mobilisation and transport the number of merchant ships either requisitioned or chartered grew rapidly. Captain John Wilkins joined me, as did a young male clerical officer (whose name sadly escapes me), who as a Territorial soldier was a member of the Intelligence Corps.

Our task was to liaise between Commercial Shipping Owners and the MOD. We arranged onward shipment of crew members, spares and stores to their ships, which on sailing were under Naval Military orders and communication regimes – therefore owners were denied direct contact.

My first and probably only dramatic step was to send a fax to all the shipping companies involved (it is of note that we ended up with fifty-two ships on our books) to explain my task briefly, and to ask for the name and contact details of the person who would wish to be the first to know if something untoward should happen to their ship. This, I believe, concentrated minds upon the gravity of the situation.

Colonel Mike Bowles MBE, Port Squadron Commander from 17 Port Regiment, RCT, has some startling memories concerning the loading of one of these STUFT:

The first few days were feverish activity for Marchwood. First, the LSLs were loaded – at least those that were in UK. *Bedivere* was in Vancouver and the *Tristram* languishing in the balmy waters off Belize, with nothing more war-like than tropical kit to wear! Two were loaded in Marchwood and the remaining two in Devonport, and by the Monday evening they were sailing to join the hurriedly assembled Task Force. Each LSL sailing had on board a detachment of twelve stevedores and plant operators from the Regiment as well as a Mexeflote raft with a crew of six. A couple of ships also took workboats with a further crew of four. So quickly, the numbers deploying from the Regiment were increasing. We next started the task of loading commercial ships taken up from trade (STUFT) in various ports around the country. I remember a particular one, the MV *Elk* of P & O, which loaded in Southampton. A large Ro-Ro ferry, she was soon looking decidedly war-like with Bofors guns fitted to the foc'sle and parts of her upper deck combing cut away to allow decent arcs of fire for Scimitar armoured vehicles of the Blues and Royals which were strategically parked to give added firepower to the vessel – well, an air defence capability anyway! Down below on the main vehicle deck a block stow of some 2,500 tons of ammunition of varying hazard categories was being finished off and when I arrived to check on the work of our busy stevedores, the shoring of the cargo was being carried out by REME shipwrights, sitting on top of the four-pallet-high stow, cutting the dunnage timbers with a petrol driven power saw. And all this in Southampton, a port with no ammunition licence at all! I am pleased that the Health and Safety Inspectors did not choose that particular night to attend! I was accompanied on this visit by my trusty Sergeant Major, Mike Cahill, who took me to one side and in his inimitable cockney way said, 'Cor blimey, Sir, if this lot goes up Winchester'll have a beach!' Many of the merchant ships deploying also took teams of stevedores from Marchwood with them, which further boosted numbers from the Regiment deployed.

Preparations continued on both sides. On the islands, the Argentine 5th Marine Infantry battalion, complete with full artillery support, arrived in Stanley on 8 April, even as General Haig and Prime Minister Thatcher had their first meeting.

At sea, RFA *Grey Rover* was established as 'resident work-up' tanker in the Portland area to be used by many STUFT for replenishment trials and training in Portland exercise areas.

Further south, HMS *Antrim, Plymouth* and RFA *Tidespring* were detached from the Main Battle Group (TG 317.8) with orders to 'proceed with dispatch' to Ascension, where the main RNSTS party were just arriving, ready to deal with the mountain of stores awaiting them.

Good Friday in 1982 was Friday 9 April, the same day that Britain announced its proposed Maritime Exclusion Zone (MEZ) around the Falklands. At the same time the Argentine military ordered that no troops on the Falklands were to initiate hostilities, possibly because the Argentines were still trying to keep the occupation low key thus making Britain's response look like over-reaction. And diplomatic activity continued with General Haig arriving in Buenos Aires to talk to General Galtieri and the Junta. He was to continue to London two days later, where Mrs Thatcher made it very clear that the only solution, as far as she was concerned, was a complete return to the *status quo*.

Britain's military build-up did not slow, however, and Good Friday was also the day that *Canberra*, her conversion complete, left Southampton, Ascension-bound, carrying 40 and 42 Royal Marine Commandos and 3 Para, together with MV *Elk* and her load of ammunition.

At Northwood, a combined RN/RNSTS movements cell was set up, specifically to oversee logistic support for the Task Force, thus freeing the staff of Empress State Building to return to their normal duties.

And at Ascension, RFA *Fort Austin* embarked three Lynx and two Wessex helicopters, along with 120 men of a combined SAS/SBS force and an RN surgical team, before heading south for her long-awaited rendezvous with HMS *Endurance*.

RFA *Stromness* and *Resource* caught up with the *Fearless* Group on 10 April, and while the EU was imposing sanctions on Argentina for the first time, *Stromness* began a major VERTREP with the other ships of the force, in the process transferring her SBS contingent to *Resource*.

HMS *Antrim, Plymouth*, and RFA *Tidespring* had by now arrived at Ascension, where *Tidespring* quickly embarked her two designated Wessex and their crews, together with 'M' Company, 42 Commando. The Marine Company had been flown out to Ascension Island beforehand and were tasked with re-taking South Georgia. Expecting to be the first British troops to see action, they were to be disappointed.

A mixed force of Royal Marines, SBS and SAS, amongst others, captured Grytviken on 25 April, almost without a shot being fired, while 'M' Company, through no fault of its own, was still 200 miles away aboard *Tidespring*. To add insult to injury, instead of then rejoining their Commando for the amphibious assault on San Carlos, 'M' Company were ordered to garrison South Georgia, remaining there for the rest of the war, which surely must have seemed an odd and frustrating use for the talents of those highly-trained and able young men.

The facilities at Ascension were being rapidly enhanced, much to the relief of the RNSTS working party, with the arrival of a complete set of mechanical handling equipment, including some much-needed fork lift trucks and an RNSTS mechanical handling expert.

Arrangements were also made to fly Geneva Convention Identity cards to RFA and to RNSTS personnel in RFAs.

More support ships were on the way, with the immensely powerful motor tugs *Salvageman* and *Irishman* sailing from Britain, and perhaps more importantly for the Task Force, the requisition by STUFT 1 of an oilfield repair ship, the *Stena Seaspread*. This was a peculiar-looking but immensely well-equipped vessel, and after a working-up period which included practising the techniques for changing a warship's Olympus turbine at sea, an operation never before undertaken outside a Naval dockyard, the *Stena* went south. She carried a full RN working party of 160 men and the Fleet Clearance Diving team as well as nearly 500 tons of specialised stores, mostly spare parts.

Admiral Woodward, on board HMS *Glamorgan*, arrived at Ascension on April 9 with TG 317.8/ Group II, consisting of HMS *Glasgow*, *Sheffield*, *Coventry*, *Arrow*, *Brilliant* and RFA *Appleleaf* along with *Glamorgan*. A few hours earlier, Captain Brian Young's *Antrim* task group, TG 317.8/ Group I, including RFA *Tidespring*, had set sail from Ascension, heading south. *Tidespring* was joined by her embarked flight, as their Flight Commander, Lt Mike Tidd, remembers:

845 'C' Flight joined RFA *Tidespring* off Ascension on 11 April 1982, along with a company of Marines from 42 Commando, and we almost immediately set sail with HMS *Antrim* and a detachment of 'D' squadron 22 SAS and HMS *Plymouth*, for South Georgia.

As the Flight Commander it was a bit of a culture shock as not only was 'C' flight not my normal team, but I and most of the team had never worked as an embarked flight on a Royal Fleet Auxiliary before. As we sailed south towards the Antarctic we were not only rapidly shaking-out as a team but also adapting to the differences between operating from a naval warship and a fleet auxiliary.

The first thing that I had to get my head round was the chain of command. Normally when embarked in a warship I took orders and tactical direction/advice from the ship's command team. However on *Tidespring* the situation was somewhat different as, whilst I was answerable to Shane Redmond, *Tidespring's* Captain, for the conduct of the flight whilst embarked, the military command was across the water in *Antrim*. Shane however proved to be an excellent ally and worked very hard to ensure that the ship gave us all the support possible. This was later to be an invaluable partnership when we ended up operating as a prison ship for three weeks, taking the prisoners from South Georgia to Ascension for repatriation.

Tidespring was a fairly battered old lady of a fleet tanker, which was shortly due to be sold off under John Nott's defence cuts. She had just come from a NATO exercise where she had been sideswiped whilst refuelling a German frigate, which had left her with a badly dented port side, which didn't exactly enhance her looks. For all of that she was a pretty rugged old bird and she stood up well to the pounding that she got from the awesome seas in the South Atlantic.

As we sailed south we quickly realised that improvisation was going to be the order of the day, as many of the services that we would take for granted on a warship were just not available. Shane Redmond and I would pore over the Met chart each day and cobble together a forecast between us. This was not made any easier by the fact that I hadn't worked in the southern hemisphere before, where weather systems work the opposite way round to our end of the globe. The flow of intelligence to the tanker was also sketchy to say the least and we got our most up-to-date information from the BBC World Service each night.

The *Tidespring's* flight deck was a single spot deck, which meant that we could only range one aircraft at a time, and was often wreathed in the sulphurous smoke from the funnel just forward of it. The lads got very good at ranging and spreading the second aircraft in record time, but it still meant that it took us approximately fifteen minutes to get both aircraft airborne or recovered; something that was to give us some anxious moments later on.

The crew culture on board the tanker was also considerably different to what we were used to on a warship. The captain and officers were professional Royal Fleet Auxiliary, whilst the bulk of the crew were standard merchant seaman. The ship's ratings lived in single cabins with ensuite facilities whilst the flight ratings lived in a single communal mess deck, which caused some friction from time to time. My team of officers lived in double cabins in the officers' accommodation; roughing it by RFA standards but luxury compared to what we were normally used to.

Andy Pulford, an RAF pilot on exchange and my second-in-command, probably found the culture the hardest to get his head around. He was totally overawed by Ronnie, our cabin steward, who was very camp and would bustle in the mornings with his golden ringlets streaming out behind him and cup of tea in each hand. 'Good morning Flight Commander, and how is my Flight Commander this morning?' he would inquire with a little flourish. Meanwhile 'Pullthrough' would have disappeared under his bedcovers with his backside pressed very firmly to the bulkhead. I found this highly amusing and so when Ronnie innocently inquired as to whether Flt Lt Pulford would like a cup of tea, I would urge him on with: 'Oh I'm sure he would, Ronnie. He doesn't seem to be awake yet so you'll have to give him a little shake.'

As Ronnie's hand gently touched Pullthrough's shoulder he would appear from under his bedcovers like a Jack-in-the-box! No matter how much I reassured him that he wasn't Ronnie's type, I'm sure he slept most nights with one eye open!

My other two officers were Lieutenant Ian 'Jock' Georgesson and Sub Lieutenant Andy 'Boy' Berryman. Ian was a laid-back and highly reliable Scot, who had been a Wasp pilot at the same time as me, and was therefore well used to life at sea. He decided early on that, as he was going to war, he would shave his hair down to a crew cut. This quickly earned him the nickname of 'Bullitt' as he was the spitting image of Steve McQueen in the film of that name.

'Boy' Berryman was a tall, lanky sprog pilot whose boundless energy reminded me of a large red setter puppy as he rushed round knocking things over in his eagerness to please. He loved it when, to the great amusement of the RFA officers, we had a 'rumble' in the officers' bar to let off steam. The Boy was a big strong lad and would often emerge victorious from the sweating, panting pile of naval aircrew, having knocked over virtually every stick of furniture in the room.

Two days out of Ascension we rendezvoused with RFA *Fort Austin*, from whom we obtained rocket pods and GPMGs [General Purpose Machine Guns] but no rockets. 'C' Flight's flight commander Nick Foster was aboard the *Fort Austin* and was meant to transfer to *Tidespring* to take over his flight. However we both agreed that, as I was the squadron warfare instructor, it made sense for me to retain command of 'C' Flight and continue with them down to South Georgia.

RFAs continued to work-up their military capabilities and bring their embarked helicopter flights up to full capability. One example was RFA *Resource*, with the *Fearless* group, where her embarked flight practised loading drills and firing their 'cabin' gun. According to her Captain, the aircrew set about: '. . . strafing the smoke floats (previously dropped as targets) with commendable accuracy.' Next day was even more interesting when the helicopter crew practised firing live missiles.

On 10 April Britain turned up the political pressure by bringing into effect the previously-declared Maritime Exclusion Zone (MEZ) which extended to 200 miles around the Falklands.

One the same day RFA *Fort Austin* replenished HMS *Endurance*, the latter having been down to one meal a day for some days until the RFA arrived. All went smoothly until one of *Fort Austin*'s Wessex developed engine trouble and had to ditch a pallet of meat, weighing approximately one ton, into the sea. At least one of the SBS men took the accident philosophically, being heard to remark to his mate: 'Lucky it wasn't the beer.'

The Chief Officer describes the atmosphere aboard *Fort Austin*:

The day before we arrived at Ascension, I remember being given various signals which detailed changes to the SHOL for both Lynx and Wessex Helicopters, which gave a slight clue as to what might be happening on the next day when we arrived at Ascension. A further signal stated that a helicopter would be arriving at about 04.00 hrs. It soon became apparent when we anchored off Ascension on the morning of 6 April, that a build up at Ascension had already started, as many different people arrived onboard stating that they were going to embark on *Fort Austin*. Over the period of the next few days we embarked some 192 persons from all three services with their equipment, including two Wessex HU 5's and three Lynx helicopters.

The task was then to find accommodation for them all. This initially fell to the Purser's Department, but then this was off-loaded upon me. My other task was to try and keep a track of who was boarding and staying and who was only visiting etc. A rather daunting task as one had to be continually going to Flyco, Hangar Top, Flight Deck, Pilot ladder and the Purser's Office.

We eventually left Ascension after two and a half days to meet up with HMS *Endurance*, having accommodated most of the embarked personnel in cabins, doubling up where necessary and using daybeds in some cabins. We even had to use one of the holds for a section of SAS. So leaving Ascension we had four flights (one Wessex flight of two helos and three single Lynx flights), approximately 80 SAS, 22 SBS and about 15–20 RAF personnel!

During the run south to meet *Endurance* we had some interesting experiences. We spent many hours trying out the best way to get as many helicopters into the hangar as we could, and eventually managed to get to the best possible stowage of a Lynx and a Wessex in each side of the Hangar with the third Lynx parked to one corner of the deck near the Hangar door. We also had a day when the various troops put their boats and parachuting skills to practice. It was very nice to see that they all got on reasonably well together, and there was much help and assistance given by the ship's staff to get such things as outboard motors to work, and I believe the SAS were most grateful for the assistance of an Engine Room Cadet, who managed to fashion a firing pin for a Milan or such like missile launcher, and to see it successfully fired.

On meeting up with *Endurance*, *Tidespring* and *Plymouth* on or about 12–13 April, we offloaded the SAS and SBS plus our Armilla RN medical team to the three ships plus a lot of essential stores to *Endurance*. We took a number of civilians off the *Endurance* for return to Ascension. These included a TV crew. Another day we met up with the first group of escorts going south and we started off on one of those epic RASs that went on for about twenty-seven hours. Everybody mucked in, helping in the holds, on the points and anywhere else that they could be of assistance. People worked until they dropped, went away had a quick nap and were back again. I even believe that some worked right through. Ships just kept on coming round for more loads until they had got what they wanted or were full.

It was noticeable that some of the loads were what probably became the staple diet for many weeks, Argentinean corned beef! Needless to say the RNSTS wags had penned a few comments to these loads as well as on some of the others. I suppose there was as much going off the back end as there was the points, but I never got the chance to go up there. After that hectic period it was off back to Ascension for more stores. We arrived back there to find the anchorage fairly full of ships: Navy, RFA and STUFTS.

Argentina sent new proposals on 13 April, apparently offering more flexibility, while the RNSTS London movements cell finally reverted to normal working, leaving all South Atlantic movements to be controlled from Northwood.

At sea, RFA *Brambleleaf* was by now off the Cape of Good Hope, heading south, while RFA *Tidespring*, with *Antrim*'s South Georgia task group, made her expected rendezvous with *Fort Austin*. *Fort Austin* first replenished fuel from *Tidespring*, before transferring food and ammunition (178 loads) to the RN ships along with the SAS and SBS teams she'd embarked at Ascension. Food and the Naval surgical team were then transferred to RFA *Tidespring*, before *Fort Austin* turned north, heading for a rendezvous with the *Brilliant* Group. On the same day MV *British Tamar*, MT *Yorkshireman* and MV *British Tay* sailed from the UK.

The next day the *Antrim* group rendezvoused with HMS *Endurance*, and *Tidespring* improvised a fuel rig which she then used to replenish *Endurance* with Dieso. HMS *Endurance* was something of a problem for the RFA, because she was one of the very few ships in the Royal Navy not equipped for fuel transfer at sea. The reasons for this were fairly obvious, of course, in that *Endurance* always bunkered from the fuel tanks in Stanley, which the RFA kept topped up for her.

Tidespring's Master describes the problems the RAS(L) with *Endurance* posed:

Not being fitted for replenishment at sea, refuelling *Endurance* in the ASI [Ascension Island] area posed a unique problem. There was too much swell coupled with the generally poor manoeuvring characteristics of a single-propeller vessel to warrant the risks involved in Rafting-up, there was also a further problem with a mismatch of connections. The solution was to transfer one of my Officers to *Endurance* and carry out an assessment of the situation. My XO [Executive Officer], Chief Officer Alec Bilney and Seaman Chief Petty Officer Ron Kennedy were then able to develop a way forward. The solution was relatively simple in the end – the engineers made the connections, we passed two quarter lines across, towed *Endurance* astern at steerage speed of six to eight knots and passed a home-made rig by float and gunline. A slow, but simple and effective piece of improvisation.

After refuelling, the *Antrim*'s Group I headed for South Georgia, accompanied by *Endurance*. Group II, consisting of HMS *Brilliant*, *Sheffield*, *Coventry*, *Arrow* and *Glasgow*, left Ascension, followed by RFA *Appleleaf*. Commanded by *Brilliant*'s Capt J Howard they would eventually proceed at twenty-five knots to a position 1,200 miles south of Ascension, acting as the Carrier Group screen and cover for *Antrim*'s attack on South Georgia.

However, the whole group were short of ammunition and food, so a signal was sent to the long-suffering *Fort Austin*, requesting a RAS (S) on the 16th. As one of the Fort's embarked RNSTS stores team put it: '. . . demands flooded in and it soon became obvious that the forthcoming RAS would dwarf all that had gone before.'

In London, the War Cabinet discussion on 15 April came to the conclusion that '. . . blockade of the Falklands was impossible.' Luckily, nobody told the Navy or the RFA that, although they probably would have taken no notice, since both services have a reputation for doing the 'impossible'.

On West Falklands, the largely uninhabited part of the island group, the Argentines continued with their preparations, which mostly took the form of establishing observation posts (OPs). General Haig went to Buenos Aires for more talks, which resulted in a telephone conference between US President Reagan and President Galtieri, and while Galtieri was explaining his peaceful intentions, the Argentine Fleet (TF 79) quietly put to sea.

HMS *Glamorgan*, which had left Ascension the day before, rendezvoused with the *Hermes* group, which included RFA *Olmeda* (Capt G P Overbury), the latter carrying FFO specifically to refuel the older carrier. Admiral Woodward transferred to *Hermes* by helicopter and the whole Group, having been previously joined, on passage, by HMS *Alacrity*, *Broadsword* and *Yarmouth*, proceeded towards Ascension.

After another meeting between Haig and Galtieri, Argentina decided on another set of concessions on 16 April but there was some concern in Buenos Aires over US bias.

In the UK, RFA *Blue Rover* (Capt D A Reynolds) sailed from Portsmouth and there was a call for munitions production, particularly, Sea Wolf, Sea Dart and the other Navy missiles to be accelerated, since the Navy's projections for consumption of such items during the conflict indicated a serious shortfall.

Fort Austin rendezvoused with the *Brilliant* Group and began what became known to the RFA's crew as the 'MEGARAS'. In the words of Jim Quirk, *Fort Austin*'s Supply and Transport Officer (Naval):

It started at 20.30 on 16 April and finished at midnight on the 17th – at the time it was referred to 'Operation Insomnia'. Ten consecutive jackstay transfers were carried out, each ship in the group connecting twice – once for general stores and provisions and once for ammunition. Fifteen Sea Dart missiles were issued in three consecutive transfers, as well as Sea Skua, Sea Wolf and Seac Cat missiles, lightweight torpedoes and a wide range of conventional ammunition. Since the Group was steaming to an operational area they back-loaded all excess paints, other inflammables, corrosives, ceremonial equipment and practice ammunition – in total some 200 loads, making a grand total for the evolution of 580.

When the jackstay work finally finished it was still necessary for a lot of the returned items to be stowed and secured, in particular the ammunition; some of my working party stayed at work to tidy up until 04.00 on Sunday 18th, which meant that they had been on continuous duty for forty-six hours. The achievement of the MEGARAS was all the more remarkable because it was performed by men who had already spent two of the previous four days conducting large scale replenishments at short notice and in particular were very short on sleep.

Together with her normal stores, *Fort Austin* also back-loaded the Group's 'special weapons', taking one 600 nuclear round from *Brilliant* and one 600 (S) (surveillance) round from *Sheffield*.

While the *Brilliant* Group were being replenished, the carriers HMS *Hermes* and *Invincible* arrived at Ascension, in company with *Alacrity*, *Broadsword*, *Yarmouth* and *Glamorgan*, having spent the trip working up air crews and carrying out drills to reduce the time to get to action stations. Most ships in the Group eventually achieved a fully closed-up state to action stations in about four minutes.

Other RFA activity included *Olmeda*, which had been previously detached from the Carrier Group and sent north to rendezvous with HMS *Fearless*, eventually finding herself in company with HMS *Antelope* and the LSLs instead. And reinforcements continued to be sent from UK dockyards, including MV *Stena Inspector* and MV *Stena Seaspread* after their conversion to repair ships, while another tug, MV *Wimpey Seahorse*, sailed from Devonport.

The next day the British nuclear submarine *Conqueror* entered the northern iceberg limit, while RFA *Resource* arrived at Ascension and was immediately tasked to replenish HMS *Glamorgan* at sea. While this was in progress a Russian Tu-95 'Bear' reconnaissance aircraft made several passes over the vessels. *Resource*, having finished her RAS, returned to Ascension's SW anchorage, just off the airfield, where she transferred forty-two loads aboard by helicopter.

On Sunday 18 April, RFAs *Olmeda* and *Resource* left Ascension as part of the Carrier Battle Group (TG 317.8) in company with HMS *Hermes*, *Glamorgan*, *Broadsword*, *Yarmouth*, and *Alacrity*. HMS *Invincible* sailed later but soon caught up with the main group.

Before leaving, *Resource* refuelled from *Olmeda* and while talking over the sound-powered telephone, it was learned that *Olmeda* had only one month's food left, her No 8 rig was being worn out and she was steering from the command shelter. So, it wasn't just *Tidespring* that stood in need of TLC.

The trooping vessels were also gathering, and on 19 April five of the LSL landing ships, escorted by HMS *Antelope*, arrived at Ascension, together with HMS *Fearless*.

The day before, *Canberra* had reached Freetown, making a refuelling stop before heading on to Ascension, and, in Britain, another BP River-class tanker, *British Trent*, left Portsmouth for the South Atlantic.

Captain Phil Roberts, Master of *Sir Galahad*, describes their journey:

On the passage south to Ascension we prepared ourselves for war by exercising our NBCD [Nuclear, Biological and Chemical Defence] teams, action stations, working up our Gazelles (only the Flight Commander had previously done any deck landings; all the other pilots were new to the game). As far as possible, we tried to integrate the Royal Marines into the day-to-day running of the ship; Officer Commanding Troops attended my daily Heads of Departments meetings where a lot of problems were ironed out. LSLs had not originally been built to embark so many troops for such a long period. There were few facilities for relieving the boredom and making life easier in very cramped dormitories. There was very little upper deck space left, due to deck cargo, for physical training; even the flight deck was overcrowded with three Gazelles. I have to admire the spirit of the Royal Marines. They remained unremittingly cheerful throughout the journey south. I received very few moans or complaints from them; they were all desperately keen to get down there and get on with the job.

Much the same happened to *Sir Percivale,* as Captain Tony Pitt recalls:

The period at anchor in Lyme Bay was spent conducting routine drills for the embarked force and generally settling down. The Embarked Force (EF) comprised of 'B' Echelon 45 Cdo, 7, 8 and 148 Batteries Royal Artillery, Condor Troop 59 Cdo Sqdn, 'M' Flt BAS and the LSL & Mexe Detachments RCT from Marchwood, totalling 310 Persons. It was also a period for taking stock to see what we might have missed. It was realised that food, water, beer and minerals would be a problem in the long term and, from day one, these were all rationed. The opportunity was also taken to commence flying operations and it was soon discovered that problems would be encountered with positive control of the helicopters due to no transponder being fitted on the aircraft and no receiver on the ship.

This phase of the operation started at midnight on 6 April with a rendezvous with other vessels of the Task Force, off Eddystone Lighthouse. The period was spent working up the ship in all aspects of its task. A lot of time was spent with flying operations in order to familiarise the aircrews with operations at sea. Many internal exercises were held dealing with the safety of the ship, and those of the EF [Embarked Force] who being suitably trained were incorporated into the ship's organisation. Replenishment at Sea (RAS) approaches were also practised with other ships including stern RAS which was considered the most suitable method of refuelling in the waters of the South Atlantic.

On the maintenance front, time was spent painting out any high visibility colours on the ship that stood out, including the white areas.

On the operational side the following points are of interest:

a.   During flying operations on 9 April one Gazelle had an accidental inflation of one flotation bag. The pilot quickly inflated the other bag and returned to the deck for a precautionary landing. Flotation bags were not again used.

b.   It was thought that it would be possible to fire a 105mm gun from the vehicle deck and 7 Battery were given permission to set it up for inspection.

c.   On Saturday 10 April we carried out an extensive Vertical Replenishment (VERTREP) with *Resource,* transferring all stores that were held by us for many ships further south.

   d. Replenished bunkers from *Pearleaf* on 15 April and provisions from *Stromness* on 18 April.

During the trip down we received information on future intentions, the most important of which were as follows:

   a. The mix of ammunition and vehicles on all ships was unsatisfactory and there would be extensive reshuffling of cargo throughout the force on arrival at Ascension Island (ASI). *Sir Percivale* would be loaded in a logistic configuration and used for resupply.

   b. During the period at ASI the LSLs would be fitted with air defence weapons comprising Bofors 40/60 and GPMGs.

   c. After leaving ASI the Mexeflote raft would not be side-loaded but broken down and stowed on deck. This would mean that the raft size would have to be reduced to sixty-six feet.

   d. Official clearance was given to operate Sea King helicopters from the after Flight Decks of LSLs.

On 15 April *Fearless* left the group and *Antelope* took over control and proved very conscientious, calling a meeting of all RFA Captains to investigate any problems and holding an Operation Awkward (counter underwater swimmer actions) brief prior to arrival at ASI. A considerable amount of cross-decking took place during the passage and *Sir Percivale* was visited by most of the senior officers who were embarked with the Force.

By now the crisis was in its sixth week, with no sign of a political settlement. British military preparations continued, and by 18 April all ships in the Carrier Battle Group were now working in the routine of 'Defence Watches', a twenty-four-hour shift system. Woodward needed time for his fighting ships and aircraft to inflict as much damage as they could on the Argentine Navy and Air Force before the vulnerable, lightly-armed LSLs arrived to make their invasion run.

The LSLs and their escorts, now designated the Amphibious Group (TG 317.0), remained at Ascension until nearer the date set for the landing with 3 Commando Brigade (TG 317.1), who were then able to receive some extra training ashore and afloat.

In the South Atlantic, *Conqueror* was surveying South Georgia, while back in Britain, RFA *Regent* sailed from Devonport and the old supply tanker RFA *Plumleaf* left from Portland. Both RFAs then joined HMS *Argent* and *Argonaut* for the voyage to Ascension.

Her dockyard work finished, SS *Uganda*, now converted to a hospital ship, left Gibraltar for her station in the Red Cross Box. No one, especially not the politicians who started the whole business, could know how soon this hurriedly-converted 'floating bedpan' was going to be needed. Nor how desperately.

In a last flurry of diplomatic activity 20 April saw the formulation by General Haig of a 'Memorandum of Agreement' which he intended to be put to both sides. Needless to say no agreement was ever reached or discussed on the basis of this document.

Meanwhile, RFA *Stromness* arrived at Ascension, some little way behind the *Fearless* group, while *Resource*, now at sea with the Carrier Battle Group, transferred one 600 special weapon from HMS *Broadsword* to her secure containment facility. *Canberra*, soon to be christened 'The Great White Whale', and MV *Elk* also arrived in the Ascension anchorage. Her commandos quickly disembarked to begin training, while HMS *Fearless*'s artificers began to modify *Elk* for helicopter operations.

Subtlety was not a major factor in *Elk's* conversion: the Navy men simply cut away several hundred feet of her seven-foot high gunwale before building covered stowage for three Sea King helicopters. The space provided for the helicopter deck turned out to be sufficient to land even the big twin-rotored Chinook.

Ships continued to arrive or be despatched from the UK. *Salvageman*, the powerful ocean-going tug anchored off Ascension, had been delayed by a fire in the galley. Fortunately, Royal Navy artificers got to work and she was rapidly made ready to sail. And in the UK, MV *Fort Toronto*, the only water tanker to serve in the South Atlantic, set sail, also heading for Ascension.

Operation Corporate was coming together. With *Antrim's* group on the way to South Georgia, the Carrier Battle Group approaching the Falklands and the 'bayonets' of the invasion force ashore at Ascension for training, the stage was set for what all the military theorists said couldn't be done: a successful invasion by a force inferior in numbers of troops, aircraft and supplies against an entrenched enemy.

It remained to be seen if the quality and training of the British would make the difference.

CHAPTER FIVE

ASCENSION ISLAND

L YING AS IT DOES about eight degrees south and fourteen degrees west, Ascension Island enjoys a mild, warm climate whose main feature is the southeast trade wind which, blowing almost continually, serves to make the incessant dust and ash an everyday feature of life there.

Named from the date of its discovery, Ascension Day, 1501, it is volcanic in nature, the thirty-four square miles of the island consisting predominately of lava, with a covering of fertile soil on places like Green Mountain, known locally as 'the Peak'.

This is the island's highest point, boasting one of the few areas of cultivated land, which once supplied meat and fresh produce to the population. Their numbers vary anywhere between 1,000 and 1,200 individuals, and are made up of St Heleneans, Europeans and Americans.

The British arrived in 1815, establishing a Marine garrison in 1821 in order to deny the place to anyone intent upon attacking nearby St Helena, where Napoleon was housed after his Waterloo defeat.

In 1982, Two Boats, in the centre, and the American camp near Wideawake airfield were the other main centres of population. Facilities included a 10,000-foot runway, operated by Pan-Am for the American military at Wideawake, and the BBC's short wave relay station, together with a manual telephone exchange run by Cable and Wireless. Otherwise, resources were found to be severely limited when the Royal Navy turned up in the early spring of 1982, intent upon converting this peaceful chunk of Atlantic lava into an intermediary airhead, training ground and naval base from which to retake the Falkland Islands.

Arriving almost on the heels of the first group of RN helicopter maintainers came the newly appointed Commander British Forces, Ascension Island, Captain Bob McQueen CBE RN. He was soon to be known as 'Captain One In, One Out' because of his firm intention not to allow non-essential personnel to remain and use up the island's sparse resources, particularly accommodation and water, which were to remain in short supply for the whole of the war.

He found himself in charge of a threefold organisation, consisting of: RN operations, including helicopters; RAF operations, predominantly the C-130 Hercules of Transport Command; and the hugely complex RNSTS logistics effort.

Soon, however, under the direction of McQueen and his team, order began to prevail out of initial chaos. Aviation fuel (AVCAT) was, to begin with, one of the main logistic headaches, but with the arrival of the Royal Engineers, a pipeline was quickly laid from the shore installation, serviced via the offshore fuelling buoy, to a flexible 'tank farm' on the airfield. Over twelve million gallons of AVCAT were eventually delivered in this way, from the various American tankers, which were connected in turn to the buoy. Despite this, AVCAT was always in short supply during the war, although it never became the limiting factor it might have been without the pipeline.

Accommodation was provided, at first, using tents and then by the loan from the US Government of flat-packed cardboard huts, complete with services and mop and bucket. These clever designs unfolded for erection, their peculiar conformation leading to the huts being dubbed 'concertina city'. Reverse osmosis units were imported to supply potable water, although water was never plentiful. At one point, these makeshift arrangements were catering for the needs of over 1,400 service personnel, with a team of Royal Navy Regulators responsible for their smooth operation.

Food supply was also initially a problem, but the RNSTS team, whose responsibility this was, soon arranged to borrow a dry store from Cable and Wireless which was quickly racked out for use. Along with the importation of two refrigerated containers from the UK, adequate stocks of both fresh, tinned and frozen food stuffs were available, although without some of the variety many were used to. Lettuces, particularly, tended to be in short supply.

Fixed-wing sorties and the innumerable daily helicopter deployments were also swiftly and ruthlessly co-ordinated, with safety a priority.

They needed to be, because RNSTS personnel were soon organising the mountain of airlifted stores that seemed to grow daily, into lanes on the south-east corner of the runway apron. These all had to be marked according to destination and made ready to be loaded into cargo nets for airlift to the waiting ships. Six million pounds of freight were dispatched by air to Ascension between 2 April and 11 July, all to be re-packed and organised by the RNSTS.

One particular worry during this period was the lack of a designated area for the storage of ammunition. This, unfortunately, led to the ordnance being piled at one end of the runway, almost directly under the helicopter-landing path, where any personnel nearby would have been extremely vulnerable in the event of an air attack or special forces raid, both seen as distinct possibilities by the Task Force commander.

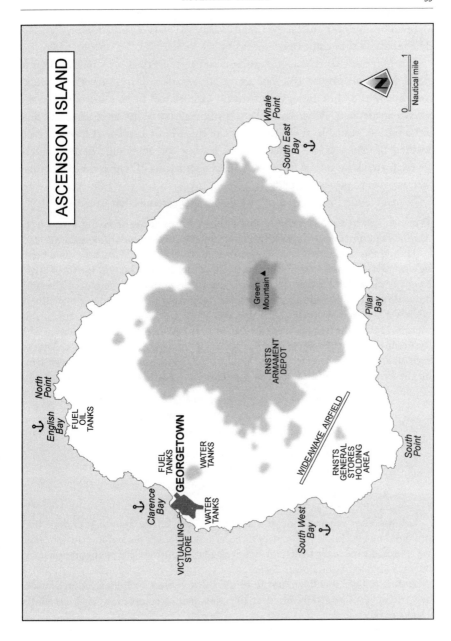

Fortunately, an area was quickly designated about a mile from the airport and a secure containment facility was dug out of the side of a hill and placed under the control of a qualified member of the RNSTS team.

In addition to the stores, the island 'welcomed' over 6,000 additional visitors or 'tourists' as they came to be known by the locals.

Not only were the LSLs, ammunition and store carriers, which arrived on 19 April as part of Amphibious Task group 317.0, expected to cope with this backload but at the same time, their existing cargoes had to be reorganised in the wholly inadequate Ascension Island anchorage, so as to have essentials like ammunition available from the moment the troops landed. Added to their loading problems was the necessity of leaving the anchorage every night to forestall attack by special forces or midget submarine, of which the Argentines were known to possess several.

Captain Tony Pitt, Master of RFA *Sir Percivale*, recalls that time:

We anchored in Clarence Bay at first light 19 April, before receiving a visit from Marine Superintendent Captain D Thompson concerning our Chinese crew.

Throughout the period in ASI redistribution of cargo took place, interrupted only by a small hiccup on 22 April when, for a short time, it was thought the force might have to sail early. Further delays were experienced from the night of the 26th onwards as all ships had to proceed to sea every night because of the possibility of underwater swimmer attack. Each ship was given a sector to patrol in darken ship routine. During the first night of this dispersal we had a close-quarters situation with the ocean-going tug *Irishman* who seemed to be wandering about aimlessly. After an exchange of messages on VHF radio we de-conflicted without damage. Much later, off the Falkland Islands, we received a missive from the Master that was as follows:

> 'We regret our intrusion in the midst of the night
> It was not an illusion there you're quite right
> But the Irishman seeking a place for safekeeping.
>
> We've had time to ponder and make up our mind,
> Not the oceans to wander or sector and kind,
> So without any rancour we'll stay here at anchor!'

He obviously had a keen sense of humour!

On the ship defence side the armament was fitted. Standing Orders were produced by CPO Harvey (Gunnery Officer) and, although the system had to be tried we appeared to be ready to defend ourselves. Due to the foredeck configuration it was only possible to fit one Bofors 40/60.

A stern anchor was flown out from the UK to replace one damaged in previous operations. This was duly fitted at the port quarter so enabling an Operational Defect to be cleared.

It had been hoped that the EF [Embarked Force] would be able to put in some training but due to various circumstances only one exercise was completed. This involved transporting 7 Battery and their guns by helicopter to the airfield for a mock assault. From the point of view of ship organisation it seemed to go very well.

On logistics the lub-oil stocks were replenished from *Blue Rover* in the early hours of Tuesday 27th and fresh water was fully topped up from the tanker *Fort Toronto* overnight Thurs/Fri whilst lying alongside. On completion of watering at 05.20 Z Fri 30 April, the ship was, in all respects, ready to proceed to the Falkland Islands area. *Sir Percivale* steamed to the southwest of Ascension and waited until the early hours of Saturday morning for all the other LSLs to be watered.

Some passengers had been transferred before departure. We had lost 148 and 8 Batteries and 59 Cdo Sqdn Condor Troop, and embarked Cdo Log Reg, Main 'B', total passengers now 335.

RFA *Sir Galahad*'s experiences were similar, according to her Master, Phil Roberts:

At Ascension we spent ten days frantically cross-decking Royal Marines and our cargo. By now it had been decided which LSL would be doing what at the landing. This meant considerable reshuffling of the cargo which had been hurriedly loaded at Plymouth and at the other ports where our sister ships had been loaded. We did get a Bofors, six GPMGs [machine guns] and a Blowpipe missile launcher fitted here, together with crews to fire them. We were also allocated sandbags, which after a great deal of hassle we managed to fill and place on the upper bridge deck as protection for the GPMG crews.

In our role as logistic support ship we sailed from Ascension loaded with WMR [War Maintenance Reserve] and a mixed array of vehicles and with the following embarked: Commando Logistic Regiment, HQ and Sigs, elements of the Field Dressing Station. We knew of the very large Argentinean Air Force yet to be neutralised and also of the many Exocet missiles they were capable of deploying against us.

Given these loading problems, it is hardly surprising that the back-load did not all get done. The Rapier missile systems, for example, had been sensibly loaded in the bottom of the LSL holds, wrapped in plastic so as to minimise the effects of salt corrosion, but the delay entailed in finding and moving such equipment meant they couldn't be checked at Ascension, resulting in a long wait before they became fully operational at the beachhead.

The LSLs did, however, receive some welcome means of self-defence in the form of Bofors guns and a Royal Artillery Blowpipe detachment, as the gunners' commander, Lt Colonel Roger Dickey, explains:

If there were doctrine and tactics to cover the air defence of LSLs, no one appeared to know what they were or where they could be found. The most helpful advice offered was to get hold of a video copy of *The Longest Day* and to read *The Cruel Sea*. One section of 'D' Troop, 43 Air Defence Battery Royal Artillery with the Battery Captain as LSL Air Defence advisor to COMAW [Commodore Amphibious Warfare], was ordered to catch up with the Fleet at Ascension Island and, with Commando GPMG gunners and the promise of 40/60mm Bofors to follow, hatch an air defence plan to cover a beach assault on Stanley. The landing ships chosen to lead the assault (the plan changed later) were *Sir Lancelot, Tristram, Percivale* and *Galahad*.

Each was allocated a Blowpipe detachment with up to ten missiles, six GPMG gunners and one or two Bofors with ammunition mostly dated as 1940. A fully-laden LSL makes for a very crowded firing platform, with wire hawsers getting in the way and limiting firing arcs to the front and with vehicles, helicopters and refuelling apparatus getting in the way of Blowpipe's severe efflux zone to the rear. With each ship loaded differently, a compromise saw missiles on the flight decks, machine guns on the roof of the bridge and Bofors on their bow mountings, giving, one way or the other, 360 degree coverage.

Inevitably there was an uneasy alliance between everyone aboard and at least initially, by ships' officers and crew alike, air defenders were treated as a very dangerous addition to the embarked troops roll. Talk of engaging ground targets with all systems on the run-in to the beach did nothing to allay fears. A combination of test firing on Ascension and the successful engagement of splash targets towed by the ill-fated HMS *Antelope*, briefings, day and night watches and the general 'mucking in' of the air defenders started to shift the perception balance from 'embarked troops' to 'ship's roll'. Gunners, Royals, loggies and matelots were never going to particularly hit it off, though, during the relative inactivity on the long voyage south. A spoof signal from COMAW, concocted in the wardroom by officers tired of endless board games, had Officer Commanding Raiding Squadron asking around the Fleet for lime green, duck egg blue and sand coloured paint so as to prepare his raiders for any type of landing conditions. While on the freezing windswept bridge roof, wearing every spare piece of clothing in the Pusser's store and looking like grotesque Michelin men, an altercation between a Royal Artillery signaller and Royal Marine machine-gunner was allowed to be played out as neither pugilist could land a blow on his Sumo-like opponent.

As the convoy joins the main fleet and moves into a defensive formation we are an impressive sight and a timely replenishment of GPMG and Bofors rounds is wel-comed. Blowpipe missiles, as was to be proved, were a different matter. Baked in the equatorial sun, moved regularly by MHE [Mechanical handling Equipment], helicopter or manhandled, the ready missiles were now subjected to ship's vibration, the huge seas, freezing temperatures and salt air. On Ascension, detachments had undergone hundreds of simulated engagements while standing on a rocking surface in order to prepare them for future engagements at sea, but it was not the firing conditions but the aircraft pilots that were to really test the operators.

Unfortunately, while this redeployment and cross-decking was going on, the usually reliable crews of the LSLs began to be uneasy about the role they might be called upon to play and a certain amount of unrest appears to have developed. A senior officer, Captain David Thompson RFA, was despatched from Empress State Building to assess the situation, but by the time he arrived, the men had settled down into normal working. The problems clearly hadn't been fully resolved, however, because trouble was to develop once again, weeks later, on the San Carlos bridgehead.

Helicopters and the landing craft (LCUs) eventually got almost everything where it was needed and this period did prove invaluable, allowing the RFAs and STUFT practice in both damage control and air defence. Troops were able to practice embarkation drills and to zero all their weapons, including the RA's 105mm field guns, weapons that proved essential later on.

Other benefits were more nebulous but no less important, best expressed in the words of Commodore Michael Clapp, COMAW, who wrote later that, during the Ascension stopover, which lasted nearly two weeks: '. . . a huge degree of confidence and trust was achieved.' Which was to make an incalculable difference later, in the hell of San Carlos, better known to the crews who endured it as 'Bomb Alley'.

The LSLs of the Amphibious Task Group finally sailed on 1 May, followed by the *Canberra* group on the 7th, but the logistics effort slowed not at all, with a tanker designated to refuel the visiting Task Force vessels remaining on station. For much of this period, it was MV *Alvega*, which began duty on 21 May. As well as the station tanker, RFAs like *Fort Austin* visited periodically for replenishment, while *Tidespring* also arrived in mid-May with a cargo of nearly 200 Argentine POWs.

Offshore, during 25–27 April, another station tanker, RFA *Pearleaf*, set what was believed to be a record when she spent fifty-two hours continually connected to MV *British Tamar* in a marathon pumpover. Both the station tankers and the tank farm ashore were replenished by periodic visits from American tankers.

The war's end did not see the end of Ascension Island's usefulness, either. Despite its being over 3,000 miles from the Falklands, the RAF's Transport Command still used Wideawake as a forward operating base, refuelling the C-130 Hercules in flight on their way to the new strip mat runway at Stanley.

One RFA man, Jim Keller, has somewhat alarming memories of his trip south:

I was on leave during the war, but arrived on one of the first flights in. We left Brize Norton on a VC 10, there were about ten of us in total as passengers and I was the lowest ranking.

Once we had taken off I asked the others if they minded if I smoked my pipe. Someone else piped up – cigars? Anyway nobody objected and we all started to smoke our favourite tobacco.

The next thing the steward came amongst us and requested that we put out our smoking implements. 'OK,' we all said, 'but can you please explain why?'

'That green tarp in the alleyway is covering the live ammo'.

'Shit!' we said, or words to that effect. Eventually we arrived at Lagos Airport to top up with fuel for the trip to Ascension Island.

We landed at the end of the runway very far from any buildings or persons. As soon as the aircraft stopped and the Captain said it was OK to get out, but not to go away from the tail of the aircraft, we shot out and had a good smoke.

Fuelled up and on our way to Ascension to spend the night under canvas.

Next day it was on to a 'Herkie-bird' and on our way to the Falklands. Forty-thousand rivets flying south in loose formation but we landed safely ... thirteen hours later!

During the flight they had to refuel and I was lucky enough to observe the refuelling from the flight deck. The pilot looked as if he was in his fifties – the RAF had pulled him out of retirement, so I was informed, and also that he had only one eye, which I didn't believe, but confirmed that was so at a later time. We started the refuelling at thirty-something thousand feet and ended up at about a hundred feet from the oggin, perhaps less. The Vulcan tanker's slowest speed, with brakes on and going downhill was the same as the Herkie-bird's top speed going downhill.

The operation was exciting and interesting to see so close up. The pilot was in total control of it all, feet on pedals, hand on yoke and the other hand on the throttles. Lined up with the markers on the Vulcan and socked into the probe first time. When the RAS was nearly complete I was requested to go back to my seat and it was then that I noticed that the pilot's jumpsuit was soaking with sweat, and it wasn't because of the heating!

As I left to head back to my seat the pilot asked what my interest was and I told him that the RFA did the refuelling at sea; that was when I noticed that one of his eyes didn't move in accordance with the other, in fact it didn't move at all!

Undoubtedly Ascension's role was crucial.

Without the island base, supply lines from the UK would have been impossibly long and air cover, except for the over-worked Harriers, all but non-existent, and there would have been no convenient half-way house to allow troops essential time to train, zero their weapons and rest after their sea voyage from the UK. On a more mundane but no less essential note, even mail delivery would have been next to impossible.

All these factors made Ascension an essential logistic prerequisite to both Operation Paraquat, the attack on South Georgia, and the vastly more complex Operation Sutton, as the Falklands invasion itself was designated.

CHAPTER SIX

SOUTH GEORGIA

O N WEDNESDAY 21 APRIL, while the ships of the Amphibious Task Group and the troop-carrying STUFT were organising themselves in the Ascension anchorage, they had an unexpected visitor in the shape of RFA *Fort Austin*. Still carrying the 'special weapons' she had back-loaded from *Broadsword* several days previously, she began a hasty but all-embracing re-store, almost before her anchor was secure. Her Chief Officer describes it:

After the hectic period of the MegaRAS, it was off back to Ascension for more stores. We arrived back there to find the anchorage fairly full of ships: Navy, RFA and STUFTs.

Very soon after arrival, the flight deck was busy again with loading stores. The STO(N) [RNSTS Supplies and Transport Officer (Naval)] and his team went ashore and earmarked the stores that would be the optimum value and use to us, and very soon afterwards the loads started appearing and it was soon realised that the only way to get them below was to have both lifts up and working. At times we had anything up to nine helos lining up to drop off loads. Some with passengers would offload on deck and then drop off the passengers on the hangar top. It was absolutely vital that we watched both places at once. It was pretty hectic! Then suddenly it would all go quiet as helos were re-tasked to move troops around the fleet, then when that was over, back they came in dribs and drabs. It was a relief to leave FLYCO at the end of the day, but then one had to go midships and sort out accommodation and other matters. Eventually after a couple of days, we returned to the south.

In the Commons, Francis Pym made a statement about the Government's intentions toward Argentina, implying that force would only be a last resort, which he was then forced to retract, having suffered the humiliation of being ordered to return to the House.

Farther south, RFA *Appleleaf* left the safety of the Carrier Group to undertake the role of 'motorway tanker', sailing a box course in the region of forty degrees south, where she replenished southbound ships of the various Task Groups until relieved on 26 April.

And off South Georgia, Capt Brian Young of *Antrim* and the men under his command were assessing the situation they found there.

The trip south had not been uneventful. There had been a number of dubious sonar contacts, at least by those ships with working sonar, which did not include either of the RFAs, and although some of these were identified as whales or thermal layers, enough were doubtful to keep most of the crews on edge.

Shane Redmond of *Tidespring* was emphatic about the submarine menace. In his own taped log he recorded on 20 April: 'Several red contacts from the Navy last night. Personally, I am convinced that we have had company since the 17th.'

There was something else exercising Shane Redmond's thought processes that freezing autumn day off South Georgia. With a cargo of 200 Royal Marines of 'M' Company, his own crew and a swimming pool full of AS 12 missiles neatly surrounded on all sides by fuel tanks full to the brim, he had the grand total of four machine guns for ship defence.

Off Gibraltar, just before deploying south, Captain Redmond had a conversation with Admiral Woodward, on the subject of arming RFAs, which left him considerable food for thought:

Immediately before the South Georgia Task Group split from the main body returning to the UK, Admiral Woodward asked if I needed anything. My response was 'Yes, some weapons', to which he responded that we would probably be more of a danger to ourselves than an enemy. In hindsight, how wrong can you be!

Gordon Wilson, the new RFA Fleet Manager for Personnel and Operations, also had some worries about RFA armament:

In 1982, RFAs were unarmed. Originally guns manned by naval personnel could be fitted if required, but in the event there was usually neither the time to fit and test them, nor could sufficient trained naval personnel be spared. Thus the policy was to rely on the protection of naval vessels against attack. During passage south most RFAs acquired hand-held machine guns (GPMGs), manned by servicemen. These provided some morale boost, but were not terribly effective in protecting the ship. And, as it turned out, warships had many other priorities in addition to the close protection of RFAs, which thus could be fairly vulnerable targets. Major debate following the Falklands Conflict resulted in the decision to equip RFAs with their own defensive armament, mainly manned by trained RFA personnel. This change led to a major increase in personnel training and was seen as altering the essentially civilian nature of the RFA Service. It brought the RFA into ever-closer co-operation with the Royal Navy, and led to the development of its potential to contribute substantially to any military operation in which its ships participated.

One of *Tidespring*'s Petty Officers (PO), Peter Robinson, recalls how the Royal Marines made themselves at home, despite her lack of weapons:

One of my memories of 42 Cdo was when I was coming back off the flight deck as we approached South Georgia. I had been to pump up the AVCAT tank, and as I came round the for'ard end of the flight deck, there were two Marines sitting in the

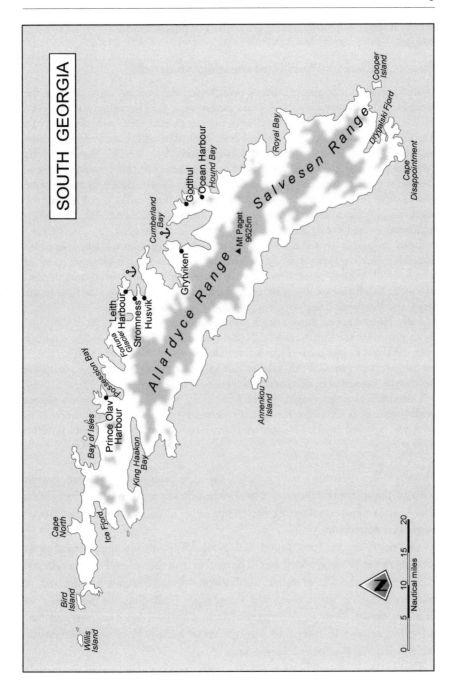

SOUTH GEORGIA

Cooper Island

Drygalski Fjord

Royal Bay

Cape Disappointment

Salvesen Range

Ocean Harbour
Hound Bay

Godthul

Cumberland Bay

Mt Paget 9625m

Grytviken

Allardyce Range

Leith
Fortuna
Glacier Harbour
Stromness
Husvik

Possession Bay

Bay of Isles

Prince Olav Harbour

King Haakon Bay

Annenkou Island

Cape North

Ice Fjord

Bird Island

Willis Island

N

0 5 10 15 20
Nautical miles

dry swimming pool, busily arming grenades. The pool at this time was full of AS 12 missiles.

One of 'M' Company remembered one of those men well:

Unfortunately one of the gentlemen which you were talking about arming the grenades in the swimming pool is no longer with us. His name was Sgt Mac McCleman, not too sure of the spelling of the surname, he was Troop Sergeant of 9 Troop, 'Mike' Company. I can remember we queued up on the shade deck armoury to 'ammo up' at about four in the morning, and Mac asked me how many L2 grenades I wanted. I asked him how far I had to throw it so that I would not get to wear any of it, to which he replied 'about 150 yards'. I then asked him what else he had on offer. 'White phosphorous' was the reply and it depended on which way the wind was blowing whether you were going to get your skin burned off!! I ended up with what seemed like a ton of link for my GPMG [machine gun].

I can remember that the Chef was on more money than us, and I can also remember that we spent most of our journey south moving trillions of boxes of ammo, of all different types, from one end of the ship to the other. It became a bit of a joke: 'What you are doing today: moving boxes of ammo from the bow to the stern, and tomorrow if we have finished, we are going to put it back.'

I also remember practising getting into Rigid Raiders in the middle of the night down the side of the ship in the middle of the Atlantic. Climbing down the scramble nets, the Rigid Raider seemed like it was miles below us, so we went further, then a bit further, then a swell would take us and we would have to scramble back up the nets, hence the name. Soaking wet and freezing cold, lots of fun.

I also remember abseiling down the front of the bridge. I think there are photos of this in the book *Operation Paraquat*; unfortunately we did not have a camera until after we captured South Georgia so I don't have any pictures of our time on *Tidespring*.

However, the RFA don't tend to dwell on little problems, like being shot at without the wherewithal to shoot back, when there's a job to do, whether it's a fifty-hour pumpover or landing 200 troops on an unknown shore in the face of Argentine opposition.

The next day, 22 April, found *Tidespring* off South Georgia, preparing to disembark her Wessex, which was to be used to land the SAS on Fortuna Glacier.

This wasn't the first plan that the Navy and Royal Marines had devised. A number of other suggestions had been made, including the possibility of beaching one of the ships, allowing the Marines to abseil down her bow and then using her engines in reverse to drag the vessel back to deep water, while the troops assaulted the Argentine positions.

Eventually, however, Fortuna was the preferred option, although the experienced mountaineers amongst the task group, like Guy Sheridan, were concerned about the ability of even the SAS to walk off this glacier.

Tidespring's two Wessex duly departed with the SAS embarked. Lt Mike Tidd RN, *Tidespring's* Flight Commander, was piloting the leading aircraft and now takes up the story:

South Georgia, a crescent-shaped island, 105 miles long and 18.5 miles wide, rises sheer out of the sea to a height of between 7,500 feet and 9,500 feet at its spine. Over half its land mass is permanently covered by ice in the form of glaciers. It lies in the South Atlantic on the edge of Antarctica at virtually the same latitude as Cape Horn and bears the full brunt of the wild weather that sweeps around the Cape.

Operation Paraquet (or 'Paraquat' as it was unwittingly dubbed by all involved) was the codename given to the operation to retake South Georgia in April 1982, at the start of the Falklands campaign. Having been the first piece of British territory to be captured by the Argentineans it was planned to be the first objective to be recaptured, partly for political reasons, but also to provide a cross-decking point for civilian ships acting as troop transports.

Tucked away on the edge of Antarctica, few people had heard of it. Certainly none of 845 Naval Air Squadron 'C' Flight would have claimed to have been able to point it out in an atlas before we embarked in the fleet tanker RFA *Tidespring* at Ascension Island to join the Task Group which had been charged with its recapture. 'C' Flight consisted of two Wessex 5s and about thirty personnel, with myself as Flight Commander, Flt Lt Andy 'Pullthrough' Pulford RAF, our tame Crab, as my second-in-command, Lt Ian Georgesson and Sub Lt Andy 'Boy' Berryman, and Leading Aircrewmen Tug Wilson and Jan Lomas.

The maintenance team was led by the fiery but very reliable Chief Bill Raines. Our two aircraft, Yankee Alpha (XT473) and Yankee Foxtrot (XT464) were standard Wessex 5s but fitted with SS 11/AS 12 rocket rails and M 260 missile sights as it was envisaged that we might be required to provide the Royals with fire support against bunkers or other strongpoints at some point during the operation. The Wessex 5 was a basic battlefield utility helicopter, completely devoid of any navaids or self-defence systems, but much loved by all who flew her. She was getting pretty long in the tooth by now, but was still a very rugged, manoeuvrable and reliable airframe that could absorb a lot of punishment and was forgiving enough to let many a young pilot off the hook when he mishandled her.

The Task Group consisted of the County class destroyer, HMS *Antrim*, the Task Group leader, with 'D' Squadron SAS embarked, RFA *Tidespring*, with 'M' Company of 42 Commando Royal Marines embarked, and HMS *Plymouth*, a Rothesay-class frigate, with elements of the SBS. The senior aviator of the group was *Antrim's* flight commander, Lieutenant Commander Ian Stanley, a very experienced 'Pinger' [anti-submarine] pilot. His Wessex 3, known as 'Humphrey', was quite an old airframe but, equipped with radar and a fairly sophisticated Automatic Flight Control System (AFCS), well-suited to the task of acting as a pathfinder for our Wessex 5s.

On the way south 'The Red Plum' (HMS *Endurance*) joined up with us and we received detailed briefings from Tony Ellerbeck, her Flight Commander, and David Ives, the Senior Hydrographer, on the terrain and the sort of weather conditions that we would find there. Having trained in northern Norway we were used to operating in Arctic conditions, but even so the sheer violence and unpredictability of the weather that Tony described sounded unpleasant to say the least. In spite of Tony's eloquence however, I don't think that any of us realised just *how* unpleasant until we experienced it at first hand. I suppose, looking back, that initially we mentally equated the conditions that he described with the worst of the weather that we had been used to operating in the Arctic. As it turned out this was a bit like equating a tabby to a tiger!

The first phase of the operation was to carry out a detailed reconnaissance of the Argentine positions. Our mission, code-named 'Dandelion', was to insert Captain John Hamilton's SAS patrol 2,500 feet up on Fortuna Glacier, from where they planned to make their way along the spine of the island to a point from which they could observe the Argentine garrison at Leith. Our lack of a realistic appreciation of the conditions is borne out by the fact that the initial thoughts were to use a night formation approach and a covert insertion of the SAS team onto the glacier. The Wessex 5s were fitted with beta lights and we even hatched a plan to do an airborne join-up with Humphrey, *Antrim's* Wessex 3, which would lead us in using its radar. We practised the airborne join-up with the two Wessex 5s on the night of 15 April and succeeded in frightening ourselves fartless. As Boy Berryman had not done any night formation before, I decided to put him in the right-hand seat and to demonstrate from the left. The process of the airborne join was tricky under the best of conditions, but peering round an M 260 sight and eventually flying with my head half out of the cockpit window in air temperatures of several degrees below zero made it very sporting indeed. Eventually we decided that discretion was the better part of valour and opted for a daylight insertion.

We arrived off the northwest tip of South Georgia on the morning of the 21st and, after Ian Stanley had carried out an initial recce in 'Humphrey', we embarked the troops and then got airborne in a three-ship echelon and set off through driving snow showers towards the coast. In accordance with normal 'Jungly' operating procedures, our two Wessex 5s flew with a single pilot and aircrewman, myself in Yankee Alpha with Tug Wilson, and 'Pullthrough' in Yankee Foxtrot with Jan Lomas.

Our first sight of the coast, as we made landfall at Cape Constance, was pretty awe-inspiring as black cliffs rising 1,000 feet vertically from the sea appeared through the driving snow. We skirted round through the low ground at the landward end of Cape Constance and emerged into Antarctic Bay, where the foot of the Fortuna Glacier disgorges into the sea. The turbulence was impressive: we would be using full power just to maintain height one moment and then be in full autorotation (no power applied) and still going up the next.

The weather on the glacier was wall-to-wall snow and, after orbiting in Antarctic Bay for some time, Ian Stanley made the decision to return to the ships and refuel. We headed back through heavy snowstorms, Ian Stanley to *Antrim* and 'Pullthrough' and I to *Tidespring*. *Tidespring's* deck could only operate one aircraft at a time, so I landed first and then watched while CPO Raines' team quickly folded the aircraft and stowed it in the hangar. In the meantime 'Pullthrough' was hovering off the port quarter with his aircraft building up an impressive accumulation of snow and ice!

At 11.45 we tried again. This time we were able to make better progress and climb up on to the upper slopes of the glacier, though it was still very murky and there was severe turbulence and a lot of snow being whipped up from the surface by the wind. To add to our deep joy and happiness, we could see that the surface of the glacier was heavily crevassed which meant that, whilst we might gain some visual references from the surface once we got close enough, we would have to be careful about where we put down. Ian Stanley led us up to near the top of the glacier and then turned into wind and made his approach using his Doppler and Automatic AFCS to let himself down onto the surface. As I turned into wind I realised how few visual references were going to be available to me, particularly as the last 200 feet of the approach was partially obscured by flying snow, and that the standard snow-landing approach would not be feasible. I overshot and went round again while Tug Wilson, my aircrewman, and I discussed the problem.

On the second approach I kept the aircraft orientated as best I could using the few distant references available, while Tug did a sterling job of talking me down gradually to the surface. It was a challenging approach to say the least. Apart from the lack of visual references, we were on the updraughting slope of the mountain and had to go into virtual full autorotation to persuade the aircraft to descend. Once we got close to the surface we could see that the crevassing was even worse than we had thought. We eventually touched down with a crevasse about ten feet away on our starboard side and started off-loading the troops. Despite having the collective lever fully down (no power applied), I found that we were being moved sideways and backwards by the wind. Sat on the surface we still had sixty knots of airspeed on the clock and I ended up having to fly the aircraft to try and keep it in position while Tug off-loaded as quickly as possible before we slid into the neighbouring crevasse. As soon as the off-load was complete we bounded into the air and scuttled off down the glacier and back into Antarctic Bay to wait for the others, before breathing a sigh of relief and returning to the ships. Back on board *Tidespring* 'Pullthrough' and I debriefed, agreed that we had never flown in conditions like these before, and said: 'Thank Christ we'll never have to do that again!' How wrong can you be!

Overnight we were meant to keep one aircraft on Casevac (Casualty Evacuation) standby, but as night came the barometer dropped thirty millibars in an hour and the wind rose to peak at gusts of eighty knots. The weather changed so fast that we were unable to fold the rotors on the deck alert aircraft and the tipsocks, which were meant to anchor the tips of the rotor blades to prevent them thrashing up and down in the wind, started to tear themselves apart. In the end we anchored the blades with heavy manilla mooring lines, lashed everything else down to the best of our ability and then wedged ourselves into our bunks to get what rest we could overnight.

When morning came and the wind eased down to just a full-blown gale we were quite surprised to find that the aircraft was still in one piece. However, up on Fortuna Glacier things were not looking so good. Overnight the wind on the glacier had peaked at over 100 knots and John Hamilton's team had had their shelters torn away. They were now cold, wet and starting to become hypothermic. We were not all that surprised when, at 10.00, they called for urgent evacuation as they were suffering from frostbite and exposure.

Our planned duty roster would have put Ian Georgesson and Boy Berryman in the frame to fly. However, though I was quite happy that Ian (the world's most unflappable and likeable Scot) was experienced enough for the task, the Boy, though a very competent young pilot, was still too new to the game to operate in the sort of conditions that 'Pullthrough' and I had experienced the day before. In addition I felt that someone with previous knowledge of the conditions and the lie of the land should go. I could hardly ask 'Pullthrough' to do something that I did not want to do myself, so I put myself down to fly the first of our two Wessex 5s, Yankee Foxtrot, with Tug Wilson as my aircrewman, and Ian and Jan Lomas to fly Yankee Alpha. It would be fair to say that neither of us was looking forward to the trip but, if I had to go up there again, I was glad to have Tug with me. He and I knew each other from our time flying Wasps and I had great respect for his calm reliability and unfailing sense of humour.

We launched between snowstorms at about 10.30 and headed off into shore. As we entered Antarctic Bay the weather over the glacier looked pretty awful so Ian Stanley ordered our two Wessex 5's to land on the low ground at Possession Bay while he recce'd ahead. Ian Georgesson, in his inimitable fashion, soon had Jan Lomas out wading about in the snow taking happy snaps of all of us with Ian's camera. Eventually Ian Stanley returned to say that he had been unable to find a break in the weather over the glacier and so we returned to the ships to refuel and wait.

An hour or so later we tried again and this time we arrived at the foot of the glacier to find a break in the cloud. As we set off up the glacier we were acutely aware that we were going to be very short of escape options up there. Normally, no sensible pilot flies himself into a situation where he does not have escape options. In this case, if we got caught in the air by the weather we might be unable to land because of whiteout; we would be unable to climb as we were already experiencing icing; the only route in or out was the one we were taking as we had mountains on either side of us, and in the Wessex 5s we had no radar, doppler or Automatic Flight Control System.

Ian Stanley led us up through the clear patch and, as we approached the top of the glacier, we spotted the smoke grenades that the SAS team had fired to mark their position. They had only moved a few hundred yards from where we had dropped them and were now huddled in the lee of some rocks in an area that was relatively free of crevasses. Their smoke grenades had stained the snow around them making the approach and landing relatively straightforward this time. We landed facing our escape route down the glacier, which at this point was a fairly shallow ice slope leading down about a mile to a ridge, on the other side of which the ice dropped away much more steeply. Tug got weaving down the back and soon had our stick of tired, half-frozen troops loaded. As soon as they were all onboard he shut the door, and broke out some hot soup that he had brought along to get some warmth back into the 'grunts'. Meanwhile I had radioed Ian Stanley and asked permission to depart as I could see a fresh belt of cloud and snow brewing up near our escape route.

As soon as I got the OK I lifted and headed off down the valley at about sixty knots and 100 feet, which should have given me the option of landing on again if the weather got too bad. As it was, the speed with which South Georgia weather changes proved too quick for me. About half a mile along the valley the wind suddenly shifted and without warning I was in complete whiteout in thick driving snow. The effect of whiteout is very difficult to describe adequately to anyone who has not experienced it. Basically the flying snow over a white and featureless background obscures all visual references and leaves you totally disorientated. If this happens to you on skis it can be quite frightening, but airborne over a glacier with 'cumulo-granite' mountains on either side and no ability to climb up and out of trouble it was very bad news indeed! The only option available was to try and get the aircraft back down on to the ground if I could just find a reference to land by.

I had passed a small clump of rocks a few seconds earlier so I called down to Tug to let him know that we had a problem and banked to the left – a 50/50 decision that probably inadvertently saved both of our lives. Tug threw open the cabin door and leaned out to look for the surface as I tried to turn and regain a landing reference. Unfortunately, what neither of us could see was that we were in a dip in the ice and, as I glanced in at the instruments halfway round the turn, I saw the radalt (radar altimeter) winding down at an alarming rate. I had no idea where the ground had suddenly come from but realising that a collision was inevitable I pulled in power and flared the nose up to cushion the impact. The aircraft hit the ground, left wing low and tail first, doing about thirty knots, sheering the port undercarriage leg off and crashing down and grinding along on its left side. I remember lying in my straps, with a feeling of intense frustration, watching the left-hand side of the cockpit filling up with debris and snow and thinking 'Mrs Tidd isn't going to like being a widow!'

Eventually the aircraft ground to a halt. The inertia switches in the nose had crash-stopped the engines and apart from the wind and my windscreen wiper, which was still squeaking away, it was relatively quiet. I reached down beside me to turn off the fuel cocks and electrics only to find that the whole lot was buried under snow and broken glass. Tug called through from the cabin that everyone seemed to be in one piece, so I hauled open the starboard cockpit door, climbed up onto the side of the fuselage, and helped Tug get the cabin door fully open.

By this time the other two aircraft had arrived and were able to use the wreckage of mine as visual references to land by. I staggered across to the cabin door of Ian Stanley's Wessex 3 and plugged myself into the intercom lead that Fitz, his aircrew-man, handed to me. Ian's first words were: 'You messy bastard, you've left your windscreen wiper on!' to which I replied with some feeling: 'If you're so f—ing clever you go and turn it off!' Fitz bounded off into the snow and, with the help of Tug and Jan Lomas, the survivors were divided up between Humphrey and Ian Georgesson's Wessex 5, which was busy jettisoning fuel to bring the aircraft weight down so that it could lift the extra load.

Once all survivors had been loaded the two aircraft waited for a break in the weather and then lifted off in formation and headed off down the glacier. By this time the press of bodies in the back of the Wessex 3 had forced me to unplug from the intercom to make room, and I was probably lost in my own thoughts, as I don't remember much about the flight back to the ships until we landed on *Antrim*.

Once onboard I climbed out of the aircraft, gave Ian Stanley a thumbs up, and made my way across the Flight Deck and round the superstructure into the hangar.

Inside, First Aid parties were busy laying out stretchers, making up saline drips and obviously preparing to receive casualties. I took my bonedome off, grabbed hold of Chief Heritier, Ian Stanley's Senior Maintenance Rating, and told him that it was okay he could relax, our only casualty had suffered nothing worse than a cut cheek. He looked at me for a moment and then took me by the arm and said: 'You obviously haven't heard, the other Wessex 5 crashed into a cliff on the way out. We don't know yet if there are any survivors.'

The shock hit me like a blow to the stomach and for a moment I felt physically sick. Jock Georgesson, Jan Lomas and Tug were good friends of mine and to hear that they were probably dead on top of what I had just been through left me feeling cold, dazed and weak.

I heard Humphrey lift off again and, in something of a daze, I was taken up to debrief with Brian Young, *Antrim's* captain and the Task Group Commander. Considering that he had just seen the whole operation come off the rails and blow up in his face he was very sympathetic. I think Ian Stanley must have talked to him about the conditions on the glacier the day before, because when I told him how we had been overwhelmed by the speed with which the weather changed he seemed to understand and told me not to blame myself. I was led away to the wardroom and given a hot drink while we waited for news.

I don't think I registered much more until the Ops Room announced that Humphrey's crew had made contact with Yankee Alpha's crew and that they had all survived. I cannot describe the relief that I felt when I heard. It was some time later before Ian Stanley managed to find a hole in the weather to get in and pick up Ian Georgesson and his team, and the story of that remarkable piece of flying is best left to Ian Stanley himself to describe. Suffice to say that he and his crew managed to pack sixteen armed men into an aircraft cabin that normally feels cramped with four people in it, fly back and land on a heaving deck at well above his normal maximum all up weight. Ian was later awarded the DSO and in my opinion it was richly deserved (even if he was a Pinger!).

Once Ian Georgesson was dried off we sat down to debrief and he filled me in on what had happened. Having embarked the survivors from my aircraft they had started off down the glacier through a break in the weather with the Wessex 3 in the lead. Within half a mile however, the weather had closed in again and they were in whiteout. The Wessex 3 with its radar and FCS was able to continue using its automatic height-hold to maintain height over the surface, and initially Ian had been able to formate on it. Unfortunately, what neither crew could see was that they were approaching a ridge of ice and, as Humphrey's height-hold caused it to descend on the far side of the ridge, Ian Georgesson suddenly found himself having to descend to try and hold on to his reference, only to find his radalt winding down to indicate that the surface was coming up to meet him. He pulled in power to cushion the landing and probably would have got away with it if the wind had not been blowing at 40–50 knots from his side. He touched down hard and then the aircraft rolled over because it was still moving sideways. What Stewart Cooper, the co-pilot in the Wessex 3 had mistaken for the aircraft running headlong into a cliff had been the cloud of snow that was thrown up as the blades hit the ground!

Luckily no one was hurt, with the exception of the sergeant who had got a cut on his cheek when he was struck by the cabin-mounted machine gun (GPMG) in the crash in my aircraft and who now got a matching cut a couple of inches further down his cheek from the GPMG in Ian's! Ian and Jan Lomas soon had the troops mustered out on the ice and, after persuading them to take a photo of the crew sitting on their wrecked aircraft (only Jock Georgesson would have thought of that!), inflated the aircraft dinghy and got everyone in out of the weather. For the next few hours they kept everyone occupied playing cards until Ian Stanley's crew finally managed to reach them and rescue them.

The loss of two-thirds of the Task Group's troop-carrying helicopter assets was a major blow to the operational plan but, as it turned out, not a fatal one. HMS *Brilliant*, a Type 22 frigate with two Lynx helicopters embarked, was diverted from the main Falklands Task Force to reinforce the South Georgia Task Group.

Ian Stanley's skill and the rock-like unbreakability of the Wessex 5 airframe had saved the Paraquat operation from total disaster, but next day *Tidespring* faced her severest challenge yet, with the arrival of RFA *Brambleleaf*.

Having replenished the *Antrim* group on the trip south, as well as *Endurance*, and finally, *Fort Austin*, *Tidespring*'s fuel stocks were running low. Consequently, she and *Brambleleaf* were ordered to move out to sea about 100 miles off South Georgia, where they could safely attempt to pump over both Dieso and AVCAT.

The situation was slightly critical because *Plymouth*, who went with them, had only enough fuel left for about twelve hours' steaming. Things began to go bad from the start, when the RFAs ran in to a force 10 gale, with giant waves, produced by the unique contours of the Falklands shelf, breaking with monotonous regularity over both ships.

This RAS (L) certainly wasn't a simple operation, as Shane Redmond, RFA, OBE, Master of RFA *Tidespring*, explains:

During the South Georgia phase it became clear the part weather would play in the resupply of all units and that some rethinking of how RFAs operate would be essential. The pumpover on 22/23 April emphasised the point that long duration replenishments under the prevailing weather conditions had to be avoided wherever possible. Not withstanding this, it was also realised that given the ability to select the replenishment course and speed, RAS between two large and cumbersome ships could be achieved in very much worse conditions than would previously have been thought possible. A further consideration on that day (and throughout the campaign) was the risk of attack when two mission-essential units were in such close proximity. (Subsequent discussion with Lt Cdr Horatio Bicain AN, Commanding Officer of the [Argentine submarine] *Santa Fe*, indicated that such concerns were not without foundation: in fact he was able to state *Tidespring*'s course and speed during the pumpover with a surprisingly high degree of accuracy). One may well wonder what the effect of a successful attack might have been on the forthcoming deployment from the UK, particularly in the political sense. On 22/23 April 1982, given the critical fuel state within the group and the absence of any other source of supply, there was simply no option but to press on and get the job done.

The pumpover had barely begun, however, when *Endurance* signalled the presence of an Argentine C-130 (Hercules), also quickly detected by *Antrim*. The Hercules flew away from the coast of South Georgia and soon found the replenishment group, despite the mist and low cloud. This aircraft was replaced some hours later by a second, while, at 14.56, *Endurance* reported the presence of an Argentine submarine within 100 miles of her position and probably even closer to the RFAs.

Given the vital role the RFAs were set to play and their vulnerability, Captain Young had no option but to order the captain of *Plymouth* to order an emergency breakaway.

Unfortunately, only about 700 tons of fuel had been transferred before *Plymouth*, as commander of the Group, ordered the RFAs to terminate the pumpover.

The ships headed southeast at their best speed of seventeen knots, which soon placed them in amongst the icebergs. The lack of adequate protective clothing issued to both ships' companies added to their difficulties because lookouts and RAS parties could not spend more than about half an hour on deck.

Shane Redmond explains:

Climatic conditions in South Georgia and the Falklands Operational areas made the near absence of proper protective clothing a major concern.

Bridge lookouts, Flight Deck and RAS personnel work in highly exposed positions where temperatures can have a serious detrimental effect on a ship's overall efficiency. *Tidespring* received twenty outfits of cold weather clothing at Ascension Island. Due to variations in size this provided sufficient outfits for some sixteen personnel – a woefully inadequate allocation. On a lighter note, a flood of gloves socks and woolly hats were eventually received onboard courtesy of wives, mothers, the WI and numerous other charitable sources at home. These were most gratefully received!

Equipment shortages were so acute that the only night vision aid *Tidespring* had was a Royal Marine's rifle sight borrowed for the occasion. Frayed nerves weren't helped, either, when *Antrim*, joining at speed, fired a star shell, illuminating both RFAs in the mistaken belief that she was approaching a surface target.

In addition to those caused by the Royal Navy and the icebergs, Captain Farley, Master of *Brambleleaf*, had his own problems after a stormy passage around Cape Horn:

We received a signal, 'Be prepared in all respects for war.' Bridge and engine room watches were doubled, and two days later we arrived at our final rendezvous, which was well inside the MEZ, and stopped the ship. We had no idea why we were there, nor who we would meet there – we had a calculated guess that it would be another RFA. During the early hours of the morning I was called to the bridge, and informed that a darkened ship had flashed at us with an Aldis lamp. We flashed back at the undistinguishable shape, using a challenge code. No reply. The waiting was nail-biting, would the next sign be orange flashes from a gun? When dawn lightened the sky, it was some relief to find RFA *Tidespring* there.

The pumpover was quickly organised, and we started to transfer fuel. We had operated on local times, whereas the Paraquat group had remained on Zulu time, so when the CO of *Tidespring* said we would RAS after breakfast, it seemed strange as we had already had our breakfast some hours before! The OTC [Officer in Tactical Command] ordered an 'Emergency Breakaway' then ordered us in a southerly direction at best possible speed. I was ordered at one point to make, 'Best possible speed'. When I replied that I was making the best possible speed, I was then ordered, 'Make more than your best possible speed.'

We were by this time running amongst icebergs and growlers, in darkened conditions with no radar being used. We were then given a zig-zag course, and this was all happening within sight of South Georgia. There was a suggestion that *Tidespring* and ourselves would anchor in a small bay in South Georgia, raft up and complete our pumpover. We both declined this scheme. At one point we were illuminated by star shells from one of our warships, so what with speeding south in the dark, amongst bergs, in the dark and no radar, I had the feeling my own people were going to get us killed. At this time we received an intelligence signal, which indicated that the Argentinean submarine *Santa Fe* was in the area with orders to land his marines and then sink all the British ships in the area. (Not a thing to tell the crew!)

The OTC of the group arrived back at this point, took control and ordered the tankers to proceed north, and clear of the MEZ [Maritime Exclusion Zone]. The next day we completed the pumpover with *Tidespring*, and were then ordered north to Ascension to replenish from the *British Esk*.

One point that I heard later was that *Tidespring* carried as a POW the captain of the *Santa Fe*. The captain stated that he was in the vicinity, with torpedoes loaded and ready, and he had two large targets, the only reason he did not fire was that both *Tidespring* and *Brambleleaf* were zig-zagging. Should this be true then one of our ships could have been the first casualty of the war. A sobering thought. I must admit I gained a few grey hairs that night.

The government may have been still trying to handle the situation with kid gloves but the consensus in the Navy was for getting on with it, neatly summed up by Captain John Coward RN of *Brilliant*, when he said bluntly: 'It suited the Navy to be frozen well down the track, rather than at Ascension.'

Brilliant, having been ordered to detach from its own covering group on the 22 April, arrived off South Georgia on the 24th while *Tidespring* and *Brambleleaf* completed their pumpover, in force 10 weather, transferring about 2,000 tons of Dieso as well as some FFO (Furnace Fuel Oil) and water. *Tidespring* then replenished both *Antrim* and *Plymouth* before the RFA was ordered northwest to rendezvous with *Brilliant*, a meeting which took place late that evening. The *Antrim* group had by now received instructions that they could fire on any enemy aircraft that posed a direct threat.

This order was repeated to *Endurance* while she lay at a position off South Georgia's Barff Peninsula, just as she was being overflown by an Argentine Boeing 707. An incensed Nick Barker was forced to watch helplessly as it flew into the mist, despite the fact that his Electronic Detection staff could hear the pilot relaying his position to the nearby submarine, in plain language.

After refuelling the Type 22, *Tidespring* was left to loiter outside the Maritime Exclusion Zone, while *Brilliant* turned southwest, hurtling through the Southern Ocean in order to catch up with *Plymouth* and *Antrim*.

RFA *Brambleleaf*, her job complete, headed back to the UK.

Next day, 25 April, saw a dramatic improvement in the fortunes of the Royal Navy.

On the previous day, *Antrim* had received an assessment from Northwood to the effect that if the *Santa Fe* was in his vicinity, it must have a specific purpose, probably to land reinforcements. Logical enough, but where was the submarine going?

Young and his team realised she could have only two possible destinations, Leith Harbour or King Edward Point. His assessment of the submarine's likely position having been confirmed by another signal from Northwood, he set his only radar- and sonar-equipped helicopter, *Antrim*'s well-worn Wessex 5 (callsign 406, known to all as 'Humphrey'), searching off East Cumberland Bay, supplemented by *Brilliant*'s two Lynx.

At 07.30, *Plymouth* intercepted a Spanish language transmission on a civilian frequency, which could only have been *Santa Fe* announcing her imminent departure. *Brilliant*'s Lynx and Humphrey the Wessex, now with full anti-submarine warfare kit re-installed, were in the air less than half-an-hour later, while *Endurance* had her AS 12 missile-equipped Wasp ready for instant takeoff.

Humphrey swept through Cumberland Bay, quickly finding the submarine on the surface about five miles north of Barff Point. Ian Stanley and his crew instantly attacked, dropping two depth charges when directly overhead.

Clearly damaged by Humphrey's attack and circling erratically, the Guppy-class *Santa Fe* turned back to shore, apparently in an attempt to return to Grytviken. Now under prolonged attack from the other helicopters of the Group, the *Santa Fe* was eventually berthed at the tiny BAS jetty at Grytviken and the crew swiftly evacuated.

With the garrison and submarine crew demoralised by the savagely efficient attack on the submarine, Young and his military staff, Major Guy Sheridan RM and Major Cedric Delves SAS, decided to act quickly.

Plymouth and *Antrim* began to fire intimidatory salvoes at the Argentine positions while Humphrey and the two Lynx landed troops in a succession of drops. With the Royal Marines and SAS beginning to move on the Argentine positions, a white flag was suddenly seen flying from King Edward Point.

That was more or less the end of the operation. The Royal Marines took down the blue and white of Argentina and hoisted the Union flag in its place, capturing the tiny Leith garrison later that day. The detachment's commander was the infamous Lieutenant Alfredo Astiz, wanted by France and Sweden for human rights violations during Argentina's so-called 'Dirty War'.

This is what the books call the 'Battle for South Georgia' but in reality, it wasn't won by the soldiers when they occupied Grytviken. Its outcome was decided two days before, 200 miles away during the *Tidespring/Brambleleaf* pumpover, when Lt Cdr Bicain, Commander of the submarine *Santa Fe*, thought that HMS *Plymouth* was making a depth charge run in his direction when, in fact, she was joining *Tidespring* for an essential fuel replenishment. Bicain broke off his attack, abandoning his self-confessed plan to put four torpedoes into *Tidespring*. The two RFAs completed their pumpover, *Tidespring* having replenished *Plymouth* simultaneously.

Had Bicain succeeded in torpedoing Redmond's ship, she would, as her master succinctly puts it, 'have disappeared in a blue flash', having, amongst other highly inflammable supplies, that swimming pool full of AS 12 missiles. The 'blue flash' would certainly have destroyed *Brambleleaf* along with *Tidespring* and left the *Antrim* group stranded, without fuel and about 1,000 miles from the nearest chance of getting any.

Needless to say, the operation to regain South Georgia would have had to begin again from scratch. And South Georgia couldn't have been left because although it looked like a sideshow from the point of view of certain elements in the UK armed forces, from a logistics point of view, it was essential for a number of very good reasons.

First, because the STUFT needed a reasonably sheltered anchorage to transfer dry goods, mainly food and ammunition, to the Fleet Store ships such as RFA *Fort Austin*. Second, the troopships, particularly the *Queen Elizabeth II*, also required a safe haven out of flying range of the Argentine mainland to rest their passengers and transfer troops to the smaller vessels making the run into San Carlos Water. South Georgia was also ideally placed to act as the anchorage for a 'station' tanker, a role RFA *Blue Rover*, amongst others, filled for a time.

Food, men and fuel. Three essential ingredients for invasion. And without a safe anchorage like South Georgia, where else were they to come from?

During the attack on South Georgia, *Tidespring* and her cargo of 200 Royal

Marines from 'M' Company had been kicking their heels 200 miles away, outside the MEZ, although she had still been at defence stations, with the hospital ready for casualties.

One of her crew, Petty Officer Peter Robinson, recalls the routine:

When enemy aircraft were detected, the alarm would be given:
  'Hands to defence stations, hands to defence stations, this is not a drill.'
  'Close all X and Y openings.'
  'Close watertight doors.'
  'Crash stop ventilation.'
  'Damage control parties stand to.'
  'First aid parties to the sick bay.'
  'Gun crews close up at the rush.'
This is what I can remember, then all members of the crew would run to their allotted station, in addition the threat would be piped through the ship, something like, 'Enemy aircraft off port beam, gun crews engage', or 'Enemy submarine sighted.'

Every member of the crew was issued with lifejacket, survival suit, gas mask and anti-flash gear, which we had to carry at ALL times, eating, sleeping, working, and when you went to the bathroom, it was NEVER allowed to be out of reach.

My action station was with the Engine Room Damage Control Party, and we mustered on the port side of the aft accommodation block, outside the Engineer's office.

Finding out how the war was going was difficult but generally, we listened to the BBC World Service when we were able, and we also got news from the aircrew or anyone who came on board. We also got newspapers but they were usually days old.

By 26 April *Tidespring* was in Cumberland Bay, engines running to help the anchor hold, while she unloaded her cargo of Royal Marines and ammunition, using a combination of helicopters and her ship's lifeboats. She left again before nightfall, leaving the Marines to what Redmond described as '. . . one hell of a mess.'

Next day saw *Tidespring* back in the bay ready to take on her first load of POWs, the crew of the *Santa Fe*, despondent after the unfortunate death of one of their colleagues which had occurred while moving the submarine to a safer location.

Tidespring's role as a prison ship had begun with a signal from Captain Brian Young RN, to Shane Redmond, Master of *Tidespring*, asking if he could accommodate some POWs. Redmond, in proper RFA style, responded with the single word: 'Delighted'.

He claims it is the shortest signal he ever wrote, but he might be excused for also claiming it to be the one that led him into the most trouble.

Capturing South Georgia, although it took Whitehall pressure from Young's already overburdened shoulders, added crushingly to the logistics nightmare he found himself facing. Scrap workers, the crew of Bicain's *Santa Fe*, the commando garrison of Grytviken and Alfred Astiz's special forces unit from Leith all had to be processed, which included trying to identify them, and then incarcerated somewhere where they could do no harm before being returned to Ascension for repatriation to Argentina.

Fortunately, he had a possible option on hand.

Tidespring, the old fast fleet tanker, had sufficient space aboard to accommodate the 185 POWs if the holds and magazines were converted; and with the loss of their Wessex, Mike Tidd's weapon-trained flight were available for duty as prison guards.

Of course, using an old RFA as a POW transport wasn't without drawbacks. The Geneva Convention stated that only a commissioned officer could supervise POWs, so Lt Tidd had to be placed tacitly in charge of the Argentineans, although Captain Redmond still had overall responsibility, including being the one everyone would blame if anything went wrong.

Apart from the massive logistics problems of feeding, washing and exercise, the men had to be guarded twenty-four hours a day, and the twenty-five Royal Navy artificers who comprised Tidd's total force seemed rather inadequate, given that the prisoners would have to be confined in four separate compartments. Borrowing *Antrim*'s nine-man Royal Marine detachment, thus bringing Tidd's force up to thirty-four, alleviated the manpower problem, although this was still no great number to guard the 185 prisoners that *Tidespring* eventually held.

Almost immediately another problem arose. Tidd's men had all been trained to handle the British Self Loading Rifle (SLR), but the round this fired was easily powerful enough to penetrate the fuel tanks surrounding the POWs' cells, which could have resulted in a fire or explosion. Tidd borrowed a number of Sub-Machine Guns (SMG) and arranged a quick familiarisation lesson for his flight. Despite this, there was only one incident where a young air mechanic tried to clear a round from the chamber of an SMG while the magazine was still attached. The weapon discharged itself but fortunately no one was injured.

No better option than *Tidespring* offered itself, however, and after dispatch of Redmond's signal agreeing to the transfer, the ship became a hive of activity, all hands turning to, so that by 27 April, when Bicain's men began to come aboard, the battered old tanker had begun to be converted, temporarily at least, into a prison ship.

The first problem was deciding where everybody was going to go. Bicain's men and the scrap workers did not present much of a problem, but the commandos who made up the majority of the garrison needed careful supervision, while Astiz's special forces were a tough lot who could be relied on to make trouble when and if they could.

One of the magazines, with heavy-duty doors, was cleared out for Astiz's men, while a second held the *Santa Fé*'s crew. The marines, being the largest group, went in the fore hold, with its newly erected bunks. This presented its own problems since Redmond was forced to flood the bunker tank below this hold to prevent the prisoners interfering with essential controls sited there, which, in turn, dropped the temperature of the metal deck close to freezing.

Perhaps the easiest group to accommodate were the scrap workers, who built their own bunks in the now vacant Wessex hangar on the upper deck.

Redmond's men turned over most of their spare clothing, bedding and mattresses so that by the time *Tidespring* left South Georgia on 1/2 May, every prisoner had been showered, identified and assigned a bunk and lifeboat station. They each had their own knife, fork, spoon, plate and cup and were eating at least as well as the crew, on three meals a day.

Security was tight, Tidd's men operating in shifts and doors only being opened upon receipt of a five-tap signal. Bicain had been previously informed in no uncertain terms that if any of his men were told to stop at any time by a guard they had to do so. Otherwise, they might be shot. With 185 prisoners aboard, Redmond and Tidd were taking no chances.

Mealtimes were also strictly regulated, and after feeding each group, the men were supplied with a bucket of hot, soapy water to clean their utensils. At the first mealtime, it soon became quite clear that some sort of system needed to be introduced because the Argentine officers pushed to the front of the queue and ate far more than their share of the food, leaving their men with almost nothing. From then on, food allocation was strictly supervised, a necessity which surprised the British officers present, whose first lesson in command had been that their men always came first.

After meals, the POWs were issued cigarettes and allowed the use of a lighter for one hour, it being deemed too dangerous to allow unrestricted access to a source of fire, especially on a ship crammed with inflammable cargo.

Redmond, Tidd and Bicain, who was the senior Argentine officer, met every day to allow Bicain to voice any grievances he had and for the British officers to modify any protocols already in place.

Every two days the prisoners were allowed to shower under supervision and they were also given two exercise periods a day on deck. They were also supplied with soft drinks, and hot rolls for breakfast and a selection of magazines and films, these latter shown from a projector mounted on the rim of the fore hold.

Not a single casualty occurred during the largely uneventful, ten-day voyage to Ascension, and upon reaching the island base, its anchorage now crowded with ships of all shapes and sizes, every man was sent ashore in clean clothes, freshly laundered.

The International Committee of the Red Cross inspected the ship and interviewed the prisoners and concluded that, in the circumstances, their treatment was reasonable. Captain Redmond was, however, informed of a number of infringements under the Geneva Convention, which had been committed during his carriage of the prisoners. Redmond was understandably annoyed:

Probably enough has been written about the subject of the POWs already, even so a few maybe not so well known facts are worth recording. After the recapture of South Georgia Captain Brian Young (CTG) [Commander Task Group] asked if we could possibly accommodate a few prisoners. Being the only ship available I responded with the shortest signal I have ever sent, one word: 'Delighted'. My enthusiasm quickly mellowed when a seemingly endless stream of Argentinean soldiers, special services personnel (Astiz), sailors and scrap metal merchants, totalling 185 arrived. Having accepted the commitment, I sent an urgent signal to the Group asking for anything they could spare in the material sense, for example bedding, clothing, and cooking utensils, plus a number of other items my staff sorely needed to cope with the needs of our new 'guests'. Contrary to the views expressed in another publication, the material help was not that generous! We did however receive a small detachment of Marines to supplement Mike Tidd's flight personnel with the guarding of the POWs – more mouths to feed, albeit welcome ones!

Included in this number was a pair of Uruguayan nationals whom I was instructed to treat as passengers. Shortly after embarking, their presence in a restricted area and a generally over-inquisitive nature suggested that a form of house arrest was more appropriate!

The visit by the IRC [International Red Cross] prior to disembarking the prisoners injected a note of caution in my mind. While the prisoners' complaints related to matters over which *Tidespring* had no control, the Head of Mission, a Dr Tershiling (spelling uncertain) made it abundantly clear that he believed there had been infringements of the prisoners' rights under the provisions of the Geneva Convention. Broadly speaking they were:

a. Failure to remove prisoners from a combat zone – I think we remained in area for five days after embarkation and before departing for ASI.

b. Prisoners held under degrading conditions – accommodation, toilet and washing facilities, minimum time on deck for exercise.

c. That a policy of demoralisation was in force – citing an incident where two Marines within earshot of some rating prisoners suggested that the entire Argentine Navy had been sunk by the RN!

d. Collective punishment had been applied to military personnel on three occasions – citing an incident involving the special forces element.

e. No lifejackets had been provided.

f. That as a non-military officer I could not be in charge of POWs. I countered by stating that Lt Mike Tidd, Royal Navy was running the POW element. However the IRC said that it was quite obviously that I was in overall command and the point stood!

The list amounted to nine specific points, none of which had been made as a formal complaint at the daily meeting with the prisoners' senior officers. In fact the only formal complaint made was by the submarine's Executive Officer, which Mike Tidd and I were unable to agree to (recorded on daily tapes). I took particular offence at the suggestion of a policy in (c) above. All that had been said was that the *Belgrano* had been sunk and the rest of the Argentine Navy had run for home – a statement of fact! With regard to lifejackets we had insufficient onboard to provide each prisoner with one, however efforts were made to obtain adequate supplies from another RFA 'Leaf' who had arrived on station. Though I knew that they held a quantity in excess of one per man the Captain refused to release any. Not my favourite person on that day! No other opportunity presented itself.

I made it quite clear that my overriding concern was the safe delivery of all prisoners and that this was second only to the safety of the ship. With the ever-present possibility of a breakout it was of paramount importance the prisoners clearly understood the position and that any such action would not be tolerated. The situation onboard was such that neither Mike Tidd or I could take any chances and so the regime had to be strict, but humane and properly enforced. All the prisoners reached ASI safely. They were in a fit and well state departing in newly laundered clothing. As they left *Tidespring* a number of prisoners made a point of thanking us for what we did for them (given the resources available). Three had asked for political asylum.

Mike Tidd, nicknamed 'Angel of Death' by the Argentine POWs, also remembers those times well and describes his experiences here:

Tidespring rejoined the task group in Grytviken Sound as the dust settled and we set about the task of reinforcing the troops ashore. *Antrim* flight were good enough to get me airborne again to help me get over the effects of the crash, and then Ian and I volunteered to run the airhead ashore and were soon established on Grytviken Point marshalling in helicopter-loads of troops and stores. We spent an extremely cold night in the BAS building, which had lost most of its windows in the firefight, before returning to *Antrim* the next morning.

Back onboard *Antrim* on the 27th Brian Young was wrestling with the dilemma of what to do with the Argentinean prisoners. At this point, as far as I was aware, they should have been about ninety of them in accordance with the original intelligence estimates, so I happily suggested to Brian that, as my twenty-five weapons-trained flight personnel had run out of helicopters to look after, we could guard the prisoners for him. He was delighted with this solution and Ian and I were despatched back to the *Tidespring* to prepare for this, with the first sixteen prisoners arriving soon after.

It was at this point that I first became aware that there were 170 other prisoners heading my way, which I have to admit, caused a bit of a sharp intake of breath! Some very rapid planning was called for, and over the next eighteen hours the crew of the Tidespring worked miracles clearing the main hold of stores and then building tiers of shelves to act as sleeping accommodation for the prisoners. Meanwhile my team and I were working out how we would process the prisoners as they came aboard, distribute them across the available holding areas and then guard them.

It quickly became obvious that we were under-resourced and, after some negotiation, I was able to persuade Brian Young to lend me *Antrim*'s nine-man Marine detachment as well as a supply of SMGs [Sub-Machine Guns] (our rifles would be too unwieldy to use in the confines of the areas below deck and if any shooting was to be done I preferred that it should be with 9mm ammunition rather than high velocity 7.62mm!).

The following morning, with the ship still resounding to the sound of hammers hard at work in the forward hold, we started embarking the main body of prisoners. Each one had to be documented and then searched and then moved to a holding area to await completion of the work in the hold. Luckily it was a cold clear day with little wind so we could process them initially on the flight deck. Led by the Marines our lads did an excellent job and by 20.30 all of the prisoners were safely housed below decks. It's worth remembering at this point that the majority of our lads were young aircraft maintainers who had been trained to use weapons for self-defence, but were certainly not professional soldiers.

The ship's team led by the Chief Officer, Alec Bilney, displayed great initiative in creating habitable accommodation with very limited resources. The sleeping shelves in the main hold were put together in very short order and then the entire RFA crew gave up the cushions from their day beds to provide mattresses for the prisoners as well as bedding and clothing. Forty-gallon drums were cut in half, fitted with wooden seats, and then screened off in part of the hold to act as toilets. The next problem was trying to keep the hold warm and, despite heating the tank beneath its floor, we had to issue the prisoners with all the spare clothes and blankets that were available to keep them warm.

By now we had subdivided the prisoners, with twenty special forces in the port magazine, the crew of the *Santa Fe* in the starboard magazine, thirty scrap merchants in the hangar, and the main force of Argentinean marines in the hold. Security was a major headache as my small force of thirty-five was well and truly outnumbered. We had rigged the main hatch over the hold, which weighed over a ton, so that it could be dropped very quickly at the first sign of trouble and had explained to the prisoners that any attempt to break out of the hold would result in us dropping the hatch and a lot of people getting very sore heads! We had also managed to get hold of a supply of tear gas grenades, which we kept ready to drop down the ventilation scuttles if we lost control below decks. All of my lads were armed at all times and I slept with my 9mm Browning tucked under my pillow.

About this time I had an interesting 'discussion' with one of my Petty Officers who informed me that he had joined up to mend aircraft and not to shoot people. I advised him that if that was the case he had no place in an armed service and I would see him disrated and returned to the UK forthwith. I gave him a full thirty seconds to think it over and I'm pleased to say he came to his senses and gave me no further trouble.

I shall always be deeply grateful that, during this period in Grytviken Sound, Tony Ellerbeck came across and briefed me on the leader of the Argentine special forces detachment, Lieutenant Alfredo Astiz. Tony warned me that although the man was outwardly disarmingly charming, he was a very nasty piece of work who would need careful watching. Astiz was wanted by the UN for the torture and murder of two nuns. Over the next few days he continually fomented trouble amongst the special forces prisoners, constantly challenging the authority of his guards. To ensure that he knew where he stood I had the doors of the port magazine opened and then briefed the guards, with Astiz and his team listening, that if any prisoner stepped out of the magazine without permission he was to be shot. He got the message and the special forces team quietened down after that, though Astiz himself remained a thorn in our side until eventually we persuaded Brian Young to hold him separately on board *Antrim*.

At 16.00 on 1 May we left South Georgia and sailed northwest to rendezvous with the main Task Force en route to Ascension Island. The move north to relatively warmer waters was very welcome as it was proving extremely difficult to warm the main hold whilst in the icy waters around South Georgia.

With the immediate business of getting the prisoners accommodated and secured now behind us, we could draw breath and take stock of the situation. Shane Redmond, as captain of the *Tidespring* was responsible for the prisoners' safety whilst I, as the senior military officer, was responsible for their security and for ensuring that as far as possible they were treated in accordance with the terms of the Geneva Convention. This may sound relatively straightforward but apart from an outline knowledge of some of the basics, I certainly did not know the detail of the Convention's requirements with regard to POW handling – my team and I had never been trained to be prison camp guards. Luckily, Captain Redmond was able to lay his hands on two copies of this wondrous tome, one of which he gave to Captain Bicain, the captain of the *Santa Fe* and senior officer prisoners, whilst he and I pored over the other.

I should explain at this point that the terms that the Geneva Convention laid down were written in 1949 and were 'Directions for detention barracks and military prisons in which prisoners of war are detained.' In other words they were written for use in land-based prisoner of war camps and not with temporary prison accommodation aboard a ship at sea in mind. Many of the provisions, such as the issue of cigarette rations and prisoners' pay would just not feasible in a hastily-converted fleet tanker at sea.

Shane and I set up a regular daily meeting with Captain Bicain at which we discussed all aspects of the prisoners' conditions. These became a regular battle of wits as Captain Bicain studied his copy of the Geneva Convention and then made demands that we comply with some of its more obscure provisions, whilst Shane and I had to decide which we could practically comply with whilst still maintaining security. It was an interesting game of mental chess, which stretched all three of us.

It was very noticeable that the Argentine officers treated their conscripts like dirt.

Most of the officers were regulars of European extraction whilst the vast majority of the conscripts came from Indian peasant backgrounds. We had noticed that, on one of the first occasions when we fed the main body of the prisoners down in the hold, the officers pushed their way to the front and the young troops weren't allowed to feed until they had had their fill. There was considerable dismay amongst the Argentine officer corps when we explained to them that, whilst they were in our care, they would observe the British tradition of ensuring that the lads were fed first, before the officers.

On 3 May the rapid rearming of our lads with SMGs came back to bite me in the backside when one of my young air mechanics had a Negligent Discharge in hangar. Luckily the only casualty of the stray round was a large aircraft maintenance manual, something for which I was immensely grateful! Under the circumstances I felt that I had no option but to charge the young man, as he had disobeyed one of the most basic rules of weapon handling in that he had attempted to clear his weapon without first removing the magazine. In the meantime we set about re-briefing all of our troops on the correct weapon-handling drills for the SMG.

On the BBC World Service that night we heard that the *General Belgrano* had been torpedoed and sunk by a British nuclear submarine. After a lot of heart-searching we decided not to make this known to the prisoners as the morale of some of them was low enough already. Our own morale took a knock the next day when HMS *Sheffield* was hit by an Exocet and had to be abandoned, and Lieutenant Nick Taylor, a good friend of ours, was killed during a Sea Harrier attack on Goose Green.

On 5 May my young Naval Air Mechanic and I were flown across to HMS *Antrim* for him to be 'weighed off' for his negligent discharge. To my intense annoyance at the time the Commander of *Antrim* let him off on the basis that he was unfamiliar with the weapon that he was handling. In retrospect it was a fair point but at the time I did not feel that it would help me maintain the sort of very tight discipline that I needed amongst my troops to deal with the situation that we found ourselves in.

By the 6 May the weather was starting to warm up and we set about rewriting our routines in order to get the prisoners up into the open air to get some exercise as often as possible. The flight deck was the only viable area in which to achieve this, and so this entailed moving batches of prisoners from the forrard 'tween decks along the catwalks over the tank decks and up through the hatch onto the flight deck. We were able to secure the flight deck by establishing a GPMG nest on top of the hangar roof, but guarding the POWs moving around the ship placed more strain on our already stretched manpower.

On the 7 May we had to keep the POWs below decks all day as *Tidespring* rendezvoused with, and helped to refuel the main Task Group on its way down to the Falklands. The sight of this vast armada of ships as it came up over the horizon was very emotional and we were acutely aware that we were watching history in the making. It is most unlikely that any of us will see that many grey warships sailing together again in our lifetimes.

The 8th dawned clear and bright and the lads worked hard all day shuttling the prisoners up to the flight deck for exercise or to the showers for a wash. The only minor hiccup occurred when Major Lagos, the senior officer of the Argentine marines, objected to being made to trot round the flight deck by one of my Marine corporals. He felt this was very demeaning and we weren't able to make him see that it was for his own good!

The previous close relationship between Britain and Argentina threw up some interesting situations between ourselves and the prisoners. One of the Argentine marines, Lieutenant Richardson, commented to me that it was pretty ironic that his father had been a decorated Spitfire pilot with the RAF in the Second World War and now forty years later the son was a prisoner of the British! One of the young Argentinean marines down in the hold, who acted as our prime interpreter because of his excellent English, had been due to start a degree course at Oxford that summer. He was greatly saddened that the conflict had made the likelihood of this happening pretty remote.

On 12 May we finally arrived off Ascension and, as soon as we were within helicopter range, delegations from the Red Cross, SIB [Army Special Investigation Branch], and all sorts of others arrived on board to quiz us on every aspect of the prisoners' time with us. At the time it felt a bit like the Spanish Inquisition but, at the end of it all, the overall impression seemed to be that we had done a pretty good job.

Once we got closer to Ascension two of the Wessex based on the island finally began the offload of the prisoners. I can't remember the detail now, but the first aircraft to arrive radioed in with the objection that what we wanted to do would break some peacetime rule or other. By this time it was early evening and I was tired and the burst of invective that I unleashed down the radio was probably very unprofessional. It had the desired effect though and we soon had a regular shuttle going, transferring the prisoners ashore to the aircraft that would fly them to Montevideo.

I was quite touched when several of them, including Major Lagos, came over and shook my hand and thanked me for the way that we had looked after them. One notable exception was Captain Bicain who left without a word and looking very miserable. I guess his mind was on the treatment that he would receive from his own people for losing his submarine.

Almost immediately, *Tidespring* re-stored, filled her fuel tanks and, having collected two new Wessex to replace those lost on Fortuna, headed south again to rejoin the main Carrier Task Group, having once again displayed the versatility and professionalism which has been a characteristic of the RFA throughout its long history.

Tidespring stayed with the main group for the rest of the war, replenishing the warships and STUFT as and when required.

CHAPTER SEVEN

THE TEZ AND MOTORWAY TANKING

ADMIRAL WOODWARD'S Carrier Battle Group continued south after leaving Ascension 18 April. The trip began uneventfully, except for the initially disastrous news about the Fortuna Glacier offensive from South Georgia.

On the 23rd, the British Government issued a statement, declaring their intention to operate a Total Exclusion Zone around the Falkland Islands and clearly stating the conditions that would apply to any Argentine vessels found within it. The relevant points were that any Argentine warship or aircraft inside the TEZ was liable to attack, and any vessel posing a threat, whether inside or outside the zone, was also liable to be attacked. Although the *Belgrano* incident will be dealt with later, it should be noted here that HMS *Conqueror*'s attack met the conditions noted in this statement.

With the Carrier Battle Group, the Task Force sustained its first casualty, when an aircrewman was lost during a VERTREP between HMS *Hermes* and RFA *Resource* using two of the carrier's Sea Kings, when one of the helicopters was forced to ditch. Despite a search and rescue operation that went on all night and was continued by RFA *Olmeda*, RFA *Resource* and HMS *Yarmouth* into the late morning of the next day, only one aircrewman was recovered alive and at midday, the three detached ships regretfully followed the Carrier Battle Group south. The same day, RFA *Fort Austin* left Ascension Island, heading south once more to join the Carrier Battle Group.

Next day, back in the UK, Mrs Thatcher's War Cabinet rejected the new Haig proposals. Cleverly, however, and at what is believed to have been the instigation of John Nott, the Haig proposals were not officially rejected, but the British asked Argentina to react first, knowing they would probably reject them, thus making Buenos Aires appear to be the intransigent party. They also issued the full text of the TEZ statement while the Junta was sending more reinforcements to the Falklands in the shape of the 3rd Infantry Brigade.

By 25 April not just the diplomacy was swinging Britain's way. South Georgia had been recaptured and the Argentine submarine *Santa Fe* attacked and run aground.

By now the Carrier Battle Group, including *Olmeda* and *Resource* (the latter still carrying a nuclear round), were only 1,500 miles from Port Stanley, having rendezvoused with what was the *Brilliant* group, TG 317.8.2, and now led by HMS *Sheffield* after *Brilliant* had been detached to South Georgia.

The Carrier Battle Group now consisted of: the carriers *Hermes* and *Invincible*; four guided-missile destroyers, *Glamorgan, Sheffield, Coventry* and *Glasgow*; three frigates, *Broadsword, Arrow, Alacrity*; and one tanker, RFA *Appleleaf*.

HMS *Yarmouth* and RFAs *Olmeda* and *Resource* were also in the vicinity, only sixty miles astern, catching up after their fruitless search and rescue attempt.

At Ascension, RFA *Pearleaf* had by now left the anchorage to begin her record fifty-four-hour pumpover with *British Tamar*, the latter having just arrived. Captain Brian Waters aboard *British Tamar* remembers the incident:

It was to be about a week into our voyage south that we heard of our first tasking which was to be a pumpover with RFA *Pearleaf* who was accompanying the aircraft carrier group towards Ascension Island. This meant that we were to meet a well-depleted tanker and fill it up again! It also meant no immediate business for our well-checked and exercised stern RAS rig; this task would be done abeam, exactly as we had trialled back in 1977. As the information started coming in, I could see this was going to be a long and complicated evolution. Nevertheless I recall a real air of purpose about the ship – something was happening at last. The integration with the ship's company was by now well embedded and everyone showed a willingness to get stuck in together. I believe an RN communicator was seen with a spike, a shackle and well-greased hands!

Looking at my diary has brought a wry smile to my now ageing features. I see we met up with RFA *Pearleaf* on Sunday 25 April at 06.30, a little north of Ascension Island, to start the operation. In later years as a captain I was sometimes faced by a grumpy sailor wanting to know: 'Why is it always on Sundays, Captain? Can we have a half day when we get in?!' Rien ne change. I see that the weather back then was bright with a light breeze from the southeast and a low swell. This was to turn into an epic evolution but at least the weather was kind.

The challenge was in the fact that only one double six-inch hose rig could be used and there were several thousands of tons of three different oil grades to transfer, as well as a back-load of ballast from her tanks. While all this was going on each ship had to take care to preserve her stresses and trim within reasonable bounds. For the sad tankermen among you readers the *British Tamar* plan went something like this: issue FFO (heavy oil) from five wings then back-load ballast into five wings; continue to issue FFO and issue the bulk of the Dieso (light gas oil); flush the Dieso hose then issue AVCAT (aviation fuel) through it; complete issue of Dieso then finally back-load sullage and a little ballast through the FFO hose.

As we pumped our way through Sunday and all day on Monday (when RFA *Blue Rover* briefly joined us to take fuel from *Pearleaf*) we were now well south of Ascension Island so at 08.00 on Tuesday we broke off, turned the ships round and started again, heading back towards Ascension. By now, everyone was getting a bit ragged round the edges. Each ship really only had one team so we had to improvise ways to cover the events such as tank and grade changes. Fortunately the weather was balmy which allowed people to catnap on deck and the galley was available throughout, producing meals, snacks and drinks.

Truth to tell though, with another twenty-five years of experience and hindsight under my belt, and influenced by the modern obsession with all things 'Health & Safety' it cannot have been a safe evolution, though I see I reported it as such. To have the ships connected up for what has been quoted as 'a record-breaking fifty-four hours' became risky in the extreme – half those involved had never even seen it before so if an emergency had arisen we would not have been well placed to react to it. But what the heck – we were at war (or nearly) and enjoying being minor maritime heroes! Many of our colleagues were to face much worse in the days and weeks to come.

RFA *Blue Rover* and RFA *Tidepool* both reached Ascension next day (26 April), the former leaving almost immediately for the South Atlantic. *Tidepool*'s crew had not been wasting their time, as one of them explains:

The long passage from Curacao to Ascension was a very busy time as we tried to order all the stores that we would need for whatever lay ahead. This was made more difficult than usual as we did not have access (as did all other RN and RFA ships) to the stores manuals that gave all the reference numbers normally needed to order anything from the Naval Stores System. That the shore authorities coped with our best efforts so well is a great tribute to the people involved.

There was a certain amount of excitement amongst the ships anchored in Ascension when they were all ordered to make an emergency departure. *Stromness*'s diary explains the reason for it succinctly:

00.15 Zulu: Emergency departure from Ascension. During the afternoon, merchant ship transited north of ASC. In full view. Helo eventually dispatched for recce and photographed it (identified as Argentine merchant ship).

Photographs showed the ship using a common method for towing sophisticated two-man subs into operations. The Argys are expert at this sort of operation.

Later, it records that the ship: 'Disembarked Commandos to search Ascension for special forces.' Clearly, Ascension wasn't quite as safe as many seemed to think.

Back in the UK, RFA *Sir Bedivere* had arrived at Marchwood, its home port, was restored in record time and, within days (29 April), was on her way south, while RFA *Bayleaf* and HMS *Intrepid* also left for the South Atlantic. *Intrepid*, the second Landing Platform Deck or assault ship, had been re-commissioned in just twenty-two days by Portsmouth Dockyard and Portland Naval Base.

Two more STUFT, the ill-fated *Atlantic Conveyor* and the *Europic Ferry*, also left the UK on the 26th, carrying Harriers, helicopters, equipment and personnel, and were followed later that day by the STUFT tankers MV *British Wye, British Avon, Anco Charger* and *Shell Aburna*.

General Haig's 'Memorandum of Agreement' was presented to both sides next day. Markedly in favour of British interests, many observers saw it as simply more time-wasting to allow the British to move their forces into position. Thatcher's government said nothing, once again waiting for Argentina's response.

Next morning, 28 April, General Haig and Argentine Foreign Minister Costa Menendez began their discussion of the Memorandum. It seems fairly clear that Haig attempted to bully Argentina into accepting, and when this approach failed, issued an ultimatum, stating that he was going to put out a press release saying that negotiations had failed and it was Argentina's fault. The following day the US Senate passed a motion backing the British unreservedly, the so-called 'Haig's tilt'.

It is clear that almost from the beginning, Haig's mediation was seen by many in the British Government, particularly those in diplomatic circles who had had many dealings with Argentina, as a convenient way of 'filling the vacuum' as the British Ambassador to Washington politely put it, until the military option was in place. Whether there was any real intention to negotiate seriously, by either side, is still a matter for debate.

In Buenos Aires, the US Senate's response was, not unnaturally, felt to be extremely hostile.

With the Task Force, Admiral Woodward gave his response to the recapture of South Georgia: 'This is the heavy punch. As we get closer the options become fewer. The sands are running out.' And later in the same interview, he had a warning for the Argentine conscripts: 'If you want to get out, I suggest you do it now. Once we arrive, the only way home will be courtesy of the Royal Navy.'

Back in Britain, RFA *Sir Bedivere* left Marchwood, in something of a rush, as her Master, Captain Peter McCarthy OBE, remembers well:

On the morning of Friday 2 April 1982, RFA *Sir Bedivere* sailed as planned from Vancouver for Marchwood. Earlier radio programmes had reported that Argentina had invaded the Falklands: the Argentine freighter previously berthed astern of us had hurriedly slipped, and with skilful handling had turned around and headed for sea – perhaps the Master suspected that she would have been detained! However after being held by Canadian authorities for a short while she was allowed to proceed with a pilot: by that time *Sir Bedivere* wasn't far behind and overtook her – she kept in to the US coast until we had overtaken – perhaps she thought we were belligerent.

We were given a priority transit of the Panama Canal and made a fast passage to UK. Our day at Marchwood was hectic as extra equipment was fitted and we loaded everything we could carry until we sailed for Ascension Island. There we cross-decked with other ships and sorted ourselves out before embarking a 'full load' of troops and sailing southwards. On passage we replenished a flotilla of Trawler/Minesweepers, which gave our passengers some diversion as did King Neptune and Court on crossing the line.

At Ascension, the 'Hospital' group, after only a day at anchor, was on its way south once more, as the repair ship *Stena Seaspread* arrived. MV *Wimpey Seahorse* also left Ascension today, heading, by way of South Georgia, for what would eventually become the Tug, Repair and Logistics Area (TRALA).

HMS *Plymouth* and HMS *Brilliant* joined the Carrier Task Group from South Georgia, returning the special forces units, 'D' Sqn SAS and SBS No 2 to the carriers. And with the arrival of these last two warships the Carrier Task Group, once again in company with RFA *Olmeda* and RFA *Resource*, began a massive replenishment operation for fuel, ammunition, and stores so that each ship would have reasonably high reserves before entering the TEZ, the Group now being only 500 nautical miles from Port Stanley.

RFA *Resource* carried out VERTREPS with HMS *Coventry* and HMS *Glamorgan*, as well as jackstay transfers with HMS *Brilliant* and a transfer using the special Sea Slug missile rig, number 7, to HMS *Arrow* and HMS *Plymouth*, although these last two were not logged as missile transfers.

This giant replenishment finished the next morning (30 April), as the TEZ came into force and General Haig held a press conference blaming Argentina completely for the failure of the negotiations and claiming that Britain had been ready to accept his deal. This wasn't actually the case, as Mrs Thatcher makes clear in her autobiography *The Downing Street Years* (p. 207). Argentina also announced the establishment of its own TEZ, encompassing a 200-mile zone around its coast and the Falkland Islands.

With its major replenishment exercise now finished, the Carrier Group turned and made for the TEZ. *Resource*'s log noted the day's sea and weather conditions:

Noon position: 510 33'S, 0470 13'W, Average speed: 9.58 knots, Atmospheric pressure 1012.3 millibars9 (high), Temperature 3.2 degrees C, Weather: Dry, Sea temperature: 6.1degrees C, Wind strength (Beaufort): Force 5.

In all not a bad day for the South Atlantic. Lots worse were to come.

Still with the Carrier Task Group, RFA *Appleleaf* pumped over her remaining AVCAT to RFA *Olmeda*, then, at noon, detached to replenish her supply tanks from *British Esk*. Like all the 'Leaf' boats, *Appleleaf* was only intended as a support and depot supply tanker, although during the war she frequently replenished warships, in all supplying fuel on eighty-one occasions.

British Esk was now deployed on 'motorway tanking' duties, a job most crews found tested their patience and tolerance to the limits. Although they came to

the job of motorway tanking sometime later, the experiences of the crew of
British Wye were typical:

We arrived at Ascension seeking a spare part for our only crane. Peter Breeze, the
RFA Bosun, hitched a ride ashore, waded through endless cases and packages and
found the part, he claims, when he tripped over it. We were sailed from Ascension
after collecting the spare parts and mail. We received our sailing orders by v/s [visual
signal] from HMS *Fearless*: 'PIAWPO'.

'What,' said Captain Bundle 'is PIAWPO?' [It means Proceed In Accordance With
Prior Orders.]

I told him we had none as yet. So we slipped away and headed south. We received
our orders a couple of hours later.

We were sent to a holding position at about thirty-five [degrees] south, and hung
around waiting. We met a couple of other STUFTS, all tankers, but mostly it was just
waiting.

Looking back through the signals, I realise what a logistical nightmare it must
have been especially for the FOL [fuel and lubricants]. There was a preoccupation
with our issuable cargo; every authority was busy housekeeping. The other
preoccupation was mail.

At Ascension, things were hotting up with the departure of the first part of
the Amphibious Task Group, consisting of the slower LSLs, escorted by HMS
Antelope and accompanied by RFA *Pearleaf*. *Sir Galahad*'s Master, Captain Phil
Roberts, remembered the trip south very well:

So, on 30 April, in company with four other LSLs, RFA *Pearleaf*, and our escort, HMS
Antelope we set sail from Ascension Island in the direction of South Georgia.

Commander Nick Tobin, captain of *Antelope*, referred to us as his Chinese Navy
(all the ships he escorted were manned by Hong Kong Chinese crews – approximately three hundred men in all), and through his good leadership and particularly
his strict EMCON [Emission Control – restriction of radio or radar transmissions to
avoid detection] policy we achieved our passage south without detection. He also
very bravely allowed us our first Gunex, firing at star shells he put up. A lot of Bofors
ammo was put up by the five LSLs, some of it landing remarkably close to him!

Nearer South Georgia, HMS *Antrim* and HMS *Plymouth* took over duties as
escorts, by which time we were getting down into the roaring forties and were
receiving our first real taste of bad weather.

Sir Percivale (Captain Tony Pitt) was also involved in that target practice:

As with the previous sea passage, after leaving Ascension, an extensive amount of
training took place during this period, building up to Action and Shelter Stations at
any time of night or day. Response was good, both from ships personnel and EF
[Embarked Force]. Further flying training took place with emphasis on night flying
with minimal or no deck lighting. The firing of rockets and GPMG was also practised
from the Gazelles.

The ship's defensive capabilities were also tested when HMS *Antelope* bravely towed a splash target down a line of LSLs with itchy trigger fingers. During this exercise we also had the opportunity to loose off two 105mm shells. The trial was very successful and it was thought to be the first firing from the deck of a ship and certainly an RFA. Further air defence training was conducted by HMS *Antelope* to familiarize the LSLs with the sequence of events and methods of communicating these, culminating in live firing at a star shell.

Provisions were topped up from *Regent* on 6 May and *Stromness* on 18 May. Bunkers were supplied by *Pearleaf* on 8 May and AVCAT on 18.

On 13 May the Task Unit was advised by COMAW [Commodore, Amphibious Warfare] that ships should now have adjusted their routine to suit conditions in the Falkland Islands although remaining on GMT.

Over the next few days the routine on *Sir Percivale* was 'eased to the right' and the working day finally commenced at 10.00 Z with lunch at 14.30 Z and dinner at 20.30 Z. Daybreak was, at this time, around 11.00 Z and once settled, this new routine seemed to suit. On Sunday 16 May a two-watch system commenced on the bridge, with doubled-up watch keepers.

Strangely enough, there doesn't seem to have been much in the way of planning about the early deployment of ships to the South Atlantic. A number of people involved with the early stages have said that it was basically a question of getting as much south as they could and relying upon that being enough.

This probably explains why fuel was never a limiting factor at any stage, although a number of warships had only enough shells left for two days' consumption by 14 June.

Food supply was also a problem, as by 10 June *Sir Percivale* had only two days' food left at full rations, while others were also quite badly off.

And food and ammunition could have been even more of a problem if either RFA *Fort Austin* or RFA *Resource* had been sunk. As one of the shrewder RFA officers put it: '. . . the loss of *Fort Austin* or *Resource* might then have turned out to have been even more significant than the loss of a carrier or landing ship.'

CHAPTER EIGHT

THE SEA PHASE – SOFTENING UP

HAVING COLLECTED TOGETHER all his forces in a cohesive group near the Falklands, Admiral Woodward's first objective was to convince the Argentine military that he was about to immediately attempt a landing. He hoped that this would encourage both the Argentine Navy and Air Force to attack the Task Force in an attempt to stop the British invasion. His task would then be threefold:

Firstly, to fight a battle of attrition with the Argentine Navy and so reduce their strength such that they would be unable to interfere with British repossession plans.

Secondly, to fight a similar battle with the Argentine Air Force, similarly reducing their effective strength to a negligible level.

Thirdly, having assured himself of the destruction and/or incapacity of those two branches of the Argentine armed forces, to blockade the military population and reduce their effectiveness then repossess the Falkland Islands by invasion and restore British sovereignty with minimum military and civilian casualties.

Admiral Woodward himself put it most succinctly:

My initial plan was to lay on a major demonstration of force well inside the Exclusion Zone to make the Argentines believe that the landings were about to take place and thus provoke a reaction that would allow me to conduct a major attrition exercise before the amphibious force actually arrived to complicate my problem.

At the very least, I might discover whether they had a coherent defensive plan.

The trouble, of course, with attrition exercises is that they can work both ways. Woodward was gambling that the skill and nerve of his men as well as the quality of their training and equipment would be sufficient to outweigh the Argentine superiority in aircraft and numbers, even given the disadvantage of operating from a carrier base 8,000 miles from home.

And, in the final analysis, he was right. Just. Although what might have happened, if for instance, the Argentine Navy, particularly their submarines, had been better deployed, or if the Junta had managed to buy a few more Exocet still remains an intriguing question.

1 May was a busy day for all concerned. The Carrier Task Group entered the Total Exclusion Zone at 07.00 GMT (04.00 local) and almost immediately, an RAF Vulcan from Ascension bombed Stanley airport, cratering the runway in at least one place.

This attack was an incredible piece of organisation, requiring no fewer than five refuellings from Victor tankers on the way down with a similar number on the way home.

Later that morning, the Harriers of *Hermes'* 800 squadron, and *Invincible's* 801 squadron, also cratered Stanley and Goose Green airstrips making them unusable, at least for C-130 transport planes. This left the Argentineans temporarily unable to airlift supplies, and effectively cut off from the mainland.

While this was going on, the Argentine fighters and bombers had not been slow in attacking the Task Force, although for them the results weren't encouraging.

The Harriers' first attempts at the incoming Mirages were unsuccessful but in the mid-afternoon, a Combat Air Patrol (CAP) from *Invincible* shot down two Mirages heading for the carriers. Minutes later, *Hermes'* CAP accounted for a single Dagger which had been escorting three aircraft of the same type who were attacking HMS *Glamorgan*, *Alacrity* and *Arrow*. The warships were patrolling off East Falkland and had bombarded Port Stanley airfield with their 4.5-inch guns in an attempt to convince the Argentine forces that a seaborne invasion was imminent.

This turned out to be the first and last dogfight of the war, where Argentine aircraft flew air-to-air sorties against the Harriers. The rapid loss of two out of their dozen R.530 missile-equipped Mirages worried the Air Force command so much that in future, Argentine aircraft would decline air-to-air combat . . . if they could.

Meanwhile, HMS *Brilliant* and *Yarmouth*, following a presumptive submarine contact, were forced to break off the search after dark in order to return to the Carrier Task Group, not, however, without seeing *Hermes'* CAP down one of a group of Canberra bombers, apparently intent upon attacking the warships.

The first day of combat had ended well for the British, although, in the Commons, Francis Pym was assuring anyone who would listen that the Task Force's activities were '. . . concentrating Argentine minds . . . no more activity would be expected from the Task Force . . .'

The Junta, however, had not been idle, although at a top-level meeting, which included most of the country's generals, the call was still for negotiation, avoiding all out war at any cost.

Incidentally, the suggestion has been made elsewhere (Gavashon and Rice, p. 82) that the US Government (and therefore Mrs Thatcher) knew about this reluctance on the part of Argentina for all-out war via a CIA bug, although she could hardly have been able to act upon it, given the Argentine's public belligerence.

Late on the afternoon of 1 May, Rear Admiral Allara, in command of Argentine aircraft carrier *Viencentio de Mayo* and its accompanying Task Group, is thought to have received orders from his superior, Contralmirante J J Lombardo, the officer in overall command of the Navy's defensive operations, to use the two northern groups of his TF 79 against the British. Too late to take action that day, Allara waited for morning and enough wind to get his heavily-laden aircraft airborne from the old carrier.

Adding confusion to the picture, it was also later claimed, by certain Argentine sources, that the naval representative on the Junta, Anaya himself, ordered the withdrawal of all Argentine Fleet units back to home port today.

For the RFAs, information was scanty. RFA *Resource*'s diary records:

Today there was the first air-raid warning between 13.30 and 14.30. Hands went to Emergency stations. Men were closed up two to a machine gun, in anti-flash gear and very alert. There had been a bombing raid by our own Harriers and Vulcan bombers over the Falklands.

The very first warning of the alert came over the helicopter control net and it was noticed on the radar screen that chaff blooms were appearing all around the major warship targets, also our own Harriers were seen streaking across the radar display, returning to their respective carriers, following the raid on Stanley.

The atmosphere was very tense but everyone was very calm.

As might be expected, the counter-claims about numbers of aircraft shot down began at once, with the Argentines claiming anything from two to four Harriers destroyed. All this speculation came to nothing however, when, in one of the most effective pieces of spontaneous propaganda of the war, Brian Hanrahan told millions in Britain watching the BBC News: 'I'm not allowed to say how many 'planes joined the raid but I counted them all out and I counted them all back.'

Admiral Woodward summed the day up neatly: 'We did not want this fight. I'd hoped we could put it off but we've shown our colours and it's been our day.'

Next day was another busy one for the RFAs. RFA *Regent* left Ascension, soon to provide another much needed specialist Ammunition, Explosives, Food and Store (AEFS) ship in the South Atlantic. RFA *Tidespring* finally got away from South Georgia with her 185 Argentine POWs embarked. Ascension bound, she was escorted initially by HMS *Antrim*. Almost immediately, the big fast fleet tanker made a planned rendezvous with RFA *Appleleaf*, in the course of which *Tidespring* replenished the 'Leaf boat with what was left of *Brambleleaf*'s winter aviation fuel (AVCAT), previously pumped over to *Tidespring* at South Georgia.

HMS *Plymouth* and HMS *Antrim* remained with the RFAs as escorts.

Several hundred miles to the north of the Falklands, the Argentine Navy was preparing its counter-offensive, soon to be nicknamed 'Lombardo's Fork'. For much of the period between the successful completion of Operation Rosario and the arrival of the Task Force in the TEZ, the Argentine Navy's Task Groups, designated TG 79.1, TG 79.2, TG 79.3 and TG 79.4, were in Puerto Belgrano, not sailing again until 27 April, when the ships left their base and took up positions to the north and south of the Falklands.

Led by the carrier *Vienticinco de Mayo*, TG 79.1 also comprised the latter's defence screen of two British-built Type 42 anti-aircraft destroyers, while TG 79.2 consisted of two Exocet-armed destroyers, the *Segui* and the *Comodoro Py*.

A third group, TG 79.3, made up of the 6-inch cruiser *General Belgrano* and two Exocet-armed anti-submarine destroyers, *Piedra Buena* and *Hipolita Bouchard*, were to the southeast of Port Stanley, in a holding position off Isla de los Eatados (Staten Island).

Finally, a more recently formed group, TG 79.4, consisting of three twenty-four knot A.69 corvettes, *Drummond*, *Granville* and *Guerrico*, this latter recently repaired after being all but shot to pieces by the Royal Marines defending Grytviken, was to the north of TG 79.1 and TG 79.2, who had remained in company. The French-built corvettes of TG 79.4 had a 100mm automatic gun and four Exocet, as well as modern Bofors guns and anti-submarine torpedoes. Each group also had a tanker in support.

In response to Admiral Woodward's successful attack, Admiral Lombardo ordered the carrier from its original position off Deseado, some 400 miles north west of Stanley, so as to bring it within flying range of the British.

While carrying out this position change, Rear Admiral Allara also attempted to fly his jets off of the carrier but, fortunately for the British, the wind wasn't strong enough to allow the heavily loaded, conventional fixed wing aircraft to take off.

The British VSTOL (Vertical/Short Take Off and Landing) Harriers had no such problems and were able to fly their usual two-aircraft CAPs in all weather conditions.

With the *Belgrano* group to the southwest, Woodward's Task Force were caught in a potential pincer movement. The heavily-armed WWII cruiser *General Belgrano*, with its 5-inch and 6-inch guns and possible Exocet fit, only needed to cross the nearby Burwood bank to evade HMS *Conqueror* and become an instant threat to the Task Force.

The vital RFAs, being significantly slower than the warships and without armour, were particularly vulnerable and at least one of them, RFA *Resource*, was carrying a nuclear depth charge in its secure containment facility. Coupled with a northerly attack by the carrier's aircraft, the cruiser's bombardment could have decimated the Task Force and destroyed any likelihood of a successful outcome to Operation Corporate.

Consequently, a change to Woodward's Rules Of Engagement (ROEs) was sought and obtained, resulting in HMS *Conqueror* launching three torpedoes at the cruiser and sinking her in the late afternoon of 2 May, with the loss of 321 lives.

This enormous loss of life was thought to be due to failure by the crew to take ordinary precautions rather than the effectiveness of HMS *Conqueror*'s torpedoes. Important anti-flash doors, in particular, appear to have been left open, which allowed a fireball to enter a crew compartment where the major losses occurred.

There can be no question that the *Belgrano* posed a real threat to the Task Force and that her sinking was necessary. Although over forty years old, she had guns with a range of thirteen miles, and which outranged the 4.5-inch guns of the Task Force. Her armour was between three and eight inches thick, making her virtually impervious to British shells and missiles, including the deadly Exocet. And with a twenty-nine knot top speed, she could have run down any of the vital RFAs at will.

Woodward's only option against her was either a Harrier with a 1,000 pound bomb or a submarine. Sensibly, he chose the latter and used it sooner rather than later.

Interviewed on British television some months later, even Admiral Allara was forced to admit that, in the same position, he would have sunk the *Belgrano*, especially after the clear warning of 23 April.

The men of the Task Force had no doubts about the reality of the threat, although their knowledge of Argentine religious customs was patchy, as RFA *Resource's* diary explains:

As the first light of dawn broke, the Battle group was expecting a raid from the Argentine aircraft carrier, *De Mayo*. Our course was east at sixteen knots, away from the threat. However, at 15.00 hrs GMT, course was reversed.

... The air attack from the Argentine aircraft carrier never materialised. We wondered if, for religious reasons, the Argentines were not prepared to fight on Sundays.

Even then, it was still business as usual, the diary finally recording:

VERTREPS were carried out today with HMS *Alacrity*, *Arrow*, *Yarmouth*, *Brilliant* and *Glamorgan*. The RAS with *Glamorgan* was carried out on Rig 7 (The dedicated Sea Slug rig). Forty-five unit loads were passed.

During this period, despite the incessant activity, replenishment of the warships went on almost continuously, especially helicopter delivery of food and ammunition.

Monday 3 May was a quiet day for the Task Force, although the sinking of the *General Belgrano* meant that negotiation between the two sides was never really attempted in earnest again and a military solution was now inevitable.

Bad weather prevented any offensive action by the British Task Group, so the ships spent the day replenishing.

This spell of high winds also kept the *Vienticinco del Mayo* from operating its aircraft, and following the loss of the *General Belgrano*, the Argentine fleet began to pull back to shallow water, where they would remain, taking no further part in war.

In retrospect, it is clear that the Royal Navy effectively won the surface war today, since the Argentine Navy would never again allow any of its major units to leave port again, thus effectively achieving the first of the Task Force's major objectives. Although the Argentine capital ships never ventured out again, Admiral Woodward was still forced to detail a nuclear submarine to watch them for the duration of the conflict, thus tying up a valuable resource at a time when it could have been of use elsewhere.

RFA *Fort Austin* (still carrying a nuclear round) also rejoined the Carrier Battle Group today, while RFA *Plumleaf* left the Ascension area, heading south. No rest was allowed to Commodore Sam Dunlop's big stores ship. With 250 loads of transit stores, 200 bags of mail and twenty tons of fresh food, she immediately embarked on what seemed to the crew like a continuous round of replenishment by helicopter, which lasted for a period of ten days. During this time, some of the 845 NAS Wessex pilots flew anything up to twenty miles to deliver their loads. One of her crew explains:

Much of the next few weeks prior to the invasion, was at most periods very quiet, except for a few diversions and busy days. One busy day was the arrival of about 130 personnel from HMS *Sheffield*, which had been hit by an Exocet missile. This brought our levels of accommodating people to the highest yet. It was sad in some ways because at various levels the ship had come to know the ship's company of HMS *Sheffield* ever since we had first met up with them in Mombassa in January. The *Sheffield* contingent was on board for nearly a week, before transferring to the *British Esk* for their journey home via Ascension. If one considers the *Fort Austin* being overloaded with people, that ship went to Ascension with nearly 240 extras and they only had a crew of thirty-five! The *Sheffield* crew, once they had settled on board the *Austin*, helped out in many departments without any problems.

By this time I had gone round the ship many times with clipboard and plans and had my very own comprehensive plan as to who was where and even measured up the daybeds and settees etc, to see where people could be accommodated. It was to come in very useful later. Using watchkeeper's cabins was considered the last straw, but on the whole nobody objected to fitting an extra person in their cabin if required.

Another memory of this period was being detached 400 to 500 miles north of the

Falklands to await an airdrop. On a beautiful calm afternoon, a Mk 4 Sea King arrived and wanted to shut down on the Hangar Top, which it did, soon to be followed by a Hercules that dropped personnel and equipment. I seem to remember the Sea King was piloted by an RAF officer, who managed to have an hour or so sunning himself on the Flight Deck before the drop. The helicopter was eventually loaded up and away it went. It was more than likely refuelled on the Hangar Top, as by this time we had realised that it was possible to do this, by rigging a spare HIFR [refuelling] rig up there, as by this time we had at least three or four on board. Talk about being flexible!

Another day was spent transferring the Wessex and Lynx to other ships, including to the *Atlantic Conveyor*, and embarking a flight of four Sea Kings ('Pingers'). More re-organisation of the accommodation lists and adjustments to the Souls on Board Lists. Another memory of this period was the arrival of an RN Chief Petty Officer with an interesting piece of kit, namely a thermal imaging camera that was being tested. It was fitted to a Lynx. I remember talking to him and he told me that he was having problems with the camera and could not protect it from the elements very well, as the cling film that covered the casing would not withstand the pressures etc, on take off. A suggestion was made that in the holds the RNSTS had large quantities of clear polythene, so he paid a visit to get some, and I believe the problem was solved. I did manage to see videos of earlier trials of this camera, and it clearly showed the hotspots on a Type 42 Destroyer, in blacked out conditions.

As mentioned in the account above, 4 May had been a day of terrible tragedy for the Task Force. Almost before first light, Vulcans from Ascension once again tried to bomb Port Stanley's runway, this time, however, inflicting no damage on the airfield.

Meanwhile, the Carrier Battle Group had run to within 100 nautical miles of Stanley, with Sea Harriers flying CAPs (Combat Air Patrols) from first light. Unfortunately, the Group was found by an Argentine Neptune reconnaissance aircraft, which called up two Exocet-carrying Super Etendards, who managed a successful attack on the British vessels. HMS *Sheffield*, hit while on duty in what was known as the 'picket line', some twenty miles up-threat from the carriers, lost twenty of her crew, with another twenty-four wounded, the rest being evacuated by HMS *Arrow* and the Sea Kings of HMS *Hermes* and RFA *Resource*.

One of the crew of RFA *Olmeda* has hair-raising memories of the incident:

One event that I feel was never explored was that Lieutenant Phillipi was reported to have launched two Exocets in the attack on HMS *Sheffield*.

If he did, where did the second go?

I think it landed between the *Olmeda* and, I think it was, HMS *Antrim* probably a mile astern of the Olmeda. Only some three people saw it (we did not recognise it for what it was) a QM [Quartermaster], Captain Gil Overbury OBE RFA from the bridge wing and myself from the flight deck.

Later that day, the first Harrier loss was recorded when the second of a pair of 800 Squadron Sea Harriers, piloted by Lieutenant N Taylor, was shot down as they crossed the coast near Goose Green, prior to making an attack on Port Stanley's airstrip. Lt Taylor was killed and subsequently buried with full military honours on the edge of the airfield. Honourable men, it seems, weren't confined to one side.

Interestingly, communication around the Group seems to have been patchy, RFA *Resource*'s diary recording:

A terrible day for the Task Group. One Sea Harrier was lost and HMS *Sheffield* was hit by an Exocet missile. We heard the news echoing back to us from home, 8,000 miles away, on the BBC World Service.

Sheffield's Lynx, which had been flown off as soon as the missile hit, had been collected by RFA *Fort Austin* where it was soon joined by some of her ship's surviving crew.

RFA *Fort Austin*'s crew quickly applied the lessons learnt from their accommodation difficulties during their first visit to Ascension, as one of the crew explains:

In all some 170 men from *Sheffield* were embarked . . . All were quickly allocated a cabin to share with a ship's officer or rating, kitted out where necessary with clothing and toiletries where available and, where possible, allocated to a Department for duty purposes.
    We found them all remarkably cheerful and anxious to help out where they could. One Petty Officer set up shop as a barber in the Supply Office, another spliced wire strops and yet other helped out in the holds.

It wasn't all quite so pleasant, however, although RFA humour, served dark and dry, did prevail:

Many [of *Sheffield*'s crew] who joined *Fort Austin* had flash burns around the eyes and sometimes hands where they had not been wearing anti-flash clothing, which became a very popular item of loan clothing on board overnight!

Fort Austin's doctor remembers one of *Sheffield*'s casualties in particular:

Later on in the conflict we received casualties and survivors from HMS *Sheffield* and HMS *Coventry*. One of the uninjured was a young Doctor from the *Sheffield* which pleased me greatly at the time as I was on my own without any medical help. He was very wet so, without asking, one of my shipmates gave him a brand new pair of his own pyjamas to wear under his survival kit.
    When our survivors were evacuated including the young doctor, he took the pyjamas with him. We all felt very sorry for our shipmate who will have to convince his wife that they are not in some other lady's bed!
    In my casualty queue I had also noticed an injured rating with a jacket with four

stripes on his sleeve. I did not realise until afterwards that he was the captain of the *Coventry*, refusing to assert his rank.

At the end of the day, the Task Group then withdrew from the TEZ (Total Exclusion Zone) to conduct another major replenishment (RAS). Further north, RFA *Blue Rover* joined the *Tidespring/Appleleaf* group, while, in the UK, MV *Lycaon*, loaded with ammunition, sailed for the South Atlantic.

Wednesday 5 May was another quiet day for the Task Force, with the RAS still in progress. RFA *Resource* took 150 of *Sheffield*'s survivors on board, after they had spent a comfortless night aboard HMS *Arrow* and *Yarmouth*. The *Sheffield* was still afloat, acting as a 'tethered goat', to attract submarine or air attack, but the mainland weather prevented the Argentine Air Force from operating today.

RFA *Resource*'s diary records the impression the *Sheffield*'s survivors made on her crew:

Survivors of the *Sheffield* gave vivid descriptions of war to our crew. It made a great impression on them, reflected at the next Emergency Stations.

We also learned that respirators had provided a great relief from the acrid smoke and had provided a vital 30–40 seconds to enable enclosed spaces to be evacuated when they filled with toxic fumes.

Claiming she had engine trouble the *Viencentio de Mayo* crept north towards her base at Puerto Belgrano, hugging the coast to avoid submarine attack. Once there, she remained in port, not putting to sea again until after the surrender.

Atlantic Conveyor and HMS *Intrepid* also arrived at Ascension on 5 May and, much to the relief of the Task Force Commander, two other air-defence Type 42 destroyers, replacements for *Sheffield*, were on their way, with HMS *Exeter* ordered to leave Belize and HMS *Cardiff* ordered to Gibraltar for maintenance and restoring before going south as part of the *Bristol* group. This latter consisted of two Type 21 frigates, HMS *Avenger* and *Active*, three Leander-class frigates, HMS *Minerva*, *Penelope* and *Andromeda*, and the Fast Fleet Tanker RFA *Olna*. The group was led by HMS *Bristol*, the Navy's sole Type 82 destroyer.

The next day saw more tragedy for the Task Force, when a CAP from *Invincible* vanished without trace. The two aircraft were last seen disappearing into thick fog after being directed to investigate a contact reported fifty miles to the south of the group. It is believed the two Sea Harriers collided in poor visibility. No trace of either pilot or their aircraft was ever found.

Continuing bad weather prevented any further activity by the Task Force, so Admiral Woodward ordered RFA *Olmeda* north to rendezvous with RFA *Appleleaf*, the latter having finished pumping over what was originally RFA *Brambleleaf*'s winter AVCAT.

The *Tidespring/Appleleaf* group separated, with RFA *Blue Rover* and *Appleleaf* going south towards the Task Group, escorted by HMS *Plymouth*, while RFA *Tidespring* and her escort HMS *Antrim* turned north, making for Ascension.

RFAs *Tidepool* and *Plumleaf* left Ascension to join the Carrier Battle Group, escorted by HMS *Ardent* and *Argonaut*, while in a move which some observers in Britain saw as better late than never, France finally halted delivery of Super Etendard aircraft to Argentina.

One of *Tidepool*'s officers, Graham Ferguson, had a big job:

We arrived some days later at Ascension to find a large fleet of ships already at anchor. This was very impressive even though the carrier group had already left. Shortly after our arrival we embarked a Wessex 5 helicopter and started to receive stores, most of these by helicopter. Given that I was the only qualified FDO/HCO I spent all the daylight hours, and some night ones too, on the flight deck! One of the first items to arrive was the Marisat satellite communications aerial that was flown out underslung from a Wessex 5 and dropped onto the ship's monkey island. The loading continued for some days during which more ships arrived and some left. It was an extraordinary scene enlivened by the continuous stream of aircraft landing at Wideawake airfield which was sufficiently close that we watched the aircraft land and take off. At one stage there was a report of an Argentinean submarine in the area and we all up-anchored and cruised around in the vicinity. In our case this was to the south of the island and late that night we watched as a continuous stream of aircraft took off one after the other. Rules change in wartime! This later turned out to be the famous Black Buck raid that targeted the Port Stanley runway.

We left Ascension on 6 May, with elements of the amphibious force led by *Fearless* and *Intrepid* and including many ships taken up from trade (STUFT). Most notable, and noticeable, was *Canberra* with her white hull, now getting very stained with rust. One of our first replenishments was with her and this was rather protracted as the RFA is normally the 'guide' that steams at a set course and speed determined by the senior naval vessel that is to be replenished, bearing in mind the tactical situation. In this case *Canberra* would be the guide and *Tidepool* would have to draw alongside. RFAs, especially at that time, were not really equipped and trained for the fast approach that is normal and very desirable in a real war situation. Our lengthy approach from the beam was not the most spectacular RAS I have been involved in! Our performance in this respect was brought into sharp focus by the approach of the P & O ferry *Elk* which had a four-ring RN captain on board advising her civilian Master.

The logistics effort began to gather momentum again on 7 May, with the departure from Ascension of the main body of amphibious assault vessels, although bad weather prevented any activity by the main Carrier Group. This Amphibious Group included HMS *Fearless*, HMS *Intrepid*, RFA *Stromness*, MV *Atlantic Conveyor*, MV *Europic Ferry*, and SS *Canberra* as well as MV *Elk*, the ammunition transport, although the latter vessel was not part of the Amphibious Group. RFA *Stromness*'s diary recorded the event:

21.40 Zulu (GMT) co-ordinated silent departure i.e. ships weighing anchor and proceeding in formation with no radio or radar transmissions.

Clearly, the Commodore Amphibious Warfare (COMAW), Michael Clapp, was taking no chances about losing the element of surprise. *Stromness*'s crew were issued, en route, with anti-flash gear, cold weather clothing, survival suits, respirators and, more worryingly to some minds, Geneva Convention (prisoner of war) identity cards. Many had their eye on another sort of emergency, one of her crew remembering that: 'The NAAFI also reported an increase in the sales of Mars Bars for secreting away "just in case".'

This Group, including MV *Elk*, had HMS *Ardent* and *Argonaut* for escort.

MV *Norland* was also meant to be part of the Amphibious Group but her UK departure had been delayed and she only arrived at Ascension today. She stayed only long enough to give her troops some much needed time ashore before leaving in the wake of the rest of the Group.

HMS *Antelope*, RFA *Pearleaf* and the LSL landing ships, still waiting at about thirty degrees south for the rest of the Amphibious Group, were overtaken by RFA *Regent* and the hospital ship *Uganda* and later this whole group rendezvoused with HMS *Antrim* and *Tidespring*. It had been previously decided that HMS *Antelope*, one of the Type 21 frigates, did not offer enough protection to the LSLs, so she exchanged passengers and her single prisoner, Lt Astiz, with HMS *Antrim*, who then assumed escort duties for the whole miscellaneous collection of vessels, while HMS *Antelope* accompanied *Tidespring* to Ascension. Perhaps significantly, the same day saw the TEZ extended to within twelve miles of the Argentine mainland.

Resource's diary shows that 'Emergency Stations' were starting to have an air of routine about them:

The use of damage control equipment was further demonstrated by the ship's officers i.e. breathing apparatus, splinter boxes, 'Yankee shores'. Also, escape routes were discussed with the ship's company so as to gainfully employ the time during the long Emergency Stations.

Plymouth's group, which included RFA *Appleleaf* and RFA *Blue Rover*, rendezvoused with RFA *Fort Austin* and RFA *Olmeda* on Saturday 8th, RFA *Olmeda* immediately beginning a pumpover from *Appleleaf*.

Off the Falklands, HMS *Brilliant* was detached from the Task Group to patrol the north entrance to Falkland sound, while HMS *Alacrity* shelled Argentine bivouacs on Port Stanley Common. HMS *Coventry*, on patrol with HMS *Broadsword*, claimed two Skyhawks shot down while HMS *Yarmouth* took HMS *Sheffield* in tow around midnight.

The Harriers scored another success, turning back another Argentine

Hercules and its Mirage escort before it could reach Port Stanley.

And the RFAs were in the thick of things, as *Resource*'s diary records:

A RAS took place with HMS *Invincible* from 14.58 until 15.38 . . . While *Invincible* was alongside, we heard her order 'Scramble the Harriers!' Hostile aircraft had closed to within thirty-eight miles of us. And we witnessed, at very close quarters, the Harriers roaring off the deck to defend us.

Next day saw the Task Force back in action with the Harriers trying to attack Stanley with 1,000 pound bombs attached to their fuselage pylons. Flak and the Argentineans' Roland missiles meant the bombing would be carried out from a high level, but when the aircraft arrived over the target, they did not release their bombs due to an unacceptable risk that they might have hit the settlement. Their time wasn't wasted however, because, barely twenty minutes later, HMS *Coventry*, whose operations room was controlling the CAP, detected the Argentine trawler *Narwhal*. This was subsequently attacked by the Harriers with bombs and cannon fire, before being captured by a party of SBS from HMS *Hermes* and a prize crew from *Invincible*, who abseiled onto the trawler's deck from Sea King helicopter.

During this attack, a Mark 4 Sea King was forced to land and refuel on HMS *Glasgow*'s Lynx-sized flight deck. The pilot managed this landing and the subsequent take-off, despite having only a metre's clearance between the Sea King's rotor tip and *Glasgow*'s hangar door!

Meanwhile, HMS *Coventry* and *Broadsword* were in action off Port Stanley, shelling the Argentine troop positions there, HMS *Coventry* claiming a 'double kill', in the form of two A-4C Skyhawks. Later that evening, HMS *Brilliant* and *Glasgow* arrived off Stanley to relieve the HMS *Coventry/Broadsword* combination, and ensure another sleepless night for the Argentine garrison. HMS *Alacrity* and *Arrow* were sent to blockade Falkland Sound and ensure no supplies reached the defenders by this route.

Earlier, another attempt to fly a Hercules transport into Stanley was turned back by a Sea Harrier CAP, while, within the Task Force, *Fort Austin* transferred a nuclear round to HMS *Hermes*.

In the UK, MVs *Baltic Ferry*, *Nordic Ferry* and *Alvega* left Britain for the South Atlantic, while in South Georgia, RFA *Blue Rover* arrived in Cumberland Bay to act as Station Tanker.

The operation to recapture the Falklands was now nine weeks old. And this ninth week started badly for the British, when on Monday 10 May HMS *Sheffield* finally sank under tow just to the east of the TEZ, on her way to South Georgia. The Type 42 might just have made Cumberland Bay but a thirty-five-knot wind and five-metre waves proved too much for her. Much had been learned, however, about the effects of fire and explosion on a modern warship and her loss resulted in removal of some materials which had been found to emit toxic fumes, and the eventual issue of a superior pattern of emergency breathing apparatus to every man in the Task Force.

Later that afternoon, HMS *Alacrity* and *Arrow* were sent to conduct inshore operations, the latter tasked to reconnoitre East Falkland, while *Alacrity* sailed clear through Falkland Sound, from south to north. Coming out of the north end, HMS *Alacrity* fired on and sank an Argentine transport, the *Isla de los Estados*.

She rendezvoused with HMS *Arrow* off Cape Dolphin, both ships then proceeding back to the Task Force, unaware that they had been fired on by the Argentine diesel submarine *San Luis*, using a wire-guided torpedo. The torpedo's control wire broke after a couple of minutes; otherwise the submarine might have squared accounts for the coaster.

Unfortunately, the badly damaged *Narwhal* also sank that day, despite the best efforts of her prize crew, who were airlifted to safety at almost the last moment.

In the UK, RFA *Engadine* (Capt David Freeman), the Navy's helicopter training ship, sailed from Devonport for the South Atlantic, with 847 NAS 'A' flight and maintenance team embarked, while RFA *Olna* sailed from Portsmouth in company with the *Bristol* Group, consisting of HMS *Bristol* (Capt A Grose RN), the Type 21 frigates *Avenger* and *Active*, and the Leander-class frigates *Minerva*, *Penelope* and *Andromeda*. The Type 42 destroyer HMS *Cardiff* was also ordered to join, en route, from Gibraltar. At the same time RFA *Sir Bedivere* arrived at Ascension, the authorities there also establishing a 100 nautical mile Terminal Control Area around the island.

David Bolton, one of *Engadine*'s cooks, recalls the journey south:

On our way down to the Falklands, we started doing more boat drills and fire and emergency drills, gunnery drills and everything drills that the top had decided we needed to be up to speed on for the war.

While at Falmouth, we loaded many more helicopters than we were supposed to carry and all the flight cabins were full of extra pilots and maintainers etc. We left with far more bodies on board than we were cleared for by Lloyd's Registry.

As a training ship, *Engadine* was fitted with stabilisers and it was decided by the tops to take these in to give us a bit more speed, so we were warned that the ship might roll a bit more than usual, although it did not.

During our voyage south, *Engadine* crossed the equator for the first time in her career. A massive party went on for the day with everyone enjoying the weather and a day off to relax and party. Games and stupidity went on all day with many a bad head from too much drink.

We stopped at Ascension Island to take on more supplies, mainly engine spares as we had a cracked cylinder on the main engines.

It had been sent to Gibraltar for us, but we had left by then, so it had gone to the UK and missed us there, so it caught us in Ascension.

After a stop at Ascension, we then started getting into the war spirit, and the inside of porthole lids were painted black, so as to reduce reflection. We did as asked, though no one could really see the point as the ships were highly visible. All burnables were collected. Porthole curtains, door curtains etc were turned into packing in case there was a breach of the hull, when they would be used to partially block it.

The thick rubber mats used in alleyways to reduce noise as flight crews worked round the clock were dumped overboard as they were a huge risk if they caught fire.

During the second leg of our trip, a parachute drop of the new Stingray torpedoes was arranged so that we would have these for the war. Not quite ready when we left the UK, they were flown out and parachuted down to us for distribution to the fleet.

There was a rumour going round that the Vulcan bombers which were supposed to have bombed the runway at Stanley had in fact failed and it was secretly done by an American bomber, with the RAF getting the credit.

One of the problems of going this far with extra crew on board was water, and all sorts of requests were made to save water and not use so much. Many comments along the lines of, 'I'm not showering with my mate to save water!' were heard. I even made up a poster from magazine cutouts which was posted on all notice boards, I still have the original in my scrap book.

One place used to store water I believe was the ballast tanks, which, although used for seawater usually, were filled with fresh water. It tasted OK although it was a bit murky. Must have been OK as the engineers were drinking it, and if it was OK for them, then it was OK for us!

Another thing we did to keep morale up was to organise an eating competition. The galley started this one by putting up notices, then making up a raffle for charity.

The raffle was for ordinary ship's items, luxuries and anything donated. Sold loads of tickets.

Then we set to, to make up a feast for the contestants. It was good food, bulky, in large portions. If you refused an item because you did not like it, you were out.

The RAF lads went at it with gusto, the various squadrons on board were competing against each other. One of the tricks used by the squadron chaps was to have a helper beside them, then, when they were getting full, they would just put the fingers down the throat and regurgitate it into a bucket, held by their helper. There was talk that this might be cheating, but it got by.

I cannot remember the menu, terrible really, but I do remember the sweet that I made. Large sweet/soup bowl of the old naval style filled with a thick, very sweet rice pudding, surrounding a largish lump of bread pudding, very dry. On top of this was put a nice coating of meringue to disguise what was underneath. This was toasted in a hot oven then decorated with tomato slices.

They tucked into this dish with relish, ah, a nice rice pudding, but they got bogged down with it then as they came upon the bread pudding in the middle that slowed them down and stopped some of the eaters.

Ah, what a good night that was.

Then we grew up and went into our first war for many of us.

By 11 May, the Amphibious Group, ploughing its way south, had been joined by RFA *Tidepool*. Off the Falklands, RFA *Regent* joined the Carrier Battle Group today, along with *British Esk*, the latter immediately being tasked to pump over her cargo to RFA *Olmeda* and *Appleleaf*, before taking the *Sheffield*'s unwounded survivors aboard and returning to Ascension. Off West Falkland, HMS *Broadsword* and *Coventry* waited hopefully to catch an Argentine Air Force sortie, but bad weather kept the aircraft grounded. At the same time the hospital ship *Uganda* arrived on the on edge of the TEZ. Unable to come closer to the Task Group because of her non-combatant status, she waited to embark HMS *Sheffield*'s wounded.

In the UK, Lloyds decided to withdraw insurance cover from any ships in a large area of South Atlantic.

Next morning, with the weather still poor, HMS *Brilliant* and *Glasgow* took their turn to bombard the Argentine positions around Port Stanley. During their period on the gunline, they were attacked twice from the air by Argentine Skyhawks. *Brilliant*'s Sea Wolf missiles accounted for two of the first wave when *Glasgow*'s Sea Dart and 4.5-inch automatic gun both jammed, although the second wave, weaving in at sea level, confused *Brilliant*'s Sea Wolf computer so much that, in David Brown's words: 'the system folded its arms and retrained the launchers fore and aft.'

One 1,000 pound bomb skipped over *Brilliant*, while the other tore a hole through *Glasgow*'s hull, three feet above the waterline, before exiting the other side without exploding. One of this second wave was shot down by the Argentines themselves as the raid fled over Goose Green, while a third wave of Skyhawks turned back without attacking.

After dark, the two warships returned to the Task Force, beginning a nightmare few days for the crew of *Glasgow*. By the evening of the next day, the damage to her hull was repaired but she could only operate one Olympus turbine, which had only manual speed control. The RAS hose had been shot away, too, so a lash-up rig was improvised before she replenished, in a full gale, with one engine and a single hand-controlled propeller.

No record is available of what the RFA involved felt about this procedure. Doubtless, to quote Gordon Butterworth, the RFA's Chief Marine Superintendent, they '. . . just got on with it. When all is said and done, if a ship needs fuel, it can't wait and you have to do the job, gale force wind and thirty-foot seas not withstanding.'

Anyone who had previously doubted it, Royal Navy included, was certainly finding out that RFA really did mean: 'Ready For Anything'.

Within the Task group, sixty-three of *Sheffield*'s survivors were transferred to
MV *British Esk* for passage to the UK, while in Britain, Cunard's RMS *Queen
Elizabeth II* and MV *Balder London* left for the South Atlantic, and RFA
Brambleleaf arrived in Portland for repairs.

Off Ascension, RFA *Tidespring* was preparing to disembark nearly 200
Argentine POWs after a not entirely uneventful trip, while, just north of
Finisterre, RFA *Engadine*'s elderly propulsion unit failed her, keeping her hove to
until the engine room staff managed to pull off a major component change, an
operation usually reserved for a fully-equipped dockyard.

Thursday 13 May saw RFA *Tidespring* finish disembarking her POWs and, with
a heartfelt sigh of relief, she stayed only long enough to embark two brand new
Wessex, food and fuel, before turning her bow south again a couple of days later
on 16 May.

Bad weather prevailed in both the TEZ and Argentine mainland so Admiral
Woodward's group were free to try and deal with HMS *Glasgow*, although HMS
Hecla, the Royal Navy ocean survey ship, which had been hurriedly converted to
an ambulance for the transport of wounded, did manage to join *Uganda* in the
Red Cross Box, the hospital ship having embarked *Sheffield*'s casualties, mostly
burns victims, the day before.

Early on the morning of 14 May, the Argentine airbase on Pebble Island was
attacked by the SAS, in a classic commando-type raid. Both the air base and
eleven aircraft were destroyed, the teams being extracted under a precisely-
controlled barrage of fire called down from HMS *Glamorgan* by a Naval Gunfire
Spotting team, landed with the SAS for just that purpose.

In Britain, final terms were sent to Argentina by the British Government, and
the Declaration of Active Service in the South Atlantic was formally announced
at midnight. This placed every individual on a Task Force ship, even the media
correspondents, under Service discipline. Reassuringly, this meant that, amongst
other advantages, if the worst happened, no one's estate would attract death
duties.

That same morning saw RFA *Fort Grange* leave the Clyde early, bound for
Ascension Island, while SS *Atlantic Causeway*, sister ship to the ill-fated SS
Atlantic Conveyor, also sailed from the UK. The last of the LSLs, RFA *Sir Bedivere*,
left Ascension, carrying not only the Navy's No 3 Fleet Clearance Diving Team,
but RAF and Army bomb disposal experts as well.

With the Task Force still experiencing bad weather and unable to operate,
RFA *Resource* transferred a nuclear round to *Invincible*, receiving a single training
round in exchange.

Despite the weather, it was, once again, business as usual for the RFAs,
Resource's diary recording:

VERTREPS took place between *Hermes, Arrow,* RFA *Appleleaf* and *British Esk* and our dentist sent to treat patients on HMS *Yarmouth*. Later, he was collected by helicopter.

Weather was still poor on May 15. *Resource* recorded a wind strength of force 9, although she still managed to transfer one special weapon and a surveillance round to RFA *Regent*. The Carrier Battle Group was now well to the east of the Falklands, the rough weather ensuring that they were not troubled by Argentine air activity. HMS *Glasgow* was repaired and operational again, with two working Olympus turbines.

Late in the afternoon, the weather began to clear and HMS *Alacrity* and *Brilliant* were detached for inshore operations, while VERTREP began again in earnest. HMS *Alacrity* repeated her transit of Falkland Sound, dropping off a group of SBS on her way, while HMS *Brilliant* sent her Lynx to investigate Fox Bay, both ships returning to the Battle Group before dawn.

Argentine transport runs, made overnight to Stanley by C-130 Hercules, had now become well organised, but in a further blow to their capability, today their sole remaining Neptune was declared non-operational and remained so for the duration of the war. Now Argentine attack aircraft, especially their Super Etendards, were without a vital reconnaissance link, depriving them of an up-to-date source of targeting information.

Next day, the whole of the Amphibious Group would rendezvous prior to its final approach to the TEZ. Then the next phase of the war would begin: Admiral Woodward's 'heavy punch'.

CHAPTER NINE

THE LAND PHASE – SAN CARLOS

T HE BUILD-UP FOR THE land offensive really began on Sunday 16 May with
the arrival of the Amphibious Group and its concentration, some 700 miles
southeast of Mar del Plata, for the final approach to the TEZ.

This group now included five LSLs, plus RFAs *Tidepool, Stromness, Pearleaf,*
and *Appleleaf* as well as the STUFT troopships SS *Canberra* and MV *Norland,*
together with the supply vessels MV *Atlantic Conveyor,* MV *Europic Ferry,* MV *Elk*
and the water tanker MV *Fort Toronto.*

Leading the Group were the landing ships HMS *Fearless* and *Intrepid* with
escort provided by HMS *Antrim, Plymouth, Ardent* and *Argonaut.*

RFA *Plumleaf* had previously been dropped off from the Amphibious Group
to act as a 'motorway tanker', operating in a region around forty degrees south in
order to replenish ships bound to and from the Task Force.

At Ascension, RFA *Tidespring* began her voyage south today, having collected
two replacement Wessex and with an escort in the shape of HMS *Antelope,* while
Glamorgan began her period bombarding Darwin, Fitzroy and Port Stanley
areas.

During the previous period, between 1 May, when the Carrier Battle Group
entered the TEZ, and the 15th, the day prior to the Amphibious Group's final
approach, the RFAs had been almost continually at work replenishing the
warships or each other. Now, with the arrival of the troopships and the
imminent landing, the demand for replenishment increased even further, RFA
Resource's diary entry for the 16th recording:

VERTREP with RFAs *Regent* and *Fort Austin* and HMS *Alacrity, Yarmouth* and
Brilliant as well as a RAS [Liquid] with RFA *Olmeda* and a jackstay transfer with RFA
Regent.

This last transfer looks like the two special weapons which are listed in the MOD
document (*see* Bibliography) for 15 May. The MOD document is probably in error
since the diary is based on log entries and there is no RAS to *Regent* for the 15th.

With the Carrier Battle Group, four of *Hermes'* Sea Kings were transferred to
RFA *Fort Austin,* while the carrier took in return five smaller helicopters and a

Wessex 5 'gunship' of 848 NAS. New arrivals at this time included RFA *Pearleaf*, which, according to her log, arrived off the Falklands to begin operating in the area.

With her new helicopters comfortably stowed, RFA *Fort Austin* transferred two special weapons, one 600 (S) and one 600 (T), to RFA *Regent* while the destroyer HMS *Coventry* also transferred a 600 (S) to *Regent*. The old 'R'-class RFA was now carrying one 600, two 600 (Surveillance) and three 600 (Training) rounds.

Having completed her transfer the *Fort Austin* was detached to the northeast to collect an air drop from a C-130 Hercules out of Ascension, which turned out to be a number of highly-specialised troops and their equipment.

The Argentineans did attempt a Super Etendard attack today, but it came to nothing, the Carrier Group's vastly-experienced team of senior naval flyers having taken precautions against the dangers posed by regular flight patterns of aircraft using carriers. So when the Etendards put their head momentarily above the radar horizon, they found nothing to shoot at. Although HMS *Brilliant* detected their Agave Radar signals, by the time the CAP arrived, the Etendards had gone home, taking their missiles with them.

Later that afternoon, HMS *Hermes* and *Invincible* parted company, the former to collect her Harriers from *Atlantic Conveyor*, while *Intrepid* had been tasked to fly off a heavily-laden Sea King, on what became a one way mission to mainland Chile. Its purpose has never been revealed but all three members of the aircrew were decorated after the campaign, which seems unusual, since, by their own admission, all they appear to have done was get lost and crash their aircraft.

By the next day, 18 May, RFA *Olna* had arrived off Ascension, and during the morning, Harriers from *Atlantic Conveyor* began to be flown off to the *Hermes*, a total of eleven Naval and RAF aircraft arriving during the day.

British Esk left the Battle Group today, northbound, with *Sheffield*'s survivors and one correspondent, and later that evening, the Carrier Battle Group and Amphibious group rendezvoused in the TEZ, 700 miles east of Mar del Plata.

Over fifty ships were now in company and the RFAs were busy again, RFA *Resource*'s diary recording VERTREPs with four of the LSLs and RFA *Pearleaf* as well as HMS *Ardent*, *Antrim*, *Plymouth*, *Fearless* and MV *Elk*. Later that night, *Glamorgan* again bombarded Port Stanley, ensuring yet another disturbed night for the garrison.

RFA *Bayleaf* arrived at Ascension next day, while with the Task Force now only 300 miles east-north-east of Port Stanley, 19 and 20 May saw a period of intense activity by the RFAs, the ships transferring fuel, food and ammunition in an apparently endless stream to the warships and troop carriers. RFA *Resource*'s diary alone recorded nineteen VERTREPS with the LSLs, STUFT and warships.

Major troop movements were also carried out between SS *Canberra* and the assault ships HMS *Fearless* and *Intrepid*, mainly using the latter's landing craft, a form of transport not particularly popular with the soldiers transferred in this way. Tragically, two hours after sunset, an 826 Squadron Sea King crashed into the sea, with the result that twenty-two men from 'D' Squadron 22 SAS were lost.

Glamorgan was inshore again on the night of the 19 May, and by next morning, after another intense period of activity, the invasion force was assembled for the landings.

Commodore Sam Dunlop OBE, CBE of RFA *Fort Austin* addressed his officers, petty officers and crew that night. Perhaps most memorably, he said: 'The next thirty-six hours will be the most decisive in the Falklands Campaign.' Not words to be taken lightly, coming, as they did, from a veteran of every RFA deployment since WW II.

Prior to the arrival of the landing force, Woodward had already achieved two of the three major British objectives, namely that Argentine troops on both East and West Falklands were cut off from resupply except by transport aircraft and that the Argentine Navy had been neutralised as a serious opponent.

Worryingly, his third objective, removal of the Argentine Air Force, seemed as far off as ever, although the British had inflicted significant losses. Just how significant these losses were would be made clear to the landing force during the next few days.

Codenamed 'Operation Sutton', the assault on the Falklands was to begin with a seaborne landing at San Carlos Water, a sea loch opening off the east side of Falkland Sound. The landing force itself included a large number of RFAs, including: RFA *Fort Austin*, tasked as anti-submarine and helicopter support ship and refuelling facility, RFA *Stromness*, still in her role as troop carrier, and the five LSLs, *Lancelot*, *Geraint*, *Percivale*, *Tristram* and *Galahad*, carrying troops but also to be used for the assault.

The STUFTS, *Canberra*, *Norland* and *Europic Ferry*, also carrying troops, would be part of the first wave, while MV *Elk* was needed to land her cargo of ammunition. HMS *Intrepid* and HMS *Fearless* were to provide the landing craft, both LCUs and the bigger LCVPs, and HMS *Antrim*, *Broadsword*, *Brilliant*, *Plymouth*, *Yarmouth*, *Argonaut* and *Ardent* were assigned as escorts.

One of *Fort Austin*'s crew remembered that night vividly:

The next big event was the entry into the Falkland Sound and San Carlos. The evening before I had issued everyone with anti-flash [clothing] for the first time, mainly because we barely had enough for our own use and I don't think there was much left in stock in the holds. We spent most of the night at Emergency Stations and as daylight came we found ourselves anchored in Falklands Sound launching Sea Kings to patrol the approaches, as it was believed that possibly there was at least one

Argentinean sub in the area. The ship was at Emergency Stations for an air raid when suddenly there was a pipe for the anchor party to close up. Leaving HQI in the care of the Chief Engineer, I rushed up forward and was told to get the anchor up quickly as we were going inside San Carlos, as it obviously appeared to the Commodore that we were rather exposed in the sound with only one GPMG [machine guns] and a few rifles to provide defence. As we were heaving up the anchor, we suddenly heard the sound of aircraft, so we all dived for cover. What fools we felt when one of our Sea Kings flew past the foc'sle. Nobody on the bridge had thought to warn us that one was about to launch from the Flight Deck. So we went into San Carlos Water and found a gap amongst the ships, hoping that we would be better defended than outside.

The Landing Group and escorts detached from the Carrier Battle Group at 14.15 GMT (or Zulu) on 20 May to begin their westward run, sailing to the north of the Falklands and arriving outside Falkland Sound after dark, bad weather having covered their approach.

HMS *Ardent* and *Antrim* had detached earlier and reached their ordered positions, where the latter would land an SBS strike force and the *Ardent* would cover an SAS diversionary attack on Darwin.

By 10.15 GMT, HMS *Antrim* and *Yarmouth* had established a patrol line between West and East Falkland and confirmed the absence of enemy submarines. *Antrim* now closed to Cat Island, covering the assault ships of the first group as they made their run.

HMS *Fearless* led *Intrepid* into the Sound at 10.45 (local). Turning towards the shore of East Falkland, they anchored at about 11.20 and began to 'dock down' ready to disembark their LCUs (landing craft). Meanwhile, the troopships *Canberra*, *Norland* and RFA *Stromness*, with RFA *Fort Austin* last and escorted by HMS *Plymouth* and *Brilliant*, arrived and anchored in the Sound soon after the LPDs at about 12.10, almost immediately disembarking their troops to the landing craft.

Gunfire from HMS *Antrim* and a ruthless assault by the SBS took care of the OP on Fanning Head, which was safely in the hands of the Royal Marines by 1.30, ensuring that the ships of the Amphibious Group were safe from the mortars and 106mm recoilless cannon deployed there.

Having collected their troops and led by Major Ewen Southby-Tailyour RM, the landing craft made the eight-mile trip down San Carlos Water, the guns of the Blues and Royal's light tanks jutting over the bows of the LCUs. The Marines and Paras landed almost without a shot being fired and occupied their assigned positions in San Carlos bay. Diversionary attacks being made at Goose Green and HE and star shells off Stanley persuaded the Argentines that British were attacking elsewhere, directly at their greatest troop concentrations.

With Port San Carlos and San Carlos Settlement occupied and the beachhead established, the LSLs, led by *Sir Percivale*, moved directly into San Carlos Water, the other ships raising their anchors and following soon after, at about 6.30 GMT.

The LSLs anchored and prepared to spend the day unloading. RFA *Sir Percivale* had anchored off Ajax bay, with her single 40mm Bofors gun pointing shoreward, ready to support 45 Commando, then landing, slightly later than planned, from the LCUs.

San Carlos was now designated the Amphibious Operations Area (AOA). Commodore M Clapp, RN, was responsible for operations there.

Captain Tony Pitt, Master of *Sir Percivale*, remembers the trip well:

Met up with *Fearless* group on 16 May during late afternoon. This group, which included all the captains, took place on *Fearless* outlining the intentions regarding the planned assault in the San Carlos area. It was turning out to be quite an operation and it was beginning to look as if it was really going to happen.

At first light all ships of the Assault Force formed up into a tight box formation with both ships and columns half a mile apart and headed west for the Falklands. The sky was overcast with moderate visibility and ideal for the task. This formation was maintained until 21.00 when the various groups broke away to carry out the tasks allocated in the operational orders. *Sir Percivale* remained with the other LSLs and the *Europic Ferry* and cleared to the NW of Falkland Islands to await their planned entry into Falkland Sound at approx 10.00. *Broadsword* was in charge although she was not programmed to enter the Sound.

It was *Sir Percivale*'s lot to anchor furthest south in San Carlos Water so we had to lead in all the other ships of our group. No specific route had been given to enter Falkland Sound and it was up to the respective captains to decide the safest. We took a route to the west of Sunk Rock, which was unmarked, in order to put maximum distance between Fanning Head and ourselves. Point X was reached on time at 08.45 and we assumed Action and Shelter Stations. At this time tracer was sighted in the vicinity of Fanning Head so the passage was approached with some trepidation. On approaching the entrance to San Carlos Water two ships at the north end were identified as *Norland* and an LPD assault ship, but other ships that should have been in the same area were still anchored in Falkland Sound. It became obvious the operation had been somewhat delayed but to what extent we did not know. We checked with *Fearless* and were told to proceed to our designated anchorage, No 14, off Ajax Bay (Red Beach).

It soon became apparent that Red Beach had not yet been assaulted as a Landing Craft (Utility) LCU full of troops came alongside and proceeded with us to the anchorage. The assault had been planned for 09.45 and it was now approaching 11.00. On arrival at the anchorage the LCU carried on and we were in a position to watch the assault take place whist attempting to cover it with our own weapons. Fortunately there was no opposition and we heaved big sighs of relief and congratulated ourselves on having overcome the first hurdle.

The Mexeflote raft was discharged to the water, assembled and prepared for forthcoming operations. The first Air Raid Warning occurred at 12.40 and throughout the rest of the day, for varying periods we were at Action Stations. The last 'all clear' was at 20.14. It was soon discovered that the operation that had started so easily was not going to continue that way. The first air attacks were to the north of the inlet where *Norland* and *Canberra* were anchored, but later they concentrated on the ships in Falkland Sound that were less protected by the terrain. Many RN ships were hit during the day but nothing came near the south of San Carlos Water and *Sir Percivale* did not fire a shot in anger.

During the day it was decided that *Sir Percivale* would be off-loaded first due to the cargo being more accessible. It was also realised that the off-load would have to continue despite the air raids, only stopping when the aircraft were in the vicinity.

During the early hours of the next morning (22 May) *Ardent* blew up and finally sank, with the glow from the fire visible in the sky over the hills to the west of San Carlos Water. During the night RFA *Stromness* and the STUFT cleared the area to the Total Exclusion Zone (TEZ). Before first light *Sir Percivale* was relocated to No 20 berth, half-way up the Inlet to the west. Air raid warnings occurred throughout the day but no aircraft reached San Carlos Water and the off-load continued.

Sir Galahad fared similarly as Phil Roberts, her Master, explains:

On 19 May we rendezvoused with *Fearless* and the rest of the amphibious Group close to HMS *Hermes* and her carrier Task Force. It was on my way by helo to *Fearless* that I was able to get a bird's eye view of this tremendous force of ships.

The D-Day plan was that the landing would take place at San Carlos in the early hours of 21 May: *Sir Galahad* was required to anchor in San Carlos with the rest of the LSLs, *Canberra, Norland, Europic Ferry* and *Stromness*.

One hour before dawn, the LSL group approached the northern entrance to Falkland Sound. We were in the last of the groups; *Fearless* and *Intrepid* had gone ahead and inserted landing craft to secure the beachhead. The first sign of any activity was tracer flickering across the headland at Fanning Head. We anchored in our assigned anchorage just after launching our Gazelles, which had been tasked on duties in support of 2 Para. As the sun rose over the hills at San Carlos, it could have been spring on a Scottish Loch. However, this peaceful scene did not last for long.

Pucaras flew in and out of the hills and we fired our first shots in anger. The sound of that gunfire was surprisingly exhilarating. However, our confidence was short-lived. One of our Gazelles returned with very bad news that the other two Gazelles had been shot down, both pilots and a crew member killed. Our first reactions were of shock and anger but at the same time it put into perspective our reasons for being there and gave us a greater sense of purpose: to rid the islands of their unwanted invaders.

Apart from off-loading ambulances and men of the Field Dressing Station to Ajax Bay, no further cargo was discharged on D-Day.

It was not too long before all the ships in San Carlos came under heavy air attack from A4 Skyhawks and Mirages [Daggers], bombs landing within a quarter of a mile. These air attacks continued all day and we were all relieved when night time came as we had been told that the Argentineans did not fly at night. This proved true of their fighters. The other threat that we had to contend with was underwater swimmers: we dropped scare charges to counteract this.

By dawn, the warships had formed a 'gunline' across the mouth of San Carlos Inlet and Falkland Sound ready to deal with air attacks, while the Mount Kent helicopter base and Goose Green airfield had also been successfully attacked.

The Battle of 'Clapp's Trap'

Nothing loath, the Argentine Air Force joined battle almost as soon as they had light enough to get their aircraft off the ground.

The first aircraft was a Pucara from Goose Green although he did not get close enough to the AOA (Amphibious Operations Area) to be seen by the British. Next up was a Naval Macchi MB339, which fired on HMS *Argonaut* before flying up the Port San Carlos valley, catching a glimpse of the activity in San Carlos as he went, pursued by machine gun fire, *Canberra*'s Blowpipe missile, a Sea Cat missile from *Intrepid* and shells from *Plymouth*'s 4.5-inch guns.

Despite Harriers being operational over both ends of San Carlos Water, the topography limited the effectiveness of their warning radar, making the lack of an Airborne Early Warning system even more crucial.

Soon Argentine Daggers were coming thick and fast, one of them making a run for RFA *Fort Austin*, only to be blown out of the sky 1,000 yards from the big store ship which had been shooting at it with a couple of machine guns and two dozen rifles that 'Black Sam' Dunlop had liberated from who knows where.

Lt Colonel R Dickey, RA, recalls events on the LSLs:

On D-Day (21 May) the LSLs moved in line-astern towards Falkland Sound. Although still dark, the crews closed up and all weapons were laid on Fanning Head where a firefight between the SBS and an Argentine outpost was taking place as the ships passed below. The day passed quickly for those unloading the ships but the air defence crews became increasingly frustrated while watching the outer gunline ships being heavily attacked and, because of the range, being unable to influence the battle. Their first engagement was not until late afternoon when a flight of four Mirage IIIs appeared on a run towards the LSLs.

Gnr Wyllie on *Sir Lancelot* had his view partially blocked by the superstructure and stepped into the flight deck safety net, sending a Blowpipe missile along the side of the ship to the consternation of all on the bridge and bridge wings. Sgt Dawson on *Sir Tristram* also fired, the two missiles scattering the planes which jettisoned bombs harmlessly over land.

On 23 May, the LSLs score their first kills: an A-4 Skyhawk, from Lance Bombardier Hargreaves on *Sir Tristram*; and a Mirage III by *Sir Lancelot*'s Bofors, the only weapon system firing at the time according to HMS *Fearless*. That night,

HMS *Antelope*'s exploding bomb forced all the LSLs to move as she burned fiercely, and to the surprise of the air defenders, the following morning sees *Sir Lancelot* as the southern guardship. Inevitably, for the first time, the air attacks are over the Sussex Mountains. Bombardier Johnson's Blowpipe misfire on *Sir Lancelot* is rewarded with three 1,000 pound bombs, one of which bounces off the water and up into Captain Dickey's cabin, coming to rest under the telephone kiosk, cutting all electrics and starting fires. *Sir Galahad* is similarly hit and Gunner Davies is wounded by shrapnel and evacuated with the rest of the crew but only after Bombardier Currie downs a Mirage. On *Sir Percivale*, Gnr Groves finds a Sea King full of pressmen between his missile and an A-4 Skyhawk and has to manoeuvre it around the helicopter. He acquires a second Skyhawk and hits the tailplane. Finally, while covering the evacuation of *Sir Lancelot*, Gnr Wyllie adds to the day's tally by damaging a Mirage with his missile.

The cohesiveness of the air defence plan is then disrupted as evacuated crews join different ships for different tasks. RFA *Fort Grange* is reinforced with Blowpipe and GPMGs, Teal Inlet is mineswept and the move of ammunition and men forward through Teal inlet and Port Pleasant begins. *Sir Lancelot* becomes a prison ship for Darwin's Argentine Air Commodore and the new home to 'D' and 'G' Squadrons SAS, who bring with them a seemingly endless supply of Stinger missiles.

This first wave having departed, the vessels took advantage of what was to prove a priceless two-hour lull. HMS *Antrim*, which had been hit repeatedly, soon had her fires under control and moved into San Carlos Water to effect repairs, along with RFA *Fort Austin*, whose Master, Commodore Sam Dunlop, had decided his position off Chandos Point was too exposed.

During subsequent raids, HMS *Ardent* was sunk and HMS *Argonaut* hit. RFA *Fort Austin* also claimed to have hit an Argentine Dagger/Mirage with machine gun fire later that afternoon, although this has never been corroborated.

In San Carlos Water, the LPD assault ships and LSLs were frantically unloading via landing craft and Mexeflote rafts, taking full advantage of the Argentine Air Force's failure to realise the importance of the landing ships.

In addition to their almost unique flatbottom design, the LSLs also carried what are known in the RFA as Mexeflotes (this name derived from 'Military Experiment Equipment'). Technically, they are called 'Class 60 load carrying pontoon equipment' and consist of a single 120-foot, 90-ton pontoon, powered by two Hydromaster six-cylinder 75hp outboard diesels. These motors are stowed separately and lowered into their housings once the pontoons are in the water.

Mexeflotes may be disassembled and transported as deck cargo or, more usually, they are winched vertically and carried flat against the side of the LSL. In use they are dropped or lowered into the water and the engines fitted. The raft is available to transport men and equipment ashore. Rafts can also be joined together to form a bridge between ship and shore if conditions do not allow the

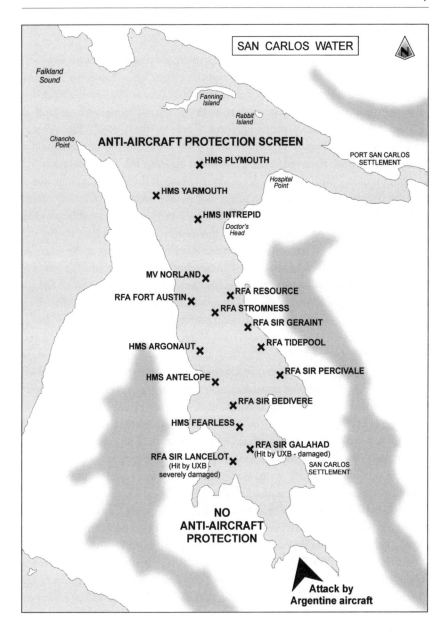

vessel to beach. When used as transport, each raft can carry about one ton per foot of length.

In 1982 the Mexeflotes were not crewed by the RFA but by specially-trained personnel from the Army's Royal Corps of Transport (now part of the Royal

Logistic Corps) based at Marchwood Military Port (renamed Marchwood Sea Mounting Centre in 2000), home port to the LSLs.

Now both the RFA and RCT were at full stretch, moving essential stores ashore to the nearby beaches. Despite this enormous effort, when *Canberra, Norland, Europic Ferry* and RFA *Stromness* sailed from San Carlos Water overnight, the first two took with them 90,000 man days of rations, along with 40 and 42 Commandos' and 2 Para's front-line stores. *Canberra* (the 'Great White Whale') and her fellows departed at 22.30, escorted by HMS *Antrim*, her unexploded bomb having been removed in a tedious and dangerous ten-hour operation.

Commodore Clapp's concern during every phase of the initial landings was to get the irreplaceable, highly vulnerable, and mostly unarmed RFAs and STUFT out of the Amphibious Operations Area (AOA) as soon as reasonably possible, hence the early sailing of the troopers. He was aided in this, at least during day one, by the tactical failure of the Argentine Air Force in targeting the warships and all but leaving the RFA and STUFT alone, thus allowing the landing forces to gain a logistic foothold and an impetus they never really lost.

This failure was, however, soon pointed out to them by the UK media, along with the fact that the fuses on their 1,000 pound bombs were incorrectly set.

Argentine air losses to date were: nine Mirages, five Skyhawks, two Pucaras and five helicopters. It was estimated that they still had left: thirty-eight Skyhawks, twenty-four Daggers, six Canberras and seven naval Skyhawks, these latter with crews which had trained against naval targets, specifically warships.

Despite this intense activity at San Carlos, the pace of the logistic effort was also being forced elsewhere. Still with the Task Force, RFA *Resource* carried out a single RAS with RFA *Tidepool*, while her diary records: 'The Press were on board RFA *Resource* today.' Media communications were to be greatly facilitated by the modern satellite communications in the RFA's Fort-class vessels, a system which was used extensively by the embarked Press.

At Ascension, MV *Alvega* took up duty as Base Support Tanker, while *Baltic Ferry* and *Nordic Ferry*, carrying 5 Infantry Brigade's heavy weapons and military stores, called briefly at Ascension before leaving for South Georgia.

Further south, RFA *Tidespring* rejoined the *Bristol* group and, in the UK, MV *Geestport*, carrying an essential load of fresh and frozen food, departed for South Georgia. In London, the Ministry of Defence had completed a review of ammunition status, which was giving cause for concern.

Next day, 22 May, was quieter, with bad weather on the Argentine mainland preventing attacks on the AOA, although the weather did not stop a four-aircraft Harrier GR3 strike on Goose Green. Commodore Clapp took advantage of this lull to land all the Rapier batteries and make them operational as well as landing more troops to reinforce the Paras.

Unloading was still going on from the LSLs via Mexeflote, landing craft and the Marines' own rigid raiding craft. Further east, on the edge of the TEZ, RFA *Resource* and MV *Elk* were embarked on a major RAS with RFA *Stromness*, MV *Norland* and *Europic Ferry*, transferring hundreds of loads with the help of every helicopter the Task Force possessed, including the clumsy anti-submarine Sea Kings, prior to the troopships' return to San Carlos the next day.

Further north, RFA *Fort Grange* had arrived at Ascension, while MV *Scottish Eagle* was leaving the UK, southbound for Ascension, to assume station tanker duties.

Off Goose Green, in the early hours of the morning of 23 May, at about 02.00, the Falkland Island Company vessel *Monsunen* was spotted by British warships. At that time she was in Argentine hands and being used as a supply ship. HMS *Yarmouth*, then in company with HMS *Brilliant*, illuminated her with star-shell, causing her to be run aground and abandoned by her crew. The *Monsunen* suffered no damage from her adventures and was quickly taken over by an RN crew and used by the Task Force for coastal supply movements.

RFA *Stromness*, *Norland* and *Europic Ferry* returned to San Carlos at first light, having completed their load transfer from RFA *Resource* and MV *Elk* at the edge of the TEZ along with HMS *Antelope* as escort.

RFA *Resource*'s diary records:

A VERTREP took place with *Canberra* to transfer about 100 Marines to *Resource*. The ship's company prepared for front line action supplying the bridgehead. . . . It is worth noting that, during the RAS with *Canberra*, 150 tons in loose packages were transferred when the Deck Dept, Embarked Flight etc all assisted the working party to clear the loads. This showed great teamwork.

Nor would it be the last time job descriptions went by the board. RFA *Stromness*'s diary for this day records significantly:

12.57: Anchored. Commenced discharging EFHE [Emergency Fuel Handling Equipment] and 'Airport 82'.

This, of course, was the mile of steel mesh runway, and its accessories, which was to become HMS *Sheathbill*, the Falkland Islands' first Naval Air Station.

With clear weather both over the Amphibious Operations Area (AOA) and the mainland, the RFA and STUFT were fortunate to be able to off-load without interruption from Argentine aircraft, although there were a number of attacks on the escorts, during one of which, HMS *Antelope* was hit by two Skyhawk bombs, both of which failed to explode.

Sadly, one bomb exploded during an attempt to defuse it, killing the Royal Engineers' bomb disposal expert, Staff Sergeant Prescott, and badly wounding his colleague Warrant Officer Phillips. *Antelope* sank after the explosion and subsequent fire.

Ashore, at San Carlos, the Royal Engineers had begun assembling fuel-handling equipment and landing pads (which had been brought south by the old 'Super Sampan') to allow shore-based helicopter and Harrier operation.

Overnight, RFA *Resource*, *Sir Bedivere* and *Tidepool*, the latter tasked to refuel the warships, entered San Carlos, while RFA *Sir Percivale* moved out. One of *Tidepool*'s crew, Chief Officer Peter Nelson, described their time in the anchorage and its sad ending:

On reaching the TEZ and RASing one and all, our Wessex flight then disembarked to *Hermes* taking their machine guns with them.

One of the ships I remember refuelling was HMS *Ardent*, where I conversed with John Sefton, who had been with us on the Armilla Patrol.

I arranged for the supply of a number of Mars Bars from their NAAFI. Goods passed, money exchanged, RAS over; my lasting memory is of John standing on the wing of *Ardent*'s bridge and exchanging waves. That was the last time that I saw him as he was killed the next day, with most of the flight, when the Argies bombed *Ardent*.

The night before we went in, I remember the film was *Chariots of Fire*!

We entered San Carlos the day after the landings and set to immediately, filling up rubber draccones with AVCAT [aviation fuel] which were towed ashore by Army tugs to set up the loading area. This took up a couple of days during which time we had numerous air attacks. With no defensive armament we were a sitting duck. Anyone seeing aircraft attacking in the sound would yell 'Alarm Aircraft' and all would take appropriate action. On one of these occasions an Engineering Officer exiting midships accommodation into the sunlight caught sight of a formation in the sky and raised the alarm. It was only when they flapped their wings he knew he had a red face but at least he was alert.

Due to the sparse variation of diet, I remember eating a lot of sausage and mash at this time. The other thing I remember was the stiff upper lip of the Senior Purser who insisted on dressing for dinner every evening.

We made a number of shuttles in and out of San Carlos. It was a busy time in and out. On one occasion, just after *Atlantic Conveyor* was sunk, we sailed and on our way to the TEZ fuelled one of the LPDs. Mid-RAS she launched her chaff; emergency breakaway and off like a 'scalded cat'.

We were left to pick up the pieces, the nearest ship to the Exocet. Needless to say the engineers pulled the stops out and I'm sure that *Tidepool* exceeded her 'baptismal trial speed'.

Life got into a routine: replenishments, top-up, fill draccones and harbour fuelling but it was 'B' cold on deck. Replenishment Command consisted of a 5-bum park bench constructed by the chippie adjacent to the telephone exchange on which we spent many cold days and nights. Not to say about the thigh-deep 'V' cold water on the tank deck whilst checking ullages and swinging valves. A belated thanks to the Ladies of Leeds who kindly supplied those super woolly gloves and balaclavas.

All ships were now using Greenwich Mean Time (GMT), also known as 'Zulu' time.

RTREP of stores,
scension Island, during
e period 15–30 April.

LEFT: Ascension Island anchorag embarking the 105mm guns of 8 Battery, Royal Artillery.

BELOW: RFA *Sir Tristram*: D Palin boarding a Sea King Mark 4 for conference on HMS *Hermes* (in th left background).

MAIN PICTURE: Passage south: MV *Europic Ferry*, MV *Norland* an Landing Ship Logistic in grey South Atlantic waters.

RIGHT: RFA *Pearleaf* refuelling RFA *Sir Tristram*, April 1982.

BELOW RIGHT: Tony Tompkins tries his hand with a captured Argentine .50 calibre machine gu on the flight deck of RFA *Stromne*

ABOVE: Grytviken, South Georgia, with an old harpoon gun in the foreground and RFA *Tidespring* in the hazy background.

BELOW: Lt Mike Tidd, Senior Pilot, RFA *Tidespring*, sits in the cockpit of his helicopter, waiting to take off, April 1982.

LEFT: The Wessex taking off from a rather battered looking RFA *Tidespring*.

BELOW: Two members of the aircrew sit on top of a crashed Wessex, awaiting rescue from Fortuna Glacier.

ᴛ: D-Day, 21 May:
ᴀ *Sir Tristram*
ving at San Carlos.

ᴴᴛ: 'Chalky'
hite at RFA *Sir
istram*'s starboard
dge wing machine
1.

ʟow: Half-light in
ɔ Carlos: MV *Baltic
ry*, RFA *Blue Rover*,
ɔ of the assault
ps (*Fearless* or
repid) and a Type
destroyer.

LEFT: RFA *Sir Lancelot*, just keeping score.

BELOW: Second Officer Dave Gilzean, at RFA *Sir Lancelot's* port 40mm Bofors.

RIGHT: Essential in-theatre ship repairs were supported by MV *Stena Seaspread*.

LEFT: HMS *Glamorgan*, the only ship in the Falklands to survive an Exocet missile hit, coming alongside *Stena Seaspread*, 13 June.

RIGHT: HMS *Plymouth*: note damage to funnel.

LEFT: HMS *Glamorgan*: close-up of the damage done in the hangar area by the Exocet missile strike.

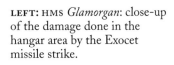

RIGHT: The repair area: frigates with *Engadine* in the background.

RIGHT: RFA *Sir Galahad,* 8 June.

INSET: RFA *Sir Galahad,*
approximately fifteen minutes
after the Argentine air attack,
8 June.

...ew and
...sualties
...acuating the
...rning
...A *Sir Galahad*.

Captain Green RFA, DSC examines his ship.

urly' Wilson on the circumstances of this famous photograph:

ook this picture with an old 110 cartridge nera after coming off RFA *Sir Galahad* on 8 June 32. Just before the attack by Argentine vhawks, I, along with the other members of nce of Wales's Company, 1st Battalion Welsh ards, had just left the tank deck of the ship to topside. We first heard the enemy planes and mediately someone shouted from above 'Air id Red!', the alarm for imminent air attack. As e we all started running for the safety of the k deck. Being quite near the door I remember ning into the hold when the world seemed to olode. The sensation of heat penetrated your s and throat and I, along with everyone else und me were picked up and tossed as if we were thers in a storm. A lot happened over the next rty minutes or so that we were on board but er doing everything we could we were ordered by our Company second-in-command, Capt opes, who seemed to me to have the evacuation he more seriously-wounded comrades under trol at the bow of the ship.

By this time all the lifeboats and rafts had long ie and I saw a small wooden launch near the p. She wouldn't come close so I jumped in the er and swam the short distance to her. Three er mates also got on board and she took us Mexeflote, a large floating platform, which making her way to the stricken *Sir Galahad*. ce on board the four of us helped, to my

surprise, dozens of injured and able soldiers get off the *Galahad*. Once the influx of men dried up this float then started its way to Fitzroy Settlement. I remember wondering at the time why she hadn't headed for the nearest piece of land but with hindsight I reckon due to the amount of wounded men we had on board the helmsman wanted to get to the Forward Aid Station which was at the settlement. When I looked back at the burning ship I had a sudden thought that my family wouldn't believe what had just happened. This was of course nonsense but as a young nineteen-year-old Guardsman my naivety took the better of me. I started to unpack my camera from its waterproof packaging then I had a decision to make. After all that we had been through I didn't know how my comrades would take to me photographing the ship whilst we were surrounded by wounded friends. As some were still armed I decided to play safe and not advertise my intrusion into the source of our hell and discreetly took one photograph from my hip. I had no way of knowing at the time whether this single shot would work but what I did know is that it was the quickest and slickest movement worthy of any Wild West Gunslinger.

'My thoughts often go back to the Falklands and the memories of 8 June are as vivid today as they were twenty-five years ago. Fifty-three good men died aboard the RFA *Sir Galahad*.'

RIGHT: Dave Palin and Cadet Halewood from RFA *Sir Tristram* at Fitzroy, 11 June.

BELOW: The liferafts from the *Sir Galahad* are towed towards shore.

BOTTOM: RFA *Sir Tristram*'s boats and liferafts.

FAR RIGHT: The burnt-out RFA *Sir Tristram*, 11 June.

ABOVE: The wrecked bridge of RFA *Sir Tristram*, 11 June.

LEFT: A close-up of damage to the superstructure of RFA *Sir Tristram*, 11 June.

BELOW: The Royal Fleet Auxiliary Memorial at Fitzroy, Falkland Islands.

Next morning, 24 May, dawned uncharacteristically clear again and the LSLs and store ships were granted two hours to unload in peace, before the first wave of Argentine aircraft arrived at 9.45 am. A member of *Fort Austin*'s embarked RNSTS complement recalls the scene:

Dawn on the morning of Monday 24 May saw the largest gathering of RFAs since the Fleet review. Lined up across San Carlos Water were *Fort Austin*, *Resource* and *Stromness* (all carrying large ammunition loads).

A little astern was *Tidepool* and the five LSLs were anchored at the head of the water.

The three solid support ships were lying abreast of each other at two cables distance (approx 400 feet) and could not spread themselves out because the burning hulk of HMS *Antelope* was ahead with its forward magazine intact.

At 11.30, a surprise attack . . . placed bombs between the three solid support ships . . . the nearest to *Fort Austin* landed fifty feet away but failed to explode.

This time the Skyhawks ignored the watchful escorts, screaming over the Sussex Mountains and launching their bombs at the anchored transports. RFAs *Sir Bedivere*, *Sir Galahad* and *Sir Lancelot* were all hit, the first by a 1,000 pound bomb that bounced off the head of its twenty-ton crane, while the last two both received 1,000 pounders through their hulls, which started fires even though they failed to explode.

RFA *Sir Bedivere*'s Master, Captain Peter McCarthy, has vivid memories of the incident:

We joined a large fleet of ships off the Falklands on a damp misty day – *Atlantic Conveyor* stood out from the rest; and a few days later went to our assigned anchorage near the head of San Carlos Water. Most of the other ships were already there and squeezing through them in the dark wasn't particularly comfortable. On a later occasion, in similar conditions, it was even less comfortable when our gyrocompass 'fell over', affecting the radar of course!

Our routine at the time was similar to that of other LSLs. Many of our marines and soldiers remained on-board whilst we discharged vehicles and stores by Mexeflote and helo and we alternated our time at anchor with patrolling north and east of the islands. In San Carlos, air raids were frequent in daytime and we had to admire the courage and skill of the Argentinean pilots, who left the valley to face a wall of fire and Rapier missiles. At our anchorage near the head of the 'loch', *Bedivere* was one of the first targets they met. 'Our' Royals put up a dense cone of GPMG tracer fire which perhaps deterred some of the pilots from passing directly overhead, *Bedivere* was only hit once and that bomb did not explode!

HMS *Ardent* sank fairly close, a horrible sight, and the loss of *Atlantic Conveyor* was deeply felt and changed the course of the war. We passed over her reported grave the next day.

The tragic damage to *Sir Galahad* and *Sir Tristram* was disheartening, especially to our Chinese crew members, but stoically they carried on, so increasing our already great respect for them.

Aboard *Sir Galahad*, the RFA's luck was holding . . . but only just. Captain Phil Roberts records the scene:

On 22 and 23 May we were subjected to air attacks during daylight, and at first light on 24 May we shifted anchorage to within half a mile of Ajax Bay in order to speed the discharge of cargo which was scheduled to start that day. We passed very close to the dying throes of HMS *Antelope*, our old friend who had escorted us to and from Ascension on the way down – a very sad sight. Not long after we had anchored, there were several heavy air raids. It was during the first of these raids that we were hit by a 1,000 pound bomb which ricocheted off the water, close to the bridge and passed through the ship's side, tore its way through four steel bulkheads and came to rest in a battery-charging room only some sixty feet from where three hundred tons of ammo lay.

Fortunately, it failed to explode; otherwise neither I nor any of my crew would be alive today.

I sent for the bomb disposal squad and evacuated all personnel to the after end of the ship. After about an hour the bomb disposal team arrived and after they had examined it they advised me that the bomb was in a very critical condition and the slightest vibration would set it off. I decided to evacuate the ship until such time as the bomb could be made safe. The embarked forces were evacuated first by lifeboat to HMS *Fearless*. As they were mustered at the lifeboats, another air attack followed and we were strafed by cannon, sustaining about twenty hits resulting in three injuries. In the same attack, several Argentine aircraft were shot down and each was followed by a tremendous cheer from the Royal Marines waiting to board their lifeboats. It sounded like Cup Final day at Wembley – it did our morale good which was starting to sag at this stage. We all eventually got off and dispersed to various ships around San Carlos water, most of us, including myself, ending up aboard RFA *Stromness*, where we were made very welcome.

On the evening of 25 May, after a day of very heavy air attacks, my Chief and Second Engineer Officers, together with a small team including an Electrical Officer and two RCT crane drivers, returned to *Sir Galahad* to provide services for the bomb disposal squad from HMS *Intrepid*. The bomb was removed from the ship in the early hours of 26 May by an extremely brave bunch of men.

Barely twenty minutes after the first attack and with RFAs *Sir Galahad* and *Sir Lancelot* still battling fire below, a second wave of four Daggers hurtled in. This time, however, the Paras on Sussex Mountain managed more warning and consequently, a warm welcome was accorded to the aircraft with the sky full of Sea Cat, Rapier and bullets from automatic weapons of every calibre and kind.

HMS *Fearless* and RFA *Galahad* caught some cannon fire and poor old *Lancelot* received another bomb, which again failed to explode, while another 1,000-pounder exploded so near RFA *Resource* that the crew thought they'd been hit! Their diary recorded the incident with the RFA's typical indifference:

14.13 [local] There was a tremendous explosion and, at first, we thought we'd been hit. Patrols were sent out to check for damage, then Captain Seymour's voice came over the intercom: 'Don't worry, we just got a bit wet.'

In fact, we later learned that we had been near-missed by at least two bombs, one of which had landed between RFA *Stromness* and ourselves, exploding twenty yards away on our port side, level with the bridge.

Fort Austin, anchored abeam of RFA *Stromness* and *Resource* (a 'nice target' as *Stromness'* diary remarked), was also near-missed, the bomb landing so close that many aboard the 'Super Sampan' thought she'd been hit, as the diary of one of her officers records:

On their first run they [the Argentine aircraft] did not hit anything but I saw one shot down (Rapier) and the others got away.

The next raid was hairier by far. *Resource* had arrived during the night. We were anchored next to her and on the other side was *Fort Austin*. During the second raid at least one plane flew between *Resource* and *Fort Austin* at below funnel height. That was frightening. One Skyhawk was hit by our own GPMG but we aren't sure if it splashed. In the third raid some hits were scored on *Lancelot* (two unexploded bombs) and *Galahad* (one unexploded bomb – very unstable). We had a fright when a bomb dropped exactly half-way between *Resource* and us. I did not connect the violent shudder with the splash until later. I thought at first that we had been hit but it was obvious from the lack of fire etc that we had not. We checked for damage and found none, but we had had a shock.

This attack could quite easily have finished the war in Argentina's favour. The British were fairly well supplied with tankers, at a pinch being able to make use of BP's modified River-class as well as the RFAs. Of the specialised Ammunition, Equipment, Food and Store (AEFS) ships, however, they had only four: RFAs *Fort Grange*, *Fort Austin*, *Resource* and *Regent*, with *Stromness* designed to resupply only food but also able to RAS munitions if required.

Fort Grange was still a week away (although she left Ascension heading south that day), while *Regent* was with the Carrier Group, but as she had special weapons embarked she could come no nearer San Carlos than the edge of the TEZ.

An explosion that day on any of the three ammunition-carrying store ships anchored abeam in San Carlos would have probably caused a chain reaction, resulting in the destruction of all three and leaving the warships perilously short of ammunition. At a time when they needed every missile and shell to fend off the still-dangerous Argentine Air Force this would probably have spelt the end of the war for the Royal Navy.

RFA *Sir Lancelot*, despite her bomb damage, claimed to have scored hits with Bofors and machine guns on a Skyhawk and a Mirage (the Mirage later confirmed) while the RA Blowpipe missile section aboard *Sir Bedivere* claimed a 'probable' victim. *Norland*, also discharging cargo in San Carlos, claimed to have been hit by wreckage from a Mirage which disintegrated above her after being hit by Rapier. She also claimed to have damaged an aircraft with her own automatic rifle fire.

That was the end of the air attacks for that day.

Later in the day crews from both *Galahad* and *Lancelot* were transferred to RFA *Stromness*. That evening, RFAs *Tidepool, Sir Tristram, Sir Bedivere* and MV *Norland* were escorted out of Falkland Sound by HMS *Plymouth* and eventually out of the TEZ by HMS *Ambuscade*.

Sir Lancelot's diary recorded her ordeal over the next few days:

24 May

At 00.30Z shifted to a temporary anchorage near the entrance and then at dawn to a new position at the southern end of SCW [San Carlos Water] off Seaview Point.

At 13.45 a wave of three Skyhawks, approaching down the valley from the south, drop six 1,000 pound bombs, one of which came inboard having bounced off the water. Entering the starboard side at Mil Off C, deflected by deckhead, fractured firemain riser and cable runs in alleyway, into E/R [Engine Room] casing, destroying generator exhaust, header tank piping before exiting across the port alleyway to end up in the film locker. No casualties.

The Air Defence team claimed two splashed bringing their total to five.

Resulting damage – no firemain, no power to Bridge/Radio room. Decision made to evacuate the ship.

The ship's company and remaining embarked force (total 240) were taken ashore to Red Beach by LCUs [landing craft] at 15.00. Welcomed, fed and watered by the Loggies, they awaited a decision on their future. None having arrived by nightfall, the ship's company bedded down in the disused refrigeration plant/field hospital.

25 May

At 00.30 they were awakened with orders to move to a ship. The Hong Kong Chinese [HKC] however, declined to move and with two exceptions could not be persuaded otherwise. Eventually the UK personnel (plus 2 HKC) arrived at *Stromness* at 03.30 to a welcome bed & breakfast, joining the *Galahad* evacuees already there.

The HKC were moved later that day by military methods. Air attacks continued and probably this is when *Sir Lancelot* was hit for the second time, causing damage to the Sgts Mess and galley on the port side. She was also strafed by 20mm cannon.

At 15.30 the two LSL Captains attended a meeting in *Fearless* where it was decided that as *Galahad*'s bomb was more accessible, it would be dealt with first. So the *Galahad*'s officers plus four 'volunteers' from *Lancelot* (Choff, CEO, 1st LO and 3EO) transferred to *Fearless* leaving the remainder to sail in *Stromness*.

26 May

Galahad's officers return to their ship. At sea *Lancelot* ship's company and *Galahad* HKC transfer to *Sir Tristram*.

27 May
The four return to *Lancelot*. FCDT3 (Lt Bruen) secured the bomb. Engineers bucket diesel to header tank to start generator. Fridges saved. Choff weighed anchor and ship is towed by 3 LCUs to 'safer' anchorage in Fern Valley Creek. It is observed that considerable looting of MOD Stores and personal effects has occurred. Some of the latter were later recovered.

28 May
FCDT3 and *Fearless* team cut route for removal of bomb, up one deck and through three bulkheads to sheerlegs near No 2 lifeboat. The four assisted where possible, continued restoring systems and Choff cooked the meals.

29 May
After working through the night, the bomb was lowered to the water at 10.00Z.
    Fearless team commenced clearing debris and fitting temporary patches over bomb holes.
    Power restored to Radio room and some communications now possible.

29 May–2 June
At sea several plans are made to return the ship's company to San Carlos, but these are frustrated by weather and other factors.
    On board, repairs continued, some cargo was discharged, food issued ashore and accommodation provided to numerous persons with convincing reasons for their presence including the RCT Mexeflote teams. Choff resigned as cook. Occasional air attacks.

3 June
Sir Tristram returned to San Carlos and the 'Lancelots' to their ship. Repairs continue, now by ship's staff, *Fearless/Intrepid* teams and FMG [Fleet Maintenance Group].

    Argentina's national day (25 May) began early and eventfully with 2 am reports from RFA *Resource* and *Fort Austin*, both still in San Carlos, of external noises. Both RFAs were checked by Fleet Clearance Diving (FCD) teams, then re-anchored on eastern side of San Carlos Water, together with *Stromness*, *Sir Percivale* and the two other damaged 'Sir' ships.

    Argentine aircraft attacked again today, sinking HMS *Coventry* and damaging HMS *Broadsword* and HMS *Argonaut*. But the rate of attrition and lack of success of the majority of their sorties meant that this was the last day the Argentine Air Force would mount regular attacks. As David Brown succinctly put it: 'The Battle of Clapp's Trap was over.'

    But not the war. Later that afternoon at 3.41 pm (local), MV *Atlantic Conveyor* was hit by an Exocet fired from a Super Etendard.

    Taken up from trade on 14 April, *Atlantic Conveyor* had been moved almost immediately from Liverpool, where her owners had her held in reserve, to the naval dockyard at Devonport. The 15,000 ton Ro-Ro (Roll on-Roll off) container cargo ship arrived on 16 April and work began immediately to convert her into an aircraft transport, incorporating repair, landing and accommodation facilities for Harriers, Chinook and Wessex helicopters, as well as their crews and maintenance staff.

Such a role ideally suited this type of vessel, with its large flat deck stretching forward from the bridge, which was situated right aft. Added to this enormous deck landing area, *Conveyor* also had six ramp-connected cargo decks, with the lower, main deck opening on to a stern ramp. She was fast, with a cruising speed of twenty-two knots, and her complement of thirty-four officers and men all volunteered for service in the South Atlantic.

She stayed in Devonport for ten days, until 25 April, and during that time containers and Portacabins were fixed four deep along both sides of her upper deck, the fore deck having already been cleared of obstructions to form a landing pad. A second landing pad was created abaft the bridge superstructure, both pads being fitted with navigational equipment and floodlights to allow aircraft to operate safely by day or night.

While this work was going on, all the ancillary fittings were also being installed. Flexible tanks for AVCAT, filters and pumps, liquid oxygen tanks for Harrier breathing apparatus, a Sat Nav system, RN communications, new living quarters and extra toilets were all crowded into the ship, along with 3,000 tons of spares, tentage for 4,500 troops and a complete airfield, including a mile of steel mesh runway.

Loading was completed with the addition of six Wessex 5 of 848 NAS and five twin-rotored Chinook helicopters of No 18 Squadron RAF as deck cargo, along with over a hundred RFA, RNSTS and RN personnel, in addition to her normal crew, making a total complement of 160.

On 25 April, she weighed anchor and departed Devonport, Ascension bound.

The voyage to Ascension Island was largely uneventful and she duly arrived on 5 May, having broken the voyage to refuel at Sierra Leone. Eight Sea Harriers of 809 NAS and six RAF ground-attack Harrier GR3s were embarked at Ascension. Special fresh water tanks had been fitted to the ship at Devonport to cater for the RAF aircraft, which incorporated considerable quantities of magnesium in their structure and were vulnerable to corrosion in the salty atmosphere.

She left Ascension on 7 May, along with the last elements of the Amphibious Group (TG 317.0), entering the TEZ on 18 May and almost immediately flying off her fourteen assorted Harriers to HMS *Hermes* and *Invincible*.

She remained in company with the Task Group until the 25th, when, while occupying a place at the northern end of the line of RFAs and warships screening the two carriers, she was hit by an Exocet, released from one of a pair of Argentine Super Etendards making an unusually well co-ordinated attack on the carriers. Despite some argument, most sources agree that she was only hit by one missile, which punched a hole in her main cargo deck on the port side aft as she was trying to turn away from it. Upon entry the missile turned, ran the length of the ship, passing through the engine control room and coming to rest somewhere under the bridge area. Here either the warhead exploded or, as seems more likely, the unused fuel ignited and set fire to a mountain of highly inflammable stores.

In moments the ship was an inferno, with dense black smoke adding to the chaos. Despite the best efforts of the crew, ninety minutes later the order to abandon ship was given. Most of the crew escaped in liferafts, many drawn away from the ship's side by the efforts of HMS *Alacrity* closing to within suicidal proximity of the giant Ro-Ro, who, in one of her uncontrolled lunges could easily have smashed in the warship's egg-shell fragile hull.

Three days later, with most of her fires burnt out, she sank beneath the freezing waters of the Southern Ocean, taking with her twelve of her crew, including all three RFA men aboard, as well as much needed supplies and all but one of her embarked helicopters. It was the loss of these vital helicopters that forced Clapp and Thompson to use the vulnerable LSLs to fill the short-range transport role, carrying supplies and troops from the Brigade Transport area to the exposed unloading areas such as Teal and Fitzroy. If the helicopters lost on the *Atlantic Conveyor* had been available, those ships needn't have been risked and the subsequent disaster at Fitzroy need never have happened.

Incidentally, RFA *Regent*, still carrying a nuclear round, was also with TG 317.8 when *Atlantic Conveyor* was hit.

On 25 May the Argentines also began operating a surveillance radar at Port Stanley which they used to detect 800 and 801 Squadron CAPs and inform their attacking fighter-bombers so they could avoid them.

The logistic chain from the UK continued to operate. Even as the troops consolidated their bridgehead, MV *British Enterprise III* set off from the UK, while at the same time RFA *Engadine*, the RFA's purpose-built helicopter maintenance ship, arrived at Ascension on her journey south.

And ships were coming out of the danger zone too. RFA *Stromness*, *Resource*, *Tidepool* and *Sir Percivale* moved out of Falkland Sound, escorted by HMS *Ambuscade*.

On the night of the 25th RFA *Fort Austin* took *Coventry*'s survivors on board before leaving, eventually carrying nearly 280 men. Each was fed, clothed and allocated a bed space, although sometimes the latter was only a patch of carpet in one of the *Fort*'s spacious lounges. One survivor recalls that night . . . and RFA hospitality:

A bedraggled survivor from *Coventry*'s sinking, I along with 200 plus fellow woebegone companions moved by LCU from *Broadsword* at about 03.00 hrs, through a pitch-black, darkened San Carlos Water to RFA *Fort Austin* – commanded by RFA Commodore 'Black Sam' Dunlop. *Austin*, despite having been held in San Carlos for overlong, with lots of raids and close-quarters splashes, and now being delayed for us when they were on the eve of escaping temporarily to the east, could not have looked after us better. Food, bunks, some chaffing, humour, cigarettes for those who wished them and so on were all provided.

I had ended up on the day bed of an Asst Pursers cabin – he had offered me vehemently his large and comfy-looking proper bed, but I had with stupidly typical British restraint, declined. We were then given a very good breakfast, menus out, no fuss or drama. I was barefoot; well, one foot clad with a gym shoe. The other emergency issue, oversize and too large, had come off on the pilot ladder clambering up to the clearway. I found a friendly storeman who gave me some DMS boots, a seaman's knife, the lack of which had almost drowned me underneath my sunken life raft (sunk by the port Sea Dart missile still on the launcher) the day before, and a leather seaman's foul weather hat which I still have to this day (still not signed for, so please don't make me return it).

Later, in the lull of another air raid we watched the film *Hurricane*, starring Charlton Heston, and his ship sinks – not another happy ending! In between we looked at the scribbled messages underneath that table in the Officers Mess, which is still in *Fort Austin*. Twenty-four hours later, after something of an obstacle course transit via Wessex and lifeboat, we made it to *Stromness*.

David Pitt was the Chief Officer, the Captain was Barrie Dickinson and Ian Pilling, the OPS/NAV [Operations Officer/Navigator] (with me in *Diligence* for Operation Telic) – what a super, well-led ship *Stromness* was.

I joined via a jumping ladder to the clearway as the ship went to Action Stations for Air Raid Warning Red and an Exocet attack. Much spooking, understandably, by some of us who had already left one sinking ship and were now on their second ammunition ship. An hour later at about 10.30 I think, I am in the Officers Mess, the AQM [Assistant Quartermaster] from 45 Commando, rear party and IC Battle Casualty replacements and the NAAFI Manager, Jan Morris I seem to recall, were giving us drinks (alcoholic) and even some of our mail which was intercepted from a passing helicopter. Two days of surreal luxury and comforting followed as we transited to South Georgia; Chinese Chefs, 'Sod's Opera' and the chance to send familygrams home to reassure our next of kin. All this totally overwhelmed the small communications office but again they could not do enough for us all. All this, and watching on the bridge how the Captain very calmly conducted blind pilotage to wiggle the ship into a hugely-crowded anchorage in Grytviken in zero visibility are abiding memories.

We then cross-decked to the *QE2* and came home, but that's another story.

Next day (26 May) was spent by the Carrier Group replenishing from RFA

Tidepool, brought from the Amphibious Operations Area by HMS *Ambuscade*. Also with the Carrier Group, RFA *Regent* transferred one 600 and two 600 (S) nuclear rounds back to RFA *Resource*. At the same time, *Resource* transferred her Press team to RFA *Regent* and RFA *Stromness* transferred the crews of *Galahad* and *Tristram* to RFA *Tristram*.

Welcome reinforcements in the form of HMS *Avenger, Active, Cardiff, Andromeda, Minerva* and *Penelope* also joined the Carrier Battle Group today.

In San Carlos, having secured the beachhead, 45 Commando, 3 Para and 2 Para prepared their breakout, with 3 Para tasked to 'tab' north overland to Teal Inlet settlement, 45 Commando sent to nearby Douglas and 2 Para directed south to attack the garrisons on the narrow land bridge occupied by the settlements of Darwin and Goose Green. These last two were the main Argentine troop concentrations outside of Port Stanley.

Back at the inlet, the unexploded bomb was removed from *Sir Galahad*, while the tug *Irishman* was detached from the TRALA and sent to salvage *Atlantic Conveyor*.

Captain Phil Roberts remembers that night . . . and several previous to it:

Stromness had to sail at short notice on the night of 25/26 May for South Georgia to meet the *Queen Elizabeth 2*. I had agreed with COMAW [Commodore Amphibious Warfare] that my Chinese crew should remain in *Stromness* until the bomb had been disposed of, but all officers, RCT ranks, RN signalmen and ship's air defence team would spend the night in *Fearless* and move back to *Sir Galahad* when it was safe to do so.

With the bomb safely disposed of, we transferred from *Fearless*. By this time, the Chief Engineer Officer had restored all services and the first thing we did was to shift to a more sheltered anchorage out of the main bomb runway. With the help of RN shipwrights we patched up the hole in the ship's side with eighth-of-an-inch steel plate and backed this up with some classic Phoenix damage control shoring.

This was a very difficult time for my officers; not only did they have to do their own duties but all the duties of the absent Chinese. The Purser was doing sterling stuff in the galley. He even put up the crew from HMS *Argonaut* for bed and breakfast while her bombs were being defused. Likewise, the Deck and Engineering Officers worked extremely hard and I never heard any of them complain. The RCT lads were invaluable during this period.

Overnight, *Sir Geraint* and *Europic Ferry* moved out of San Carlos, to meet HMS *Active*. Graham Ferguson of *Tidepool* also remembers that time and the days prior to it:

On the night of 23/24 May *Tidepool*, escorted by HMS *Plymouth*, left the Carrier Group for San Carlos. We entered the following morning just prior to dawn breaking. It was a very surreal experience, the weather was calm and we could just make out the dark shapes of various vessels already in the bay. As dawn broke on a very clear sky we saw San Carlos for the first time and were struck by the amazing similarity to Scapa Flow. As soon as it was light helicopters transited to and fro, some dropping unannounced onto our deck when it was seen to be free, to fill up with fuel. With the collection of mainly RN and RFA ships it seemed like a normal exercise.

This peace was rudely shattered whilst I was on the flight deck where our Wessex had landed back after delivering the Flight Commander to HMS *Fearless*. Expecting to be recalled at any time it remained 'burning and turning' which was, as it turned out, just as well. Idly strolling across the deck and looking southeast past the helo I was glad to see two Harrier jets coming up the valley hugging the contours of the ground. My pleasure at the sight of friendly forces quickly turned to alarm as the lead aircraft turned towards us and started to climb at the beginning of a bombing run. In doing so it exposed the pale blue under-wing tanks!!! Everyone on the air net seemed to them at the same time and all circuits were crowded with calls of 'Red Alert'. Our helo very sensibly took off horizontally to starboard and headed for a shallow fold in the adjacent valley. As NBCDO [Nuclear, Biological, Chemical and Damage Control Officer] I headed swiftly off the flight deck and proceeded forward at speed only to be brought up short. I had forgotten to take off my communications belt including headphones etc.

Arriving breathless in HQI it was just as well that the Chief Engineer had taken charge in my absence and had everything under control. We then spent what seemed like a long time with nothing to do but listen to the ship's internal broadcast system from the bridge relaying the air situation. It was interesting to note when a raid was reported as approaching from any direction that everyone glanced at the repeater compass to assess what side we might expect the bang!

After refuelling a number of vessels that came alongside (and many helicopters that dropped in unannounced) we left the anchorage as night fell. Clearing the entrance we refuelled the ships available to the north and then headed east back to the carrier group. The plan was that we would complete all of this and be out of sight of the north coast of East Falkland by dawn. But nothing ever goes to plan and most days saw us, unarmed, sailing as fast as we could to the safety of the Carrier Group. As soon as we joined we were hard at work refuelling as required before sailing further east to the Tug, Refuelling and Logistics Area (TRALA) where we replenished our depleted fuel stocks from mainly-civilian tankers. These pumpovers were always very lengthy, nearly always in bad weather. This schedule was very testing for all concerned and one wonders how we kept it up for so long with a small crew. RFAs do not have enough personnel to go into 'defence watches' as RN vessels do.

When our replenishment and any other tasks required were completed we would be ordered west to the Carrier Group to join in there and so began the race track which saw us head west as dusk arrived to be off Falkland Sound the following morning.

Thankfully, the amphibious phase of the operation was now at an end with the Commando Brigade ashore, virtually independent, and the anchorage almost empty, except for the LPD assault ships and damaged LSLs. At South Georgia, the 11th Mine Countermeasures Sqn arrived today, *Iris* (Telecom cable ship) having arrived on the 25th to begin loading steel plate and welding gas for *Stena Seaspread* in the TRALA.

Thursday 27 May saw 45 Commando and 3 Para set out for Teal, while, in San Carlos, the LPDs *Intrepid* and *Fearless* were now serving as helicopter ships, with the damaged LSLs, *Sir Lancelot* and *Sir Galahad*, also serving as landing and refuelling points. Outside the TEZ, RFA *Olna* arrived in the Falklands area to begin operations while RFA *Stromness*, having embarked *Coventry*'s survivors and *Brilliant*'s Lynx flight from *Fort Austin*, then sailed, unescorted, for South Georgia.

Antrim had earlier rendezvoused with *Queen Elizabeth II*, taking aboard the Commander, Land Forces, Falkland Islands (CLFFI), Major-General Jeremy J Moore OBE, MC, and the Commander 5 Infantry Brigade, Brigadier M J A Wilson OBE, MC. The destroyer immediately set out for the Carrier Battle Group, where the two commanders were transferred to *Hermes* for a conference with Admiral Woodward and Commodore Clapp, before moving to HMS *Fearless*, which had left San Carlos that night specifically to collect them.

Later that day, the Brigade Maintenance Area was attacked and hit, the Argentine parachute-retarded bombs failing to explode on the Ajax bay refrigeration plant where the Field Hospital, nicknamed the 'Red and Green Life Machine' by the troops, was located. Fires were started amongst stacks of ordnance at San Carlos but these were quickly dealt with. Five men of the Commando Logistics Regiment were killed and twenty others wounded.

Overnight, RFA *Tidepool* entered San Carlos to replenish ships in the Amphibious Operations Area, in company with MV *Elk*, which was sent in to continue discharging her load of ammunition, whilst HMS *Avenger*, on patrol off Port Stanley, may have been the target for the Argentine's first shore-based Exocet firing.

Sixty-four Argentine aircraft had been lost by today, while in South Georgia, *Queen Elizabeth II* had arrived in Cumberland Bay and begun transferring 5 Infantry Brigade to SS *Canberra* and MV *Norland*. Meanwhile, at Ascension, RFA *Bayleaf* departed for the South Atlantic.

Next day, both RFA *Tidepool* and MV *Elk* left San Carlos just before daylight. Further east, the presence of shadowing aircraft caused HMS *Bristol* to be detached from the Carrier Group and designated LOLA (TRALA) 'manager', tasked to defend and manage the RFAs and STUFT there, ensuring that ships bound for the Battle Group or Amphibious Operations Area were available, with the correct instructions and ready to leave on time.

RFA *Resource* was detached from the Carrier Battle Group and deployed to South Georgia, there to rendezvous with MV *Saxonia*.

Goose Green and Darwin were captured by the 2nd Bn The Parachute Rgt (2 Para), tragically at the cost of their popular and enthusiastic commanding officer, Col H Jones, who was killed while leading his men against an Argentine machine gun post.

The northerly advance was also going well, 45 Commando having reached their assigned position at Douglas Settlement early in the afternoon while 3 Para were even further east, resting before their entry into Teal Inlet Settlement next day. Grasping a strategic opportunity, something they are famous for, an SAS patrol had already occupied the abandoned Argentine positions on Mount Kent.

Earlier, just before dawn, SS *Atlantic Conveyor*, her bows blown off by exploding ordnance, finally sank under tow, despite the bravery and best efforts of *Irishman* and her crew.

At South Georgia, RFA *Blue Rover* sustained slight damage while replenishing *Norland*.

Saturday 29 May saw lots of activity in the Amphibious Operations Area. The unexploded bomb was finally removed from *Sir Lancelot* and dropped safely overboard, while *Sir Percivale* came back into San Carlos today, back-loading stores for Teal Inlet. The trip to Teal was due to be dangerous, the slow (seventeen knot) LSLs being an easy target, but the loss of helicopter support with *Atlantic Conveyor* meant Commodore Clapp had no alternative.

RFA *Tidepool* also returned today to replenish ships in the Amphibious Operations Area, in company with *Elk*, still intent upon discharging her dangerous cargo of ammunition.

While *Uganda* anchored in Grantham Sound, in order to decrease ship motion while surgery was under way, further north, MV *British Wye* was bombed by a lone Hercules, although the aircraft achieved only one glancing hit on the vessel's deck with no damage or injuries for the eight bombs it dropped. One of her RFA crew gives a typically off-hand account:

We were finally sailed from our holding position (at forty degrees south) by a route that swept south east and crossed to the north of South Georgia to arrive in the logistics area, about 150 miles east of Port Stanley.

It was en-route that we had our meeting with an Argentine C-130 Hercules. The aircraft had been modified and fitted with bomb racks under the wings. The initial target was Grytviken South Georgia, but low cloud and poor visibility had defeated that plan. I met with Captain Barker from HMS *Endurance* some months later. He told me that they heard the aircraft circling while they were having lunch on the *Queen Elizabeth II*. I think that story may need checking out. I cannot imagine all those RN types settling into lunch on a luxury liner.

We however were caught in clear visibility by the Hercules, the signal log tells the story, as do the BP newsletters. After the attack we took a more rapid and direct route to the logistics area.

At South Georgia, RFA *Blue Rover* left to rendezvous with Task Group, while RFA *Stromness* arrived in Cumberland Bay and began taking on troops, ammo and Rapier missiles from MV *Lycaon*.

Sunday 30 May saw San Carlos almost clear of ships, although *Sir Percivale* was being used as temporary Argentine POW accommodation. Well before dawn, RFA *Tidepool* and MV *Elk* left the Amphibious Operations Area (AOA) anchorage. The land attack was progressing well, with 45 Commando having secured Douglas Settlement, 3 Para being firmly ensconced at Teal Inlet and 'K' Company, 42 Commando relieving the SAS on Mount Kent.

By 11.00, RFA *Tidepool* and MV *Elk* were on their way back to the AOA, being due to rendezvous with *Atlantic Causeway* and *Europic Ferry*, then due from the TRALA, but the latter were forced to turn back in heavy seas. MV *Elk* left San Carlos before dawn but RFA *Tidepool* remained, while the remaining LSLs, *Sir Galahad* and *Sir Lancelot*, also left San Carlos Water.

In Gold Bay, South Georgia, weather conditions were still preventing the replenishment between RFA *Resource* and MV *Saxonia*. RFA *Resource*'s diary recorded at one point:

At first light a RAS was attempted with MV *Saxonia* but excessive rolling caused the RAS to be abandoned because the suspended loads swung dangerously to and fro in *Saxonia*'s hold with a pendulum motion.

Stromness, meanwhile, had finished her RAS with MV *Lycaon*, her diary recording:

15.12 FAOP [Full Away on Passage]. On sailing SG, embarked 415 troops & 108 Rapier missiles, assorted 200 tons ammo. Holds filled and remainder of ammo double-banked on either side of clearway for almost entire length.

It was a good job 'Health and Safety' did not drop by!

Monday 31 May started eventfully with a strike by an RAF Vulcan, using Shrike anti-radar missiles against the TPS-43 radar operating near Port Stanley. Unfortunately the attack was unsuccessful and the Argentines quickly encased their precious radar in a surrounding and enveloping layer of earth several feet thick, thus rendering it safe from further attack.

In San Carlos, RFA *Tidepool* supplied AVCAT to the Forward Operating Bases at Port San Carlos and San Carlos Settlement, while MV *Elk* had returned and was still unloading her cargo of ammunition.

Further north, RFA *Fort Grange* was attacked by an Argentine C-130 on its way to Carrier Battle Group, while in South Georgia, RFA *Resource*'s crew had finally given up any idea of berthing on *Saxonia*. In the slightly calmer waters of Husvik harbour they set about transferring *Saxonia*'s load using the five trawlers of the Mines Counter Measures Squadron.

Overnight, *Elk* and *Tidepool* departed San Carlos, while *Baltic Ferry*, *Atlantic Causeway* and RFA *Blue Rover* moved in, the latter carrying fuel for the Army's vehicles and their Rapier generators. *Norland*, carrying 1/7th Gurkha Rifles and HMS *Hermes'* Commando detachment, these latter to act as POW guards, followed behind without an escort.

Meanwhile and also under the cover of darkness, *Intrepid* transported her LCVPs and LCUs to Port Salvador for minesweeping operations, it being thought that the plywood hulls of the landing craft would not trigger magnetic mines. By dawn, the LPD was back in San Carlos, now redesignated the Transport Area (TA) and so falling the under command of Commander Land Forces, Major General Moore.

By now, the sea war was effectively over, and all the efforts of the RFA and their Naval colleagues were being directed to supply and support of the infantrymen currently closing in on Port Stanley.

Tuesday 1 June saw RFA *Appleleaf* reassigned to motorway tanking duties, cruising between thirty-five to forty-five degrees south until 18 July, while RFA *Plumleaf*, operating off South Georgia and well within range of the Argentine Boeing 707s, was moved north to twenty-five degrees south, some 1,100 miles southwest of Ascension, safely out of range.

During her time off South Georgia, she took part in a number of replenishment operations, including one with the *Brilliant* Group, which took over thirty hours, during which the big tanker was connected to one or other of the warships for a total of twenty-two hours in total, most of her deck crew remaining on duty for the whole of that period.

In the TRALA, RFA *Sir Galahad* was now fully operational, as Captain Phil Roberts well remembered:

By 30 May we were ready to sail from San Carlos to proceed to the carrier group to get back our Chinese who by now were embarked in *Sir Tristram*. We had only discharged approximately 100 tons of ammunition in this time, plus all the vehicles stowed on the upper deck. The ship by this time was like the proverbial tip. We felt rather relieved to sail out of San Carlos that evening and hopefully to restore order if not some decent food, and above all to get out of the firing line for a day or two.

On 31 May our Chinese crew were returned by helicopter in atrocious weather conditions. They, surprisingly, were all very pleased to be back and straight away set-to to clean up the ship and within an hour had provided us all with a hot meal.

On 1 June we RAS'ed fuel with RFA *Olna*, and restored sanity to the Chief Engineer Officer by getting a fresh supply of cigars. I have never seen someone enjoy a smoke so much before. I decided that it was time I restored my own sanity and sent for my steward. He provided us both with a beautiful gin and tonic with ice and lemon served on a silver tray complete with a bowl of peanuts. Much to the amusement of all on the bridge, we both enjoyed those drinks. They were a happy relief after so much tension.

Overnight, in San Carlos, *Atlantic Causeway* arrived and began to off-load stores, helicopters and the RAF Rapier squadron, this latter being Blindfire radar-equipped and so capable of night firing. *Norland* unloaded her Gurkhas at Ajax Bay, while *Baltic Ferry* landed material for 5 Infantry Brigade.

Earlier, the Port Salvador channel had been swept by the plywood LCVP, marking a channel up to Teal Inlet that was wide and deep enough for a laden LSL.

Intrepid left San Carlos in darkness to collect her landing craft, while *Sir Percivale* made the first run into Teal Inlet, via the swept passage. *Intrepid*'s LCVP had not put up any mines but that did not prevent a certain amount of anxiety aboard RFA *Sir Percivale*, as her Master describes:

Berthed on *Tidepool* late morning to replenish Dieso and AVCAT. Resumed anchorage mid-afternoon and commenced loading cargo for supply of Teal Inlet, which was being set up as a Forward Supply Area (FSA). It was hoped to be able to load the cargo in such a way that we could come somewhere near supermarket standard and have everything readily available by type. As will be seen this did not transpire.

Tuesday 1 June

A new month, a new anchor berth. Now anchored to the west of the inlet NE of Redhill Point. Loading continued throughout the day and reached a crescendo by evening. We were planned to sail at 21.30 but due to various foul-ups and complete lack of appreciation of the coalface by those at the pit head we finally got away in the early hours of Wednesday morning.

Wednesday 2 June

Before sailing, the sixty-six-foot Mexeflote had to be side-lifted using one lifting post. It is not quite certain whether this has ever been done before so it could be another first. Weighed anchor at 03.40 and proceeded to Teal Inlet with no tank deck cargo secured and approximately 350 troops on board. A parlous state for a ship heading out to sea off the FI, even though the run was only four hours to sheltered waters. Due to the delayed sailing time there was no escort available but the trip round proved uneventful; even the swell was kind.

We arrived at the entrance to Port Salvador at 07.30 and began a very tense passage in confined, tidal and unknown waters at night which were 'thought' to be clear of mines and which passed through shores which were 'thought' to be clear of the enemy. Needless to say the ship was at Action Stations throughout the passage. Thanks to good navigation and lack of foresight on the part of the enemy we made it safely to anchor a half-mile off Teal Inlet settlement jetty by 09.00. The Mexeflote was launched and discharge commenced. During the early afternoon we were visited by Commodore Amphibious Warfare (COMAW) and General Moore who both seemed very pleased and not a little relieved that we had arrived safely.

The discharge continued throughout the day but very slowly so ship's lifeboats were used to ferry some personnel and baggage ashore. The biggest delay seemed to be caused by the fact that the chosen beach was not, at all states of the tide, suitable for Mexeflote operations and at that time no trackway was laid.

During daylight hours we were used extensively as a helo-refuelling pad, dealing with between forty and fifty per day. The weather was overcast and misty and ideal for giving protection against enemy air attack.

Thursday 3 June
Continued discharge throughout the night and day completing late evening. Refuelling of helos continued unabated and included, by now, topping up of forty-five-gallon oil drums. Embarked some personnel suffering from 'trench foot'. Another misty day.

Friday 4 June
Sir Percivale sailed from Teal Inlet at 02.45 clearing the entrance to Port Salvador at 03.40. We returned to SCW [San Carlos Water] in company with *Fearless* who was loitering outside, inserting an LCU into Teal. No sign of *Sir Galahad* who was due into Teal shortly after we left. We arrived at anchor in SCW at 10.00, taking up previous position west of inlet. Waited patiently all day for next cargo but nothing arrived until last light. We were planned to sail at 23.00 but due to late start of loading this soon became impossible. Hospital ashore did not want trench foot cases so they remained on board.

At sea, *Elk* left the Carrier Battle Group to return to the TRALA, while *Canberra* temporarily joined the Carrier Battle Group, before leaving overnight for San Carlos Transport Area (TA) with RFA *Tidepool*.

On 2 June, the day began with leaflet raids on Port Stanley by Harriers. Within the Carrier Battle Group, HMS *Invincible* transferred one 600 nuclear round to *Fort Austin*, the big store ship having finally received orders to proceed to the UK.

RFA *Blue Rover*, having got rid of her dangerous petrol cargo, left San Carlos, while RFAs *Sir Galahad* and *Sir Bedivere* back-loaded stores for Teal Inlet. Captain Phil Roberts remembered:

On the night of 1/2 June we proceeded back to San Carlos, slightly perturbed as to whether our one-eighth-of-an-inch patch would hold out at full speed into a force 8 gale. However, only a slight amount of water seeped through and all was well. We completed loading for Teal inlet on 2 June and sailed that night for the carrier group, spending all day on 3 June trying to regain our allotted station within the task group.

Canberra and RFA *Tidepool* arrived in the San Carlos anchorage an hour before dawn and the Welsh and Scots Guards of 5 Infantry Brigade began a leisurely disembark from *Canberra*. Too leisurely for many people's liking, especially *Canberra's* master, since, because of this, she had to remain in the TA for another day. *Nordic Ferry* and *Atlantic Causeway*, however, finished unloading.

Meanwhile, 2 Para had secured Swan Inlet and Fitzroy Settlement. A telephone call earlier in the day to Fitzroy had assured Brigadier Tony Wilson that the settlement was unoccupied. Wilson commandeered a Chinook, crammed it with men and rushed to Fitzroy, which his group then occupied.

Lack of helicopters meant the planned build-up on the northern flank via Teal Inlet was now jeopardised by the need to reinforce 5 Infantry Brigade using LSLs.

Overnight, four ships departed from San Carlos, the 'Sir' ships bound for Teal, while *Nordic Ferry* and *Atlantic Causeway* returned to the Carrier Battle Group. Later and still covered by darkness, RFAs *Stromness*, *Sir Tristram*, and *Blue Rover* returned, together with MV *Nordic Ferry*, while the Argentine prisoners from Goose Green were moved into *Norland*.

At Ascension, MV *Scottish Eagle* arrived to take up duties as Station Tanker. In Husvik harbour, RFA *Resource* was still battling the South Georgia weather, having dragged her anchor spectacularly the previous evening.

One of the RFA's few breakdowns occurred next day, Thursday 3 June, when RFA *Plumleaf* developed a fault in her diesel machinery cooling system. After repairs, she resumed motorway-tanking at twenty-five degrees south, still some 1,100 miles from Ascension and well out of reach of Argentine long-range Boeing 707s.

RFA *Fort Austin* was effectively relieved by *Fort Grange* on the same day, the latter joining the Carrier Battle Group from the TRALA along with *Elk* and *Tidepool*. Taking advantage of *Fort Austin's* return to the UK, special weapons were transferred to her. HMS *Brilliant* transferred one 600 round, HMS *Glamorgan* one 600 (T), RFA *Resource* one 600 round, two 600 (S) and two 600 (T), HMS *Invincible* one 600 round and RFA *Fort Grange* one 600 (T). *Fort Austin* was now carrying three 600 nuclear rounds, two 600 (S) and four 600 (T) nuclear weapons in her containment facility.

RFA *Engadine*, coming south from Ascension, was overflown by an Argentine Boeing 707, 1,000 miles northeast of the Falklands. If the aircraft had flow lower and closer it might have found out that this RFA vessel was relatively well armed, having fourteen GPMGs (General Purpose Machine Guns) and LMGs (Light Machine Guns) as well as twenty riflemen.

In San Carlos *Canberra* completed her off-load, VERTREPing over a hundred loads, while the LCUs carried on a continuous shuttle service.

At Teal, RFA *Sir Percivale* finished her off-load with the help of her own Mexeflote, one of *Intrepid's* LCUs and a detachment of Sea Kings from 846 NAS and returned to San Carlos, leaving the entrance to Port Salvador just as *Fearless* made her way in to send off an LCU. Having finished their respective jobs, the LSL and LPD returned to San Carlos in company.

While this was going on the Gurkhas marched up to Darwin, allowing the rest of 2 Para to move on and occupy the Bluff Cove settlement.

Overnight, RFAs *Stromness*, *Blue Rover* and ss *Canberra* left the TA, escorted by *Plymouth* and *Minerva*, while HMS *Intrepid*, *Elk*, and RFA *Sir Galahad* moved in, the last heading for Teal Inlet independently on the morning of the 4th. HMS *Plymouth*, having left her escort group when it was past Pebble Island, then fired 150 shells from her 4.5-inch guns into Port Howard, ensuring its garrison remained awake.

On 4 June San Carlos was relatively busy, with RFA *Sir Percivale* back-loading for Teal Inlet, while *Sir Tristram* began loading ammunition and stores for 5 Brigade at Fitzroy.

The team from *Stena Seaspread*, together with the LPD's engineering staff, were working on *Sir Lancelot*, trying to repair the elderly LSL sufficiently to allow her to resume supply operations.

Sir Galahad made her entry into Teal through the Port Salvador narrows in full daylight, anchoring and beginning her off-load soon after. Captain Phil Roberts recalled the time:

At first light on 4 June we negotiated the winding passage into Teal inlet and anchored a mile off the settlement. When daylight came it all looked rather peaceful and we could see the mountains that overlooked Port Stanley quite clearly. It was at Teal that we finally discharged our cargo of ammo and stores that we had loaded a long time ago in Plymouth. On 4 and 5 June we fuelled about 95 helicopters: they were queuing up like cars at an M1 filling station!

On 6 June after passing all our excess AVCAT to *Sir Percivale* we sailed for San Carlos, arriving at first light. The weather in San Carlos was foul, blowing gale 8 or 9, so no cargo was loaded on the 6th.

Poor weather on the Argentine mainland prevented any low-level air attacks on 4 June, although there appears to have been some high-level, possibly *Canberra*, activity.

Later in the day, *Exeter*, *Invincible* and *Brilliant* examined the land-based Exocet threat, the Argentines having, rather cleverly, fabricated a lorry-mounted launcher which could fire a missile at a target located by their TPS-43 radar. Due to the serious nature of this threat, bombardment activities around Port Stanley had been suspended.

The inbound TA convoy today consisted of *Sir Geraint* and *Blue Rover*, no outbound convoy leaving.

Within the Carrier Group, RFA *Fort Austin* began transferring all her remaining stores to *Fort Grange*, having already back-loaded most of the Task Force's special weapons.

In San Carlos, RFA *Sir Lancelot* was finally mobile again, although she was unable to play a very active role in the logistics effort just yet, while MV *Nordic Ferry* and *Elk* were still off-loading, having suffered some difficulties in transporting their cargo to the shore. RFA *Sir Geraint*, however, had managed to speed up her cargo transfer with MV *Elk*, by utilising a Mexeflote secured between stern doors of the two vessels, which then enabled a forklift to work between the ships.

Clear weather allowed some forward movement of artillery by helicopter as well as the transfer of a Rapier troop to Teal inlet, although part of the Rapier equipment had to be moved by RFA *Sir Percivale*. By the time *Sir Percivale* arrived at Teal, *Sir Galahad* was still off-loading, so *Sir Percivale* became a helicopter refuelling point, filling them up at an average rate of one every ten minutes. Before leaving for San Carlos, *Sir Galahad* pumped-over all her remaining AVCAT to *Sir Percivale*. *Sir Percivale*'s Master, Captain Tony Pitt, remembered an eventful trip:

Sir Percivale finally sailed from SCW [San Carlos Water] at 05.30 on the 5th with *Plymouth* as escort, arriving off Big Shag Island at 10.00 for passage to Teal. *Sir Galahad* had arrived Friday night and was still discharging, so [we] anchored clear to the north. *Sir Galahad* finished discharge by last light so we berthed alongside her to relieve her of her remaining AVCAT for use during the next two days at Teal. Operation only took thirty minutes: slipped, anchored and commenced discharge of cargo.

Next day, the 6th, we continued discharge of cargo and supply of AVCAT to thirsty helos, completing deck-landing 750. The honour went to a Gazelle from our own 'M' Flt.

In the early hours of the morning of the 7th we received word that the RN rates on board had heard noises very much like sonar transmissions, a noise they were used to hearing on HM Ships. Requested Fleet Clearance Diving Team (FCDT) to be sent from SCW and increased incidence of scare-charge drops. FCDT did not turn up before sailing.

Completed discharge by 11.00 but due to requirement to leave Port Salvador under cover of darkness we remained at Teal refuelling helos until our tanks were dry. Sailed from Teal at 22.30 and cleared the narrows at 23.30. Numbers of TF increased to twenty-eight and taking up valuable berths.

Sir Percivale anchored in SCW in the early hours of the 8th in a position in the middle of the inlet. Not too happy with that. When approaching the entrance to SCW we were surprised to see *Sir Galahad* just sailing when she should have been clear some four hours earlier on her passage to Bluff Cove. During the air raid warnings we tried to keep the vessel lying north/south to reduce target. However, no aircraft were sighted in SCW but both *Galahad* and *Tristram* were badly hit at anchor in Bluff Cove and *Plymouth* was hit in Falkland Sound.

HMS *Sheathbill*, the Harrier airstrip at Port San Carlos, was now operational. The same day, HMS *Intrepid* embarked 2nd Battalion Scots Guards and transported them, overnight, to Lively Island, where they were disembarked for Bluff Cove, a distance of thirty-five miles, via landing craft. In South Georgia, RFA *Pearleaf* was continuing with her replenishment activities while RFA *Resource* proceeded to sea at 11.00, having finished her consolidation with MV *Saxonia*, during the course of which she loaded 800 tons of food and some ammunition, with 100 units of empties back-loaded to the STUFT.

Tragically the only 'blue-on-blue' (friendly fire, where a unit accidentally shoots at another on the same side) incident suffered by the Task Force occurred at 04:10 on Sunday morning [6 June], involving HMS *Cardiff* and resulting in loss of an Army Gazelle helicopter of 656 Sqn Army Air Corps and all her crew as well as two passengers from the Signals Regiment.

RFA *Fort Austin*, still with the Carrier Battle Group just outside the eastern boundary of the TEZ, finished transferring stores to *Fort Grange* on 6 June, then sent her Sea King helicopter equipment to *Atlantic Causeway* before leaving next day for South Georgia and then home.

At San Carlos, bad weather had made HMS *Sheathbill* unusable early that morning while both RFA *Blue Rover* and MV *Nordic Ferry* were emptied and outbound overnight.

The remaining Welsh Guards were aboard *Fearless*, which sailed at dusk, 19.30 pm, with the intention of rendezvousing with *Intrepid*'s LCUs north of Lively Island and using them to disembark Guards. Unfortunately, the LCUs did not make the rendezvous, having been commandeered for another task.

Sir Geraint was still back-loading for Teal, but *Sir Tristram*, having completed her load for 5 Infantry Brigade at Fitzroy, hoisted in her Mexeflote for use in forward anchorage and sailed at 23.00, some hours after *Fearless*. Captain Robin Green, Master of *Sir Tristram*, remembers the trip:

After a few days at sea we returned to 'bomb alley' to load men and supplies for Bluff Cove/Fitzroy. After loading we subsequently departed overnight via Falkland Sound. *Sir Tristram* 'flew' down Falkland Sound, because although the ship was darkened, we were silhouetted by a brightly lit *Uganda* and thus visible to Argies on West Falkland.

We arrived early off Pleasant Point, keeping well to the east to clear the kelp and small islands. I had been briefed to enter Port Pleasant in the dark but on my chart the channel was no wider than a thick pencil line!! We could not hang about outside because we were in range of Exocet and 155mm guns at Stanley. Suddenly the moon came out of the clouds and after conferring with the Navigator I decided to enter by moonlight.

We *assumed* we held the land on either side but with all guns closed up we entered with the Chief Officer hanging over the bridge wing watching the kelp and me hanging over the other side looking down on the bit of low-lying island, and then we were in, and we anchored off Fitzroy.

Baltic Ferry and *Norland* were inbound to San Carlos overnight while *Active*, *Ambuscade*, *Invincible* and *Brilliant* were detached for missions inshore. Further west, *Hydra*, the ambulance ship, arrived in Montevideo, while MV *Stena Inspector* sailed from Charleston, USA, heading for the South Atlantic. And in the morning RFA *Fort Austin* finally left the Carrier Battle Group, calling first at South Georgia, then Ascension, before reaching Devonport on 29 June, where her nuclear rounds were finally off-loaded.

In San Carlos, HMS *Intrepid* had returned, having failed to collect her LCUs due to the latter being unable to make the planned rendezvous. Her two remaining LCUs took two companies of Welsh Guards ashore and were left at Bluff Cove, before she returned.

Overnight, RFA *Sir Galahad* embarked the 1st Battalion Welsh Guards, Field Ambulance, Rapier Troop and vehicles at San Carlos Water, before beginning the overnight and unescorted trip to Bluff Cove. Also embarked was a Sea King to assist her off-load.

Fearless returned to Teal at 7.30 to collect her two LCUs, while *Sir Percivale* began her own return from Teal at about the same time. *Intrepid* headed for Low Bay, Lafonia, to collect her four LCUs which had travelled there from Bluff Cove.

At sea, *Hermes* moved out of the TEZ for a much-needed boiler clean, although her Harriers remained operational by using the airstrip HMS *Sheathbill*.

Back in San Carlos, *Norland*, with over 1,000 POWs aboard, sailed overnight, with *Elk*, while *Junella*, *Pict*, and *Cordella* arrived from South Georgia and RFAs *Engadine*, *Olna* and MV *Atlantic Causeway* moved towards the TA. Chef Dave Bolton describes life aboard the helicopter ship:

We went into defence watches, as we approached the TEZ, not the ones that we use now, but similar. Designed to have most people round during the hours of greatest threat from attack.

I worked nights and had to make sure that there was always something hot to eat for those flying etc and any special requests for long flights or extended maintenance crews.

One thing I had to do, one night, was feed an SAS team.

They had done one of those HALO drops into the sea, swum ashore, done their mission, swum back out, got picked up by helo and transferred to us. I went in to see what they wanted and they were all asleep at the mess table, but one of them said, give us a big greasy breakfast, so I complied and they all woke up and ate with gusto and thoroughly enjoyed it. I did not make it too greasy as even then it wasn't good for you. These guys have some reputation, but they were still decent gents.

Working nights, I got to wander round a bit more and quite often went up on the bridge to listen to the cryptic messages being spoken over the attack radios.

Then wandered into the helo electronics repair workshop and played with their new Sinclair Spectrum computer, yes, brand new then. Someone had even written a little game for it, taking the Falklands from the Argies, quite popular it was too.

In South Georgia, the weather being kinder, RFA *Stromness* arrived in Cumberland Bay, and immediately began working round the clock to re-store from MV *Saxonia*.

Tuesday 8 June began badly, trouble with an inbound convoy causing RFA *Engadine* and the minesweepers to be ordered back to the Carrier Battle Group, and HMS *Penelope* collecting RFA *Olna* and *Atlantic Causeway* and experiencing an Exocet scare while escorting them past Pebble Island, in daylight.

Two Argentine observation posts (OP) were giving cause for concern, so today they were dealt with. Members of 'B' Company, 40 Commando landed at the Cape Dolphin OP only to find it empty while *Plymouth* moved inshore to bombard the Mount Rosalie OP.

RFA *Sir Geraint* was loaded for Teal, while *Sir Lancelot*, repairs almost complete, began rearranging her load, collected from Ajax Bay and *Atlantic Causeway*.

Ashore, in the first of a series of fatal coincidences, the STOVL strip at HMS *Sheathbill* was damaged by a GR3 Harrier crash landing, causing a lack of cover over Fitzroy which would have disastrous consequences, as covered in the next chapter.

RFA men were in danger elsewhere, as *Resource*'s diary records:

Between 23.03 and 23.52 hrs, a RAS was attempted with HMS *Cardiff* using Rig One. But at 23.40 hrs, the arm of the rig collapsed and two men were nearly lost over the side; these were the Chief Officer and the Bosun.

In fact, the Bosun was only saved from being lost overboard because he managed to grab a line or net to which he clung before he could be rescued from the ship's side.

Two other men suffered bruises and lacerations after being struck by a Sea Dart missile that had broken loose from the collapsed rig.

In South Georgia, RFA *Fort Austin* visited briefly before heading home, and the mooring vessel, *Wimpey Seahorse*, arrived to begin laying moorings.

In the only incident involving an outsider during the whole war, the US tanker *Hercules* was attacked by an Argentine C-130, some 300 miles north of the TEZ. This might have been excusable but the Argentineans actually came back for a second try at the unfortunate tanker a couple of hours later.

CHAPTER TEN

FITZROY AND THE LSLs

THE WELSH GUARDS

B Y APRIL 1982, the British Army had undergone a considerable and sometimes sharply painful transformation, which had resulted in a structure that
would have been unrecognisable to any soldier of an earlier generation.

Many of the old line regiments had gone or been reduced to single battalions,
these battalions being then grouped into new, autonomous brigade formations.

In many ways, this made good logistic sense, at least when it was done
properly, as was the case with 3 Commando Brigade. This brigade consisted of
three commandos, infantry battalions in all but name, as well as logistics,
engineers, artillery, a specialist boat unit, an air squadron and even an electronic
counter-measures unit. All these men were commando-trained. They also
exercised together and more to the point, during these exercises and any other
operations all units were controlled and co-ordinated by a central command
structure.

In other words, when the brigade operated, it operated as a permanent
formation, where every unit's operational techniques and constraints were
known to every other unit and misunderstandings kept to a minimum. Of
course, the amphibious nature of Operation Corporate made 3 Commando the
obvious first choice, but it rapidly became clear that they would need
considerable reinforcement if they were to have a chance of retaking the islands.

Consequently, the 2nd and 3rd Battalions of the Parachute Regiment were
temporarily transferred from 5 (Army) Brigade and hurriedly sent south on
Canberra with the Royal Marines. This left 5 Brigade with only the 1/7th Gurkha
Rifles, so the 1st Battalion Welsh Guards and 2nd Battalion Scots Guards were
moved in to make up the shortfall.

5 Brigade's internal organisation was not as well developed as that of the
Commando Brigade. They had no integrated artillery, no logistics regiment nor
their own heavy lift helicopters. After they had carried out a preparatory exercise,
'Welsh Falcon', in the Brecon Beacons, it became clear that the newly formed
brigade was not quite the coherent unit it needed to be.

Of course, it takes time to fully integrate any group of individuals, but the HQ staff of 5 Brigade were never allowed this essential breathing space, because, in what began the chain of decisions culminating in the disaster at Fitzroy, the MOD (Army) decided to send 5 Brigade south. Their justification was that these reinforcements would only be used for reserve or garrison duties so their lack of experience as a formation wouldn't matter.

A few minutes' conversation with Commodore Clapp or Brigadier Thompson would have immediately dispelled this notion, because what they wanted was a brigade strength unit capable of fighting its way around the southern flank, while the Royal Marines cut through to the north. Clapp and Thompson wanted 'bayonets', and 5 Brigade were certainly under no illusions about that. They were there to clear the Argentines off the island, not guard POWs and dig latrines.

The brigade departed the UK in *Queen Elizabeth II* on 12 May and, instead of the re-stow at Ascension they had been promised, were routed directly for South Georgia, the men attending what must have seemed an endless round of briefings, lectures and practical demonstrations, with gruelling sessions of fitness training thrown in for good measure. Equipment was a problem, too, the Welsh battalion having left Southampton short of 100 of their essential Arctic rucksacks or 'bergens'.

The space aboard the ship was not well designed for the battalion's needs, and, perhaps surprisingly, the consensus seems to have been that the 'Queen' was a good deal less comfortable than the *Canberra*, to which most of them later cross-decked.

The *Queen Elizabeth II* arrived in Cumberland Bay, South Georgia, on 27 May, six days after the San Carlos landings. The brigade transferred to *Canberra*, *Norland* and RFA *Stromness*, expecting to be able to rest, attend a couple of lectures and conduct their long-awaited live-firing trials on the way to San Carlos.

But the brigade's luck was out once again. The weather turned rough almost as soon as the little flotilla left the shelter of Cumberland Bay and what should have been an easy two-day trip turned into a gale-force nightmare lasting four and a half, with the upper deck off limits for all that time.

On 2 June, while 2 Para were securing Fitzroy and Bluff Cove with their rapid dash via Chinook, *Canberra* dropped anchor in San Carlos and the Guards battalions began to disembark.

This operation took a full twenty-four hours to complete, much to the annoyance of *Canberra*'s master, who was thus forced to spend a full day more in San Carlos than he plainly felt was necessary. Once off-loaded, the Guards set up defensive positions on the northern reverse slope of Sussex Mountain, above the San Carlos anchorage.

By 21.00 on 3 June, they were on the move again, this time heading for High Hill, which would put them five miles from Darwin, directly overlooking the Darwin–Bluff Cove track. Their move lasted fifty minutes, before their commanding officer, Lt Colonel J Rickett, called the attempt off as the vehicles carrying the Welsh Guards' essential heavy equipment had become hopelessly bogged down.

Incidentally, much has been made elsewhere of the Welsh Guards' lack of physical fitness, which consequently made a ship lift to Fitzroy necessary. While it is true that a number of officers were concerned about the effect of a fourteen-mile 'tab' on some of their men, the Guards had recently completed an exercise in Kenya and it was probably the unfamiliar terrain and lack of proper boots that were causing anxiety more than the men's condition.

By 5 June, it had been decided to move the rest of 5 Brigade, effectively the Scots and Welsh Guards, round to Bluff Cove by sea. The Scots arrived safely that night after a landing craft journey of six hours and so did half the Welsh battalion the following night, although poor communications meant that the other half, 351 men, had to return to make the fateful trip by *Sir Galahad*.

Fitzroy and the LSLs

The loss of *Atlantic Conveyor* and, more particularly, the Chinook and Wessex helicopters she was carrying, was undoubtedly the most important logistic setback experienced by British forces during the whole campaign.

Lacking the means to move large amounts of supplies forward from San Carlos by air, Commodore Clapp and General Moore were forced to use the vulnerable LSLs, whose shallow draught made them the most suitable vessel for such a role, to transport staples like food and ammunition by sea to Teal inlet. From here it could be distributed by helicopter to 3 Commando Brigade, who had marched around the northern flank from the beachhead, although it soon became clear that there were not enough helicopters to maintain a simultaneous advance on both the northern and southern flanks.

Brigadier Tony Wilson, in command of 5 Brigade, who were assigned to head the southern advance, was faced with a difficult situation. If he marched his brigade across country from Goose Green to Fitzroy, there were no convenient areas to rest the men or arrange the pickup of vital supplies by sea. That meant that the troops would have to carry everything they needed and, as previously mentioned, Wilson and his subordinates had very real concerns about this.

At the same time, there were good tactical reasons why his units should move without delay and Wilson was, quite naturally, impatient to begin.

His problems seemed to be solved when, on 2 June, Major Chris Keeble, second-in-command of 2 Para, suggested that a small party from 2 Para could be flown forward by Scout helicopter to Swan Inlet house and, once there, make use of the telephone link with Fitzroy to find out if there were any Argentineans at the settlement. If no enemy troops were present, then the Scouts and the Task Force's single Chinook could start moving 2 Para up to Fitzroy, which they would then occupy and fortify.

Wilson approved the plan enthusiastically and, at first, everything seemed to be going well, despite Wilson failing to inform Major-General Moore's HQ about what they were doing.

The reconnaissance force of twelve Paras quickly occupied the empty Swan Inlet House and their commander duly rang Fitzroy, only to find that the few Argentineans previously in the settlement had withdrawn.

Within the hour, the Paras had returned to Goose Green, where the Chinook was immediately taken off load carrying, crammed with its maximum complement of fifty paratroopers and dispatched to Fitzroy, while the much smaller Scouts took on four men each, before also setting off for the settlement. By nightfall, most of 2 Para and their headquarters staff were in position, having also occupied Bluff Cove. Unfortunately, their heavy support, vital to the success of such a defensive role, consisted of 'A' Company's single mortar detachment.

Mixed reactions greeted the news of Wilson's advance when it was received at General Moore's headquarters, mostly consternation at what might happen to the weakened 2 Para, without air defence or artillery, if the Argentines returned in strength.

Consequently, next day, some Sea Kings were found and the rest of 2 Para were flown forward. Helicopters being in such short supply, however, it was decided that the rest of the brigade, including the Scots and Welsh Guards, would have to be moved by sea.

But now another set of problems arose. Either of the two LPDs, HMS *Intrepid* or *Fearless*, could have brought the rest of 5 Brigade and their heavy equipment to Bluff Cove in a single night lift, but that would have meant leaving them exposed in the anchorage during daylight, less than fifteen miles from the main Argentine positions in Fort Stanley.

These LPDs, with their sophisticated communications, were, in the naval mind, almost as valuable as the carriers, and their loss would have crippled the British advance, perhaps fatally. So it was decided they couldn't be risked in daylight and that the best way to proceed was to organise a landing craft shuttle.

Intrepid would sail halfway to Bluff Cove, then tranship her four landing craft, carrying the Scots Guards and their equipment, which would sail into Bluff Cove.

The LPD would return to San Carlos and the next night, *Fearless* would make the same trip, only this time *Intrepid*'s LCUs would rendezvous with her and, together with *Fearless*'s two LCUs, move the rest of the battalion, consisting of 700 Welsh Guards, ashore.

The first night's trip, commanded by Major Ewan Southby-Tailyour, went more or less according to plan, except that the sea conditions meant that, instead of the planned two-hour trip, the LCUs actually took six.

On the next night, however, things began to go badly wrong. Difficulties with radio communications meant that the LCUs, now at Fitzroy, did not make the rendezvous and all *Fearless* could do was put half the Welsh Guards in her two remaining landing craft and dispatch them to Bluff Cove, which they reached safely some hours later. *Fearless* returned to San Carlos, taking the other half of the Welsh Guards battalion with her.

Next day, 7 June, Moore and Clapp were ordered to halt any more operations of this type involving the LPDs and so the decision was made to use the smaller and slower LSLs.

An overloaded RFA *Sir Tristram* complete with Mexeflote, having sailed round on the night of 6 June, was still in Fitzroy's Port Pleasant anchorage, discharging ammunition for 5 Brigade, her off-load difficulties compounded by a lack of LCUs or similar ship-to-shore transport.

RFA *Sir Galahad* was in San Carlos, loading vehicles and men of 16 Field Ambulance, thirty men from 'G' Sqn SAS and four Rapier launchers, the latter intended to supply air cover for the Fitzroy anchorage. She also had a Sea King helicopter embarked.

Capt Phil Roberts, master of *Sir Galahad*, was verbally instructed to embark the remaining 352 Welsh Guards and, sailing at dusk, disembark those troops at Bluff Cove in the early hours of the morning, under cover of darkness, then get back to Fitzroy to offload the Field Ambulance and the Rapiers before dawn, so both operations would be carried out safely under the cover of darkness.

Capt Roberts explains some of the accommodation problems this entailed:

Sir Galahad sailed from San Carlos with over 500 passengers and crew embarked, over 150 in excess of her passenger certificate. COMAW gave signalled approval for the exemption.

The Welsh Guards had to be billeted in the tank deck as the port side troops accommodation had been wrecked by the unexploded bomb on 24 May. As well as accommodation problems, these extra personnel put a great strain on the catering staff and other ship-board resources.

Both the Rapiers and Guards units were loaded quickly but lack of transport and communications difficulties meant that the Field Ambulance and their vehicles weren't aboard until five hours after dusk.

Sir Galahad's Master, Captain Phil Roberts, knowing that he could not make

Bluff Cove, discharge the Welsh Guards and get back to Fitzroy in darkness, signalled Clapp's staff that he intended to stay in San Carlos and sail at dusk the next day. Soon after, however, he received a signal ordering him to sail but only as far as Fitzroy, where he was to disembark both the Rapiers and the Field Ambulance.

Capt Roberts described the situation he found himself in:

The signal I received from Clapp's staff was not copied to 5 Brigade Headquarters, although my Executive officer did inform the O/C troops of the change of destination.

Having already turned in, there was nothing to be gained from calling the Welsh Guards at the time of sailing from San Carlos and this new information would be passed to them in the morning when they were called.

The passage to Fitzroy was conducted in total radar and radio silence so as not to alert the Argentineans of our presence, which meant that the Welsh Guards could not have sent a signal to the rest of their battalion anyway.

Capt Roberts was also quite clear about Commodore Clapp's involvement in this incident, as he explains here:

It should be made clear that Commodore Clapp never intended Sir Galahad to go to Bluff Cove. As far as he was concerned, and as he in fact signalled in his initial orders on 6 June, Sir Galahad was required to go to Fitzroy (Port Pleasant) on completion of the off-load at Teal Inlet by way of San Carlos.

It was a misunderstanding by one of his staff that led to a verbal briefing to Capt Roberts, in San Carlos on 7 June, to the effect that Sir Galahad was to proceed to Bluff Cove, discharge the Welsh Guards and then proceed to Fitzroy's Port Pleasant, anchoring before daylight in order to off-load the Field Ambulance, SAS and Rapier batteries.

Commodore Clapp was never advised that the low cloud and bad weather that had been affecting Stanley and the east coast of East Falklands, had, in fact, improved considerably, resulting in excellent visibility.

Had he known this, he would never have allowed Sir Galahad to sail from San Carlos, as he has made clear elsewhere. [See Bibliography: Clapp and Southby-Tailyour.]

Sir Galahad weighed anchor at 02.00 Zulu on the 8th, anchoring in Port Pleasant sometime after first light, at 08.00 local time (approx 12.00Z), about 3 cables (600 metres) east of Sir Tristram and a mile from Fitzroy, the 150-mile trip having proved uneventful.

The weather was bright and sunny with the hills around Port Stanley clearly visible and the single remaining LCU and Sir Tristram's Mexeflote were both loaded with ammunition and waiting for the tide to turn. There had been six LCUs working in the anchorage the previous day but four had returned to Intrepid and the other one was making a run to Goose Green to collect 5 Brigade's signal vehicles.

Those responsible for the off-load from Clapp's staff, Majors Todd (RCT) and Southby-Tailyour (RM), immediately boarded *Galahad* in order to get the Guardsmen ashore as soon as possible.

Discussion became heated as a number of alternatives were considered but finally it was decided that the LCU would unload its ammunition and move as many Guards as possible round to Bluff Cove, along with their heavy equipment, which they were understandably reluctant to be separated from, although Major Southby-Tailyour has made it clear elsewhere that he would never have allowed such a move in daylight.

Along with the LCUs, they could also use local tractors and trailers, as well as a twenty-foot cutter the Engineers had requisitioned. Meanwhile the single available Sea King was unloading the Rapier units, but this was slow work, requiring eighteen helicopter lifts to get all four units ashore.

At noon the LCU was alongside *Galahad* but Lt Colonel Roberts, commanding 16 Field Ambulance and senior ranking officer, insisted that his unit should go first. An hour later, the last of the medical team was ashore but now another snag appeared. The LCU's ramp had been damaged on the last trip and couldn't be lowered to allow the heavy equipment to be loaded via *Galahad*'s stern doors. Tragically, it was decided to leave the troops aboard while their heavy equipment was off-loaded by crane.

Five hours had elapsed since *Galahad* dropped anchor and in that time the Argentinean troops on Mount Harriet, ten miles away, had signalled the mainland, with the result that the Argentine Air Force was on its way.

One group bombed HMS *Plymouth* in Falkland Sound, but the jets were too low, none of the bombs exploded and *Plymouth* escaped with superficial damage.

The five Skyhawks of the remaining group had been given the location of the LSLs as Port Fitzroy, which is an inlet to the north of the settlement, while the two vessels were actually in Port Pleasant, to the south.

Finding Port Fitzroy empty and being low on fuel, the jets swept out south over the sea to return home, and while making a rising turn, the leader's wingman caught a glimpse of the LSLs.

Simply tightening their turn brought them in line with the ships and the Skyhawks swept in to the attack, three attacking *Sir Galahad*, while the two remaining went for *Sir Tristram*. With his weapon disabled by a broken tracker optic, the sergeant commanding the Rapier troop covering Fitzroy's eastern approach could only watch the ensuing carnage helplessly.

Aboard the LSLs, the aircraft were sighted and heard at about 17.15 Z. 'Action Stations' was immediately piped but barely seconds later, the aircraft struck.

Lt Colonel R Dickey takes up the story.

Off Fitzroy, Sgt Dawson is horrified to find that he can see Argentine positions on Two Sisters and Tumbledown and prepares for the worst when Sir Galahad's arrival blocks his view to the east. [This seems debatable given the relative positions of the ships.] That afternoon they are inevitably attacked. Gunner Lush on *Sir Galahad* fires at the second Skyhawk in line but is knocked down as a bomb from the first aircraft explodes on board. Similarly, Sgt Dawson fires at a second Skyhawk and only his detachment see the deck being ripped apart on either side of him by cannon shell. Oblivious to the aircraft, he is picked up by the slipstream and thrown the length of the deck. With no signal, his missile explodes harmlessly and the third Skyhawk releases its bombs with further tragic results.

Sir Tristram was hit by two bombs, both on the starboard side towards the stern. One went straight through the ship without exploding while the other burst inside a compartment, killing the Bosun, Yu Sik Chee, and a crewman, Yeung Shui Kam, and buckling the steel wall of the tank deck. There were soon fires in the steering flat, above where there were several pallets of ammunition, and forward, close to a quantity of ammunition and explosives.

The three Skyhawks attacking *Sir Galahad* were slightly higher and consequently their bombs developed a more vertical trajectory. One went through an upper deck hatch and deflagrated, causing a massive fire-ball which swept through the tank deck, where most of the Welsh Guards were waiting to disembark. The second exploded in the galley area, killing the butcher Sung Yuk Fai instantly and wounding several other crew members, while the third burst in the engine room, killing Third Engineer Officer A J Morris. This last explosion produced clouds of thick, extremely irritant smoke, trapping Second Engineer Officer Paul A Henry, Third Engineer Officer C F Hailwood and Junior Engineering Officer N Bagnall in the Machinery Control Room. Junior Engineer Officer Bagnall was driven back by the smoke while attempting to escape but was given the only set of breathing apparatus by Second Engineer Officer Henry and ordered to try again. Bagnall eventually succeeded in getting out but Second Engineer Officer Henry, Third Engineer Officer Hailwood and a crew member who was also present, Electrical Fitter Leug Chau, were not seen again.

Meanwhile, on deck, Firesuitman Chiu Yiu Nam, realising that there were still men trapped below, pulled on his asbestos suit and went into the flaming tank deck. He managed to lead to safety ten of the Guards, who would undoubtedly have died but for his efforts. Third Officer Paul Gudgeon also entered the smoke-filled accommodation, wearing breathing apparatus, although his attempts to save one man, trapped by falling debris, were unsuccessful. Both Paul Henry and Chiu Yiu Nam received the George Medal for their actions while Paul Gudgeon received the Queen's Gallantry Medal.

Captain Roberts quickly realised that there was no possibility of saving *Sir Galahad* and, given the vast quantities of ordnance aboard, his only course was to abandon ship. He managed to give the order over the ship's broadcast system and, having done this, set about organising the launching of liferafts and lifeboats. He described events thus:

At first light we negotiated the narrow entrance to Port Pleasant and anchored off Fitzroy Settlement about three cables to the east of RFA *Sir Tristram*, who was still unloading ammo and stores. The weather was bright and sunny with good visibility – the hills and landmarks around Port Stanley looked very close. *Sir Tristram* had filled both the Mexeflote and one LCU to capacity with ammunition. So the Guards had to wait on board until assets had proceeded to shore, discharged and returned to the ship. The Welsh Guards were anxious to be landed at Bluff Cove where they had originally been ordered to, not Fitzroy. They had been told that the bridge at Fitzroy over to Bluff Cove had been blown and was not yet repaired. So it was that only a handful of RAMC managed to get ashore, and none of the Welsh Guards, by 17.15 when the OOW [Officer of the Watch] observed two very low-flying aircraft approaching the ship fast on the starboard beam. He immediately piped 'Action Stations' and at the same time I entered the wheelhouse. We both hit the deck behind the chart table.

The ship shuddered with the explosions.

Seconds later, two more aircraft flew low over the ship and again we felt explosions. All ventilation was crash-stopped; fire alarm bells were ringing furiously on the bridge panel. Smoke immediately started to appear through the chartroom door, which had been blown open by the force of the explosions. My immediate reaction was to rush out to the bridge wings to assess the damage. On the starboard side there were flames and an enormous amount of black smoke coming out of the accommodation and engine room vent fans, and it was much the same on the port side. On looking forward, flames and smoke were shooting out of the after hatch. I tried phoning the engine room by sound-powered telephone but there was no reply. It became immediately apparent to me that fires were burning out of control in many places and that the ship could not be saved.

Instinctively, I grabbed the ship's broadcast system microphone, not knowing if it was working, and made the pipe 'Abandon Ship, Abandon Ship'. I learnt later that this pipe had been heard in most parts of the ship. I felt it very important that the after accommodation be evacuated as quickly as possible.

No 4 lifeboat was swung out over the side and had to be lowered shortly afterwards because it was being enveloped in smoke. I proceeded forward to supervise the launching of liferafts. By this time, helicopters were already arriving to take off the wounded, the Mexeflote and LCU were also quickly on the scene as were two lifeboats from *Sir Tristram*.

By 17.50 all the non-seriously injured personnel and crew had been evacuated from the ship. By this time, the whole of the bridge front was burning furiously, with smoke billowing high into the sky. Loud explosions, flames and shrapnel were erupting from the after hatch.

All the remaining injured had been evacuated to the forecastle and were being cared for by 16 Field Ambulance medics, before being winched into a Sea King. The evacuation of the badly wounded was a slow and painful operation. The pilots of the helicopters showed great courage and determination, hovering close to the deck despite the loud explosions and the debris which was being blown into the air. It was very fortuitous that our foremast had been lowered in order to increase our arc of fire. This enabled the helos to hover four or five feet above the deck, so speeding up the evacuation of the very badly-burned Welsh Guards.

At 18.15, the last of the wounded had been lifted off. I bundled my Chief Engineer Officer who had also been wounded up into the helo and then hooked myself on – I was the last to leave my ship. It was a desperately sad moment for me. A well ordered, happy and disciplined ship one moment and a burning inferno the next, and obviously at that time I did not know which or how many of my officers or crew had been killed or injured.

The full story was, of course, well recorded by the BBC camera team and reported on by Brian Hanrahan. For me, and probably my officers, crew and all those troops that we were carrying at the time, and the relatives of those who were killed, it was one of those sad moments of timing because the media used those pictures as their theme for the whole of the Falklands war, showing them time and time again. It certainly is disturbing for me to see them, as it must be for others who were there.

Captain R Green, Master of *Sir Tristram*, had clear memories of the attack, too:

We discharged all that day [7th] and *Sir Galahad* arrived next morning 8th June. Both ships were bombed about 14.00 local time. *Sir Galahad* was very badly hit and so I sent my lifeboats across to assist her.

We apparently had an unexploded bomb in the steering flat, which was on fire with the entrance blocked off by debris, and the stern trunking above, getting very warm, full of ammunition and cased diesel. I subsequently decided to abandon ship and leave it to the Bomb Disposal people to come and sort out the bomb.

We were evacuated from Fitzroy to *Fearless* and *Intrepid* in San Carlos by helo through the mountains in pitch dark and then a few days later, to *British Trent* via *Atlantic Causeway* by helo for the passage to Ascension. Then RAF to Brize Norton where there was a welcoming committee and our families to meet us.

Some of *Sir Galahad*'s crew had been forced to jump from the poop deck after being cut off by the flames, and liferafts had to be floated to these men while the uninjured troops were being evacuated from the tank deck by LCU, lifeboat, liferaft and helicopter.

The helicopter pilots in particular took incredible risks, bringing their aircraft to within feet of the burning deck and exploding ammunition. At one point, seeing the liferafts being sucked back towards the fiercely burning ship, some of the pilots positioned their machines to produce a down draught, drawing the liferafts away from the hull, despite the explosions and the pall of black smoke surrounding their machines and reducing visibility to almost zero.

By 17.50 Zulu, all non-injured personnel and most of the ship's crew were off *Galahad* and the wounded had all been moved to the forecastle at the extreme front of the ship. From the bridge front aft, the ship was a mass of flames and smoke, with exploding ammunition and flames erupting from the after hatch.

Of necessity, helicopter evacuation of the wounded was a difficult process, made extremely dangerous for both aircraft and crews by the debris and explosions, which periodically ripped the sky apart. Twenty-five minutes later, at 18.15 Zulu, the last of the injured had been removed and, after bundling his badly wounded Chief Engineer into a helicopter, Captain Roberts hooked himself onto the winch cable and was hoisted away from the deck, the last man to leave his stricken ship. By now, Captain Green, Master of *Sir Tristram*, had also ordered his men to abandon ship, the fires around the remaining ammunition having proved impossible to control.

In all, 43 soldiers and 7 RFA men were killed at Fitzroy.

Wounded from both ships were eventually transferred to SS *Uganda* for treatment, while the remainder of both crews went first to MV *Atlantic Causeway*.

Two days later, *Galahad*'s crew were transferred to MV *British Test* while *Tristram*'s crew moved to MV *British Trent*, both vessels then proceeding to Ascension Island, from where the crews went home by air.

After some hasty repairs RFA *Sir Tristram* remained in the Falklands as an accommodation ship until 16 May 1983, when she was transported back to the UK on the heavy lift ship *Dan Lifter* for rebuilding. She later re-entered RFA service.

RFA *Sir Galahad*, after a commemorative service on board, was deliberately sunk on 25 July, where she will remain as a designated war grave.

'Curly' Jones, a Welsh Guardsman who nearly died on RFA *Sir Galahad*, has been kind enough to write about his experiences, despite the obvious trauma it involved him in:

I served with the 1st Battalion Welsh Guards as a 19-year-old Guardsman during the Falklands Conflict in 1982. We were part of 5 Infantry Brigade, along with the Scots Guards, Gurkhas, and other units. After being dug in on Sussex Mountain near 'bomb alley' for several days we were taken aboard the assault ship HMS *Fearless* to be projected forward towards Bluff Cove. During the night of the 6/7 June a failed rendezvous with landing craft, due to extreme weather conditions, meant that only half the battalion could embark for the seven-hour journey through horrendous seas.

At the time, I remember feeling quite a sense of relief that I did not make the cut, and so would have at least another day of hot food and shelter aboard Her Majesty's Ship. On 7 June, during daylight, we crossed over to the RFA *Sir Galahad* in the waters of San Carlos. We entered through the rear ramps, and again I was looking forward to hot food and shelter, little realising what lay ahead.

We sat amongst fuel, ammunition, vehicles and other front-line materiel, and made use of the cramped space available to us. I remember sailing during the night, and our information was that we would be going to Bluff Cove to join up with the rest of our battalion.

By daylight on 8 June it was very obvious to us that the ship had anchored. After a long wait, with several orders to don our kit and then to stand down, we were told we were at Fitzroy and not Bluff Cove. We were also told that there were problems with the rear ramp. Eventually we were ordered to place our backpacks on netting, and then in order move to the deck of the *Sir Galahad*, where we would use scrambling nets to disembark the ship. The covers on the deck had been opened to lift our packs up and out of the ship.

I had left the tank deck to climb the stairs when I heard the low flying jets scream over the *Sir Galahad*. We all knew that they were Argentinean, and immediately started to run back into the cargo hold. What happened next was everyone's nightmare. I won't go into the details about the scenes or the fight for life we had; however, it was some considerable amount of time before we came out of the ship. On behalf of about twenty-five injured and able Guardsmen, I will here thank the Royal Fleet Auxiliary Officer whose name none of us discovered, who led us to safety wearing just a towel (I presume he was caught in the shower) after we had got terribly lost and then trapped.

June 8th, *Sir Galahad*, and Fitzroy have very emotional connections, not only to veterans and to the loved ones of those who died, but also to Wales as a nation. I believe that the images that have been shown so often in the media of the *Sir Galahad* burning have become an important part of the Welsh identity over the past quarter of a century.

For twenty years I never mentioned the Falklands to anyone, including my family. I felt as if I had been entrusted with a secret given to me by my friends who died that day. Then out of the blue my wife, Lucy, suggested that I return to the Falklands, and specifically to Fitzroy. She had seen the effects of the Post Traumatic Stress Disorder I had tried so hard to hide. Since returning in 2002 I have looked on my experiences aboard the RFA *Sir Galahad* in a positive way. I formed the Welsh branch of the South Atlantic Medal Association (SAMA Wales), which now helps many veterans and families who are still affected by their experiences of the Falklands Conflict.

By chance I recently met an ex-comrade who was with me in the corridor of the *Galahad*. During the conversation he said to me he gets dreams of a man in a white towel but can't remember how we got out. His relief on hearing that it wasn't a hallucination was a sight to see.

Unfortunately, even now, the *Galahad* may not yet have claimed her last victim. We are working tirelessly in our branch to try to make sure that she has.

During a subsequent attack, LCU 'F4' from *Fearless* was bombed and five of her crew killed, including the Cox'n, Colour Sergeant Brian Johnstone, who, days earlier, had used his clumsy craft to rescue many of the crew from the stricken *Antelope*.

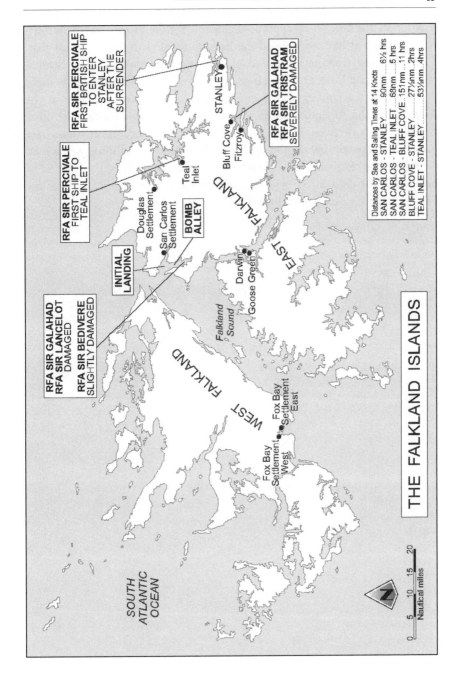

THE FALKLAND ISLANDS

After all this time, justly apportioning blame for the Fitzroy tragedy is difficult, although it has not stopped the bathtub admirals from doing just that.
There were bad decisions made, undoubtedly, but there was also a large element
of pure bad luck. If the LCUs had been able to unload *Sir Tristram* on the night
of 7 June, if the landing craft ramp had not malfunctioned, or even if the
wingman of the Argentine squadron commander had been looking the other
way when they swept out of Port Fitzroy heading for home, history would have
passed this moment by, the Guards would have landed and those young men
would now be old men, telling their Falklands tales in the local pub, instead of
being fathoms deep in the wreck of the *Sir Galahad*, where she lies off the
Falklands, with a hole from a British torpedo in her hull.

CHAPTER ELEVEN

FIRST INTO STANLEY ... AND LAST OUT

RFA *Engadine* and the minesweepers moved into the San Carlos anchorage on 9 June, and the helicopter support crews from the specialist RFA vessel immediately got to work. There was certainly plenty for them to do, as Dave Boulton, one of her crew, recounts:

I got to see quite a few of the damaged helicopters as they came in for repair, one with the entire windscreen area missing where they had been low flying and caught some cables ashore.

They brought the helicopter back in one piece, after hitting the cables, missing their blades then flying along with nothing to stop the freezing wind in their faces and the fan above blowing a storm into the cab. What experts they were, flying that machine.

Then there was another, bullet holes through the floor and they managed to get it back; quite a feat, when you consider that the floor of the cab is merely the top of the fuel tanks. See, we really trained the best flyers. Of course, the maintainers had to fix up the mess the aircraft were in and always there was the talk from them: 'You'll never get me up in one of those.'

On the night that the convoy we were in was to go in, we developed an engine problem and were immediately ordered back out of range of the enemy. We were a very valuable asset as we were the only helicopter carrier there and with all the pilots and aircraft on board. As it was, that was the convoy where the *Plymouth* got hit.

Did I mention that the ships were very cold? They were warm as usual, comfortable for casual wear and shorts etc, but after the *Coventry* got hit, because of the flash-burns it was decided to turn off all heating in the ships and encourage people to dress up warmly at all times, which probably helped to save a few lives.

We did eventually go in and spent a few days with the rest of the fleet watching and waiting for the air attacks.

HMS *Sheathbill*'s landing strip was operational again, allowing the CAPs from *Hermes* and *Illustrious* to increase their endurance over the operational area.

Helicopter operations were in full swing with the Wessex of 845 NAS (five aircraft) and 848 NAS (two aircraft) operating from Teal, along with four others from 847 NAS, moving both provisions and ammunition for both the mortar teams and the RA's 105mm guns up to the battery maintenance areas. Goose

Green was being used as a forward support area for Fitzroy with the Sea Kings of 847 and 825 NAS tasked to this sector.

Meanwhile the wounded from *Sir Tristram* and *Sir Galahad* were being treated aboard *Intrepid* and in the 'Red and Green Life Machine' at San Carlos, while more serious burns victims were taken directly to *Uganda*, which was moved into Grantham Sound to collect the wounded. This sparked, perhaps not unnaturally, a protest from the Argentineans, who claimed she was bringing in military stores.

Kevin Lawrence, a senior member of the RNSTS, remembers the night of 8 June at Empress State Building and the anxious relatives:

I was the Personnel Officer on duty in the Ops Cell in Empire State Building on the early evening of 8 June 82. I vividly remember receiving the call from Northwood asking me to go over to secure communications and the precise words of the message: 'RFAs *Sir Galahad* and *Sir Tristram* bombed, burning and abandoned.' Of course, we immediately started to make what preparations we could to inform families as soon as we had information, but we were faced with an almost impossible situation when, within a couple of hours or so, the ITN 'News at 10' broadcast Mike Nicholson's horrific report which contained those memorable images of helicopters blowing the life-rafts away from the burning *Sir Galahad* and badly-injured personnel coming ashore.

Of course, the phones started ringing immediately and although we answered every question as honestly and as best we could on the basis of the very limited information available to us, the inevitable response from frantic families was: 'It's on the television – you must know what has happened to so and so . . . What aren't you telling me?' This was one of the most harrowing periods for the personnel staff. As I recall it, it was about three days before we were able to account for all personnel. They were spread throughout the Task Force and some were ashore.

Of course, in the end it became clear that three RFA officers were killed. If I remember rightly Ron Hoole was killed separately during the attack on *Atlantic Conveyor*, and we had also lost six Hong Kong Chinese crewmen.

Despite the loss of *Sir Galahad* and *Sir Tristram*, the logistics build-up was still in progress, with RFA *Fort Grange* and *Nordic Ferry* both arriving in San Carlos. *Atlantic Causeway* and RFA *Olna* left for the TRALA, escorted by HMS *Plymouth*, the warship being scheduled for repair by the *Stena Seaspread*, which was now a permanent addition to the Area.

RFA *Sir Geraint*, *Cordella* and *Pict* also left San Carlos that evening, just after the *Plymouth* Group, heading for Port Salvador, where the minesweepers were needed to begin operations in Berkely Sound next evening, while HMS *Intrepid* and *Avenger* went south to support 5 Infantry Brigade's expected advance.

The Carrier Battle Group had spent the day replenishing and towards afternoon, MV *Europic Ferry*, escorted by HMS *Brilliant*, detached from the main group and headed north to rendezvous with helicopter transport *Contender Bezant*.

RFA *Fort Austin* arrived in Cumberland Bay, South Georgia, but after a stay of only a few hours, she was on her way north, homeward bound.

Her Chief Officer remembers the relief this occasioned amongst her crew:

During one of the many RASs I remember that there was nearly a collision between our consort and us and another RFA that had recently arrived. I seem to remember that this was during either thick fog or at night, probably thick fog. I also remember having an altercation with the Flight Commander on *Fort Grange* about getting some mail to us as we were about to leave for home, and he was saying that they were shutting down. So very quickly another Flight Commander off another RFA said that he would collect it for us, as he obviously knew more about what was going on. Eventually we left the Falklands area and went to South Georgia where other ships were collecting all outgoing mail. We then had to steam due east for a couple of days along the iceberg line until it was safe to turn north. I remember having to double up on the night watches and well remember steaming past some huge icebergs some many miles long. I was certainly glad to turn north. On the way north we met up with *Fort Toronto* and filled up with fresh water, through one of the varied rigs that had been devised in this emergency. This was positioned at one end of the so-called motorway service stations. Just before we got back to Ascension we were greeted by a Chinook to collect some of the stores for return to UK. This included at least one Pegasus engine from a Harrier, a mighty underslung load, and then it came back to collect some Lynx engines. The pilot elected to land cross deck and the engines were wheeled and carried on board. We duly anchored off Ascension for a few hours and landed the rest of the urgent returns such as mail. Certain items that we needed were taken on board and then it was back to Devonport.

We had said that we would arrive at 08.00 that morning and so we did, only because we had spent most of the previous night along the coast somewhere. We were welcomed by tugs with their fire hoses saluting us and I seem to remember it was the quickest arrival and shackling on to the buoy that I have ever participated in. Somewhere in the region of about seven minutes from rope on buoy to shackled on with lead in etc. A feat no doubt due to the excellent ship-handling capabilities of Commodore Sam Dunlop. It was very pleasing to see that there was a huge gathering of families and VIPs to welcome us as well as quite a few reliefs.

RFA *Fort Grange* moved into San Carlos next day, the 10th, to begin a provisions RAS. Supplies were getting very low on some ships: RFA *Sir Percivale*, for example, had only two full days' food left. Unfortunately, *Intrepid*'s LCUs, which would have speeded up this replenishment, were in use off Lively Island, helping to land stores at Fitzroy, so *Fort Grange*'s supply RAS was slow. Their trip south had not been uneventful, either, as her Navigator, Mike Day, recalls enthusiastically:

I joined *Fort Grange* in April 1982. She was coming to the hurried end of a refit. I had been on leave when the news came. I had telephoned my appointer at the madhouse and said 'I'm ready to come back when you have a ship.' 'Join the queue, Mike', Terry said. 'We've been inundated with calls, we'll let you know.'

The call came. 'Captain Averill wondered if you'd like to join him as navigator on *Fort Grange* in South Shields? She's got to load and go south, working up on the way with the *Bristol* group.' Of all the bars, in all the world . . . I had sailed with Don Averill twice, the last time as his navigator, standing by the building of the sister-ship, *Fort Austin*, taking her to sea for builders trials, guarantee dry-docking, acceptance trials, RAS gear trials, vibration trials, flying trials, trials trials! We had completed and calibrated every manoeuvre recommended by the Admiralty Manuals. We got to know her every characteristic and wobble, during the course of which, we had also developed a very special working relationship, quite unique in my time at sea. Sailing with Captain A, as he was usually known, could not have been better from my point of view. He was a friend. It was a dream ticket.

I drove up to South Shields with my gear. The ship was a hive of industry – I'd never seen a refit like it before. I started sorting the navigation outfit and got special help from the Hydrographer's office, probably, I thought, because I had recently done some work with them on RFA chart outfits. Then one of the Third Officers was having problems with lifeboat stores. I phoned a stores contact – no problems. After a day or two, I realised that everyone and anyone ashore was prepared to move mountains once it was hinted, 'We've got a problem. We're due south and . . .'

We sailed to *Plymouth* to load victualling and naval stores. Captain Averill, the SRO and I went to Northwood for our briefing. The energy was amazing and contagious. I took my car home prior to sailing to Glen Douglas to load the heavy stuff. In a Happy Eater on the A38 I saw the TV news – 'HMS *Sheffield* has been hit by an Exocet missile and abandoned . . .' I was not a happy eater anymore. This was not going to be an exercise. Taking leave of my family was different this time. My will had been made and signed. Dad, who had been at D-Day +3, aged 18, shook my hand and I felt we connected as equals for the first time ever.

There had been a fire on board during the refit, which had damaged the degaussing [demagnetising of the hull to protect the ship from magnetic-fused mines]. It had been repaired and after I had drawn the minefield on the chart at the entrance to Port Stanley, Captain Averill agreed we needed to recalibrate the DG before going south. A staff officer could not see the point. I assured him that, sitting on top of 5,000 tons of HE, we could, so please arrange it or my Captain would be on the phone.

We sailed from Glen Douglas after having loaded in triple time – the 'Stonnery' were working miracles. Rumour had it we had every last 4.5-inch shell, 500 pound bomb and anything else you could think of, scoured from every depot in the UK. Those wonderful rumours kept the people on board focused, excited, wondering . . .

STO(N)'s men had resorted to tomming down cargo in the holds – a good old Merchant Navy practice which I had drawn nice diagrams of to pass my Board of Trade 1st Mate's exams. When we checked the draft marks prior to sailing we knew the STO(N) team had done VERY well. As far as the Board of Trade was concerned, we were EXACTLY on our marks, nudge, nudge.

We picked up the flight, embarking 824 'C' Flight from Culdrose. Apparently the flight had not existed a couple of months before. We went to Portland for flight instrument calibrations, flight and ship safety exercises, the DG calibrations and the last bits of essential items still outstanding for STO(N).

The timetable for sailing with the *Bristol* group had never worked out. We were on our own. We drew up a two-week programme of testing every bit of gear including the Type 182 sonar and the chaff rockets. We planned a very fast passage to Ascension with only essential periods of slowing down for streaming and recovering the sonar to test the bodies, sea boat exercises and the like. 'Sail Friday PM', said QHM. I got very swift feedback that the lads were not happy – 'Friday, unlucky, not on.' I spoke to Captain Averill. 'Sort it, Mike.'

I explained to the chap in QHM s office: 'The lads are not happy . . . Superstition . . . Friday sailing . . . Sorry to incur overtime but . . .' A silence, some thinking, and then: '10.00 Saturday OK?' We parted such good chums.

For the last few weeks you felt everyone was going that bit extra. As a result they all felt they were doing their part for the war effort. It was magic.

We left Ushant on our port quarter with a plan that the lighthouse would be the last contact with land before Ascension. Avoid the shipping lanes, avoid all ships. And thus began our self-imposed work-up; tougher than any staff-imposed work-up at Portland. Reading manuals, checking SOP cards; meetings about flying, RASing, air defence (one GMPG, one LMG and twelve SLRs!), anti-sub strategy, anti-Exocet tactics . . .

Exercises, exercises, exercises.

In '79 whilst building *Fort Austin*, Captain A had released me for RNR training at *Dryad*, the Navy's Operations school. 'You are invited to a special warfare course for RNR List 1, including the operating of the new AEFSs as CCH replacements (*Blake* and *Tiger* were going, going, gone)'. Some parts of Navy Ops saw the 'Forts' as Sea King platforms with a RAS(S) capability. There were not that many ships with Sea King capabilities – except RFAs. We had also learned and practiced the operational deployment of Chaff Charlie and Delta in the role of an anti-Soviet surface-to-surface missile defence. How useful. I drew up a paper explaining how it could save us against the Exocets for the Captain and bridge team. That made them happier.

We steamed, sorry guys, motored south doing incredible daily runs and very grateful for the brand new Satnav MOD had fitted – there was a lot of thick cloud this far out in the Atlantic. Sextants stayed in their boxes. We tested ourselves, tested gear, found faults and fixed them. The Flight drew up a plan for ripple three or ripple two ASW patrols ahead of the ship; we would have anti-torpedo sonar towed astern. The bridge team got familiar with anti-torpedo manoeuvres (no green grenades this time, lads!) and the chaff rockets were loaded, tested and the panel lights lit.

'We'll need extra lookouts,' said someone at a meeting, 'they won't like that.' I put up notices on the messes and 120 people volunteered. That summed up how 350 souls gelled as one amorphous mass and *Fort Grange* became an enthusiastic unit of the Task Force. Now to find it, the Task Force that is.

We anchored at Ascension and the flight VERTREPed urgent stores here and there. Boats and craft scurried over the flat blue sea. That had to be savoured. The

QE2 came from the north, and steamed by, not stopping, with helos zapping around her like flies around . . . a honey pot? She looked as though she was on a Caribbean cruise in her Cunard livery and the glorious sunshine; had she always had those flight decks?

We pressed on south, with some strangers in the cabins behind the chart room. Ask no questions. Need to know? We had other things to focus on. ASW exercises – intelligence reports to read – a complete change of mindset. We had crossed a border, the South Atlantic began here, and we aimed for Point 'X-ray', 1,000 miles due east of the Falklands, to await further orders.

In the roaring forties now, and they roared. Thinking about some breakfast and bang, the ship seemed to stop. Everything went silent, then alarm bells went off. We had been hit by a wave on the port bow. The port for'd RAS pocket door had been forced in. Tons of sea water had gone down a lift shaft and ingressed electrical switchboards. Temporary chaos, then more work for some people to repair the damage and a sense that we had to be more careful. There was a huge crack one-and-a-half inches wide, across the deck between the amidships accommodation and the funnel. The ship had been stiff and created her own expansion joint.

We continued south. Grey seas, grey skies. We rendezvoused with *Glasgow* in foul weather conditions, to back-RAS useful stores by VERTREP. She had been hit by a bomb which had entered just above the starboard waterline, gone through the auxiliary machinery room and after engine room and out through the other side without exploding but doing an incredible amount of damage. She had stayed until *Bristol*'s group arrived and then headed north, somewhat reluctantly. We saw the entry hole, patched up of course – my first photos of the real war.

She had a big black line painted vertically down the funnel and continuing down the hull. Useful for the Argie pilots to line up on said one wag on the bridge, the first remembered comment that the black humour of warfare would generate. The bomb hole was close to it – the wag was right.

We continued south again. Point 'X-ray' ahead and closing. Another grey morning, cloud continuous, level about 1,000 feet. A call on a sound-powered phone from the flight deck. Are we rendezvousing with a Hercules? It sounds like there's one around. The Joint Services Recognition Journal had had pictures of Pakistani Air Force Hercules with underwing equipment for slinging 500 pound bombs on. Intelligence said that the Argies had bought some of the equipment for their own Hercules. It couldn't be, could it? There goes breakfast again.

'Hands to Action Stations. This is no drill. Unidentified aircraft in the vicinity. Air raid warning red. Hands to action stations.'

'Oh my God', I think, 'Is this where it all ends? What to do? Send a flash signal to CTG with our position for a start! Portland, Thursday War, it's all coming back. Thank you, staff.'

The Flight close up and break out the SLRs, etc. (I have a vision of a picture I saw as a child, of Italian Alpine soldiers, under a trellis, using the spars to support their rifles as they aim at an Austrian biplane in World War 1). I suggest to Captain A that if it is that special Herkie bird, showing him the picture, it will probably approach from astern (Why am I thinking of the Ranger-class with their off-set funnel, bridge and forward mast? Wishing ours were.) The best thing we can do is once it's sighted, presuming it will have to break through the cloud base for a visual run, at about two miles go hard a port and turn a quick ninety degrees off course, hoping the bombs will fall where we aren't any longer. It is agreed. We wait, and wait, and wait. Nothing. Let's stand down.

'Aircraft visual astern!' from the flight FDO link. It's the Hercules. 'Stand by hard a port, stand by, stand by' – and the aircraft breaks starboard and climbs through the clouds and disappears. What is going on? Did she think we were a warship? Grey is such a glorious livery! How my Merchant Navy colleagues laughed at our dull scheme. Who's laughing now?

Not the crew of the BP tanker *British Wye*, on whom the Hercules deposited the bombs later that morning. Fortunately the Argentinean Air Force still had not got the fusing right and Second Officer Peter Breeze RFA, the on-board liaison officer, had the frightening pleasure of seeing one bomb hit the foc'sle and bounce overboard, as he told me years later.

What now? 'Head west, best speed, and close the Task Group' says CTG and we head into the sea and swell, grateful someone cares.

The Ops team group in the chart room at noon Zulu time, to listen to BBC World service and plan the next twenty-four hours. 'What's Saatchi and Saatchi got planned for us today?' asks Ben, the Flight Ops Officer, grinning. That's how we are coping with the realisation that there is danger around.

Captain A chats over a cigarette and a cup of coffee. 'I started my career in a lifeboat, Mike. I wonder if I'll end it in one?' Strangely, that is reassuring. This man has done it all before. What's to worry about? A tangible link to World War Two standing right next to me. Special.

We joined the Task Group at night, in fog, whilst *Fort Austin* was back-RASing to an 'R'-boat. Darken ship (of course), I-band radar silence, long-leg zigzag – TAC-bay working over-time and yet not quite sure we were aware of everything. The previous three weeks had been a doddle compared to this challenge. We caused a few heart-stoppers and eventually got sorted with clandestine use of radar and a report to the Commodore in the morning – oops.

Then began a RAS(S) programme of immense proportions – the ships were short of so much, some on hard tack. Food, stores, ammo. VERTREP helped relieve the situation. Not quite what the young pilots had expected. Underslung loads of pairs of 500 pound bombs to *Hermes*, a few fiddles on the flight deck, then slung under the wings of a Sea Harrier and straight on for delivery to Stanley, Goose Green and the like.

Bristol was assigned as our buddy ship. A technical PO and a couple of lads came across and suddenly we had secure speech. Those sockets had been fitted to RFAs since the sixties but were always 'for' and not 'with'. One headset in the Chart Room. As I listened in for the first time I realised we really had been like a stranger at a dinner table. This was where it all happened. This is where you asked, received, planned, were turned down, whatever. Not in written immediate signals taking six hours to arrive and getting lost on someone s table because of an inappropriate DIG. This is how the Task Group had broken down the barriers and become a cohesive body. Thank you, Commodore, *Bristol* and (Sir) Caspar Weinberg, as it was rumoured.

There was a daily signal of lessons learned where frank advice was given to counter the daily threat as it changed.

'In the absence of operating chaff launchers, take the aluminium strips out of the chaff rocket and stuff them down the barrel of a Schermuly line-throwing gun and fire when chaff is ordered.' So advised the Chief Officer of one ship. Thank goodness we had no problems with the chaff launchers, rockets or resupply, sitting on the biggest magazine in the South Atlantic.

'Tie a biscuit tin on a long line underneath your Lynx helicopter and have her stationed up-threat. At the appropriate Zippo warning . . .' Flight Commander did not see the funny side of my suggestion that we could use the radar reflectors from one of our Board of Trade lifeboats in lieu of the biscuit tin, slung under a Sea King. I was only joking, honest.

There was some very valuable advice in those signals, and probably more importantly, they gave us a feeling of everyone in it together. We could think out loud to find new ways of overcoming our problems. We were all part of a team, and any judgements would come later.

The next fortnight was an intensive series of events: adventures, dramas, tragedies, heroism, futile gestures and purposeful acts. The *Grange* ran like a well-oiled machine, everyone did more than pull their weight, they punched above it.

On 14 June the final peace agreement was signed. I overheard a staff officer on secure speech say, 'Well, it has been the planned day for six weeks now, so that's not bad.' If that was true I would have said it was brilliant. My Dad said it was the best birthday present he'd ever had.

Captain A left shortly afterwards, by Hercules and in-flight refuelling (rather than in-flight entertainment) to Ascension and a more conventional aircraft home. He had not been well for some time, losing his night vision just after Ascension, and other problems accruing unfairly. *Grange* turned out to be his swan song.

I stayed with her for another thirteen months, getting two weeks' leave in October, finally leaving the Falklands in May 1983. I only saw Captain A once more, in retirement at his home in Dorset. Our three-month stint together had been a most intensive and dare I say it, an exciting period. For me, nothing at sea would ever be quite the same again.

The *Grange*'s people on board had bonded as a team. It had been a unique experience for everyone. When we arrived in *Plymouth* one Sunday morning in October '82 there was a certain sadness to see that bond broken, as people left to rejoin their families. The very families and friends who had come out in three Fleet tenders to welcome us home on that grey morning, so similar to a fine day in the Falklands.

One of the STO(N) men came to see me before he left. 'I wanted to let you know, as I will probably never come to sea again, my abiding memory will be your noon announcements on the Tannoy and talking us through the air raids. You sounded like someone reading the news on the BBC. Thank you for the memory.' I don't think I told him, I really had been imagining myself as one of the famous Home Service war news announcers in particular: 'Here is the news and this is Alvar Lidell reading it.' AL had passed on to the Home Service in the sky the year before, at Northwood, Middlesex, where this Falklands conflict had been directed from, in a bunker at HMS *Warrior*.

Fuel for both ships and aircraft was in short supply too, so RFA *Blue Rover*, having completed her pumpover from the STUFT in the TRALA, rejoined the Battle Group during the day, leaving for the San Carlos anchorage, with *Ambuscade*, in the late afternoon, arriving after dark.

A forward helicopter operating base had now been established at Fitzroy, with four Wessex of 847 NAS operating from it continually. The big RAF Chinook was tasked to keep the fuel dumps here and at the San Carlos Settlement base topped up, a job which occupied most of its flying hours.

The LSLs were still making the run into Teal Inlet, with RFA *Sir Geraint* finishing her off-load there today.

The Argentine Air Force had not completely given up, either, attempting a rocket attack on the Royal Artillery battery at Mount Kent, under cover of smoke from their own guns, without, however inflicting any damage. They also attempted a number of raids from the mainland, although none of these were pressed home once the Port Stanley radar station had detected activity from the Battle Group's Harriers.

RFAs *Fort Grange* and *Olna*, along with MVs *Atlantic Causeway* and *Baltic Ferry*, moved out of San Carlos tonight (10 June), heading for the Carrier Battle Group, while HMS *Active* and *Arrow* moved inshore to bombard Stanley overnight. And aboard RFA *Resource*, the mail arrived, bringing with it a nice new addition to the ship's library, as her diary records:

The mail today included the new edition of an Approach Chart to Port Stanley, its timely appearance suggesting *Resource*'s possible future movements

Today, 11 June, saw final preparations made for the push on Stanley. The airfield came under attack early in the morning by four of *Hermes*' Sea Harriers. Meeting intense anti-aircraft fire, the Harriers lofted their bombs at the dispersal areas, in what was to be their last attack. The bombs caused damage and fires but did not destroy any of the Pucara fighter-bombers that were their intended targets.

This wasn't the only air attack of the day. Almost as the Harriers began their climb away from the airfield, an 848 NAS Wessex 5, armed with AS 12 missiles, and accompanied by a second Wessex gunship of 845 NAS, moved in from the north and fired two missiles at Stanley's police station, which the British commanders believed was being used as the Argentine military HQ. Unfortunately, the first AS 12 malfunctioned, landing a bare 200 yards from an

Argentine hospital ship, the *Bahia Paraiso*, anchored on the waterfront. The second, however, functioned perfectly, entering the top storey of the building and inflicting heavy casualties on the Argentine Intelligence Section officers still asleep there.

Later in the day, the RAF's GR3 Harriers bombed Two Sisters, Mount Harriet and Mount Longdon, in preparation for the assault that night, while the Sea Harriers spent an uneventful day flying CAPs over the area.

In San Carlos, *Sir Percivale* finished loading and left for Teal in the evening, escorted by HMS *Exeter*, which returned with *Sir Geraint*, while *Blue Rover* spent the day replenishing ships and topping up the onshore fuel dumps.

Intrepid repeated her overnight run to Lively Island, dropping three LCUs for Fitzroy and returning before dawn, while RFA *Sir Bedivere* and MV *Elk* left the Carrier Battle Group in company, San Carlos bound.

The survivors of *Sir Galahad* and *Sir Tristram* also left the TA today aboard *Atlantic Causeway*, from where they were transferred to *British Test* and *British Trent* respectively for the journey to Ascension. SS *Uganda* was also busy, regularly moving into Grantham Sound during daylight for casualty evacuation. Today, she had the *Hecla* for company.

In South Georgia, RFA *Fort Austin* finally turned her bows north, departing for Ascension, while, in the UK, MV *Avalona Star*, carrying both fresh and frozen provisions, left Portsmouth, heading south.

At 23.00, 42 Commando attacked Mount Harriet Ridge and 3 Para assaulted Mount Longdon and Wireless Ridge. 45 Commando attacked Two Sisters an hour later, at midnight. By early morning on 12 June all objectives had been achieved and the troops had gone firm in their new positions. Now within striking distance of Stanley, preparations began for the final assault.

On that same morning HMS *Glamorgan* was hit and set on fire by truck-mounted Exocet, fired from Port Stanley High Street. The ship had detected the inbound missile and had tried to evade by turning away from it. The missile hit astern, entering the hanger where it exploded, destroying the ship's Wessex 3 and starting fires in the galley and the gas turbine gear room. This latter was quickly put out by steam drenching, so the ship experienced no loss in speed or manoeuvrability, although the galley and hangar fires proved more of a problem. By 7.00, however, all fires were out and *Glamorgan* was on her way back to the Carrier Battle Group.

In San Carlos the logistics effort was still progressing normally, with *Sir Geraint* back-loading ammunition for Teal from MV *Elk* and AVCAT from RFA *Blue Rover*, while, at Teal, *Sir Percivale* was getting on with her off-load. MV *Norland*, playing a somewhat unexpected role, was off the River Plate, unloading casualties.

Replenishment activity remained intense, *Resource*'s diary for the 12th recording:

Replenishment operations were carried out with the following warships:
HMS *Active* between 12.14 and 13.34 . . . Rig 2, fourteen loads.
HMS *Avenger* between 17.16 and 18.29 . . . eleven loads.
HMS *Ambuscade* between 23.46 and 04.26 [next morning] on rigs 7 and 5, fifty-five loads sent across.

The Marines and Paras were secure in their new positions by 08.00, although continual artillery and mortar fire was still causing casualties. Sea King 4s of 846 NAS moved the 105mm guns of the Royal Marines' own 29 Commando Artillery Regiment up to new firing positions to discourage the enemy's gunners.

Later that evening both RFA *Blue Rover* and *Sir Geraint* left the Transport Area (TA), the latter bound for Teal inlet, which she reached some hours later, having passed RFA *Sir Percivale*, on her way out through the Port Salvador Narrows, at 10.00, while RFA *Olna* moved in to San Carlos for replenishment activities.

By next day, 13 June, everything was set for the infantry's final push, although the Argentines still managed to supply a fortunately minor distraction with an air attack on 3 Commando Brigade's Tactical HQ on Mount Kent. Either by luck or good intelligence, this attack coincided with an Operations Group briefing, attended by Brigadier Thompson, his unit commanders and Major General Moore. No one was injured although a Scout and a Gazelle helicopter, parked in the nearby helicopter operating base, were damaged.

In the early afternoon, an awkward landing by the RAF Chinook damaged HMS *Sheathbill*'s landing area, forcing two of *Hermes*' Sea Harriers to make use of the LPD's deck landing space, apparently the first time Sea Harriers had done so.

It was business more or less as usual in the TA at San Carlos, with *Baltic Ferry* and the ammunition transport MV *Lycaon* moving in, while *Nordic Ferry* left, accompanied by HMS *Penelope* and also covered by HMS *Cardiff*, on duty as the anti-aircraft guard-ship, somewhere outside the north entrance to Falkland Sound.

While on passage, the warships detected a group of aircraft flying along the southern coast of East Falkland, and the *Cardiff* used Sea Dart to shot the leader down. This was the last successful missile engagement by a British warship before the cease-fire.

In Port Stanley, after the last transport aircraft left, the CO of VYCA 2, the Argentine radar station, rendered his TPS-43 radar unserviceable before the final assault.

Meanwhile, at 22.00, after a sustained artillery and mortar barrage, 2 Para moved forward to assault Wireless Ridge, while the Scots Guards attacked Mount Tumbledown.

By midnight, 2 Para had taken their objective and were seeking General Moore's permission to move forward. Tumbledown was proving harder to crack, being garrisoned by Argentine Marines, who exploited their deep, well-sited positions to utmost advantage. Heavy shellfire from the RA, the Para's own mortars and the guns of HMS *Active* and *Avenger* shifted the balance in the end and the Argentine Marines finally began to retreat as day broke and as the Gurkhas outflanked them with their capture of Mount William.

With the coming of daylight, 40 Commando's 'Alpha' and 'Charlie' companies prepared for an opposed helicopter assault on Sapper Hill, but the first lift was barely down before an order to cease fire came through.

Menendez, the Argentine Governor, was asking for peace terms.

At 8.00 local (midnight GMT) on 14 June 1982, Menendez and Major General Moore signed the formal Instrument of Surrender.

In the UK, the business of administration continued as normal. In a somewhat ironic twist of fate, on the same day the surrender was signed in the Falklands, the Death and Injury Compensation Agreement for merchant sailors serving with Task Force was finally agreed back home.

Next morning, 15 June, the 2nd Battalion, Parachute Regiment entered Port Stanley and hoisted the Governor's flag on the flagstaff outside his official residence. After an absence of seventy-four days, the British were back.

The fighting may have been over but the war, especially for the RFA, still had some way to run. Back with the Task Force, the 16th saw RFA *Plumleaf* relieved from motorway tanking and heading north to Ascension, while *British Wye* found herself still in the TRALA, as one of her embarked RFA crew describes:

Our first r/v [rendezvous] and RAS(L) was with *Olmeda* on 5 June. We started at 13.45 and completed at 02.58.

Next RAS started at 14.20 and completed at 01.18, I think with *Tidepool*. She had winch problems so we finished for the night and tried again next day. Starting at 09.20, we finished at 15.40, including an emergency breakaway when *Tidepool* lost her boilers and nearly lost her rig. We spent the next couple of days waiting in the logistics area, and were lined up for our next RAS(L) on 12 June.

One of the stranger sights in the TRALA box was *Canberra*. Having landed her troops in San Carlos she was sent to wait with the rest of us. I remember one calm clear night seeing her fully lit up, rather like that scene from *A Night to Remember* just before the *Titanic* hit the iceberg; you could almost hear the band playing.

Again 14 June was a long day, we started with *Olna* at 09.50 and completed at 14.31, then *Tidepool* from 14.26 to 06.49 next morning. This included two BIG Corpen Novembers.

A couple of days respite then we met with *Olna* for a RAS(L), we started at 16.10 and completed at 18.12, bad weather being the problem.

We tried again next day, starting at 10.30 and finishing at 23.29. Looking at the logbook it seems we had a few moments with gyro problems. We returned to the TRALA box and VERTREPed drummed lub-oil to *Olna* and *Eburna*.

By this time we were completely out of cargo. We were directed to join the main body of the task group, and we were given a screening position that had Peter Breeze and me rabbiting though ATP1. I sometimes wondered just what the RN expected of merchant ships, with tactical maneuvering, RAS and flying operations. There were a lot of ships around *Hermes* but we found our station. We then embarked about thirty passengers from *Hermes*, all part of 899 NAS, mostly pilots and ground crew. *Hermes* finally released us on the 20 June at 16.48.

Our return to Ascension and UK was uneventful, we fitted in our passengers, and Peter Breeze squared up the cargo accounts. After a few hours in Ascension to collect mail and food etc we sailed for Portland and berthed at OCP.

Captain David Rundle was awarded an OBE in the Falkland honours list.

On 17 June RFA *Sir Percivale* had the honour of being the first ship into Port Stanley after the cease-fire, as her Master, Captain Tony Pitt, well remembers:

Sir Percivale received final instructions to proceed to Port Stanley to arrive at the narrows at 12.30 in company with *Sir Bedivere*. We assumed we would meet them somewhere off Port William. Cleared Port Salvador narrows at 06.40 and proceeded to Stanley. We kept our fingers crossed that the stated minefield areas were correct and nothing had been laid in Port William. There was no sign of *Sir Bedivere* in the area and at first light we turned into Port William on the final leg. The only vessel in sight was the Argentinean hospital ship *Admiral Iridzar* which was at anchor to the west of Port William. We thought that *Sir Bedivere* might already be lying alongside in Port Stanley but no, as we passed through the narrows at 12.30 precisely, preceded by a 'V' formation of helicopters, we realised we were the first to arrive and were very honoured to be doing so. We anchored off the Public Jetty and had our several blasts on the ships whistle answered by the cathedral bells. This was a better day for the RFAs, and the LSLs in particular.

Launched the Mexeflote and awaited instructions. We resumed our service as a refuelling deck once the helos realised we were around and, appropriately, we achieved landing 1,000 during Operation Corporate. A Sea King, callsign 'VS', took the final reward.

Later in the day, 'X', 'Y' and 'Z' Companies of 45 Cdo were embarked for 'R and R', all very dirty and tired. Relaxed water rationing for the first time since leaving UK and resolved to make them as comfortable as possible. We sailed Port Stanley at 19.30 bound for San Carlos Water and an important meeting with RFA *Fort Grange* for resupply of provisions, both solid and liquid.

The other RFAs weren't so far behind, either, as one of RFA *Tidepool*'s crew remembers:

Then it was all over and we moved round to Stanley, discharged the remainder of our cargo and awaited what was to happen to us. In view of *Tidepool* being due a refit and major survey when she was sold, her certificates had little life left when we sailed for Chile originally. Now they were well out of date. During some of the alongside harbour fuellings we had suffered various bumps and bruises, the worst I think from an LPD that tried to get into our laundry one dark night. Only two of the six lifeboats were serviceable, the others suffering davit damage. Luckily we had acquired plenty of liferafts. Cosmetically we were looking like a rust bucket.

RFA *Engadine* was quickly moved into the Port Stanley anchorage as well, as cook Dave Bolton explains:

When the truce or whatever was signed, we were sent round to Stanley straight away and were one of the first ships in there because they needed our helicopter facilities. Of course, we were anchored out and at the time, if we wanted to go ashore, we had to go up on the flight deck, wave to the flight deck captain to let him know we were there, then as helos were landing and a space was available, we were waved forward and got the chance to get ashore.

Even that had its problems: we had just got airborne, when there was a whiteout as the snow came in and the pilot decided to land on one of the little islands around the harbour. An aircrewman had to look out of the door as we came in to guide the landing and also to look for mines!

Once the snow had passed, we then landed at the local racecourse, as that was the landing centre.

Wandered around, and had to keep in the roads and paths marked by white tape as these were areas clear of mines. Took a few photos, got cold, saw the helos and Harriers do a victory flypast, got the camera out just in time to get a picture.

Then it was a case of standing there and holding up your arm till a helo landed and picked you up and you gave them your destination. One of the things very noticeable was that as soon as you mentioned your ship and job, you got very good treatment, sometimes preferential. It was good to be a cook down there.

Once we got round to Stanley, a signal went out to all the fleet that clocks would be changed to local time. We had been on northern time, just one of the ploys to fox the enemy, so, on one day, once we had finished breakfast, it was time to do dinner, with no lunch in between. But it all got sorted out and made for an interesting time.

In the UK, things seemed to be quickly returning to normal, with the National Union of Seamen in dispute with the RFA management over what war bonus was payable to RFA personnel.

Operation Corporate wasn't quite over, however. South Thule still had to be dealt with.

In 1977 Argentina had secretly established a scientific base on the South Sandwich island of South Thule. This island was then part of the Falkland Islands Dependencies, which made it British Crown territory.

Completely ignoring this fact, the Argentines erected a number of pre-fabricated buildings and imported some very sophisticated equipment to enable the base to function as a meteorological and communications centre as well as being involved in monitoring sea and ice conditions.

Usually, the base had a staff of about forty, mostly naval personnel, although it could comfortably accommodate about twice that number. Between April and October, the southern hemisphere winter, staff numbers were usually reduced to about ten.

It may also have been used as an advanced base for the Falklands invasion because, in what many observers saw as a premeditated initial move in the invasion of South Georgia, the ARA *Bahio Paraiso* called here, in March 1982, to collect men and equipment before taking part in the 3 April attack on King Edward Point.

Obviously, once the formal surrender of the Falklands had taken place, the occupation of South Thule could not be allowed to continue, so on 15 June, Admiral Woodward was ordered to re-occupy the place.

This was easier said than done. The vanguard of the seasonal pack ice was less than thirty miles from the island, which meant that, within weeks, the whole island would be encircled by an ice field so dense that any Task Force ship, even the ice-strengthened RFAs, would have the greatest difficulty breaking through it.

RFA *Olmeda*, HMS *Yarmouth*, HMS *Endurance* and the tug *Salvageman* were selected for the job, designated 'Operation Keyhole'. Overall command was in the hands of *Endurance*'s captain, Nick Barker.

Together with the ships, Barker also had four helicopters. RFA *Regent*'s Wessex was crammed into half of *Endurance*'s hangar, the rest being occupied by her two Wasps, while *Olmeda* had retained one of her two precious Sea Kings.

To carry out the actual invasion, Barker had *Endurance*'s own Marine detachment, a large part of 'M' Company and two Blowpipe detachments, the whole force commanded by Captain Christopher Nunn RM.

Barker left South Georgia, where he and his ship had been acting as Harbour Master, on 17 June, together with *Salvageman*. *Yarmouth* and *Olmeda* left the Task Group on 16 June, rendezvousing with *Regent* on the 18th. *Olmeda* took on a large volume of food from *Regent* by jackstay, and thus prepared, if necessary, for a long stay in the ice, she and the Type 12 frigate entered Cumberland Bay, embarked 'M' Company, and sailed south the same evening.

On their way to South Thule, the Marines and helicopter crews occupied their time stripping the helicopter interiors so that twenty-four armed Royal Marines could be dropped on the island in one lift. To avoid unnecessary loss of life, a message calling upon the Argentines to surrender was broadcast as *Endurance* and *Salvageman* left Cumberland Bay, but South Thule offered no reply.

Barker's two ships reached their destination early on 19 June. A reconnaissance party was landed, prior to a bombardment by *Yarmouth* when she arrived on the 20th.

Battery Sergeant Major Brum Richards, of 148 (Meiktila) Commando Battery RA, was lifted in by helicopter and had just taken up his spotting position on the island when the shoot was called off because a white flag had been seen flying over the Argentine positions, almost as soon as *Endurance* put in an appearance off Ferguson Bay.

Landing by *Olmeda*'s Sea King, 'M' Company's Marines swiftly cleared the buildings, capturing one civilian and nine military personnel, who were then evacuated to *Olmeda* by helicopter. With the prisoners aboard, the tanker and *Yarmouth* departed immediately for South Georgia. *Endurance* and *Salvageman* remained a further three days while the base's buildings were searched and sealed by the former's Marines, eventually leaving on 22 June to arrive in Cumberland Bay on the 24th.

In the mean time, *Yarmouth* had refuelled from *Olmeda*, making this the furthest south RAS on record, while another record for the furthest south 'splicing the main brace' was also claimed by the group on the birth of HRH Prince William on 22 June.

Some days later, aerial photographs showed South Thule completely encircled by impenetrable pack ice. Keyhole had been a close-run thing.

Back in the Falkland Islands, the Port William anchorage was soon crowded with ships, although the Royal Navy did not have a chance to relax since no acknowledgement was received from Argentina of an end to hostilities.

By 21 June, however, after most of the Argentine POWs had been transported home in *Canberra* and *Norland*, the new President of Argentina, General Bignone, agreed that the ceasefire should be observed although he added that peace could not be declared until the Malvinas were returned to Argentina. In light of this declaration, it was clear that a significant British presence would have to be maintained in the area.

Canberra was on her way home by 25 June, carrying most of 3 Commando, while *Norland* and *Europic Ferry* had also left, with the two Parachute Battalions as passengers.

And in a farewell of a different kind, RFA *Sir Galahad*, still carrying many of the Welsh Guards who died aboard her, was towed out of Fitzroy Cove and scuttled off Port Stanley, torpedoed by HMS *Onyx*. A sad end to a parfait, gentle knight and to some of the men who served her so long and so well.

The rest of the RFAs were still hard at it even then, with RAS and VERTREP going on day and night. In typical RFA style, though, their crews had quickly returned to normal, as *Resource*'s diary for 24 June makes abundantly clear:

Many of the ship's company took the first opportunity they had had since 5 April to leave RFA *Resource* and explore a new hull! And the NAAFI shop on *Fort Grange* proved most popular, with cinema-style queues building up to gain items previously unobtainable.

During the day, the first girl that some of us had seen for many weeks was noticed at the port forward end of *Canberra*'s No 24 lifeboat. All binoculars on RFA *Resource*'s bridge were in use at this time!

Meanwhile, in Stanley, some of the RCT men from the LSL's home port of Marchwood were having some interesting times, as their Commanding Officer recounts:

I have a couple of odd memories of those times:

– a particular MN Mate (this is after the conflict when I was working with my Squadron to discharge the enormous line of ships remaining to be discharged) who whenever I went on board always greeted me at the top of the pilot ladder in his bedroom slippers! Slightly odd in the prevailing weather conditions!

– going with cap in hand to the *Bedivere*, probably two days after the surrender, when I was trying to set up my Squadron ashore in Stanley, and unsuccessfully trying to persuade my good friend (or at least he was!), the Ch Off Richard Williams, to let us have some lunch five minutes after lunchtime on board had finished!

– told by my boys on the *Galahad* – prior to the disaster at Fitzroy, when a 1,000 pound bomb hit the ship and was lodged somewhere up for'ard and did not explode. It was decided to lift the bomb off the ship and so a crane operator, Driver Brough, duly was detailed, someone else hooked it up and the offending item was lifted gently over the side into a Gemini which had been pre-lined with boxes of cornflakes to soften the ride! The Gemini was then driven carefully away from the ship and at a respectable distance, the bomb was slipped over the side harmlessly. I wonder if Mr Kellogg ever knew the alternative use for his main product?

– our main point of discharge, post conflict, was a slipway 300 metres east of the main jetty in Stanley harbour. Thousands and thousands of tons of stores, vehicles, etc were discharged over this slipway in the months immediately after the conflict. A notable commodity in the early days was compo rations, huge numbers of which had been shipped to supply and feed not only the Task Force but also the huge numbers of POWs.

– one of the priority items to discharge immediately after the conflict was AM2 runway matting, which was needed urgently to lay down over the Stanley airport runway and make a surface good enough for C-130s to land on. This matting came in strips measuring six feet by two feet and was delivered in bundles of ten or twelve strips at a time. Because of the urgency of the requirement I was tasked to get the matting ashore with all possible haste. The standard method of moving kit ashore was to lighter it ashore by Mexeflote, a slow and time consuming method particularly because most of the ships had to stay in the outer harbour because of their size. It was therefore at least a two-mile transit to the slipway and in the prevailing Falklands weather that was a lengthy transit. There were a few Chinook heavy-lift helicopters around and so we decided to try and short-cut the normal system by lifting bundles of matting directly from the hold of the ship. The ships carrying the matting (two of them) were large five-hatch freighters with tall derricks, but despite the height, the Chinooks could just reach the cargo in the hold using a 100-foot strop – the longest they work with. The wind is always a factor in the Falklands and inevitably as the helicopter lifted the first load clear of the deck, the wind caught it and swung it dangerously close to the rigging. The pilot was concerned for the safety of his aircraft and jettisoned the load, causing some Marchwood stevedores to jump quickly for their lives! Thankfully they were paying attention! Plan B – well if lifting the loads directly from the ship was not possible, I thought perhaps we could put some on to a Mexeflote, move it away from the side of the ship, and pick up by Chinook from there – no rigging to worry about. So, we loaded a Mexe with some bundles of matting, moved it to a suitably clear piece of water and called in the Chinook. Now this aircraft has a huge downdraught, especially as it approaches and goes into the hover – you can probably guess the rest – the helicopter never actually caught up with the Mexeflote, which was blown down the harbour by the downdraught ahead of the approaching helicopter! The fastest Mexeflote in the west was born! Plan C was adopted – take the cargo ashore and use the tried and tested (and slow) method.

Next day, 26 June, saw *Resource* homeward bound, having previously consolidated her stores with her sister ship *Regent*. RFA *Stromness* was Full Away on Passage the next day as well, having embarked the men of 45 Commando during the previous two days. RFAs *Sir Geraint* and *Sir Percivale* also left for the UK around this time, the former sailing for Ascension on the 30th, while 'Sir Percy' left the day before on the 29th.

Stromness's trip home wasn't completely uneventful. One night (6 July), the men of 45 Commando presented a theatrical production of their very own, entitled 'The Sod's Opera', which was to become famous or infamous throughout the entire RFA. Unfortunately no copy of the scripts seems to still exist. The day after, 45 Commando presented the ship's company with an Argentine rifle and a working .50 calibre Browning machine gun for self defence, which her crew jubilantly took turns in firing until the ammunition ran out.

July saw the departure of *Sir Lancelot*, RFA *Engadine* and RFA *Appleleaf* for the UK, while RFA *Pearleaf* was tasked to 'motorway tanking' off Ascension.

RFA *Regent*, RFA *Bayleaf* and RFA *Tidepool* left the Falklands in August, the first two UK bound while *Tidepool* resumed her interrupted trip to Chile, described here by a crew member:

It was finally decided for us to return to Chile and we set off for Puenta Arenas with two escorts, HMS *Euryalus* and HMS *Charybdis*. It was learnt that the Argies were trailing us down so courses were altered to round the Horn. *Euryalus* and *Charybdis* then left us to speed homewards and we made our way around Tierra Del Fuego through the back door to Puenta Arenas, fantastic scenery, excellent navigation by our Nav, Les Coupland, all reminiscent of the *Beagle* voyage. From there we took the inside passage, up the fjords to the Chilean Naval Base at Talcahuano.

The Chileans greeted us like battle-scarred veterans and the state of the ship did not seem to matter: their ship had survived a war! It was overheard from one of the RFA sailors explaining that some of the starboard side damage was caused by an Exocet bouncing off.

The Chileans were relieved to see that their goodies were unharmed and intact as was the Embassy car.

Captain Rex Cooper was there and organised our repatriation. Chief Engineer Brian Stalley remained behind to get everything stuck back together whilst everyone else flew home via Valparaiso and Brazil to Gatwick. A reception team headed by Captain Butterworth met us. Some of the officers, including myself were asked to wear uniform – the only problem was that after the official welcome and customs there was nowhere to change, so I ended up journeying to my parents in uniform. I arrived just as JR was shot! I finally got home to Spain a few days later for an enjoyable leave, but I had missed the World Cup.

Another of her crew remembered that trip and particularly their homecoming:

We joined in the immense relief that everyone felt when we heard that white flags were flying over Stanley. It was not long before everyone's main area of operation was Berkeley Sound to the north of Stanley and in sight of the airfield. We anchored there and refuelled spasmodically as required but this was intermittent as many vessels headed north back to the UK. We saw many new vessels arrive with additional stores and, much appreciated by all, the Canadian Pacific tanker *Fort Toronto* that was a new vessel loaded with fresh water.

The days passed and even some of the new arrivals had unloaded and departed but still we waited for orders from MOD. Eventually they came with the instruction to proceed to Chile and hand the ship back to her owners! But which way? From the Falklands it is almost the same distance to proceed back the way we had come to the east of South America and through the Panama Canal as it would be to go via Cape Horn and up the east coast of Chile. Each was fraught with difficulties. How would people react during the transit of the Canal? Or, alternatively, was it wise to go south of Cape Horn, which was very close to Argentina, particularly their large air force base at Rio Galagos. We were very aware that the government of Argentina had not accepted the surrender or even a cease-fire. After a further delay we were told to go to Punta Arenas, which is the Chilean port and naval base, about halfway through the Magellan Straits close to the border with Argentina. We obviously could not enter the Straits from the east as it is Argentinean territory and they might not be too well disposed to a vessel that had contributed to their humiliation. And so we went to the south of the Falklands and, as quickly and quietly as we could, south of Cape Horn.

It is an amazing sight, a single black and very bleak rock rising sheer out of the sea. We were escorted to this point, which is where Chilean territorial waters start, by a very reluctant frigate who was very glad to leave us to proceed on our own and to return east as fast as possible!

We travelled northwest along the coast until we came to a lead that threaded through the spectacular landscape. Everyone who saw it was struck by the immensity of the landscape, much of which will never have been trodden by man. The nearest comparison is a Norwegian fjord but even those spectacular places do not have the same sense of scale which resulted in many feeling very awed.

After travelling for some time we approached the Magellan Straits just to the south of Punta Arenas and, at this point, a Chilean naval tug approached with a substantial number of the previous crew who were astonished to see the poor state we were in. When they had last seen their vessel it was in pristine condition shortly prior to the formal handover in Santiago. Now there was this rusted and battered vessel. They wondered how many times we had been hit but we had to confess that the damage was inflicted by the British Navy (during replenishments!).

We then proceeded to the west and exited the Magellan Straits proceeding north using the inner channel with the assistance of a Chilean pilot. It was a fascinating journey that took some time, which emphasised the length of the Chilean seaboard.

We arrived at the main Chilean naval base of Talcuhana where we handed the vessel to her proud new owners in a startling ceremony. The respective crews lined up either side of the flight deck. They made a fascinating contrast with the Chileans to starboard in their best and very smart naval uniforms lined up in neat rows with a band at the front. The RFA crew were a very mixed bunch with many of the officers in uniform but the rest of the crew in civilian dress as they were due to embark into tenders immediately after the ceremony. The RFA ensign was lowered and *God Save The Queen* played in a moderately recognisable form. There were speeches from various Chilean senior naval officers and their ensign was raised to the sound of their national anthem sung most lustily by the Chilean crew. Of course all uniformed personnel saluted at this point which caused us a bit of a problem as we were not familiar with the Chilean national anthem. Assuming that, like ours, this would be one verse long we ceased the salute only to have to quickly return as another verse followed, and then another and another. We ended in an equally farcical situation, with us still saluting when they had finished.

We all disembarked and were bussed to the local airport and flew north to Santiago, the Chilean capital, where we were accommodated in a large modern hotel in the centre of the city. As we were staying overnight we had a chance to walk around and admire a very cosmopolitan city, very similar, as one would expect, to an equivalent Spanish one.

The following day we boarded a British Caledonian overnight flight to Gatwick where we arrived the following morning. Shortly before we left the hotel we were told that a number of officers had to be prepared to don uniform for disembarkation. Given that we were well and truly packed this was not well received. The flight, taking longer than usual as a UK aircraft could not, at that time, overfly Argentina, was uneventful. Shortly before we landed the Captain (who had been in Club class) and a small number of us changed one at a time into uniform. This caused much amusement to the passengers in Club class as each in turn entered in, rather crumpled, civilian costume and emerged shortly after in (one hopes) very smart uniform. As we taxied into the terminal we were informed that the crew of the

Tidepool were to remain seated as all other passengers were to disembark first. A fine thank you for returning heroes who had laid their life on the line we thought. Much muttering was interrupted by a crew member saying that a stairway was being pushed to the middle door just ahead of the wing. At this point we began to realise that something was up! Indeed it was as we emerged from the aircraft we saw for the first time a large crowd on top of the terminal building with the sort of placards of welcome that had become familiar for other returning ships and forces. But, of course, we were blissfully unaware of this. The noise was deafening as the British Airports Authority had laid on a large selection of vehicles in a semi-circle and when we emerged they put their blue lights and sirens on. It was very moving and emotional. As we staggered down the steps we found a welcome committee present which was marvellous but it is a bit difficult to salute a Rear Admiral and shake hands at the same time as holding civilian garb over one arm. This rather spoilt the smart effect that had, presumably, been intended for the media.

As we met our relatives in the VIP lounge and then made our way home the weariness set in. For me it was some weeks before I became a normal human being. You do not know how much strain you had been under until it ceases!

The last Task Force RFA, RFA *Sir Bedivere*, did not come home until November, when she returned to Marchwood carrying the bodies of those men whose relatives wished them to be buried at home. And, of course, the very last RFA home, although not under her own power, was *Sir Tristram*, brought back on the heavy-lift ship *Dan Lifter* for rebuilding in the UK. *Sir Bedivere*'s Master recalled the time after the surrender:

The day after the Argentinean surrender *Sir Bedivere* was ordered into Port Stanley inner harbour and then to berth alongside the small island steamer jetty there. I was doubtful about this for various reasons, but we managed and actually repeated the procedure a number of times, as we needed to go to the outer harbour to replenish fresh water from a tanker. Fresh water supplies had been a great worry since leaving Ascension, until it eventually arrived by tanker.

Whilst alongside we issued direct to shore and also by Mexeflote and helo – the ship became a transit point and the flight deck became very busy. The helo piloted by HRH Prince Andrew visited and he quenched his thirst with orange juice in the bar. The military accommodation was full – flag and general officers embarked (and enjoyed *Bedivere* food) until suitable quarters were available ashore.

An out-of-the-ordinary request was received. Could we arrange a bath for a large party of Argentinean POWs? A large canvas bath was rigged on the tank deck and filled with warm water. A bedraggled crowd of very young lads arrived and had a marvellous time. Later, *Sir Bedivere*'s engineers boated daily to the badly damaged *Sir Tristram* and succeeded in restoring her troop deck hotel services so that she could be used as an accommodation ship until she was carried to UK and rebuilt.

RFA *Sir Bedivere* was I believe the last ship of the task force to leave the Falklands. In doing so she was honoured with a sad duty – she carried back the bodies of the fallen, which their relatives wished to be buried at home, so to the end she fulfilled the service motto that she was 'Ready for Anything'.

This wasn't the end of the RFA s involvement with the Falklands, though.

During the next year, almost as many merchant ships were under charter to transport supplies to the Islands as had been used during the war, all these activities still being organised by the London STUFT cell. Six Auxiliary Support Tankers supported the naval operations and there were also five static Depot Tankers, three in the Falklands and two at Ascension, supplying a variety of fuels and fresh water.

As well as the tankers, some vessels had a more specialised function. *Tor Caledonia* was there as the REME workshop, with *Stena Inspector* providing similar services to the Navy ships as well as acting as a diving support vessel when required. Food storage was taken care of by two 'reefers' [ships with refrigerated storage], *Avelona Star* and *Andalucia Star*, which alternated between the UK and Stanley, while MV *Rangitera* continued its role as an accommodation ship.

A number of ferries were also in use between Ascension and Port Stanley, since, despite regular Hercules flights into the enlarged airport, most personnel were transported to Stanley by ship.

Since the war, every ounce of food, water and fuel used on the Falkland Islands still has to come from the UK via Ascension. So even now, twenty-five years on, RFAs still regularly visit, replenishing the patrol vessels, the shore-based fuel tanks and refrigerated food stores which maintain the Fortress Falklands.

CHAPTER TWELVE

LESSONS LEARNED AND THE NEW RFA

FOLLOWING HARD ON the heels of the 1981 Defence Review, Operation Corporate found the RFA ill-prepared and inadequately equipped to undertake the major logistics operation required by the Navy, away from its well-understood North Atlantic scenario. Allied to this lack of preparation, they were also generally without any means of self-defence, so the RFAs often found themselves in vulnerable positions because the Navy, with few enough ships for the job in hand, could not always be there to protect its civilian support vessels. Nor were there enough of the specialist RFAs to operate the supply chain required without help from the totally defenceless STUFT, which only added to the Navy's burden.

Mr Nott's 1981 Defence Review had, of course, already designated several vitally important RFAs for immediate sale as well making over 1,000 RFA personnel redundant – just before the war began. RFA vessels, however, had been suffering under the Government's financial constraints for a considerable period prior to this Review and it had been equally obvious to many RFA and Royal Navy personnel that major changes were long overdue.

With the two exceptions of the new Fort-class, the fleet was old and most of the vessels were certainly beginning to show their age. Refits had, in many cases, been left incomplete, with little or no attention paid to the important details which make an RFA fit for war duty, such as the integrity of gas-tight citadels and the adequate operation of torpedo and mine countermeasures systems.

These financial constraints also meant that most RFAs had antiquated radar and sonar equipment, sufficient for commercial needs, when the gear worked, but wholly inadequate for dodging icebergs in the freezing waters off South Georgia.

Added to this, a large percentage of RFA ratings were drawn from the Merchant Navy Pool, which meant they often had little or no specialist RFA training, leaving the Captain and his Heads of Department with a very serious shortfall of trained personnel in vital areas. This meant that internal ship organisation was often wholly inadequate for the South Atlantic war, with no provision, at least to begin with, for manning, control or maintenance of weapons, allocation of defence watches as well as a number of other key areas. Notwithstanding, most ships quickly instituted systems, largely based on common sense, which seemed to work well.

It says much for the professionalism of the crews that, despite these shortfalls in basic equipment and training, the Task Force's supply and logistics requirements were met in full. Only two of the twenty-two RFAs deployed were lost, although there were no shortage of critics to insist that this was a matter of luck rather than judgment.

The months after the war saw the coming together of a number of committees to enquire into its conduct, most notably Lord Franks' enquiry which scrutinised the Government s role, along with much of the pre-1982 diplomacy. Perhaps of more interest to the RFA, events at Fitzroy were also the subject of a Board of Enquiry, although its results have, up until the time of writing, never entered the public domain. Even now some of the officers involved have not been allowed sight of a copy, despite numerous requests for this information.

A post-mortem of a very different type was conducted at Empress State Building, the Headquarters of the RFA. It was perfectly clear to the senior staff there, many of whom had been in the South Atlantic, that only the skill and commitment of the RFA's personnel had pulled the logistics effort through, helped by a large slice of luck.

Acknowledging that equipment and, most especially, training had shown areas which needed radical improvement, a series of discussions were held about the service's future. As a result, fundamental decisions were made during this period which set the RFA firmly on the road to the highly-trained, professional, fighting service which was to emerge into the twenty-first century.

The first and arguably the most important decision which arose from these discussions concerned de-registration, that is the removal of RFAs from the British Register and the effective loss of their merchant ship status. This would allow future RFAs to be permanently armed, rather than carrying weapons in the rather covert way which had previously been the norm. A number of other advantages went with de-registration, such as being allowed to defer a routine survey and to operate without regard to a load line, although RFAs could now no longer enter or leave port without the legal requirements warships were forced to observe.

Although this change in status was never wholly achieved, other early changes included the appointment of an RFA Defensive Weapons Officer and the establishment of an RFA Aviation Support Unit at RNAS Culdrose, to administer the RN personnel embarked on the ships who were responsible for helicopter operations and the defensive weapons.

In line with these administrative changes, training courses were improved, both in variety and content, one of them, the thirteen-week Commanding Officer Designate course run by the Royal Navy at HMS *Dryad* being one of the first especially for RFA Captains and Chief Officers. Also available for RFA officers for the first time was the Royal Navy's Principal Warfare Officer's course, in line with the service's new weapons policy.

Coinciding with improved training, employment practices were rationalised, ratings now being employed on permanent contracts, in line with the system for officers and petty officers which had been in place for many years. Terms of employment were changed as well, limiting industrial action and moving ratings and petty officers to an all-hours-worked salary scheme.

Implementation of these changes, in some cases, took place over a considerable period of time, but by 1992–93, the service was beginning to take on much of its future shape. One consequence of this was that many long-established RFA personnel found the new service not to their liking and so resigned. Foreign nationals were also largely replaced by British personnel, thus avoiding the contractual and communications problems that their employment had led to in the past. And for the first time, women began to make a significant contribution, the first female officer cadets being admitted to Warsash in 1993, before moving later to the Cadet Training Unit in RFA *Fort Austin*.

Ships were improving, too. RFA *Sir Tristram* was returned from the Falklands and re-built, becoming some twenty-nine feet longer and having a number of additional features added, the most significant being the replacement of aluminium by steel in her superstructure, as much of the loss of life at Fitzroy was attributed to the poor structural stability of aluminium at high temperatures.

A new *Sir Galahad* was commissioned and a number of the older LSLs were entered into the Ship Life Extension Program (SLEP). RFA *Diligence*, formerly the off-shore support ship *Stena Inspector*, was acquired as a heavy repair ship, while RFA *Argus* joined the Fleet as a Helicopter Training ship, replacing the elderly *Engadine*. Perhaps most significant of all, in 1992, the first of a whole new generation of RFAs left the slips of Harland and Wolff's Belfast yards, with the launching of RFA *Fort Victoria*.

This, the first wholly new RFA to be launched since the process of de-registration, clearly indicated the progress of Navalisation within the service and its move towards the 'force multiplier' concept, whereby RFAs would assume some of the duties formerly assigned to warships.

Known technically as an Auxiliary Oiler Replenishment (AOR), she is a one-stop ship, designed to deliver both fuel and dry stores, including munitions. Equipped with four RAS rigs amidships, a Hudson reel for astern refuelling, the latest 996 surveillance radar, an operations room, twelve-bed hospital and hangar and maintenance facilities for up to four Merlin helicopters, *Fort Victoria* can cope with the most exacting demands encountered in the logistics role she is required to play. Most significantly, she is well armed, being permanently equipped with 30mm cannon and two Phalanx Close In Weapons Systems (ciws), as well as two separate decoy systems, Sea Gnat and Type 182.

2000 saw the launch of RFA *Wave Knight*, the first of the new Wave-class Large Fleet Tankers. Designed as a replacement for the old 'Ol'-class vessels, they have a top speed of eighteen knots and a cargo capacity of 16,000 cubic metres, which includes aviation fuel, water and dry stores. In addition, they are equipped with 30mm cannon and fittings for Phalanx CIWS, along with aviation facilities for the big Merlin helicopter.

New vessels are still being added to the RFA fleet, the latest being something of a departure, even for the RFA. Known as the Bay-class, these vessels are designated Landing Ship Dock (Auxiliary) and are intended as a replacement for the aging LSLs, although their logistic capability far exceeds that of the older ships.

Capable of operating LCVPs and a single ninety-six foot LCU, the ships can also deploy Mexeflotes. The vehicle decks have space for up to twenty-four battle tanks which can enter or leave the ship via stern or side ramps. There is also a Chinook-capable flight deck although no hangar or maintenance support is included. Self-defence is well catered for with the inclusion of four 30mm cannon and fittings for Phalanx CIWS along with a Royal Navy party to operate them. All in all, the perfect expression of the force multiplier concept and perfectly capable of taking up either a logistics or combatant role, whichever is needed.

The RFA's traditional humanitarian role hasn't been neglected with this change in style either. When disaster threatens or happens around the globe, the RFA is often there, to such an extent that several ships in the service have received a humanitarian award in the form of the Wilkinson Sword of Peace. A recent recipient was RFA *Sir Galahad* after she took much needed supplies into Um Qasr after the 2003 Iraq war.

To coincide with the introduction of new vessels, in 1989 control of the RFA was transferred from the RNSTS under the Chief of Fleet Support directly to the operational command of the Commander-in-Chief Fleet (CINCFLEET).

The senior uniformed officer became the new Head of the RFA Service, entitled Commodore RFA (COMRFA). Subordinate to the Commodore at that time were his three specialist heads of department responsible for Operations and Warfare, Engineering and Policy, and Finance. In 1999, a further change took place with the Commodore RFA now being designated Assistant Chief of Staff (Sustainability), having responsibility for the planning, exercise and management of all matters relating to logistics and sustainability of all British maritime forces.

With the repossession of the Falkland Islands, the RFA found themselves in a new and stimulating environment, a situation described here by one of the service's senior officers:

Ever since the 1982 Campaign to successfully recover the Falklands the RFA has provided a continual presence in the region. Initially, up until late 1986, the presence was significant in the form of 'Ol' and/or 'Tide', 'Fort', 'Rover' and 'Sir'-class ships as a standard package to support an equally significant RN force of ships. The establishment however of the Mount Pleasant Airport Complex with its runways and hangar provided an opportunity to reduce the level of ships due to the newly acquired ability to rapidly reinforce and defend the Falkland Islands by air. The standard RFA presence was rapidly reduced to a single Rover-class which has seen all five of the original class serving in the area although the task has in the main been conducted by *Gold Rover* and, the now sadly decommissioned *Grey Rover*.

The main role of the Rover-class is to support the efforts of Commander British Forces South Atlantic Islands (CBFSAI) in defending the islands from potential Argentine aggression. This is primarily achieved by providing Afloat Combat Support to the resident Castle-class OPV [Offshore Patrol Vessel] and DD/FF [destroyers or frigates] as well as a plethora of other tasks including Defence Diplomacy visits to outlying settlements, South America, South Africa, West Africa and British Dependencies e.g. South Georgia and Tristan da Cunha. As can be seen the ship has a large parish effectively covering the South Atlantic from the Canaries south. Hence the title Atlantic Patrol Task (South).

Since 1982, when no facilities were available to RFAs, the amount of shore support and amenities available to ships and their ship's companies have developed beyond comprehension. A fully-equipped port was opened on East Falkland at East Cove Military Port in 1986, which has road links to the international airport at Mount Pleasant (MPA) as well as into the capital Stanley. The facilities on offer include swimming pools, sports fields, internet cafes, cinemas, bars, hire Land Rovers and a twice-weekly connection to the UK; it is now probably easier to join a ship in the Falklands than some well known Scottish ports! Logistic support is comprehensive and cargo can be loaded at a Single Point Mooring in a matter of hours.

The Falklands terrain and coastline is certainly amongst the most striking and beautiful in the world and when coupled with the opportunity to visit such places as South Georgia, Montevideo, Rio and Cape Town, to name but a few, makes it one of the most popular and operationally enjoyable drafts available to RFA personnel.

Each Rover-class spends in the region of thirty months on station with the officers and ratings changing on a regular basis at roughly four- to six-month intervals. The South Atlantic winter provides challenging weather conditions but the respite of calm conditions is only ever forty-eight hours steaming to the North. A patrol cycle with the DD/FF to and from the West African area has been established which means that it is rare to spend longer than eight weeks continuously off the Falklands. Regular maintenance visits to South American ports are extremely popular.

In summary, APT(S) provides the RFA with a highly popular, rewarding and ongoing duty. It also reinforces the ability of the RFA to provide supremely effective

Military Effect to a theatre of operations that has been in a State of Military Vigilance continuously for twenty-five years. Long may this Flexible Global Reach continue.

The Falklands campaign has been described as the RFA's finest hour, but it also marked a watershed for the service, highlighting major problems of both organisation and equipment, all of which needed urgent attention if the RFA was to continue providing afloat support to a rapidly-modernising Navy.

With a remarkably clear vision at the forefront of change, by 1993 the modern RFA had finished its initial, major evolution, becoming completely divorced from the Merchant Navy and virtually unrecognisable to anyone familiar with its pre-1982 form.

Today's RFA is a fighting service in all but name, with ships like the 'Bay' and 'Wave' classes purpose-built for a replenishment and amphibious role and including a well-designed self defence capability and up to four permanently-embarked helicopters, making them the ideal force multiplier to complement the Navy's more conventional vessels.

More important than good equipment, crew training is now a major priority, with a wide variety of courses covering both the everyday and specialist activities of the RFA.

Although the rate of change has slowed, improvement, both at a personal and organisational level, is still the order of the day, thus ensuring that the modern RFA, like its earlier counterparts, is still:

'Ready For Anything.'

BIBLIOGRAPHY

Adams T., Smith J. *The Royal Fleet Auxiliary: A Century of Service*, London, Chatham Publishing, 2005.

Brown D. *The Royal Navy and the Falklands War*, London, Leo Cooper, 1987.

Clapp M., Southby-Tailyour E. *Amphibious Assault Falklands: The Battle of San Carlos Water*, London, Leo Cooper, 1996.

Fox R., Hanrahan B. *'I counted them all out and I counted them all back': The Battle for the Falklands*, London, BBC Publications, 1982.

Freedman L. *The Official History of the Falklands Campaign: Vol I, The Origins of the Falklands War*, London, Frank Cass, 2005.

Freedman L., Gamba-Stonehouse V. *Signals of War*, London, Faber and Faber, 1990.

Gavashon A., Rice D. *The Sinking of the Belgrano*, London, Secker & Warburg, 1984.

Operation Corporate 1982: The Carriage of Nuclear Weapons by the Task Group Assembled for the Falklands Campaign, London, CBRN Policy MOD.

Perkins R. *Operation Paraquat: The Battle for South Georgia*, Beckington, Picton Publishing Ltd, 1986.

Southby-Tailyour E. *Reasons in Writing: A Commando's View of the Falklands War*, London, Leo Cooper, 1993.

Thatcher Rt Hon M. *The Downing Street Years: Vol II*, London, HarperCollins, 1993.

Villar Capt R. *Merchant Ships at War: The Falklands Experience*, London, Conway Maritime Press and Lloyds of London Press, 1984.

Woodward Admiral S., with Robinson P. *One Hundred Days: Memoirs of the Falklands Battle Group Commander*, London, HarperCollins, 1992.

APPENDICES

Appendix A: Chronology of the war

Appendix B: History of the Falklands and the war

Appendix C: In Remembrance

Appendix D: Gallantry awards

Appendix E: Chronology of nuclear weapons transfers

Appendix F: Replenishment 1982

Appendix G: Arms on RFAs

Appendix H: RFA ships in the Falklands

Appendix I: The Royal Fleet Auxiliary

APPENDIX A

Chronology of the war

Week 1

17 March

After Anglo–Argentine talks in New York, Argentineans publish unilateral communiqué with press speculation on possible unilateral action before January 1983 (the 150th anniversary of the British occupation), Galtieri giving election promise to this effect.

18 March

Scrap merchants (complete with legitimate contract) land at Leith, South Georgia, and hoist Argentinean flag, for a joke. Mrs Thatcher makes decision to order scrappers off: 'To show that we were concerned . . .'

19 March

British Antarctic Survey group arrives at Leith. Argentine supply ship *Bahia Buen Sucesco* lands 100 men.

20 March

Rex Hunt (Falklands Governor) sends message to captain of *Bahia Buen Sucesco* that landing is illegal. Hunt, Captain N Barker (Commanding Officer of Ice Patrol Vessel, HMS *Endurance*), and Lord Buxton call for tough action.

21 March

British Ambassador to Buenos Aires and Argentinean counterpart try to defuse situation. *Bahia Buen Sucesco* leaves South Georgia. *Endurance* and fourteen Royal Marines sail for South Georgia.

Week 2

22 March (Mon)

Foreign Office informs Buenos Aires that landing is illegal. *Bahia Buen Sucesco* reported to have left South Georgia but Davidoff's workers (scrap dealers) remain. Official communiqué released as situation now seems to be less serious.

23 March

Strong British press reaction. British Foreign Office concludes Argentine expedition suspicious. Argentineans still wish to avoid escalation. No military personnel on South Georgia at this point.

UK House of Commons debate also seen as provocative by Buenos Aires. Junta meet and decide on countermeasures, notably to dispatch *Bahia Paraiso* and fourteen marines to protect salvage workers.

24 March

Endurance arrives Leith.

Bahia Paraiso arrives Leith.

Costa Mendez (Argentinean Foreign Minister) tries for removal of remaining men on a civilian ship and 'white card' stamp. Hunt: 'No compromise.'

25 March

British Ambassador in Buenos Aires tells Costa Mendez that men may stay at Leith if they go to Grytviken to collect documents before returning to Leith. No reply to this ever received.

26 March

Junta today decides to invade the Falklands and orders military intervention. British intelligence in Argentina reports suspect preparations.

RFA *Fort Austin* (Commodore S C Dunlop), at Gibraltar, receives orders to replenish HMS *Endurance* on station around the Falklands. Her crew begin loading immediately. *Fort Austin* was the first surface ship ordered south.

27 March

Argentina perceives British prevarication as an attempt to covertly implement a 'Fortress Falklands' policy, leaving no room for Argentine military options. Falklands could be reinforced from Britain by 4 April so decision needed urgently.

RFA *Appleleaf* (Capt G P A MacDougall), on passage from Curaçao to UK with full load of fuel, ordered to divert to Gibraltar, embark general naval stores, then proceed south to support *Endurance* and *Fort Austin*.

28 March

Argentine invasion force sails from Puerto Belgrano. Final order for invasion still to be issued.

Week 3

29 March (Mon)

Thatcher orders nuclear submarines HMS *Spartan* and *Splendid* to South Atlantic.

SIS (UK Secret Intelligence Service) receives view from Argentine officials that military action imminent.

RFA *Fort Austin* leaves Gibraltar to replenish *Endurance*.

Argentine carrier *Viencentio de Mayo* sails, with escorting destroyers.

30 March

BBC news reports Task Force being prepared to sail.

News of British SSN (nuclear submarine) departure leaked to jittery backbenchers.

British Naval Attaché in Buenos Aires reports Argentinean warships and a submarine sailing for South Georgia and that another four ships have left Puerto Belgrano.

31 March

British request US intervention with Galtieri.

Invasion warning sent to Hunt.

All vessels of Argentinean invasion fleet at sea and heading for the Falklands.

Report of dispatch of British SSN sent to Buenos Aires, causing hardening of Junta attitude.

1 April

British Ambassador in Buenos Aires informed by Costa Mendez that South Georgia incident is closed.

Britain calls emergency session of UN Security Council.

Argentineans say they are amenable to negotiation if it is about whole sovereignty dispute, not just South Georgia. UK says this is too little, too late.

Hunt receives notice of possible invasion (15.30, local time).

Decision to send Task Force taken that afternoon and order to bring carriers HMS *Hermes* and *Invincible* to twenty-four hours' readiness is given, although *Invincible* is still being put back together after major refit.

RFA *Stromness* (Capt B Dickinson) begins preparation for return to service from pre-disposal storage.

RN ships comprising Task Group (TG) 317.8, HMS *Antrim*, *Glamorgan* (County class destroyers), *Coventry*, *Glasgow*, *Sheffield* (Type 42 destroyers), *Brilliant* (Type 22 frigate) and *Arrow* (Type 21 frigate) spend the day re-storing, off Gibraltar, from RN ships ordered to UK.

RFA *Tidespring* (Capt S R Redmond) and *Appleleaf* are ordered to accompany TG 317.8.

RNSTS begins major stores/fuel/clothing issue to ships going south.

2 April

Argentine forces land near Stanley (04.30 local time). Start of Operation Rosario (previously Azul).

Hunt surrenders (09.30, local). Company of Royal Marines captured at Stanley.

Sir Anthony Parsons (British Ambassador to UN) calls for emergency session of UN Security Council.

RFAs *Tidespring* and *Appleleaf* sail south from Mediterranean with main Battle Group (TG 317.8). HMS *Plymouth* accompanying *Appleleaf*.

RFA *Sir Tristram* (Capt R Green) sails from Belize.

RFA *Brambleleaf* (Capt M Farley) detached from Indian Ocean to join Task Group by way of Cape of Good Hope.

3 April

South Georgia invaded by Argentine forces. Royal Marines disable Argentine frigate, *Guerrico*, before surrendering.

UN demands immediate Argentine withdrawal and negotiation. Panama tries to veto.

Saturday session of UK Parliament. Government decides to send Task Force.

Three Sea Skua-equipped Lynx helicopters arrive Ascension, intended for RFA *Fort Austin*.

4 April

Argentineans learn that Americans have permitted the use of Ascension Island. Galtieri decides to reinforce military presence to force negotiated settlement.

HMS *Conqueror* leaves Faslane naval base.

Order in Council (Requisition of Ships Order) submitted, allowing the UK Government to requisition any British merchant ship or anything on board that ship for Her Majesty's service. Order approved by Queen Elizabeth II.

RFA *Tidepool* recalled from Chile.

Naval Wessex helicopters airlifted to Ascension, two for embarkation on RFA *Tidespring*.

RMAS *Typhoon* leaves UK.

Week 4

5 April (Mon)

Lord Carrington resigns as Foreign Secretary, Francis Pym appointed in his place.

Costa Mendez addresses Organisation of American States.

RFA *Olmeda* (Capt G Overbury) sails from Devonport, in company with HMS *Alacrity* and *Antelope*.

RFA *Pearleaf* (Capt J McCulloch) sails from Portsmouth, to rendezvous with Task Force.

RFA *Brambleleaf* sails from Gulf of Oman.

Carrier Task Group sails from Plymouth, HMS *Hermes* carrying eleven Sea Harriers (800 NAS) and eighteen Sea King helicopters, *Invincible* carrying nine Sea Harriers (801 NAS).

6 April

Britain demands that EEC impose sanctions on Argentina.

US stops arms sales to Argentina. Haig talks to British and Argentinean ambassadors separately in Washington DC.

Argentine 8th Regt moved by air to Falklands.

RFA *Fort Austin* arrives Ascension and embarks three Lynx, complete with Sea Skua missiles.

RFA *Resource* (Capt B A Seymour) leaves Rosyth, equipped with a Sea King, before picking up last of stores at Portsmouth, then rendezvous with RFA *Olmeda* (Capt G P Overbury) and escort.

RFA *Sir Geraint* (Capt D E Lawrence) and RFA *Sir Galahad* (Capt P J Roberts) sail from Devonport. *Sir Galahad* carries 350 men of 40 Commando, amongst others.

RFAs *Sir Percivale* (Capt A F Pitt) and *Sir Lancelot* (Capt C A Purcher-Wydenbruck) sail from Marchwood.

LSLs (Sir-class) and RFA *Pearleaf* rendezvous with RFA *Resource*, RFA *Olmeda* and HMS *Alacrity* and *Antelope*; they comprise part of the Amphibious Landing Group, which then proceeds to Ascension.

National Maritime Board (NMB) convenes to discuss Merchant Navy bonus scheme and death/injuries agreement.

HMS *Fearless* leaves Portsmouth, as Brigade HQ, with Commodore M Clapp aboard. Off Portland, they take on board Brigadier Julian Thompson and three 846 NAS Sea Kings.

Carrier HMS *Invincible* has problem with starboard main gearbox coupling.

Spares and equipment flown in by helicopter from Culdrose. Problem fixed mid-channel.

7 April

Menendez, the new Argentine Governor, arrives Stanley.

RFA *Stromness*, originally scheduled for disposal, departs Portsmouth, after rapid refit and re-storing, carrying 45 Commando RM.

Main RNSTS party arrives at Ascension.

RFA *Grey Rover* established as resident work-up tanker in Portland area.

RMS *Canberra* arrives Vospers in Southampton for conversion.

HMS *Antrim*, *Plymouth* and RFA *Tidespring* detached from Main Battle Group (TG 317.8) and ordered to Ascension.

8 April

Haig and Thatcher have first meeting.

Argentinean 5th Marine Infantry battalion and artillery arrive Stanley.

Proposed Maritime Exclusion Zone (MEZ) announced by Britain.

Stena Inspector, oil field repair ship, requisitioned.

9 April (Good Friday)

Junta issues orders that no troops on Falklands are to initiate hostilities.

Haig to Buenos Aires for talks.

RFA *Fort Austin* leaves Ascension after embarking three Lynx, two Wessex helicopters, 120 men of combined SAS/SBS force and RN surgical team. Heading for rendezvous with HMS *Endurance*.

Liner *Canberra*, now with addition of helicopter deck, leaves for South Atlantic, carrying 40 and 42 Royal Marine Commandos and 3 Para.

MV *Elk* leaves UK.

Combined RN/RNSTS movements cell formed at Northwood.

10 April

EEC sanctions imposed on Argentina.

Haig and Galtieri meet.

HMS *Antrim*, *Plymouth*, and RFA *Tidespring* arrive Ascension.

Tidespring embarks her two designated Wessex and their crews.

RNSTS working party at Ascension receives mechanical handling equipment.

Motor Tugs *Salvageman* and *Irishman* sail from UK.

11 April

Haig and Thatcher meet, Thatcher still insistent upon return to status quo.

South Georgia (*Antrim*) task group, TG 317.8/I, including RFA *Tidespring*, sails from Ascension.

TG 317.8/II, consisting of HMS *Glasgow, Sheffield, Coventry, Arrow, Brilliant* and *Glamorgan*, the last carrying Admiral Woodward, arrive Ascension Island. Have been joined on passage by RFA *Appleleaf*.

Arrangements made to fly Geneva Convention Identity cards to RFA and RNSTS personnel in RFAs.

RNSTS mechanical handling expert arrives Ascension.

Week 5

12 April (Easter Monday)

Haig returns from Buenos Aires.

Maritime Exclusion Zone (MEZ), declared by Britain (200 miles around Falklands), comes into effect.

Argentine supply ships held back to facilitate Haig's mediation.

RFA *Fort Austin* replenishes HMS *Endurance*, before proceeding north to rendezvous with *Antrim* group.

MV *British Tay* sails from UK.

13 April

Argentina offers new proposals, apparently with more flexibility.

RNSTS movements cell (London) reverts to normal working. All South Atlantic movements now controlled from Northwood.

RFA *Brambleleaf* off Cape of Good Hope.

RFA *Tidespring*, with South Georgia task group, rendezvous with *Fort Austin*. RFA *Fort Austin* replenishes fuel from *Tidespring*.

Fort Austin then transfers food, ammunition, SAS, SBS teams to RN ships and food and naval surgical team to RFA *Tidespring*, before turning north to rendezvous with *Brilliant* group.

MV *British Tamar* and MT *Yorkshireman* sail from UK.

14 April

Antrim group rendezvous with HMS *Endurance*. *Tidespring* improvises fuel rig, then RASs *Endurance* for fuel. Whole group now heads for South Georgia.

HMS *Brilliant* group, including *Sheffield, Coventry, Arrow* and *Glasgow*, leave Ascension to act as cover for *Antrim* group. Commanded by Capt J Howard (CO *Brilliant*), they proceed at twenty-five knots to 1,200 miles south of Ascension. Followed by RFA *Appleleaf*.

HMS *Glamorgan*, carrying Admiral Woodward, leaves Ascension.

MV *British Test* sails from UK.

15 April

War Cabinet decides blockade impossible.

Argentineans continue preparations on West Falklands.

Haig to Buenos Aires for more talks.

Argentine Fleet (TF 79) puts to sea.

Reagan–Galtieri telephone conference.

HMS *Glamorgan* rendezvous *Hermes* group, which includes RFA *Olmeda*. Admiral Woodward transfers to HMS *Hermes*. Now in company with HMS *Alacrity*, *Broadsword* and *Yarmouth*.

16 April

Haig–Galtieri meeting. Argentina makes some concessions.

Acceleration of munitions production in Britain.

Another outfit of mechanical handling equipment to Ascension.

National Maritime Board meet (16–19 April) to discuss pay claim.

RFA *Blue Rover* (Capt D A Reynolds) sails from Portsmouth.

Fort Austin rendezvous with *Brilliant* group. Carries out MEGARAS, known to crew as 'Operation Insomnia'.

Fort Austin transfers one 600 nuclear round from *Brilliant* and one 600 (S) (surveillance) round from *Sheffield*.

HMS *Hermes* and *Invincible* arrive Ascension, in company with HMS *Alacrity*, *Broadsword*, *Yarmouth* and *Glamorgan*.

RFA *Olmeda* previously detached from group and sent north to rendezvous HMS *Fearless*, but instead finds HMS *Antelope* and LSLs.

MV *Stena Inspector* sails from UK after conversion to repair ship.

MV *Stena Seaspread* sails from UK.

MV *Wimpey Seahorse* sails from Devonport.

17 April

Haig meets Junta.

HMS *Conqueror* enters northern iceberg limit.

RFA *Resource* arrives Ascension.

18 April

RFAs *Olmeda*, *Resource* leave Ascension as part of Carrier Battle Group (TG 317.8) in company with HMS *Hermes*, *Glamorgan*, *Broadsword*, *Yarmouth*, and *Alacrity*.

HMS *Invincible* leaves later but soon catches up with main group.

Liner *Canberra* arrives Freetown.

MV *British Trent* sails from UK.

Week 6

19 April (Mon)

New Argentinean proposals sent to London, via Haig. Deemed unacceptable.

Five Sir-class landing ships, escorted by HMS *Antelope*, arrive Ascension, together with HMS *Fearless*.

RFA *Regent* sails from Devonport and RFA *Plumleaf* from Portland. Both join HMS *Argent* and *Argonaut* for the voyage south.

All ships in Carrier Battle Group now in routine of Defence Watches.

HMS *Conqueror* surveys South Georgia.

SS *Uganda* (now converted to hospital ship) sails from Gibraltar.

20 April

Formulation by Haig of Memorandum of Agreement to be put to both sides.

RFA *Stromness* arrives Ascension.

HMS *Broadsword* transfers one 600 (L) round to RFA *Resource* in open sea.

Canberra and *Elk* arrive Ascension. Commandos disembark for training.

MV *Elk* modified for helo operations.

Tug *Salvageman* anchors off Ascension, delayed by fire in galley.

MV *Fort Toronto* (water tanker) sails from UK.

21 April

Francis Pym makes statement about Government's intentions towards Argentina in Commons, then forced to return and retract.

RFA *Fort Austin* arrives Ascension, re-stores and heads south to rejoin Carrier Battle Group, still carrying nuclear rounds.

RFA *Appleleaf* 'motorway tanking' in region forty degrees south (until 26 April).

RFA *Tidespring* arrives off South Georgia, carrying 'M' Coy, 45 Commando.

Hong Kong Chinese (HKC) aboard RFAs (crews of Sir-class ships) demand pay increase while at Ascension.

HMS *Hermes*, 2,500 miles from Falklands, buzzed by Argentine Boeing 707, which sends reconnaissance report to Argentine military.

Operation Paraquat (recapture of South Georgia) begins with SAS team landing on Fortuna Glacier, South Georgia.

22 April

Pym discusses Memorandum of Agreement with Haig, without prior Argentine knowledge.

Galtieri visits Falklands. Discussion with Menendez and Jofre. Decides to reinforce in regimental strength, changes mind and increases to brigade strength upon arrival Buenos Aires.

RFA *Pearleaf* arrives Ascension.

SAS mission crash-lands on Fortuna Glacier (South Georgia), losing both of RFA *Tidespring*'s Wessex, with subsequent rescue by third helicopter.

HMS *Brilliant* detached from Advanced Group to reinforce South Georgia Task Force.

MVs *Europic Ferry* (ro-ro ferry) and *British Dart* (tanker) sail south.

Tanker *British Tay* arrives Ascension.

23 April

British issue statement making it clear that any Argentinean warship or aircraft inside TEZ, or any vessel posing a threat, whether inside or outside the zone is liable to be attacked.

RFA *Fort Austin* departs Ascension Island.

RFA *Brambleleaf* joins Operation Paraquat. *Tidespring* and *Brambleleaf* move out to sea (200 miles off South Georgia) and attempt pumpover. Abandoned due to sub alert, subsequently found to be *Santa Fe*, whose captain later admits he intended to put four torpedoes into *Tidespring*.

HMS *Endurance* detects Argentinean sub, while *Antrim* makes contact with Argentine reconnaissance plane, either Hercules or Boeing 707.

24 April

Thatcher's War Cabinet rejects new Haig proposals.

Argentineans send 3rd Inf Brigade to Falklands.

Full text of TEZ statement issued today.

Tidespring and *Brambleleaf* complete pumpover, in force 10 gale, while *Endurance* and Task Group, now joined by HMS *Brilliant*, hunt *Santa Fe*.

RFA *Brambleleaf* leaves for UK.

UK warns surveillance aircraft will be shot down.

25 April

South Georgia recaptured. Argentine submarine *Santa Fe* attacked and run aground.

RFA *Sir Bedivere* arrives Marchwood, re-stores and leaves again on 27 April.

RFA *Pearleaf* leaves Ascension and begins record pumpover with *British Tamar*, the latter having just arrived.

Carrier Battle Group, including *Olmeda* and *Resource* (the latter still carrying nuclear round), arrive South Atlantic and rendezvous with TG 317.8/II, now led by HMS *Sheffield* and without HMS *Brilliant*.

Carrier Battle Group now consists of:

– Two aircraft carriers (*Hermes* and *Invincible*)

– Three Type 42 destroyers (*Sheffield*, *Coventry*, *Glasgow*),

– One County-class destroyer (*Glamorgan*),

– One Type 22 frigate (*Broadsword*),

– Two Type 21 frigates (*Arrow*, *Alacrity*),

– One tanker (RFA *Appleleaf*) – joined later after relief from motorway tanking.

HMS *Yarmouth* and RFAs *Olmeda* and *Resource* are only sixty miles astern.

Atlantic Conveyor and *Europic Ferry* leave UK.

Week 7

26 April (Mon)

RFA *Appleleaf* relieved as motorway tanker and heads for TEZ.

RFA *Blue Rover* reaches Ascension, leaving almost immediately for South Atlantic.

RFA *Tidepool* arrives Ascension.

RFA *Bayleaf* and HMS *Intrepid* leave UK, *Intrepid* having been re-commissioned in just twenty-two days by Portsmouth dockyard and Portland Naval Base.

MV *British Wye*, *British Avon*, *Anco Charger* and *Shell Aburna* (all tankers) sail from UK.

27 April

Haig's Memorandum of Agreement sent to both sides.

Mine clearance group (converted trawlers manned by RN crews) sails from UK: *Cordella*, *Junella*, *Farnella*, *Northella*, *Pict*.

Ferry *Norland* leaves UK.

28 April

Haig and Costa Menendez discuss Memorandum.

Hospital group, *Uganda* and HMS *Hecla*, *Hecate* and *Hydra*, arrive Ascension.

29 April

US Senate passes a motion backing UK unreservedly ('Haig's tilt').

RFA *Sir Bedivere* leaves Marchwood after returning from Vancouver, Canada.

Hospital group, *Uganda* and HMS *Hecla*, *Hecate* and *Hydra*, leave Ascension.

RFAs *Regent*, *Plumleaf*, and *Stena Seaspread* arrive Ascension.

HMS *Plymouth* and *Brilliant* join Carrier Battle Group from South Georgia, returning special forces ('D' Sqn SAS and SBS No 2) to carriers.

RFA *Appleleaf* joins Carrier Battle Group to commence RAS(L) operations.

Last major replenishment of Carrier Battle Group before entering TEZ, 500 miles from Port Stanley.

MV *Wimpey Seahorse* leaves Ascension.

30 April

Haig press conference blaming Argentina for failure of negotiations.

HMS *Conqueror* locates *General Belgrano* when it finds tanker by accident.

TEZ comes into force.

Carrier Battle Group's replenishment finishes am, and Group steams towards TEZ.

RFA *Appleleaf* pumps over her remaining AVCAT to RFA *Olmeda*, then, at noon, detaches to replenish her supply tanks from *British Esk*.

Slower elements of Amphibious Group (the five LSL Sir-class ships) sail south from Ascension, accompanied by HMS *Antelope* and RFA *Pearleaf*.

RFA *Regent* arrives Ascension Island.

RFA *Plumleaf* begins operations at Ascension.

1 May

Argentinean top-level meeting. Generals insist upon negotiation, avoiding all-out war at any cost.

Vice Admiral Allara receives orders from Lombardo to use the two northern groups of his TF 79 against British.

Claimed that Anaya himself signalled withdrawal of all Argentine Fleet units back to home port.

RFA *Pearleaf* departs Ascension, heading south.

Task Force enters Exclusion Zone at 07.00 GMT.

RAF Vulcan bombs Stanley airport (07.00–08.00 GMT).

Air battle (18.00 local), two Argentinean planes lost.

Sea Harriers crater Stanley and Goose Green airstrips making them unusable. Argentineans temporarily unable to airlift supplies, effectively cut off from mainland.

Main Carrier Group CAP (Combat Air Patrol) attacks and destroys two Mirages heading for carriers.

HMS *Glamorgan*, *Alacrity* and *Arrow* patrol Falklands and bombard Port Stanley airfield with 4.5-inch guns. Attacked by Daggers.

HMS *Brilliant* and *Yarmouth* follow submarine contact, breaking off after dark to return to Carrier Battle Group, having had air contact (Canberra bomber).

2 May

RFA *Regent* departs Ascension.

RFA *Tidespring* leaves South Georgia with Argentinean POWs, Ascension bound, in company with HMS *Antrim*.

RFA *Appleleaf* rendezvous with *Tidespring*. *Brambleleaf*'s winter AVCAT, previously pumped over to *Tidespring*, is transferred to *Appleaf*. HMS *Plymouth* and *Antrim* remain as escorts.

Argentinean Navy plans counter-attack, but light wind makes launch from their carrier impossible.

General Belgrano sunk (18.00 local) by torpedoes from HMS *Conqueror*.

Week 8

3 May (Mon)

RFA *Plumleaf* leaves Ascension area, heading south.

RFA *Fort Austin* (still carrying live nuclear round) rejoins Carrier Battle Group.

Bad weather prevents any British offensive action, so day spent replenishing.

4 May

HMS *Sheffield* hit in air attack.

RFA *Fort Austin* takes *Sheffield*'s survivors and its Lynx helicopter on board.

Sea Harrier shot down, pilot killed.

RFA *Blue Rover* joins *Tidespring/Appleleaf* Group.

MV *Lycaon* leaves UK.

Vulcans (from Ascension) bomb Stanley's runway again.

Task Force withdrawn from TEZ for major replenishment.

5 May

RFA *Resource* takes 150 of *Sheffield*'s survivors on board.

Atlantic Conveyor, HMS *Intrepid* arrive Ascension.

HMS *Exeter* ordered to leave Belize and join Task Force.

HMS *Cardiff* ordered to Gibraltar for maintenance and re-storing before going south as part of *Bristol* Group.

Argentine carrier *Viencentio de Mayo* heads north for her base at Puerto Belgrano.

6 May

Two Sea Harriers disappear, presumed collided in fog and both pilots killed.

RFAs *Tidepool* and *Plumleaf* leave Ascension to join Carrier Battle Group (TG 317.8) accompanied by HMS *Ardent* and *Argonaut*.

Tidespring/Appleleaf group split; *Blue Rover* and *Appleleaf* go south with *Plymouth*, while *Tidespring* and *Antrim* head north for Ascension.

France halts delivery of Super Etendards to Argentina.

7 May

Main body of amphibious assault vessels leave Ascension (Amphibious Group 2), includes *Fearless, Intrepid, Atlantic Conveyor, Europic Ferry,* RFA *Stromness* and *Canberra,* with escort. *Norland* arrives Ascension but departs, with troops, soon after.

Amphibious Group 1 (five LSLs, HMS *Antelope,* RFA *Pearleaf*) wait at about thirty degrees south for rest of Amphibious Group. Are overtaken by RFA *Regent* and hospital ship *Uganda*. Whole group then rendezvous HMS *Antrim* and *Tidespring*. *Antrim* transfers prisoners and takes over Amphibious Group, while *Antelope* accompanies *Tidespring* to Ascension.

TEZ extended to within twelve miles of Argentinean mainland.

8 May

Plymouth group (including *Appleleaf* and *Blue Rover*) rendezvous with RFA *Fort Austin* and *Olmeda*. *Olmeda* begins pumpover from *Appleleaf.*

HMS *Brilliant* patrols north entrance to Falkland sound. *Alacrity* shells Argentinean bivouacs on Port Stanley Common.

Yarmouth takes *Sheffield* in tow around midnight.

Twenty Harriers/Sea Harriers arrive Ascension from Yeovilton.

Argentinean Mirages attack Task Force.

Argentinean Hercules and Mirage escort turned back by Harriers between mainland and Falklands.

MV *Saxonia* sails south from UK.

9 May

RFA *Blue Rover* arrives Cumberland Bay, South Georgia, to act as station tanker.

Fort Austin transfers nuclear round to HMS *Hermes.*

Harriers attack Stanley.

Argentinean attempt to fly Hercules transport into Stanley turned back by Sea Harrier.

HMS *Coventry* and *Broadsword* shell Port Stanley and *Coventry* claims double kill, two A-4C Skyhawks.

HMS *Brilliant* and *Glasgow* arrive off Stanley to relieve *Coventry/Broadsword* combination. *Alacrity* and *Arrow* blockade Falkland Sound.

Argentine trawler *Narwhal* attacked and badly damaged.

MVs *Baltic Ferry, Nordic Ferry* and *Alvega* leave UK for South Atlantic.

Special forces teams (SAS) now established in observation hides overlooking most Argentinean positions.

Week 9

10 May (Mon)

HMS *Sheffield* sinks under tow on way to South Georgia.

Terminal Control Area (100 nautical miles) established around Ascension.

RFA *Engadine* (Helicopter training ship) sails from Devonport, with 847 NAS 'A' flight and maintenance team embarked.

RFA *Sir Bedivere* arrives Ascension.

RFA *Olna* sails from Portsmouth in company with *Bristol* group, consisting of HMS *Bristol* (Capt A Grose RN, commanding group), *Avenger, Active, Minerva, Penelope, Andromeda*. HMS *Cardiff* joins, en route, from Gibraltar.

Argentine trawler *Narwhal* sinks in heavy seas.

Alacrity and *Arrow* conduct inshore operations. Fired on by Argentinean submarine *San Luis*, using wire-guided torpedo, without effect.

11 May

Lloyds withdraw insurance cover from any ships in large area of South Atlantic.

RFA *Tidepool* joins Amphibious Group.

RFA *Regent* joins Carrier Battle Group today, along with *British Esk*.

Hospital ship *Uganda* arrives on edge of TEZ.

12 May

RMS *Queen Elizabeth II* and MV *Balder London* leave UK for South Atlantic.

RFA *Tidespring* arrives Ascension with Argentine POWs captured at South Georgia.

RFA *Brambleleaf* arrives Portland for repairs.

RFA *Engadine* has engine failure north of Finisterre, but engine room staff repair her.

Sheffield survivors transferred to MV *British Esk* for passage to UK.

HMS *Brilliant* and *Glasgow* resume bombardment of Port Stanley, during which the former shoots down two Skyhawks with Sea Wolf in Falkland Sound. *Glasgow* hit by second attack.

13 May

RFA *Tidespring* finishes disembarking POWs.

Hecla joins *Uganda* in Red Cross Box.

MV *Wimpey Seahorse* leaves UK going south.

14 May

Final Terms from UK Government issued to Argentina.

RFA *Fort Grange* leaves Clyde, bound for Ascension Island,

RFA *Sir Bedivere* sails from Ascension, carrying Navy's No 3 Fleet Clearance Diving Team, and RAF and Army bomb disposal experts.

RFA *Resource* transfers nuclear round to *Invincible*, receiving training round in exchange.

SS *Atlantic Causeway* sails from UK.

Pebble Island raid by SAS. Airbase and aircraft destroyed.

Declaration of Active Service in the South Atlantic formally announced (14/15 May).

15 May

RFA *Resource* transfers one 600 and one 600 (S) to RFA *Regent*.

Salvageman refuels at Grytviken.

Glasgow repaired and operational again.

Alacrity and *Brilliant* detach for inshore operations.

Argentine transport runs, overnight to Stanley by C-130 Hercules, now well organised.

16 May

Amphibious group concentrated for final approach to TEZ.

RFA *Tidespring* goes south from Ascension, having collected two new Wessex helicopters, escorted by HMS *Antelope*.

RFA *Plumleaf* dropped off from Amphibious group to act as 'motorway station' for southbound ships.

Glamorgan begins her period of bombardment of Darwin, Fitzroy and Port Stanley areas.

Week 10

17 May (Mon)

RFA *Plumleaf* begins motorway tanking operations in region forty degrees south.

Four of *Hermes'* Sea Kings transferred to RFA *Fort Austin*.

RFA *Sir Bedivere* arrives TEZ.

RFA *Pearleaf* arrive Falklands area.

RFA *Fort Austin* transfers one 600 (S) and one 600 (T) round to RFA *Regent*. HMS *Coventry* transfers one 600 (S) to *Regent*. *Regent* now carries one 600, two 600 (S) and three training rounds.

18 May

RFA *Olna* off Ascension.

Amphibious Landing Group joins Battle and Carrier Groups in TEZ. Thirty-two ships now in company.

Glamorgan bombards Port Stanley.

British Esk northbound with *Sheffield*'s survivors and one correspondent.

Harriers from *Atlantic Conveyor* to *Hermes*.

19 May

RFA *Bayleaf* arrives Ascension.

Battle and Amphibious groups 300 miles east north east of Port Stanley, reshuffling men, aircraft and equipment.

Glamorgan inshore again.

20 May

Invasion force assembled for landings (codename 'Operation Sutton'), includes:

- RFA *Fort Austin* (acting as anti-submarine ship, using helicopters.)
- RFA *Stromness*
- Five Sir-class ships, (*Lancelot, Geraint, Percivale, Tristram, Galahad*)
- *Canberra*
- *Norland*
- *Europic Ferry*
- *Elk*
- HMS *Intrepid*
- HMS *Fearless*
- RN escorts

This group detaches from Carrier Battle Group at 14.15 (GMT) to make westward run, sailing across north of Falklands, with seven escorts, and arriving outside Falkland Sound after dark, bad weather having covered approach.

Escorts enter Sound, followed by Amphibious Group.

RFA *Tidepool* arrives in Falklands area.

MV *Contender Bezant, Tor Caledonia* and *St Edmund* sail from UK.

21 May night/early morning:

Ships divide into three waves, entering Falkland Sound in the following order:

- *Fearless* and *Intrepid*, escorted by *Yarmouth*, anchor at about 11.20, dock down and disembark their LCUs.

- *Canberra, Norland*, RFA *Stromness*, RFA *Fort Austin*, escorted by *Plymouth* and *Brilliant*, arrive at about 12.10, before disembarking troops to the LCUs.

Later, the first three weigh anchor and move into San Carlos Water, arriving about 06.30.

LSLs (Sir-class ships) and *Europic Ferry* enter Falkland Sound and go straight into San Carlos Water, anchoring about 07.00.

RN ships form a gunline across the mouth of San Carlos Inlet and Falkland Sound ready to deal with Argentinean air attacks.

Diversionary attacks made at Goose Green.

Diversionary shelling off Stanley.

Mount Kent helicopter base and Goose Green airfield successfully attacked.

Repeated Argentinean air attacks. HMS *Ardent* sunk, HMS *Antrim* hit, HMS *Argonaut* hit.

Dagger aircraft hit by *Brilliant*'s Sea Wolf at 1,000 yards as it tries to attack RFA *Fort Austin*.

Assault ships and LSLs unloading via landing craft and Mexeflotes.

RFA *Fort Austin* claims to have hit Argentine Dagger/Mirage with machine gun fire in afternoon.

21/22 May overnight

Canberra, Norland, and *Europic Ferry* sail from San Carlos Water (depart 22.30, escorted by HMS *Antrim*).

MV *Geestport* sails from UK.

MV *Alvega* takes up duty as Base Support Tanker at Ascension.

Baltic Ferry and *Nordic Ferry,* carrying 5 Inf Bde heavy weapons and military stores, call at Ascension then leave for South Georgia today.

RFA *Tidespring* rejoins *Bristol* group.

Review of ammunition status by MOD (London) giving cause for concern.

22 May

RFA *Fort Grange* arrives Ascension.

No air attacks today, owing to bad weather on Argentine mainland.

Troops land to reinforce Paras as unloading continues from LSLs.

Falkland Island vessel *Monsunen* run aground and abandoned.

In Cumberland Bay, South Georgia, RFA *Resource* takes *Canberra*'s stores on board.

MV *Scottish Eagle* leaves UK heading south.

23 May

RFA *Stromness, Norland* and *Europic Ferry* return to San Carlos at first light, having completed load transfer from RFA *Resource* and MV *Elk* at edge of TEZ.

HMS *Antelope* hit by Skyhawk bombs, both fail to explode. One explodes later during defusing operation and sinks her.

Fort Austin's Sea Kings (from 826 NAS) join submarine hunt.

RE begin assembling fuel handling equipment and landing strip to allow shore-based helicopter and Harrier operation.

23/24 May overnight

RFA *Resource, Sir Bedivere* and *Tidepool* enter San Carlos.

RFA *Sir Percivale* moved out.

Week 11

24 May (Mon)

RFAs *Sir Bedivere, Sir Galahad* and *Sir Lancelot* hit; bombs don't explode. *Lancelot* claims hits with Bofors and machine guns on a Skyhawk and a Mirage (Mirage confirmed).

RM Blowpipe section aboard *Sir Bedivere* claim a probable.

RFAs *Fort Austin, Resource* and *Stromness* all near-missed.

RFA *Sir Galahad*'s bomb removed, ship patched up and returned to TRALA (Tug, Repair and Logistic Area) to start work again.

Norland claims to have damaged a Mirage, before being hit by wreckage.

RFA *Fort Grange* leaves Ascension.

24/25 May overnight

RFAs *Tidepool, Sir Tristram, Sir Bedivere* and MV *Norland* escorted out of Falkland sound and eventually out of TEZ.

25 May

Argentina's national day.

Resource and *Fort Austin* report hearing external noises, 02.00.

RFAs checked by Fleet Clearance Diving (FCD) teams, then re-anchored on eastern side of San Carlos Water, along with two damaged Sir-class ships.

SS *Atlantic Conveyor* hit by two Exocets, set on fire and abandoned. Three RFA crewmembers reported killed or missing, presumed dead.

HMS *Coventry* sunk. HMS *Broadsword*, HMS *Argonaut* damaged.

Argentine land-based radar first used to detect 800 NAS CAP and direct Argentine fighter-bombers away.

RFA *Engadine* arrives Ascension.

MV *British Enterprise III* leaves UK heading south.

25/26 May overnight

RFA *Stromness* leaves San Carlos Water.

RFA *Fort Austin* takes *Coventry*'s survivors on board, before leaving that night.

RFA *Stromness, Resource, Tidepool* and *Sir Percivale* also out of Falkland Sound, escorted by HMS *Ambuscade*.

26 May

RFA *Bayleaf* sails from Portland on her maiden voyage, heading south.

RFA *Engadine* departs Ascension.

MV *British Esk* lands *Sheffield* survivors at Ascension.

RFA *Regent*, with Carrier Battle Group, transfers one 600 and two 600 (S) nuclear rounds to RFA *Resource*.

Reinforcements join Carrier Battle Group.

Carrier Battle Group spends day replenishing from RFA *Tidepool* brought from Amphibious Operations Area by HMS *Ambuscade*.

Unexploded bomb removed from *Sir Galahad*.

45 Commando and 3 Para move to Teal Inlet.

2 Para move south to Darwin and Goose Green.

Irishman sent to salvage *Atlantic Conveyor*.

26/27 May overnight

Sir Geraint and *Europic Ferry* out of San Carlos.

11th Mine Countermeasures Sqn arrive South Georgia.

Iris (cable ship) arrived 25 May to begin loading steel plate and welding gas for *Stena Seaspread* in TRALA.

27 May

LPDs *Intrepid* and *Fearless* now serving as helicopter ships in San Carlos, with damaged LSLs (*Sir Lancelot* and *Sir Galahad*) also serving as landing and refuelling points.

Brigade Maintenance Area attacked and hit.

RFA *Bayleaf* departs Ascension.

RFA *Olna* arrives Falklands.

27/28 May overnight

RFA *Tidepool* to replenish ships in San Carlos, with MV *Elk* to unload ammo. Both leave before daylight, under cover of darkness.

RMS *Queen Elizabeth II* arrives Cumberland Bay, South Georgia, and transfers 5 Inf Bde to SS *Canberra*, MV *Norland* and RFA *Stromness*.

28 May

RFA *Tidepool* and MV *Elk* return to San Carlos Water.

HMS *Fearless* leaves San Carlos.

HMS *Bristol* designated LOLA (TRALA) manager.

Goose Green and Darwin captured by 2 Para. Commanding Officer Col H Jones killed.

28/29 May overnight

After completing replenishment, RFA *Tidepool* and MV *Elk* leave under cover of darkness.

SS *Atlantic Conveyor* sinks under tow.

RFA *Blue Rover* sustains slight damage while replenishing *Norland*.

RFA *Stromness* arrives Cumberland Bay, South Georgia. Takes on troops, ammo and Rapier missiles from MV *Lycaon*.

29 May

Unexploded bomb removed from *Sir Lancelot*.

Sir Percivale to San Carlos today, back-loading stores for Teal Inlet.

RFA *Tidepool* and *Elk* return to San Carlos.

Hospital ship *Uganda* anchors Grantham Sound.

MV *British Wye* bombed by lone Hercules. Only one glancing hit, no damage.

2 Para and 42 Cdo capture Goose Green.

29/30 May overnight

After completing replenishment, RFA *Tidepool* and MV *Elk* leave under cover of darkness.

Fearless joins Carrier Battle group, having collected Major-General Moore, Brigadier Wilson and their staffs from *Antrim*.

RFA *Blue Rover* leaves South Georgia to rendezvous with Task Group.

30 May

Sir Percivale used as temporary Argentine POW accommodation.

RFA *Tidepool* and MV *Elk* enter San Carlos.

Atlantic Causeway and *Europic Ferry* due from TRALA, but turn back in heavy seas.

30/31 May overnight

MV *Elk* leaves San Carlos before dawn but RFA *Tidepool* remains.

Remaining LSLs, *Sir Galahad* and *Sir Lancelot*, leave San Carlos Water.

45 Commando secures Douglas Settlement.

3 Para secures Teal Inlet.

'K' Coy 42 Commando relieve SAS on Mount Kent.

Week 12

31 May (Mon)

RFA *Tidepool* supplies fuel to Forward Operating Bases at Port San Carlos and San Carlos Settlement.

MV *Elk* unloads ammo in San Carlos.

31 May/1 June overnight

Elk and *Tidepool* depart, while *Baltic Ferry*, *Atlantic Causeway* and RFA *Blue Rover* move in.

Norland, carrying 1/7th Gurkha Rifles and *Hermes'* Commando detachment, follows behind without escort.

Intrepid transports LCVP and LCU to Port Salvador for minesweeping ops.

First Vulcan strike with Shrike missiles on Argentine TPS-43 radar.

HMS *Alacrity*, *Ambuscade* and *Exeter* detach for separate missions.

RFA *Fort Grange* attacked by Argentine C-130 on its way to Carrier Battle Group.

RFA *Resource* to South Georgia for replenishment during this week.

RFA *Engadine* enters TEZ, on way to San Carlos Water, during this week.

1 June

RFA *Appleleaf* reassigned to 'motorway tanking' duties until 18 July.

RFA *Plumleaf* leaves 'motorway tanking' operation.

RFA *Sir Galahad*, in TRALA, now fully operational.

1/2 June overnight

Port Salvador channel swept up to Teal Inlet by LCVP.

Atlantic Causeway offloads.

Norland unloads Gurkhas at Ajax Bay.

Baltic Ferry unloads.

Intrepid leaves to collect landing craft.

Sir Percivale makes first run into Teal Inlet.

Elk leaves Carrier Battle Group to return to TRALA.

Canberra joins Carrier Battle Group before leaving for San Carlos with RFA *Tidepool*.

Active, *Ambuscade* and *Exeter* leave Carrier Battle Group for missions in Port Stanley area.

2 June

Leaflet raids on Port Stanley by Harriers.

HMS *Invincible* transfers one 600 to *Fort Austin*.

RFA *Blue Rover* leaves.

RFAs *Sir Galahad* and *Sir Bedivere* back-load stores for Teal Inlet.

Canberra and RFA *Tidepool* arrive an hour before dawn.

Welsh and Scots Guard disembark *Canberra*.

Nordic Ferry and *Atlantic Causeway* finish unloading.

2/3 June overnight

Four ships depart San Carlos: Sir-class ships to Teal, *Nordic Ferry* and *Atlantic Causeway* to Carrier Battle Group.

RFAs *Stromness*, *Sir Tristram* and *Blue Rover,* and MV *Nordic Ferry* arrive.

2 Para secure Swan Inlet and Fitzroy Settlement.

Argentine prisoners from Goose Green moved into *Norland*.

MV *Scottish Eagle* arrives Ascension to take up duties as station tanker.

3 June

Canberra completes offload in San Carlos.

Gurkhas move to Darwin, 2 Para occupy Bluff Cove settlement.

RFA *Plumleaf* breaks down and after repairs, begins 'motorway tanking' operation at twenty-five degrees south.

RFA *Fort Austin* relieved by *Fort Grange*, the latter joining Carrier Battle Group from TRALA along with *Elk* and *Tidepool*.

HMS *Brilliant* transfers one 600 to *Fort Austin*.

HMS *Glamorgan* transfers one 600 (T) to *Fort Austin*.

RFA *Resource* transfers one 600, two 600 (S), two 600 (T) to *Fort Austin*.

HMS *Invincible* transfers one 600 to *Fort Austin*.

RFA *Fort Grange* transfers one 600 (T) to *Fort Austin*.

RFA *Engadine* overflown by Argentinean Boeing 707, 1,000 miles northeast of Falklands.

3/4 June overnight

RFAs *Stromness*, *Blue Rover* and SS *Canberra* leave.

Intrepid, *Elk*, and RFA *Sir Galahad* move in, the last heading for Teal Inlet independently.

RFA *Sir Percivale* finishes offload at Teal Inlet and returns to San Carlos.

HMS *Plymouth* bombards Port Howard.

4 June

Sir Percivale back-loads at San Carlos for Teal Inlet, while *Sir Tristram* loads ammunition and stores for 5 Brigade at Fitzroy.

Team from *Stena Seaspread* repairing *Sir Lancelot*.

Inbound Transport Area convoy *Sir Geraint* and *Blue Rover*.

Sir Galahad unloads at Teal Inlet, not entering narrows until full daylight. Weather on Argentine mainland prevents air attack.

Exeter, *Invincible* and *Brilliant* examine land-based Exocet threat.

National Union of Seamen meeting.

5 June

RFA *Sir Lancelot* mobility restored.

RFA *Sir Geraint* devises Mexeflote transfer, consisting of Mexeflote secured between stern doors, with fork lift then able to work between ships.

RFA *Sir Percivale* moves to Teal Inlet. *Sir Galahad* still off-loading so *Sir Percivale* acts as helo refuel point

HMS *Sheathbill*, Harrier strip at Port San Carlos, is operational.

MV *Nordic Ferry* and *Elk* still offloading.

HMS *Intrepid* embarks 2nd Battalion Scots Guards.

RFA *Fort Austin*, with Carrier Battle Group, begins transferring stores to *Fort Grange* and back-loads Task Force nuclear devices.

5/6 June overnight

HMS *Intrepid* transports Scots Guards, overnight, to Lively Island, where they are disembarked for Bluff Cove, a distance of thirty-five miles, via landing craft.

Friendly fire incident involving HMS *Cardiff* results in loss of Army Gazelle of 656 Sqn AAC.

RFA *Pearleaf* operating in South Georgia area.

6 June

Bad weather makes HMS *Sheathbill* unusable.

RFA *Fort Austin*, with Carrier Battle Group, finishes transferring stores to *Fort Grange*, then sends helo equipment to *Atlantic Causeway*. *Fort Austin* heads for South Georgia and then home.

6/7 June overnight

RFA *Blue Rover* and MV *Nordic Ferry* both emptied and outbound overnight. *Baltic Ferry* and *Norland* inbound.

Welsh Guards aboard *Fearless* sail at 19.30 to rendezvous with *Intrepid* LCUs north of Lively Island. LCUs do not make rendezvous.

Sir Geraint back-loading for Teal.

Sir Tristram completes loading for Fitzroy, sailing at 23.00.

Active, *Ambuscade*, *Invincible* and *Brilliant* detached for missions inshore.

Hydra, ambulance ship, arrives Montevideo.

MV *Stena Inspector* sails from Charleston, USA, heading south.

Week 13

7 June (Mon)

RFA *Fort Austin* leaves Carrier Battle Group for Devonport, UK, where she arrives 29 June, carrying nuclear rounds.

Intrepid returns to San Carlos, having failed to collect LCUs. Her two remaining LCUs take two companies of Welsh Guards ashore and are left at Bluff Cove, before she returns.

7/8 June overnight

RFA *Sir Galahad* takes Welsh Guards, Field Ambulance, Rapier Troop and vehicles aboard at San Carlos Water. Begins trip to Bluff Cove, unescorted, at 22.00.

Fearless to Teal at 7.30 to collect two LCUs.

Sir Percivale begins return from Teal at same time.

Intrepid to Low Bay, Lafonia, to collect her four LCUs which have travelled there from Bluff Cove.

Norland, with POWs aboard, sails overnight, with *Elk*.

Junella, *Pict*, and *Cordella* inbound to Transport Area (TA) from South Georgia.

RFAs *Engadine*, *Olna* and *Atlantic Causeway* also inbound.

RFA *Stromness* arrives Cumberland Bay, South Georgia, to re-store from MV *Saxonia*.

8 June

RFA *Sir Tristram* and RFA *Sir Galahad* bombed at Bluff Cove (fifty casualties, Welsh Guards and RFA).

HMS *Plymouth* damaged by bomb.

LCU F4 attacked.

Trouble with inbound convoy to San Carlos, RFA *Engadine* and minesweepers ordered back to Carrier Battle Group.

HMS *Penelope* collects RFA *Olna* and *Atlantic Causeway*.

Commandos deal with Cape Dolphin OP and *Plymouth* sent to bombard Mount Rosalie OP.

HMS *Sheathbill* airstrip damaged (causes lack of cover at Fitzroy).

RFA *Sir Geraint* loads for Teal.

RFA *Fort Austin* arrives South Georgia.

Wimpey Seahorse arrives South Georgia to begin laying moorings.

US tanker *Hercules* attacked by Argentinean C-130 (Hercules).

MVs *Laertes* and *Astronomer* leave UK, heading south.

9 June

Europic Ferry heads north from Carrier Battle Group to rendezvous with helicopter transport *Contender Bezant*.

RFA *Engadine* and minesweepers to anchorage. Helicopter support crews, from *Engadine*, now at work.

HMS *Sheathbill* strip operating again.

Wounded from LSLs to *Intrepid*, San Carlos medical facility and *Uganda*.

RFA *Fort Grange* and *Nordic Ferry* arrive anchorage.

Atlantic Causeway, RFA *Olna* leave for TRALA.

RFA *Sir Geraint*, *Cordella* and *Pict* leave for Port Salvador where the minesweepers are needed to sweep Berkely Sound.

10 June

RFA *Fort Grange* begins supply replenishment in San Carlos. Almost emergency situation for some ships, RFA *Sir Percivale*, for example, having only two days' food left.

RFA *Blue Rover*, replenished by STUFT in TRALA, enters during day.

RFA *Bayleaf* arrives TRALA.

10/11 June overnight

Outward from Transport Area at dusk, RFAs *Fort Grange*, *Olna*, MVs *Atlantic Causeway* and *Baltic Ferry*.

Forward helicopter operating base established at Fitzroy.

HMS *Intrepid* launches three LCUs off Lively Island to land stores at Fitzroy.

RFA *Sir Geraint* off-loading at Teal.

HMS *Yarmouth* bombards Stanley.

11 June

Stanley attacked by Harriers for the last time.

Wessex 5 (AS 12-armed) targets Stanley police station, believed Argentine military HQ.

Sir Percivale loads at San Carlos for Teal.

Blue Rover replenishes ships and tops up onshore fuel dumps.

LSL crews out of Transport Area aboard *Atlantic Causeway*.

SS *Uganda* to Grantham Sound in daylight for casualty evacuation.

RFA *Sir Bedivere* and *Elk* inbound.

Sir Percivale outbound to Teal, *Sir Geraint* returns from Teal, both escorted by *Exeter*.

Intrepid repeats LCU run to Lively Island.

HMS *Glamorgan* hit and set on fire by truck-mounted Exocet fired from Port Stanley High Street.

MV *Avalona Star* leaves UK, heading south.

RFA *Fort Austin* departs South Georgia for UK, where Commodore R M Thorn CBE, RFA is to take command.

12 June

The final attack on Stanley begins.

Sir Geraint back-loads in San Carlos for Teal from *Elk*, and takes AVCAT fuel from *Blue Rover*.

Sir Percivale unloads at Teal.

Norland off River Plate to unload casualties.

RFAs *Blue Rover* and *Sir Geraint* outbound.

RFA *Olna* inbound.

13 June

3 Commando Brigade tactical HQ attacked.

Damage to HMS *Sheathbill* strip so Harriers land on LPDs.

HMS *Intrepid* outbound to collect LCUs.

MV *Nordic Ferry* inbound forty-five miles southeast of Fitzroy.

Week 14

14 June (Mon)

Menendez asks for cease-fire at 14.21 local time.

15 June

2 Para enters Port Stanley.

16 June

RFA *Sir Percivale* first British ship to enter Port Stanley, followed by RFA *Sir Bedivere*.

RFA *Plumleaf* relieved from motorway tanking, heads north to Ascension.

National Union Seamen in dispute with RFA management over war bonus to RFA personnel.

Later

21–30 June

Sir Geraint, Sir Percivale, Resource, Stromness leave for UK.

26 June

HMS *Hermes* transfers one 600 and two 600 (T) rounds to *Resource*.

Resource departs for UK.

July

RFA *Sir Lancelot* departs for UK.

RFA *Engadine* departs for UK.

RFA *Appleleaf* departs for UK.

RFA *Pearleaf* motorway tanking Ascension.

August
RFA *Regent* departs for UK.
RFA *Tidepool* departs for Chile.
RFA *Bayleaf* departs for UK.

September
RFA *Fort Austin* arrives South Atlantic for second visit.
RFA *Fort Grange* departs for UK.

October
Sir Bedivere leaves Falklands carrying over sixty war dead.
Fort Austin leaves for UK.
Fort Grange arrives from UK.

1983
Sir Tristram back to UK aboard *Dan Lifter* for rebuilding.

APPENDIX B

History of the Falklands and the war

Occupying a position in the Southern Ocean, fifty-two degrees south and sixty degrees west, the Falklands consist of a group of two islands, West Falkland, the larger, and East Falkland.

East Falkland is almost two islands itself, joined as it is to Lafonia by a narrow strip of land upon which perch the settlements of Darwin and Goose Green. Falkland Sound runs through the middle of the group, separating it into two roughly-equal land masses.

Most of the population live on East Falkland, with settlement mainly concentrated in the coastal areas. Inland, sheep farming is the main occupation, concentrated in the area known as the Camp (from the Spanish, *el Campo*: the country).

Eight thousand miles from Britain and only four hundred from the Argentine mainland, the islands are climatically quite like Britain, with perhaps more rain and wind, even in the short summer which falls, in these latitudes, between November and March. Movement on land is much more difficult, however, since most of the land is peat which makes travelling in anything but a four-wheel drive vehicle near-impossible. Sea conditions might be charitably described as unpredictable.

The RFA has had a long association with the islands, their tankers being responsible for replenishing the tanks at Stanley, from which HMS *Endurance* refuelled on her periodic visits. *Endurance* was one of the few ships in the Royal Navy not fitted for refuelling at sea, since her replenishment was always shore based. Which proved something of a headache for her crew and RFA *Tidespring* in the spring of 1982.

At the time of the war, in 1982, two-thirds of the farms on the islands were owned by the 116-year-old Falkland Islands Company (FIC), giving them virtually total control of the region's meagre economy. Between 1951 and 1972, estimates indicate that the FIC took £11.5 million more in profit from the islands than they had invested back, with significant benefit to the British taxpayer.

By the early eighties, however, with the recession in world farming, the islands and their defence had become a drain on the Treasury, lending weight to the plans of Foreign Office officials who had been intent upon ridding themselves of an expensive and troublesome piece of South Atlantic real estate since the mid 1940s.

There's some argument about when the islands themselves were first discovered, but Britain's formal, continuous occupation began with a Capt Richard Onslow, who, in 1833, summarily ejected the Argentine garrison, led by Don Jose Maria Pinedo, and raised the Union Flag before taking possession of the islands for the British Crown.

This has been the situation ever since, with Britain effectively squatting on an island, barely two days' sail from the Argentine mainland, which they had obtained by what, in the words of one Foreign Office official in the early part of the twentieth century '. . . might be considered an act of international banditry.'

Argentina's claim to the islands rests on the argument that discovery alone isn't enough to claim sovereignty. There has to be occupation and a settled administration, which began on the Falklands with a French Colony, founded by Antoine de Bougainville, at Port Louis on East Falkland, in 1764; de Bougainville subsequently claimed all the islands for France in the name of Louis XV. A year later, in 1765, the British established a colony of their own on West Falkland, only discovering the presence of the French, who had arrived before them, in 1766.

Spain now entered the fray, with France ceding the Port Louis colony to them in 1767. By 1769, the Buenos Aires authorities had thrown the British out and apart from diplomatic wrangling and one or two set-piece incursions designed as face-savers for the British Government, the situation remained quiet, the

Argentineans even achieving a measure of short-term economic success with some farming and their exploitation of the seal fishery.

Until 1829, that is, when the Argentine-appointed Governor Louis Vernet made the mistake of arresting an American ship, the *Harriet*, confiscating some of her cargo, mostly sealskins, and then conducting the ship and her crew to Buenos Aires for trial.

Vernet claimed the *Harriet* was engaged in illegal sealing, but that didn't satisfy the American Consul. Egged on by Woodbine Parish, the British representative, the Americans dispatched the USS *Lexington*, commanded by one Silas Duncan, to settle the matter. Which Duncan did by razing the Argentinean settlement to the ground. Seeing its chance in the resulting confusion, the Admiralty dispatched Onslow and the rest is history.

So, the Argentineans claim they were there first, with their claim direct from the French who were the first settlers, and that the British only took possession after an act of American aggression.

Britain says:

1. It asserted a claim to West Falkland in 1765 and never renounced it.

2. It has been in continuous possession for 150 years and that constitutes a right of ownership.

3. The existing population have a right of self-determination, and most of them want to stay British.

And it is this last point that has proven the stumbling block in the years of negotiation between 1964 and 1982.

Despite co-operation in two World Wars, and the use of the Falklands as a Royal Navy base, there was a continual wave of niggling incidents up until 1964, which saw one of the most significant developments in the long-running saga.

In that year, the United Nations Committee on Decolonisation included the Falklands in its list of territories that ought to be encouraged to change their status, and by 1965, Argentina and the UK were being gently pressured to seek a way to resolve their differences amicably.

It was not always generally acknowledged, especially in the heady days of early 1982, that Her Majesty's Government had actually been trying to rid itself of responsibility for the islands, once and for all, since about 1940. Moreover, it was the considered view of the Foreign and Commonwealth Office, a branch of the Civil Service less than cordially regarded by the Thatcher administration, that the islands' only hope for any long-term economic and demographic stability lay in closer liaison with the Argentine mainland.

To this end, the Whitehall diplomats had adopted the so-called hearts and minds policy, perhaps best summarised by one of their brighter lights, David Scott, when he said, in talking about the 1971 Communications agreement: 'rape of the Falklands, no; seduction, by all means.'

The UN resolution, which was passed in 1965, seemed to offer a reasonable basis for some sort of negotiation, since it asked only that the interests of the islanders be taken into account, implying that while some reasonable level of concern should be accorded the inhabitants, they had no ultimate veto. Reasonable enough, when one considers that, by 1968, when the Falkland Islands Council had persuaded the Government to change the wording of the text to 'wishes', 1,800 islanders were effectively holding the joint populations of Argentina and the UK to ransom.

Negotiations stumbled on, surviving the fall of the Wilson Government and a change in Foreign Office policy, when sovereignty was removed from the agenda and the proviso added that the islanders should be involved throughout any talks. Talks were also downgraded to become the responsibility of the Under-Secretary for Independent Territories, the aforementioned David Scott.

With remarkable aplomb and no little manoeuvring, Scott managed to broker a deal, the 1971 Memorandum of Agreement, which satisfied both the islanders and the Argentine Government.

Under the terms of this new deal, Argentina would run the air service, if Britain agreed to build and maintain the necessary airstrip, as well as operating a shipping link to the Argentine mainland.

In essence, Scott had managed to avoid all the complexities of sovereignty and forced integration while hitting upon the one approach which stood some chance of success: economic interdependence. An air service meant islanders could enjoy the benefits of tourism as well as being able to use Argentine schools and hospitals. Imports would increase, particularly fresh fruit and other luxury items, previously only available via the FIC's vessel *Darwin*, which was losing money and had been earmarked for withdrawal at the end of 1971, anyway.

And his subsequent approach to the islanders was nothing short of masterly, reiterating constantly, as he did, that his major concern was a better standard of living for the islanders, not sovereignty.

This agreement, which was signed on 1 July 1971, marked the real high point in the relations between Argentina and the islanders.

At first, things seemed to be going well. The Argentineans began the agreed air service with an Albatross flying boat and the younger islanders appear to have been enthusiastic about the prospect offered by more financial and cultural links with the mainland.

It was not to be, however. No permanent airstrip was ever built and Scott's painfully constructed accord was, by 1976, in tatters. Publication of the

Shackleton Report, late in 1976, with its suggestion of a massive £13 million to increase the independence of the island community, did nothing to help, especially since Whitehall's intention had been that the report should be a basis for forcing concessions from the, by now, thoroughly disillusioned islanders.

Britain had not quite abandoned the 'Kelpers' to their fate, however. Late in 1976, a group of Argentine nationals were put ashore on South Thule, in the South Sandwich group, although the Buenos Aires administration initially denied any landing had taken place. Callaghan's government did nothing and, apparently encouraged by this and the projected removal of HMS *Endurance*, the Navy's Ice Patrol Vessel, in November 1977, the Argentine Navy cut the fuel supply to Port Stanley and declared that Argentine ships would longer fly the Union Flag in island waters.

Callaghan responded by immediately dispatching a small Task Force, comprising two frigates, a nuclear submarine and two RFAs, a tanker and a store ship, to the area, just before the yearly round of negotiations were due to begin, in anticipation of those meetings degenerating into a quarrel.

The Task Force remained on station until January when it was judged that the risk of conflict had subsided and the vessels could be quietly returned to their home ports. Britain claimed it never informed Buenos Aires about the presence of the ships, and such was the discipline of the ships' companies involved, that the deployment remained a secret until Callaghan himself revealed it, just after the 1982 invasions. Even the log books of the RFA cadets aboard the tanker were destroyed to preserve the secret.

The South Thule incident did seem to concentrate the minds of both parties and this led to a number of solutions being proposed. After a series of negotiations, chiefly involving Anthony Crossland's junior minister Ted 'Tiny' Rowlands, one of them, the concept of 'leaseback', was suggested as a way forward for the first time.

This involved sovereignty passing back to Argentina, while maintaining a long-term British presence on the islands for administration purposes, in some ways similar to Hong Kong. Additionally, all questions of nationality and constitutional rights would remain unaffected.

It was felt that such a solution, as well as going a long way to ease the tension, would also, once again, begin to encourage investment and immigration, two things of which the islands still stood in dire need, especially since the Foreign and Commonwealth Office were advocating a time course of some thirty years, at least a generation, for its implementation.

Political will, however, didn't quite match Foreign Office enthusiasm, and negotiations were still in a state of flux when the General Election of May 1979 saw the first female Prime Minister in British history boosted into office, in the person of Mrs Margaret Thatcher.

A new administration, of course, meant changes at the Foreign Office. Lord Carrington, as the only Tory remotely qualified by seniority and experience, was placed in charge here, with the unfortunate Nicholas Ridley drafted in as a junior minister.

Ridley's areas of responsibility included the Falklands, and after an initial tour of the Americas, including the Falklands, he returned home determined to sort this one out once and for all.

Ridley, like his predecessors, found himself faced with three options. He could freeze sovereignty, while continuing economic negotiations; there could be a joint Anglo-Argentinean administration (condominium); or a transfer of sovereignty to Argentina with a long-term leaseback to Britain.

Of the three, only leaseback looked like having the slightest chance of succeeding, Buenos Aires having made it clear that a freeze was totally unacceptable while the islanders would have nothing to do with the idea of a Argentine administration.

Unfortunately, despite the stark clarity of his choices, Ridley still had some problems to overcome before he could even begin any sort of negotiation. Initially, he had to convince Carrington, Thatcher, the cabinet's Overseas and Defence (OD) Committee and finally, the formidable parliamentary Conservative party that leaseback was viable.

Carrington proved remarkably malleable, although he did decide to bring the subject up with Mrs Thatcher himself, and after a period of what might charitably be described as tense discussion between those involved, it is claimed that Ridley persuaded her that some movement had to be made or, given the unstable state of its home and foreign policy, the Argentine Government would see invasion and permanent occupation as a serious option.

Mrs Thatcher finally allowed Ridley a hearing before the OD Committee, where he won approval to put a consultative document to the islanders. At this point, the parliamentary Conservative party was carefully avoided.

His trip to the islands proved difficult but eventually fruitful, finding, as he did, that many islanders, especially the younger people, conceded the need for a different, more settled relationship with the mainland. Indeed, it was reported in the *Times* at the height of the war that some islanders held the view that Argentina would put more money into the island in five years than the British had done in the last 150.

It was just a shame, for Ridley, that the Commons didn't share this pragmatic, practical view. Upon his return, he was crucified in Parliament and by the media, when he suggested both, the idea of leaseback and that, perhaps, after all, the islanders' wishes should not be paramount, although there was certainly never any question that their interests should not be considered. This adverse reaction not only sent all kinds of disquieting signals to Buenos Aires, but it had the ultimately far more damaging effect of allowing the Falkland Island Council to force the Government to insist that island representatives be included in any future talks and the sovereignty issue be frozen. This basically left both parties with nothing to talk about, since sovereignty, at least to the Argentineans, was the whole point of the exercise in the first place – sovereignty, notice, not actual possession, since Argentina had indicated it was quite willing to consider leaseback, with a long-term British administration.

The matter was further complicated when the Defence White Paper of 1981 advocated scrapping the Ice Patrol Vessel HMS *Endurance*, weakening the Government's already tenuous military links with the area.

At the same time, Buenos Aires received what it saw as more signals of British lack of interest in the islands with the new British Nationality Bill, which deprived 800 of the islanders of their British nationality, almost at a stroke.

In Buenos Aires, matters had also taken a turn for the worse.

Between 1976 and 1981, the country was ruled by a Junta of officers from the three armed forces, led by Lieutenant General Jorge Videla. Under Videla's regime, the economy was finally stabilised, with inflation falling, although the price was gruesome. Political self-expression was ruthlessly eliminated by systematic kidnap, torture and murder of any of the regime's opponents, with over 9,000 Argentineans disappearing in those six years, many, it is said, murdered by serving officers in the Argentine armed forces.

In March 1981 Videla retired, to be replaced by General Roberto Viola. Inflation once again soared and in December 1981, Viola was replaced in turn by a hard-drinking ex-cavalry officer, Leopoldo Galtieri.

Upon his election, Galtieri found himself presented with a difficult situation.

On the one hand, the British plan to allow Falklanders into the negotiations and freeze any discussion of sovereignty was seen as a hardening of their attitude and a move towards a Fortress Falklands policy, frankly acknowledged by both sides to be physically and economically unworkable. (Although, after 1982, that is exactly the situation which developed.)

On the other hand, by allowing *Endurance* to be scrapped and depriving many of the islanders of their British citizenship, Whitehall was seen as fatally limiting its military options in the area and, by so doing, was declaring an lessening of interest in the islands' future.

With considerable opposition to the removal of *Endurance*, and with the certainty that something had to be done, the Foreign Office, in what seems almost desperation, advocated a policy of education among the islanders, in order to explain the advantages of leaseback and the safeguards which such a procedure would have built in.

Even this didn't meet with whole-hearted Government approval, Carrington being doubtful of its success without, as he put it: '. . . very firm Government-approved policy.'

In other words, the Prime Minister might not like it.

General Leopoldo Galtieri inherited this unhappy state of affairs when he assumed power on 8 December 1981, at the head of a new and unstable military Junta, it having been made quite clear to him that his hold on power effectively depended upon his Government's foreign policy.

Meeting on 18 December against a background of rapidly spiralling inflation (100 per cent in December 1981), alleged human rights violations (the so-called 'Dirty War' of 1976–79) and the Beagle channel dispute with Chile, it was plain to many observers, on both sides, that some major external initiative was needed to attract attention away from troubles on the home front, much of it fomented by the Peronist trade unions.

The Falklands was the only important foreign policy issue left available, and with the 150th anniversary approaching, it was generally felt that something definite ought to be achieved in the sovereignty dispute at least.

The Foreign Minister, Dr Nicanor Costa Mendez, advocated a diplomatic assault, with invasion a possibility later in the year, when the weather would make any British attempt at reoccupation much more difficult.

The Junta agreed, although they took the precaution of ordering the current contingency plans for a Falklands invasion to be updated, in case diplomacy failed and public opinion demanded some more definite action. Although what they were to do in face of the inevitable British reaction and how they would go about hanging onto the islands once they'd been captured, in the face of action by one of best navies on the face of the earth, doesn't seem to have been decided.

Alongside Argentine error of interpretation, it is also clear that the British Government failed entirely to appreciate the depth of feeling in Argentina over the Falklands/Malvinas. Even Argentinean school children understood the nature of the dispute, and furthermore, knew very clearly who they felt the Malvinas belonged to, repossession of the Malvinas having, as one British Ambassador put it, an almost religious significance, as well as being seen as one cause which would unite all Argentineans, something probably thought very desirable by a government struggling with the sort of national problems of political unrest and economic insolvency which Galtieri's Junta faced.

In January 1982, Anthony Williams, the serving British Ambassador to Buenos Aires, justifiably alarmed by increasing press activity, signalled the

Foreign Office that a serious situation was developing, in that it appeared to be more than one of the periodic bouts of bluster which successive Argentine governments had been prone to. This advice, like so much previously passed on by the Foreign Office, appears to have been largely, if not completely, ignored by the relevant Minister.

On 27 January, Costa Mendez fired the first shot in the diplomatic conflict, contacting the Foreign Office and proposing a commission be set up, meeting monthly, with a strict deadline, its brief to discuss, amongst other things, the sovereignty of the Falkland Islands.

Argentina's stance was hardening, however, and after another fruitless meeting between Foreign Office Minister Richard Luce and Enrique Cos, the Argentineans issued a statement insisting that time for negotiation was limited and that sovereignty was, at least for the Argentine Government, the central issue and that if no satisfactory response was forthcoming, Argentina could: '. . . choose freely the procedure which best accords with her own best interests.'

It was clear something needed to be done and soon.

This already tense situation was not further helped by the appearance of an article in a Buenos Aires newspaper, suggesting the possibility of invasion.

The Foreign Office appears to have taken these moves seriously even though analysis by the relevant branch of military intelligence, the Joint Intelligence Committee, and therefore, the advice subsequently offered to Cabinet, indicated that any response was likely to take the form of a slow build-up of pressure from the Argentineans, beginning with the breaking of links between the island and the mainland and only much later escalating into some form of military action. They even went so far as to warn the islanders indirectly, via a letter to the Governor, that: '. . . unless there was a negotiated settlement, the way forward could only be downhill.'

Certainly, the career diplomats were more concerned than the majority of Mrs Thatcher's cabinet seemed to be, including the Prime Minister herself, her sole response to Costa Mendez's statement, prior to her telephone conversation with Carrington on the 28th, being to mark a telegram from the British Ambassador in Buenos Aires, dated 8 March: 'We must make contingency plans.'

What she envisaged those plans might have been is not recorded. Nor was there any further response on her part, until 31 March, when she claimed that the invasion had come out of the blue, although John Nott, the Defence Secretary, stated in the House of Commons, on 3 April, that preparations (for the Task Force) had been in progress for several weeks. The 'several weeks' of Mr Nott's statement seems contradictory when taken with the accounts of Mrs Thatcher and First Sea Lord Sir Henry Leach, who both aver that the first intimation of the need for a Task Force was made at a private meeting on 31 March, in Mrs

Thatcher's office at Westminster.

Whatever the real situation, it is quite clear than nobody in Whitehall took the Argentine invasion threat seriously until 31 March, by which time their fleet was at sea and the UK Government's sole option was to wait and see what happened.

The spark which ignited this explosive blend of Argentine nationalism and British reaction in the South Atlantic during the spring and summer of 1982, was struck by an innocent businessman called Constantino Davidoff, although the war which appeared to result from his lightweight misdemeanours should really be viewed as the end result of a long diplomatic wrangle rather than his sole responsibility. Certainly, in this context, a lot of evidence has come to light in the aftermath of the war, which suggests that the Junta were planning an invasion anyway, although much later in the year, when reoccupation would have been significantly more difficult.

Mr Davidoff, having obtained a contract to remove several old whaling stations from South Georgia, visited the island on the sophisticated Argentine ice-breaker ARA *Almirante Irizar*, without, however, reporting his presence to King Edward Point, as he should have done. Unusually for that region, the *Almirante* maintained strict radio silence throughout her voyage.

The British Embassy in Buenos Aires protested about Davidoff's actions to the Junta, without eliciting any response, and on 9 March 1982, Davidoff informed the British Embassy in Buenos Aires that he was going to begin his contract, by initially transporting forty-one men to South Georgia on the Argentine Navy transport vessel ARA *Bahia Bueno Suceso*.

The *Bahia Bueno Suceso* left on 11 March, the British Embassy reminding Davidoff, via his lawyer, of the need to report his arrival to King Edward Point, Grytviken, before proceeding.

On 18 March, the *Bahia Bueno Suceso* arrived at Leith, having failed to make the necessary stop at King Edward Point, and information about the landings was conveyed to Mr Rex Hunt, Governor of the Falklands, on 19 March.

Hunt felt the Argentineans might be trying to repeat their South Thule operation, using this presence in South Georgia to assert sovereignty at a later date, and he sent this appreciation to London. Later in the day, advice arrived from the British Embassy, Buenos Aires, to exercise restraint until the exact nature of the incident was known and whether the Junta was behind it.

Whitehall was, perhaps understandably, anxious to play down what the British Ambassador referred to later as Davidoff's 'low level and trivial mis-behaviour', but against Foreign Office advice, *Endurance* and part of the Royal Marine garrison were dispatched from Port Stanley on 21 March, although by next morning, everything seemed to be calming down. The *Bahia Bueno Sucesco* appeared to have left, taking, it was assumed, all the Argentinean personnel with it, and the British consequently prepared their first press release, stating simply that Argentine nationals had landed on South Georgia and that their own government was making arrangements to have them removed. This document was released on the evening of 22 March, just before the Argentine Government confirmed the BAS's latest information that, in fact, there were still people at Leith. By then HMS *Endurance* had returned to normal duties.

Almost immediately, *Endurance* was ordered to proceed to South Georgia and remove the Argentineans illegally present there, although these orders were later modified in light of an apparently positive Argentine response.

By 24 March, however, Argentina had reinforced the scrap workers with ten marines and by the 25th, the first time the UK Cabinet had met since the crisis, two missile-carrying corvettes had been stationed between the Falklands and South Georgia, with the clear intention of intercepting *Endurance* and removing its Argentinean passengers.

The situation was rapidly escalating and in an attempt to defuse it, Costa Mendez suggested that, although removal would involve an unacceptable loss of face for the Argentines, they would allow the workers to return to Grytviken and have their white cards stamped. The white card was an Argentinean document issued specifically for travel between the Falklands and Argentina, the dependencies, such as South Georgia, requiring a passport.

Williams pointed this out but Costa Mendez insisted on white cards or nothing, so the British Ambassador signalled London to that effect. Hunt, the Falklands Governor, insisted, however, that the white card arrangement only applied to the Falklands and that the workers needed to have their passports stamped. The Government agreed with Hunt. Costa Mendez was informed on 25 March that, if Davidoff's men would return to Grytviken they would be furnished with paperwork to allow them to continue their operation. No reply to this concession was ever received. Other events had overtaken and swamped it, because on 26 March 1982, Galtieri's Junta gave the order to invade the Falkland Islands.

The first intimation the British had that this might be taking a more serious turn was actually on the 26th, when intelligence reported suspect preparations in and around the main naval ports, although their considered assessment was that this was in line with a joint exercise taking place with the Uruguayan Navy.

Next day, 27 March, further reports were received, indicating intense activity in and around Puerto Belgrano, although one bright spot on the horizon was confirmation by *Endurance* that the *Bahia Paraiso Sucesco* had sailed from Leith, unfortunately leaving all the disputed personnel behind.

There was no significant improvement in the situation by next day, 28 March, and, in the evening, Mrs Thatcher telephoned Lord Carrington, expressing her concern. She was informed that the Foreign Secretary was seeking the intervention of General Alexander Haig, the American Secretary of State. On their way to Brussels next morning, the 29th, the Prime Minister and Lord Carrington decided to send a nuclear submarine to the area, as reinforcement for *Endurance*. Later, the Ministry of Defence confirmed that the submarine would be sent, along with the Royal Fleet Auxiliary *Fort Austin*, which would replenish *Endurance*'s rapidly dwindling supplies and remain on station to service any other ships sent to the area. On the same day, Admiral John (Sandy) Woodward was ordered to prepare to detach a group of ships from the annual Gibraltar-based 'Exercise Springtrain', ready to proceed south.

That evening, General Haig relayed his concern to the British Ambassador in Washington, that the British should show restraint. In response, His Excellency replied that the Americans could surely not stand neutral in a case where sovereign British territory had been invaded, and indicated that Argentina wasn't going to be allowed to get away with it.

There was some diplomatic activity over the next couple of days, with, significantly for the Argentineans, a BBC news broadcast on the 28th, which stated a task force was being prepared to sail south. It may be significant that this was the day the Junta confirmed the order for invasion.

On 31 March the British Naval Attaché in Buenos Aires signalled the Ministry of Defence that most of the Argentine fleet was at sea, destination unknown, and that this seemed very much in advance of the planned Easter exercises. In the early evening of the same day, Mr Nott was informed by MOD officials that intelligence had been received strongly indicating that the Falkland Islands would be invaded by Argentine armed forces on 2 April. Almost immediately, he was able to meet with the Prime Minister, together with Foreign Office and MOD officials, the latter including the then First Sea Lord, Sir Henry Leach.

It may perhaps be useful, at this point, to re-examine the Naval/MOD background against which these decisions were being made. The 1981 Defence White Paper had ordered sweeping cuts to be made to the Royal Navy's surface vessel establishment, particularly the sale or scrapping of its two remaining aircraft carriers. As stated earlier in this book, Leach particularly had been strongly opposed to their sale, and the ensuing reduction of the Navy's capability to not much more than the submarine-based deterrent.

Leach's crisp, confident claim to Prime Minister Thatcher that the Navy could put together a force to reoccupy the islands is seen as the crucial service intervention of the forthcoming conflict, and a pivotal moment in the recent history of the Royal Navy and that of Mrs Thatcher's political career.

The Argentine invasion came at 04.30 local time on 2 April, and was successful with almost no casualties on either side.

Back in London, the Government greeted the news of the invasion with shocked condemnation, and amidst extraordinary scenes in the House of Commons, whole party backing was given to the dispatch of a Task Force, fully equipped and ready, willing and able to take back the British sovereign territory.

There was a lot of newspaper talk, at the time, about 'Defenders of Democracy' and the wishes of the islanders to remain British being paramount, ignoring the fact that what had really happened was, after nearly 150 years of reasoned negotiation, the Argentines had, rather foolishly, lost their temper and indulged in a misguided attempt to make something happen.

In Buenos Aires, the Junta was convinced that Britain wasn't really concerned about the islands as a major issue and that the most they would do was make loud noises and then settle down to a diplomatic effort which would probably see Argentina in possession, with a British administration, i.e. the long-contemplated leaseback.

Investment in the islands' infrastructure could begin while at the same time, Argentine immigration would bolster the population and thus stabilise a flagging economy. Britain would have a firm, non-Communist ally in South America, and anyway, what real serious alternative did the British have? Reinvade, with the Antarctic winter coming on? And if they did reinvade, what would they do? With an unfriendly power only 400 miles away, and the problems of transporting everything in from a base 8,000 miles distant, surely they couldn't possibly conceive of the military option working?

In Britain, rightly or wrongly, the thinking was otherwise, although it does not seem that much concern was given to the situation, post-invasion. Certainly Mrs Thatcher wrote in her biography that on hearing of the invasion her first reaction was: '. . . if they are invaded, we've got to get them back.'

Understandable, perhaps, from a personal point of view, but as the leader of a country which had been trying to be rid of these islands for some years, was there another course, apart from the old colonial response, that she could have followed? One wonders just how much Argentina might have been persuaded to concede if Britain had been a bit more flexible in its attitude to what, in effect, turned out to be a policing garrison of initially just 500 young conscripts, ill-supplied with food and most of whom had insufficient training to even fire the weapons they were issued with.

In effect, Britain's next action was probably the decisive one. They went to the UN and there, despite the efforts of Panama, managed to secure a Security Council resolution (UNSCR 502/1982) which, amongst other things, demanded an instant cessation of hostilities and immediate withdrawal of all Argentine forces from the Falklands/Malvinas.

It meant that, while Argentina was ordered to leave, Britain could land as many troops as they liked, as long as they forgot about the immediate cessation of hostilities bit. The UK also considered itself covered under that part of the UN charter which gave the right of self-defence although how that applied 8,000 miles from home is still unclear.

Sending the Task Force and then obtaining Resolution 502 probably, more than any other actions, gave Mrs Thatcher ultimate victory because, from the day the invasion began, Galtieri had no option but to win.

Any but the mildest of concessions would have been seen as surrender and would have ensured his political demise. Mrs Thatcher had placed herself in a similar position, although she had left a tiny loophole when she insisted before the House that the wishes of the islanders were paramount, and, if they wished to come under the influence of Argentina, Her Majesty's Government would willingly concur. Resolution 502 allowed her to assume an impervious negotiating stance, without being seen as intransigent, at least on the domestic front, and when this failed, the old cry of 'islanders' wishes paramount' in the face of a Fascist regime didn't.

Almost immediately, Alexander Haig, the US Secretary of State, began shuttling backwards and forwards between London and Buenos Aires, trying to cobble together some sort of agreement which would prevent further conflict. Haig's mediation, which many saw simply as a stop-gap and which the Prime Minister herself later admitted served to prevent other, more even-handed peace makers becoming involved, was probably doomed to failure from the start and it was an added bonus when, after Britain had not moved one iota from its original stance on sovereignty or withdrawal, and the Argentines had offered a number of concessions, Haig finally gave up and, on 30 April, issued a Press statement blaming Argentine intransigence for the failure of negotiations.

In fact, on 24 April at Chequers, Mrs Thatcher herself admitted to defeating a peace proposal which Francis Pym had wanted to accept and she then almost applauded John Nott, who managed to find a constitutional way of putting the Argentines in the wrong, by insisting that they comment first on a plan that, she was fairly sure, neither side was ready to accept.

One wonders in the light of such actions about the seriousness of the British peace negotiation and the possible truth of the allegations made in the Press at the time that the Task Force was going to be used, whatever happened.

Could she have survived a negotiated settlement, anyway? On balance, it seems doubtful. The whole ethos of her administration was based on a refusal to give in under pressure, although there were many examples in the years before the Falklands incident where she would clearly have been more successful if she had been able to bring a little flexibility to her approach – most notably, perhaps, the Civil Service pay dispute which began in March 1981, when it took six months to achieve a settlement which unbiased observers claimed to have been possible in the first few days of industrial action.

Her bacon had already been saved, of course, in the early days of the Falklands War by Lord Carrington, when, despite having issued warning after warning in Cabinet and being studiously ignored, in the best traditions of Government ministers, he shouldered the blame for a situation which he had been predicting would happen all along. In truth, it was probably either him or the Prime Minister who had to go, so he went. Even so, after Carrington's departure, Denis Healey was still moved to call for the Prime Minister to resign as well.

Carrington's was a typically selfless action from a man to whom loyalty was clearly the first priority of those in Government. In effect, he paid for everyone else's mistakes, along with Richard Luce and Humphrey Aitkin, who resigned along with him. In his place, Mrs Thatcher, after a desperate attempt to persuade a disillusioned Carrington to stay, appointed Francis Pym. Not her first choice and certainly not a very happy one. She must have felt herself placed in some difficulty.

Haig's negotiation effectively finished on 30 April when he issued his press release, stating that it was Argentine intransigence which had prevented a settlement being reached. This, despite the recapture of South Georgia, on 25 April, and Thatcher's 'rejoice' comments which some, more even-handed observers, saw as going some way towards escalating the conflict.

It must have been doubly annoying for Haig because his resolution of the crisis was a potential career saver. In light of other circumstances, he was forced to resign shortly afterwards.

The Junta had become increasingly suspicious of Haig's motives but on 1 May, another attempt at mediation was made via Peru. Dr Belaúnde Terry, the Peruvian president, claimed to have been watching events in the South Atlantic with increasing alarm. When the Haig mission appeared to be over, Belaúnde telephoned the White House in order to offer his help in the matter. President Reagan was absent, but the Peruvian spoke to Haig and got from him a seven-point plan, which Haig gave as the British position. Belaúnde then rang Galtieri and after a long conversation, agreed to telephone again the next morning, which he did, having at the same time established a simultaneous link to Haig.

Now this is where the story gets muddled. Belaúnde claims that he thought Haig was speaking (and agreeing) for the British Government. He also claims that he thought Pym was in the office with Haig and had a direct link to Whitehall, so that negotiations were, in effect, taking place between the Argentinean and British Governments.

Pym tells a different story. He claims that there never were any hard proposals but merely a series of headings, and that further, he had no memory of any telephone conversation of the sort Haig describes and that he didn't report the Peruvian peace initiative to the Cabinet, because there was no firm initiative.

Hence the Peruvian press conference and Haig's claim that 'we're down to words, single words' which was afterwards so categorically denied by the British Government. Further moves in the debate soon became pointless, because at about 20.00 Buenos Aires time, the Argentine warship *General Belgrano* was torpedoed and sunk, just south of the Falklands, with the loss of 321 lives. The subsequent hardening of the Argentine stance made future attempts at negotiation somewhat more difficult than previously, even when Britain seemed to be unbending, after the disastrous sinking of HMS *Sheffield* and the deaths of thirty British servicemen.

Why did it happen?

For many years prior to 1982, the Falklands dispute had been between the islanders and the Argentinean Government, with the British Government acting as mediators rather than participants, while desperately trying to rid themselves of an increasingly expensive commitment 8,000 miles from home.

What faced the British was the apparently insoluble problem of convincing an increasingly sceptical group of Islanders of the advantages of living under an Argentine regime with a questionable human rights record.

At the same time, they were confronted with Argentine demands for the return of what they considered sovereign territory, albeit occupied by what Buenos Aires must have seen, at times, as simply a collection of long-term squatters.

Finally, Argentina invaded because the Junta thought that Britain had essentially had enough of the responsibility for the Falklands and its dependencies and by invading, the British could be coerced into negotiating a settlement in Argentina's favour, probably based on leaseback.

Such a move was driven by political and fiscal unrest in the country, although it appears that the Junta were aiming at an invasion date later in the year, when weather conditions would have made repossessing the islands immensely more difficult. They only moved at this time because Davidoff's misbehaviour seemed to present a favourable opportunity.

Subsequent events show that they clearly underestimated both Mrs Thatcher's willingness to run the risks, political and physical, of invasion and the Royal Navy's ability to respond to such a show of armed force.

APPENDIX C

In Remembrance

RFA Personnel on board RFA *Sir Galahad*
3rd Engineer Officer Christopher Francis Hailwood
2nd Engineer Officer Paul Anderson Henry (GM Posthumous)
3rd Engineer Officer Andrew John Morris
Elec Fitter Leung Chen
Butcher Sug Yuk Fai
Seaman N G Por

RFA Personnel on board RFA *Sir Tristram*
Seaman Yeung Shui Kam
Bosun Yu Sik Chee

RFA Personnel on board MV *Atlantic Conveyor*
1st Radio Officer R Hoole
Laundryman Chan Si Shing
Laundryman Ng Po

1st Battalion Welsh Guards on board RFA *Sir Galahad*
Lance Corporal A Burke
Lance Sergeant J R Carlyle
Guardsman I A Dale
Guardsman M J Dunphy
Guardsman P Edwards
Sergeant C Elley
Guardsman M Gibby
Guardsman G C Grace
Guardsman P Green
Guardsman G M Griffiths
Guardsman D N Hughes
Guardsman G Hughes
Guardsman B Jasper
Guardsman A Keeble
Lance Sergeant K Keoghane
Guardsman M J Marks
Guardsman C Mordecai

Lance Corporal S J Newbury
Guardsman G D Nicholson
Guardsman C C Parsons
Guardsman E J Phillips
Guardsman G W Poole
Guardsman N A Rowberry
Lance Corporal P A Sweet
Guardsman G K Thomas
Lance Corporal N D M Thomas
Guardsman R G Thomas
Guardsman A Walker
Lance Corporal C F Ward
Guardsman J F Weaver
Sergeant M Wigley
Guardsman D R Williams

Royal Army Medical Corps on board RFA *Sir Galahad*
Lance Corporal Farrell
Major R Nutbeem
Private K Preston 16 Field Ambulance

Army Catering Corps attached to 1st Welsh Guards
Lance Corporal B C Bullers
Private A M Connett
Private M A Jones
Private R W Middlewick

Royal Electrical and Mechanical Engineers
Craftsman M W Rollins
Lance Corporal A R Streatfield

20 Field Squadron RE (5th Infantry Brigade 9 Para)
Corporal A McIlvenny
Sapper W Tabard

APPENDIX D

Gallantry awards

Distinguished Service Cross
Lt N A Bruen, CO Fleet Clearance Diving Team 3 – bomb disposal RFA *Sir Galahad*.

Lt Cdr H S Clark, 825 Sqn NAS – rescue work on RFA *Sir Galahad*.

Distinguished Service Medal
CPO (Diver) G M Trotter, Fleet Clearance Diving Team 3 – bomb disposal on RFA *Sir Lancelot*.

C/Sgt M J Francis RM, Coxswain LCU FI HMS *Fearless* – rescuing survivors from RFA *Sir Galahad*.

George Medal (Posthumous)
2nd Eng Officer Paul Anderson Henry RFA, *Sir Galahad*.

Military Medal
Guardsman S M Chapman, 1st Battalion Welsh Guards – rescue work on board RFA *Sir Galahad*.

Sgt P H R Naya RAMC – rescue work on board RFA *Sir Galahad*.

WO2 B T Neck, 1st Battalion Welsh Guards – for rescue work on board RFA *Sir Galahad*.

Sgt D S Boultby, 17 Port Regiment RCT – NCO in charge of Mexeflote unit.

Queen's Gallantry Medal
3rd Officer A Gudgeon RFA, *Sir Galahad*.

Lt J K Boughton, 825 Sqn NAS – rescue work on RFA *Sir Galahad*.

Lt P J Sheldon, 825 Sqn NAS – rescue work on RFA *Sir Galahad*.

Honours and awards

Distinguished Service Order
Commodore S C Dunlop CBE – RFA *Fort Austin* (Commodore RFA).

Captain P J G Roberts – RFA *Sir Galahad*.

Distinguished Service Cross
Captain G R Green – RFA *Sir Tristram*.

Captain D E Lawrence – RFA *Sir Geraint*.

Captain A F Pitt – RFA *Sir Percivale*.

Order of the British Empire

Captain G P Overbury – RFA *Olmeda*.
Captain J B Dickinson – RFA *Stromness*.
Captain S Redmond – RFA *Tidespring*.
Captain P J McCarthy – RFA *Sir Bedivere*.
Captain C A Purcher-Wydenbruck – RFA *Sir Lancelot*.

Member of the British Empire (Civil)

J F Quirck, STO(N) – RFA *Fort Austin*.

British Empire Medal (Civil)

J A Goldie, Stores Officer Grade C – RFA *Resource*.
J Johnston, Senior Storekeeper – RFA *Fort Austin*.
P McEwan, Stores Officer Grade C – RFA *Regent*.

Mention in Despatches

Chief Officer P F Hill – RFA *Sir Percivale*.

Queen's Commendation for Brave Conduct

2nd Officer I Povey – RFA *Sir Galahad*.

Commander in Chief Fleet Commendations

Chief Officer D M Gerrard – RFA *Sir Lancelot*.
Chief Engineering Officer A Lauder – RFA *Sir Lancelot*.
1st Elec Officer C M McLean – RFA *Sir Lancelot*.
3rd Eng Officer W J Dwyer – RFA *Sir Lancelot*.
PO (Deck) J R Mount – RFA *Resource*.
SGIB G A Ferrier – RFA *Resource*.

The Permanent Under Secretary for Defence Commendations

W O Jenkins, DSTO(N) – RFA *Fort Austin*.
S J Macro, Clerical Officer – RFA *Fort Austin*.
M V Palmer, Fitter – RFA *Regent*.
D W Rogers, Stores Officer Grade C – RFA *Resource*.
F C Ross, Professional and Technical Officer Grade IV – RFA *Resource*.

APPENDIX E

Chronology of nuclear weapons transfers

RFAs involved:
Fort Austin, Fort Grange, Regent and *Resource*

Nuclear rounds designation:
600: Bomb Aircraft HE (High Explosive) 600lb MC(containing nuclear material)
600 (S): Surveillance round
600 (T): Training round

13 April
Fort Austin RAS (L) from RFA *Tidespring*, the latter on her way to South Georgia as part of *Antrim* group.

16 April
Fort Austin rendezvous *Brilliant* group. Transfer one 600 round from HMS *Brilliant* and one 600 (S) round from HMS *Sheffield*.

19 April
Fort Austin arrives Ascension, still carrying one 600 and one 600 (S) nuclear rounds, re-stores and heads south again for rendezvous with Carrier Battle Group.

20 April
HMS *Broadsword* transfers one 600 nuclear round to RFA *Resource*, in open sea.

3 May
Fort Austin, (with 600 round) enters TEZ and rendezvous Carrier Battle Group.

9 May
Fort Austin transfers 600 round to *Hermes*.

14 May
Resource transfers 600 round to *Invincible*, receiving 600 (T) in exchange.

15 May
Resource transfers one 600 round and one 600 (T) to *Regent*. This appears to be one more live round than she should have.

17 May

Fort Austin transfers one 600 (S) and one 600 (T) to *Regent*.

HMS *Coventry* transfers one 600 (S) to *Regent*.

Regent now has one 600 round, two 600 (S) and three 600 (T).

26 May

Regent transfers one 600 round and two 600 (S) rounds to *Resource*.

2 June

HMS *Invincible* transfers one 600 round to *Fort Austin*.

3 June

HMS *Brilliant* transfers one 600 round to *Fort Austin*.

HMS *Glamorgan* transfers one 600 (T) to *Fort Austin*.

RFA *Resource* transfers one 600 round, two 600 (S), two 600 (T) to *Fort Austin*.

HMS *Invincible* transfers one 600 round to *Fort Austin*.

RFA *Fort Grange* transfers one 600 (T) to *Fort Austin*.

Fort Austin now has three 600 round, two 600 (S) and four 600 (T) in her nuclear containment facility.

7 June

Fort Austin leaves for the UK, unescorted, arriving Devonport 29 June.

26 June

HMS *Hermes* transfers one 600 round and two 600 (T) rounds to *Resource*.

Resource leaves for UK, arriving 20 July.

APPENDIX F

Replenishment 1982

[BY COURTESY OF CPO (DECK) M JORDAN]

Prior to the replenishment start time, in the case of a Fuel RAS (Replenishment at Sea) all required products are flushed through the rig to ensure that clean products of the required standard are available. For a solid RAS the loads need to be made up ready for dispatch. Once this has taken place the rig requires laying out and all ropes and ancillary equipment to be connected to the rig. This includes, but is not limited to, the following equipment:

- Hose line
- Messenger lines
- Distance line
- Telephone line
- Signal bats
- Tool bag
- Gunline and rifle

The rig may also need to be altered depending on the customer's requirement.

Replenishment can be divided into three main areas, these being abeam, stern, and vertical replenishment by helicopter (VERTREP). These can then subdivided into three delivery methods dependent on customer requirements.

Beam replenishment can take the format of RAS (L) (Liquid) or RAS (S) (Solid); RAS (L) can be delivered by Large Derrick or Jackstay method. There are two Jackstay methods: firstly the Probe which is usually the preferred method of delivery; and secondly the Quick Release Connection (QRC)/NATO B method. The rig can be adapted to any of these methods. However, it is normal for it to be built and remain in one of the aforementioned states.

Large Derrick can also be delivered in two formats; as with the Jackstay this can take the format of either QRC/NATO B. The Large Derrick is a lot simpler to change from one connection to the other and it only takes around fifteen minutes to make the change.

The stern RAS (L) can be delivered by two different hose formats, depending on the ship's fit. One format consists of the conventional stern rig, which is laid on the deck of the tanker on rollers and consists of thirty-foot hoses joined together. Alternatively, the Hudson reel consists of a lay-flat hose in one continuous length, except for the last fifteen feet, which is the same as the conventional type stern hose. For the receiving vessel it makes little difference which delivery method is used.

Beam replenishment in the RAS (S) format can be divided into two main forms; Light Jackstay and Heavy Jackstay. The Light Jackstay is used for the transfer of personnel or stores up to the weight of 550 pounds (250 kilogrammes). The Light Jackstay is purely manned by personnel with no machinery involved and is therefore manpower-intensive, sometimes using all available ship's company.

Heavy Jackstay is used for the transfer of heavy loads of stores, including ammunition, up to a maximum weight per load of two tonnes. There are three main methods of delivery and these are dependent on the ship's fit. These can come in the format of fixed high point or GEC Mk 1A or GEC Mk 2. Within these fits there is additional equipment that can be used, depending on the receiving vessel's receiving position and equipment. This equipment can be in the form of drop reel traveller, which allows the lowering and recovery of loads from Heavy Jackstays to the deck on vessels which do not have the availability to lower the receiving end to the deck.

Regardless of the type of abeam rig used, or the stores to be transferred (liquid, solid or personnel), there is little difference in the basic procedures to follow. Procedures for the stern rig are, of course, different. All procedures are adaptable to suit the various rigs and reception units used, but the generic procedures are as follows:

It is normal for the receiving ship to make an approach on the delivering vessel from astern and take up the correct position, abeam at a normal working distance of between twenty-four and fifty-five metres and at a speed of between ten and sixteen knots. First contact between the vessels is by line-throwing rifle, normally fired by the receiving vessel. The rifle has been adapted to fire a soft-nosed projectile to which is connected a light, thin, nylon line. Once this has been successfully passed it is, in turn, connected to progressively bigger ropes to which are attached all ancillary lines including the messenger used for recovering equipment, telephone line for secure communication between the two vessels, and distance lines used to indicate the distance between the two vessels. All these lines are removed as they come inboard on the receiving vessel and moved to their respective points, until eventually the main wire span is hauled across. This is then attached to the receiving ship by a slip and then the rope used to heave the wire across is removed. The far end of this rope is, in turn, attached to the hose end, or the hook in the case of solid replenishment. Once the receiving vessel indicates that the jackstay is connected, the tension is gradually put on the wire using the Automatic Tension Winch (ATW). This enables the wire to be kept at a constant tension and in effect gives a ridge wire for the hoses or hook to be pulled across by the receiving vessel. In the case of the Probe rig, the probe enters the receiver on the receiving ship, and if enough momentum is available the indicators on the back of the receiver will indicate a correct connection. Should this not happen then the delivering ship will heave the probe out and have another try. In the case of a heavy jackstay QRC or NATO B rig the hoses are heaved across the tensioned jackstay and a manual connection is made on the receiving vessel's deck. In the case of a Solids RAS, once the jackstay has been tensioned there is a test weight of two tons passed across the rig to prove that all machinery is working properly and capable of supporting the weight. Once this has been done the rig is now ready for use and pumping or load transfer can commence.

Should an emergency of any description take place during the replenishment, then an emergency breakaway will commence, controlled by the delivering vessel. All lines and equipment are recovered in a rapid but safe manner to the delivering ship. Should this not be possible, the ropes will be cut or kept by whichever vessel has them at that particular time. They will then be transferred to the delivery vessel at a safer time after the incident has passed.

Once the replenishment has been completed and all intended stores or fuel have been passed, all equipment ropes and wires will be recovered by the delivery ship. First to be recovered are the hoses and hook, followed by all other ropes and connections, including the telephone line and lastly the distance line. The vessels can then move apart and continue on their passage.

VERTREP is the transfer of stores in an underslung net using a helicopter. This is a common evolution for replenishment of stores, lub-oil and certain types of ammunition.

All forms of replenishment may take place at any time of day or night and are hazardous evolutions, not least because of the close proximity of the vessels to each other. Should a vital piece of machinery fail on either vessel, for example a main engine or steering equipment, then a collision could occur very quickly. The weather can play an important part and it is not uncommon for the deck to become awash, and in extreme conditions this could sweep overboard loose equipment and even personnel. All available Personal Protection Equipment, including automatic water-activated lifejackets, is worn by all personnel involved in the evolution, and safety lines are rigged in all areas where safety rails have been removed. However, this does not always prevent the worst predicament of a man overboard; in this case the two ships would initiate an emergency break-away and launch a rescue boat to recover the unfortunate sailor.

Post-1982, replenishment operations have continued to evolve, and more efficient replenishment rigs and equipment are fitted to newer vessels. These are partially computer controlled, although they still require skilled input from a qualified operator. This automation does allow the operator to move the loads at higher speeds during a Solids RAS, as the computer equates the distance between the two vessels and stops the load on both vessels over the required spot.

Future innovations may include rigs to transfer ever heavier loads of up to five tonnes. They will present considerable engineering challenges but rapid progress is being made in these areas.

APPENDIX G

Arms on RFAs

Weapon types

– GPMG (General Purpose Machine Gun): belt-fed machine gun firing 7.62mm rifle cartridges.

– LMG (Light Machine Gun): fires 7.62mm rifle cartridges from c.30-round box. Modified version of WWII Bren gun.

– SLR (Self-Loading Rifle): semi-automatic rifle firing 7.62mm rifle cartridges from c.20-round box. Standard British service rifle at the time. Argentinean forces used the almost identical Belgian FN rifle, on which the SLR was based.

– SMG (Sub-Machine Gun): automatic weapon firing 9mm pistol cartridges from c.30-round box magazine.

– Bofors: rapid-fire anti-aircraft gun firing 40mm explosive shells. Slightly updated version of WWII-era gun.

– Blowpipe: light anti-aircraft missile fired from tube container held on operator's shoulder.

Weapons carried

A full list has proved impossible to compile but such information as is available shows the following defensive armament and where known, its origins:

Fort Austin (Comm S C Dunlop OBE, CBE)
Two GPMG.
Twenty-four assorted rifles (some claimed to be WWII-vintage Lee Enfields).
Origin of weapons unknown.

Fort Grange (Capt D G M Averill CBE)
One GPMG.
One LMG.
Twelve SLR.

Olmeda (Capt G P Overbury)
Machine guns and rifles.

Olna (Capt J A Baily)
  Machine guns and rifles.

Tidepool (Capt J W Gaffrey)
  Machine guns and rifles.
  Origin of weapons possibly Chilean, since she was not known to have been armed before she left.

Tidespring (Capt S Redmond)
  Two GPMG (from damaged Wessex 5).
  Two LMG (from damaged Wessex 5).
  SMG borrowed from *Antrim* during POW transit.
  Four 9mm Browning pistols also from *Antrim* during POW transit.
  One home-made mortar consisting of a Wessex 5 rocket pod attached to a wooden pallet, then mounted on a Wessex towing arm. Rockets fired by remote electrical control.

Blue Rover (Capt J D Roddis)
  Machine guns and rifles.

Leaf-class boats
  None of the Leaf-class boats were armed.

Regent (Capt J Logan)
  Machine guns and rifles.

Resource (Capt B A Seymour)
  Machine guns and rifles.

Stromness (Capt J B Dickinson OBE)
  None recorded, except a .50 cal Argentine machine gun presented to the ship by the embarked Commando, after hostilities ceased.

Engadine (Capt D F Freeman)
  One GPMG, one LMG and twelve SLR.

Sir-class LSLs
  Two 40mm Bofors (only one installed in *Percivale* and *Galahad*).
  RA Blowpipe troop.
  Royal Marines with hand-held SLRs and machine guns.

APPENDIX H

RFA ships in the Falklands

Ol-class Fast Fleet Tankers

Olmeda 33,250 tons.
Pennant No A124.
Captain G P Overbury (OBE) RFA.
Embarked flight: 'A' Flight 824 Sqn (two Sea King Mk 2).
Sailed Devonport 5 April 1982.
Entered war zone 25 April 1982.
Took part in recapture of South Thule with members of 'M' Coy 42 Commando.
Arrived back in UK 12 July 1982.

Olna 33,250 tons.
Pennant No A123.
Captain J A Bailey RFA.
Embarked flight: 'B' Flight 848 Sqn (two Wessex HU5).
Sailed Devonport 10 May 1982.
Entered war zone 23 May 1982.
Arrived back in UK 17 September 1982.

Improved Tide-class Fleet Tankers

Tidepool 25,930 tons.
Pennant No A76.
Captain J W Gaffrey RFA.
Embarked flight: 'E' Flight 845 Sqn (two Wessex HU5).
Returned from Chile via Curaçao, arrived Ascension Island 26 April 1982.
Entered war zone 13 May 1982.
Delivered to Chilean Navy 13 July 1982.

Tidespring 25,930 tons.
Pennant No A75.
Captain S Redmond (OBE) RFA.
Embarked flight: 'C' flight 845 Sqn (two Wessex HU5), these aircraft were lost on South Georgia. Replacement aircraft picked up in Ascension Island.
Sailed Gibraltar after Exercise Springtrain 2 April 1982.
Entered war zone 17 April 1982.

Transported 'M' Coy 45 Commando to South Georgia April 1982.
Arrived back in UK 23 July 1982.

Rover-class Small Fleet Tankers

Blue Rover 11,500 tons.
Pennant No A270.
Captain D A Reynolds RFA.
Sailed Portsmouth 16 April 1982.
Entered war zone 2 May 1982.
Arrived back in UK 17 July 1982.

Early Leaf-class Tankers

Pearleaf 25,790 tons.
Pennant No A77.
Captain J McCulloch RFA.
Sailed Portsmouth 7 April 1982.
Entered war zone 4 May 1982.
Arrived back in UK 13 August 1982.

Plumleaf 25,790 tons.
Pennant No A78.
Captain R W M Wallace RFA.
Sailed Portland 19 April 1982.
Entered war zone 10 May 1982.
Arrived back in UK 26 August 1982.

Later Leaf-class Tankers

Appleleaf 40,000 tons.
Pennant No A83.
Captain G P A McDougall RFA.
Sailed Gibraltar 2 April 1982.
Arrived back in UK 9 August 1982.

Bayleaf 40,000 tons.
Pennant No A79.
Captain A E T Hunter RFA.
Sailed direct from builders, 26 April 1982 she stretched her rigs with *Grey Rover* off Portland before sailing for South Atlantic.
Entered war zone 9 June 1982.
Arrived back in UK 31 August 1982.

Brambleleaf 40,000 tons.
Pennant No A81.
Captain M S J Farley RFA.
Sailed from Persian Gulf 5 April 1982.
Entered war zone 19 April 1982.
Arrived Gibraltar 16 December 1982.

R-class Ammunition, Explosive, Food and Store (AEFS) Ships

Regent 22,890 tons.
Pennant No A486.
Captain J Logan RFA.
Embarked flight: 'A' Flight 848 Sqn (one Wessex HU5).
Sailed Devonport 19 April 1982.
Entered war zone 8 May 1982.
Arrived back in UK 15 September 1982.

Resource 22,890 tons.
Pennant No A480.
Captain B A Seymour RFA.
Embarked flight: 'A' Flight 845 Sqn (two Wessex HU5).
Sailed Rosyth 5 April 1982.
Entered war zone 25 April 1982.
Arrived back in UK 19 July 1982.

Fort-class Stores Ships

Fort Austin 22,750 tons.
Pennant No A386.
Commodore S C Dunlop CBE (DSO) RFA.
Embarked Flight: 815 Sqn (Lynx), later replaced by 'B' Flight 845 Sqn (two Wessex HU5).
Sailed Gibraltar 29 March 1982.
Entered war zone 26 April 1982.
Arrived back in UK 28 June 1982.

Fort Grange 22,750 tons.
Pennant No A385.
Captain D G M Averill (CBE) RFA.
Embarked Flight: 'C' Flight 824 Sqn (three Sea King HAS 2).
Sailed Devonport 13 May 1982.
Entered war zone 26 May 1982.
Arrived back in UK 3 October 1982.

Ness-class Stores Ships

Stromness 16,792 tons.
Pennant No A344.
Captain J B Dickinson (OBE) RFA.
Sailed Portsmouth 7 April 1982.
Entered war zone 13 May 1982.
Arrived back in UK 23 July 1982.

Helicopter Training Ship

Engadine 8,960 tons.
Pennant No K08.
Captain D F Freeman RFA.
Embarked Flight: 'A' Flight 847 Sqn (four Wessex HU5 plus maintenance crew from 825 Sqn).
Sailed Devonport 10 May 1982.
Entered war zone 6 June 1982.
Arrived back in UK 30 July 1982.

Round Table-class (Sir-class) Landing Ship Logistic

Sir Bedivere.
Pennant No L3004.
Captain P J McCarthy RFA.
Fitted with two 40mm Bofors guns.
Sailed Marchwood 29 April after returning from Canada.
Entered war zone 18 May 1982.
Slightly damaged by glancing hit from Argentinean bomb 24 May 1982.
Arrived back in Marchwood on 16 November with 64 repatriated war dead.

Sir Galahad.
Pennant No L3005.
Captain P J G Roberts (DSO) RFA.
Fitted with one 40mm Bofors gun.
Sailed Devonport 6 April 1982 with 350 Royal Marines.
Entered war zone 8 May 1982.
Hit by unexploded bomb on 24 May 1982 which caused moderate damage and a small fire on the vehicle deck.
Hit by a bomb and aircraft gunfire 25 May; the bomb failed to explode and was removed the next day.
Hit by three bombs and badly damaged, later scuttled, 8 June 1982.

Sir Geraint.
Pennant No L3027.
Captain D E Lawrence (DSC) RFA.
Fitted with two 40mm guns.
Sailed Devonport 6 April 1982 with 450 Royal Marines and three Gazelle helicopters.
Entered war zone 8 May 1982.
Arrived back in UK 23 July 1982.

Sir Lancelot.
Pennant No L3029.
Captain C A Purcher-Wydenbruck (OBE) RFA.
Fitted with two 40mm guns.
Sailed Marchwood 5 April 1982 with embarked troops and three helicopters.
Entered war zone 8 May 1982.
Hit by two bombs 24 May 1982, neither bomb exploded, though a fire broke out in the troop accommodation and the ship was temporarily abandoned.
Arrived back in UK 18 August 1982.

Sir Percivale.
Pennant No L3036.
Captain A F Pitt (DSC) RFA.
Fitted with one 40mm gun.
Sailed Marchwood 4 April 1982 with 310 Royal Marines.
Entered war zone 8 May 1982.
Arrived back in UK 23 July 1982.

Sir Tristram.
Pennant No L3505.
Captain G R Green (DSC) RFA.
Fitted with two 40mm guns.
Sailed Ascension Island 17 April 1982 after returning from Belize.
Entered war zone 8 May 1982.
Bombed on 8 June 1982 and badly damaged.
During May 1982 she was loaded onto the heavy-lift vessel *Dan Lifter* and returned to the UK, arriving on the Tyne 15 June 1983.

APPENDIX I

The Royal Fleet Auxiliary

British dominance of the world's oceans began during the reign of Elizabeth I and this rise to prominence was mirrored by the Royal Navy's own growth and development.

As the extent of British colonial possessions grew, so however did the need for a navy capable of defending those colonies and able to transport troops who could adopt a defensive or offensive role. To facilitate these essential activities and in order to allow the Navy to remain at sea in places as far apart as Hong Kong, India and, during the early part of the nineteenth century, even Australia, a widespread system of shore bases was established.

Very quickly, however, the Navy found that warships tended to run out of essential stores at times and in situations when it was inconvenient, to say the least, to have to return to port for replenishment. In consequence, there grew up a fleet of support ships attached to the shore bases.

These fleet auxiliaries, as they came to be known, were to begin with a mixture of older warships and converted merchantmen, both chartered and Admiralty owned. Crewed by either merchant seamen or their RN counterparts, they sailed between their designated shore bases and the fleets, carrying food, cordage, ammunition and principally water, this last in specially-designed, lanteen-rigged water hoys.

By the middle of the nineteenth century, these vessels had become such a vital component of the logistics chain that an Order in Council was made, dated 9 July 1864, to the effect that the mercantile-crewed auxiliaries should fly a blue ensign defaced by the Admiralty Badge or Seal.

At about the same time, there began a series of technological advances, most notably steam power and screw propulsion, which led to the introduction of new types of warship, forcing concomitant changes in the Navy's requirements and new duties for the Naval Stores Department.

Coal began to replace wind as the Navy's motive force and coaling facilities were established at the existing shore bases while the Stores Department also started to expand its auxiliary fleet by the addition of chartered colliers.

By now, the Department's demand for shipping meant that their vessels fell into two major categories: vessels owned and operated by the Admiralty and so employed more or less full time as Fleet auxiliaries; and others taken up on charter, employed as and when needed.

In order to identify the origins of particular ships, an Admiralty circular letter, dated 3 August 1905, directed that an auxiliary vessel manned by a mercantile crew and owned by the Admiralty should in future be styled Royal Fleet Auxiliary. Thus, the history of the RFA dates from the issue of this letter.

Ships on temporary transport charter to the Admiralty were to be designated Mercantile Fleet Auxiliaries, although now they are more commonly referred to as Ships Taken Up From Trade (STUFT).

Problems with this new designation were not long in surfacing, however. When the Admiralty tried to register the hospital ship *Maine* under the Merchant Shipping Act 1894, as an RFA, it was found that their application couldn't be upheld.

Under the 1894 Act, 64/64ths of a ship had to be owned by a British subject or subjects for the vessel to be registered as British. Neither the Sovereign, whose property the vessel was deemed to be, nor the Admiralty, in whose name it was to be registered, were eligible under the Act, so RFAs were registered as the property of The Lords Commissioners of the Admiralty with the managing owner listed as the Secretary of the Board of Admiralty.

Curiously enough, RFAs weren't legally required to register, but registration confirmed their status as merchant vessels, at the same time doing away with the problems unregistered merchant vessels or warships have when entering foreign ports.

In practical terms, this means an RFA can enter a port, without special permission, collect a load of fuel or dry stores and sail again to replenish a warship, without any special documentation or time limits. This proved particularly useful during the Falklands War when RFAs and STUFT were able to take on a load of fuel at ports like Freetown, without interference from the port authorities, which would not have been the case if they had been unregistered merchant vessels.

It is perhaps also of interest to note here that during WWI, the Admiralty actually circumvented the problem of RFAs entering neutral ports to accept cargoes of fuel oil by transferring the management of some of the fleet to a commercial company, Lane and McAndrew Ltd. This legal device allowed RFAs to sail under the Red Ensign as oiler transports and so avoid complications with the neutrality laws.

It is probably fair to say that, until the introduction of fuel oil, coaling its ships was the biggest headache the peacetime Navy faced. Since ships were now forced to put into designated shore bases to take on a load of fuel, their radius of operations was significantly reduced, which meant more ships had to be deployed to make up the shortfall, using more coal, leading to more ships being needed to transport the extra fuel.

It was a particularly vicious circle and coaling-at-sea looked like the ideal way to break it. So, a series of largely unsuccessful experiments with a number of rigs was begun in 1906 with the Metcalf apparatus. The Admiralty persevered with the idea, however, in the face of disappointing results, until sometime in 1912, when RFA *Mercedes* conducted her final, inconclusive, trials with HMS *Dominion*.

By now, however, Admiral of the Fleet Lord Fisher's 1912 Royal Commission on Fuel and Engines had decided that oil-fired engines produced higher speed, increased radius of action, speedier and easier refuelling, a reduction in stokehold personnel by fifty per cent and quicker initial production of steam. They also saved in the cost of construction.

In light of these recommendations, oil was to gradually replace coal as the Royal Navy's fuel of choice, although as late as 1912, some Royal Navy ships were launched which could use both fuels.

The RFA had seen this change to fuel oil coming, however, and from as early as January 1906, had been conducting oiling-at-sea experiments, using its first tanker, RFA *Petroleum*. She was fitted for replenishment at sea using the stirrup method, and although this rig suffered from several disadvantages, most notably its tendency to break due to the high pumping pressures required, by 1908, Admiralty planners had introduced their first RFA tanker construction programme, under the auspices of the Director of Stores, Sir John Forsey.

RFA *Burma* was the initial result of this innovative idea. Although of only 2,000 tons capacity, which is fairly small by present-day standards (RFA *Tidespring*, for example, carried about 10,000 tons of FFO, with 5,000 tons of Dieso, 2,000 tons of AVCAT and water besides), she was only equipped for fuelling alongside, i.e. replenishing vessels in harbour or a sheltered anchorage.

Although oiling-at-sea trials were still being carried out by RFA and Royal Navy vessels, fuelling alongside became the predominant technique until World War II, despite the fact that the USA, Japan and most significantly the German Navy had quickly seen the advantages inherent in oiling-at-sea facilities.

1912 saw the first appearance of the term RFA on the Navy list and with the coming of World War I, the RFA underwent a phenomenal expansion, from seven vessels in service on the eve of war in August 1914, to well over seventy by the beginning of 1918.

By the end of WW I, the Fleet included:

– twenty-four overseas tankers;

– twenty-two 1,000-ton fleet attendant tankers of the Attendant-group and Cresol-class, for local port and harbour duties;

– fifteen 2,000-ton fleet attendant tankers of the Burma and Bergol class, for offshore waters and fitted for RAS by the stirrup method;

– six fast (16 knot) 5,000 ton twin-screw fleet attendant tankers of the built Trinol class.

Most of the above were Admiralty designed and built as auxiliaries.

Together with these tankers, the RFA fleet also included miscellaneous vessels such as RFA *Baccus*, the first of a line of dry store and water carriers as well a number of salvage vessels and even a collection of Port of London Authority hopper barges which were converted and used as oil carriers between 1916–17.

RNR/RNVR commissions were given to many RFA officers for the duration of hostilities and RFA personnel were also placed under naval discipline.

When the armistice came, however, it found the RFA almost non-existent, since most of the auxiliaries then in service were not being administered by the Department of Naval Stores, many being, as previously mentioned, operated by commercial companies to avoid complications with the neutrality laws.

Within months of the war's end, however, the situation had been resolved and the Director of Stores resumed administrative responsibility for the Admiralty-owned tankers and store ships, now registered under the Order in Council of 1911. This meant that, in practice, RFAs observed the normal Board of Trade regulations for merchant ships in terms of safety and radio equipment, one effect of this being to encourage recruitment to the service in a difficult post-war labour market.

Employment conditions in the RFA both before and after the war were roughly along Merchant Navy lines, with officers employed on fixed term contracts of between six months to three years, while ratings were engaged from the Joint Supply Organisation of the National Maritime Board, later known more simply as the Merchant Navy Pool, usually for a single voyage.

RFA personnel during this period received none of the specialist training which is such a characteristic of today's service, although such training was probably considered to be unnecessary since the pre-war RFA's duties consisted mainly of freighting fuel and dry stores to the numerous land bases responsible for supplying the warships of the Fleet.

During the 1930s, however, the Royal Navy began to recognise the increasingly effective role that aircraft would play in wartime and the consequent vulnerability of these established naval bases. In light of this, the Admiralty convened a Supply Ships Committee to consider what auxiliaries might be needed to supply the Navy under wartime strictures.

Recommendations from this Committee saw an increase in numbers of store ships, particularly armament carriers, modernisation of existing shore bases and fuelling depots and, most importantly in the long term, serious attempts to develop a reliable rig for oiling-at-sea. Alongside these improvements, the Director of Stores, Sir William Gick, was directly responsible for planning both the Ranger and Dale classes of modern tanker. The Ranger-class proved a particularly successful wartime design, being equipped with one 4-inch gun, a 40mm Bofors and four single 20mm Oerlikons.

World War II saw tremendous demands placed upon the RFA, which were met by both an increase in the numbers of charted merchant ships, designated Mercantile Fleet Auxiliaries, and the development of certain specialised classes of auxiliary, this last being most notably represented by the Landing Ships Gantry (LSGs).

Increasingly, during the war, the RFA began to take on crucial, highly-specialised roles, including particularly the operation of these newly modified Dale-class of Combined Operations LSGs. Alongside this, the launching of the new Ranger-class meant that for the first time RFAs were defensively autonomous, able to defend themselves rather than relying, as previously, on a vastly overstretched Navy.

As well as vessels like the purpose-built Ranger-class, many RFAs of the period were modified to carry weapons, with anything from 6-inch guns to light machine guns being fitted, this latter usually being the excellent and highly accurate Bren. Ships of this type were designated Defensively Equipped Merchant Ships, usually shortened to DEMS. By 1950, however, RFAs had been ordered to land all guns and mountings at their base port, leaving the service's vessels unarmed until the Falklands war, when a number of masters equipped their vessels with weapons on their own initiative.

The easy acceptance of their new role and the skill with which it was implemented seems to have produced an improvement in naval attitudes to the service and indeed, many of the post-war changes which have been so important in the development of the RFA may have had their beginnings with the introduction of these highly-specialised vessels and the professional way in which they operated under RFA command.

Replenishment at Sea

Up until about 1939, the RFA's predominant logistic task was freighting support, transporting fuel to the Navy's shore bases. But by 1945, with the help of captured German technology, oiling-at-sea was becoming almost routine, while significant progress had been made with experiments conducted on jackstay transfer of both dry stores and ammunition.

The first serious post WWI attempts at fuel replenishment had been conducted in 1924, using what was called the Hose Hawser method. This technique employed a hawser, by which the receiving ship was towed, passed through the fuel hose. It proved extremely unreliable and the service soon reverted to the stirrup method, whereby a 3.5-inch copper hose was suspended from the towing hawser by a series of brass stirrups, the practice now being for the tanker to tow the receiving ship.

The system was dangerous and lengthy, since the fuelling hose had to be transferred, on a series of trolleys, from a T-bar rail located on deck to the towing hawser, the whole arrangement, trolleys and all, being then passed out of a special stern chute and along the hawser to the receiving ship. Adding to the difficulty was the need to secure a cork lifebelt around the hose, halfway between each trolley, to keep it afloat in the event of a breakage, an all-too-common occurrence with this particular rig. Having secured the hose, pumping could begin, rates of about 120 tons per hour usually being achieved.

Needless to say, the RFA men who were called upon to operate it were not very keen on the system, either, their usual advice to newcomers being: '. . . keep a bucket handy for spare thumbs.'

Despite its fairly obvious shortcomings, the stirrup method remained in service until 1937/38, when experiments began with the trough system. This involved the tanker and the receiving ship steaming abeam of each other, some seventy yards apart, secured by a towing hawser and a breast rope.

While maintaining the required distance by station-keeping and adjustment of the breast rope, the tanker lowered a derrick from which was suspended a single trough containing two 5-in flexible copper hoses, through which fuel oil could be pumped at rates of about 500 tons per hour.

The next real advance came in 1941, when a German tanker was captured and found to be using a buoyant rubber hose for refuelling. British experiments quickly resulted in the production of a successful 5-in buoyant hose, which rapidly became standard equipment on RFAs. This buoyant hose, filled with compressed air and supported by a wire rope, could be towed through the water, vastly simplifying the stern replenishment process, the abeam technique benefiting by the simple exchange of the 5-in copper for a similarly sized rubber hose, with an accompanying decrease in breakages.

With the end of WWII, despite the atmosphere of austerity, development of the replenishment process continued apace. Increasing the derrick length and introducing two additional troughs meant that replenishment could now take place with the ships nearly 200 feet apart, greatly increasing the ease with which the process could be carried out in rough weather, since, in addition, the vessels maintained station by use of the engines alone, hawser and breast ropes having been quietly and unofficially dispensed with.

As a further increase in efficiency, the troughs now carried two lengths of 5-in fuel hose and a 3-in fresh water hose, all capable of being used simultaneously.

Later experiments, particularly those concerned with replenishment in heavy weather, resulted in the development of a new abeam rig, incorporating a jackstay to support the three troughs, while the newly devised self-tensioning winch kept the rig taut.

With a few modifications, this self-tensioning abeam rig is the one in use today. For the astern method, a new non-stretch bonded fuelling hose was introduced, allowing the hose to be simply trailed astern from the tanker, without any supporting wires, until it is grappled and connected by the receiving ship, at which point the pumpover can start.

A number of connecting systems have entered service over the years, with the result that now RFAs are fitted with both the USN/NATO probe and drogue system as well as the predominantly British Quick Release Mk II (QR Mk II).

This sort of technological change has been the main characteristic of the RFA post-war, along with a clear realisation of the demands which such changes make on personnel.

The first real signs of this new-style RFA was the addition, in 1952, of the first Tide-class replenishment tankers to the fleet. Admiralty designed, they were large, fast ships, built to remain at sea for long periods in all conditions. Furnace Fuel Oil (FFO), Aviation spirit (AVCAT) and Diesel (Dieso) were carried in separate tanks, with their own dedicated pumps and sufficient power to allow all these pumps to be used while steaming at fifteen knots. Three of the new jackstay systems with self-tensioning winches were fitted to these vessels, along with five large derrick rigs. They also had the capability of streaming three hoses astern, specifically for use with aircraft carriers. These new developments meant that the Tide-class vessels could easily replenish three vessels at once, even if one of them was an aircraft carrier.

In line with this new RAS technology were changes in personnel recruitment, chiefly the introduction of contracts for petty officers, so as to select and retain in the service a permanent corps of these individuals whose training and experience contributes so much to the smooth running of any RFA.

1956 saw more changes, with decisions being made at the Commonwealth Prime Ministers' Conference in London which allowed the Admiralty to begin the build-up of a force of modern auxiliaries, incorporating the latest RAS and aviation technology, this latter including vertical replenishment techniques with helicopters.

Experiments with helicopters had begun in 1950, just after the start of the Korean War, with Westland Dragonflys operating from RFA *Fort Duquesne*. By 1966, the first permanent flights had been assigned to RFAs *Regent* and *Resource* in the form of Wessex HU5s from Naval Air Squadron (NAS) 829.

The special demands all this new technology made on the officers and ratings of the RFA were accommodated by the existing naval establishments, which set up training courses in fire-fighting, navigation and communications, thus imparting more specialist skills which were outside the normal requirements of the Merchant Navy.

It has been needed because, since 1945, the RFA has supplied the Royal Navy in all its worldwide operations, including: Korea, Suez, Aden, the 'Cod Wars', the Gulf Wars and of course, the South Atlantic, as well as more unusual jobs like Operation Grapple, the H-bomb tests on Christmas Island.

Significant new additions to the Fleet came in 1963, with the completion of the two new Tide-class ships, RFAs *Tidespring* and *Tidepool*, along with the launch of the first of the Army's Landing Ship Logistics (LSLs), *Sir Lancelot*, this latter administered, for now, by the British India Steam Navigation company.

In 1965, the Royal Navy Stores and Transport Service was formed, combining the four old directorates of Stores, Armament Supply, Victualling and Fuel, Movements and Transport (Naval) under one individual, the Director General Supply and Transport (Naval). This rationalisation brought about a reorganisation which at the time of the Falklands War had resulted in the RNSTS operating via a number of supply outlets, one of which was the RFA, which handled the delivery side of the RNSTS's business.

This newly-reorganised service soon had its hands full because, with Ian Smith's 1966 declaration of Rhodesian independence, the RFA found itself assigned to the Biera Patrol, replenishing Royal Navy warships responsible for blockading the ports of Southern Rhodesia to prevent the import of crude oil.

RFAs on this assignment spent long periods at sea and the record was set by *Tidespring* during 1967. She spent ninety days continuously on the patrol, steamed 33,000 nautical miles and replenished ships at an average of six per week.

The fleet was also increased in size this year with the launch of RFAs *Regent*, *Resource*, *Engadine*, *Stromness*, *Lyness*, *Olna* and the LSLs *Sir Bedivere*, *Sir Tristram* and *Sir Galahad*. All these vessels, except *Lyness*, saw service in the Falklands.

NATO's Standing Naval Force Atlantic (STANAVFORLANT) came into existence in 1967 as a permanent multinational peacetime naval squadron. The Royal Navy contributes ships periodically, although the RFA's participation only amounts to an occasional tanker. This year also saw the Army's last two LSLs launched, *Sir Percivale* and *Sir Geraint*, and the allocation of a number of RFAs to the Aden Task Force, covering the withdrawal of British troops from the region.

Defence cuts announced in January 1968 by the Wilson Government meant the loss of the Royal Navy's aircraft carriers and a rundown in their Middle East and Far East bases, with a proportionate reduction in RFAs, although in December, Whitehall announced that from 1970, manning and management of the Sir-class LSLs would become the responsibility of the RFA.

Transfer of the LSLs was indeed effected in 1970, with Marchwood Military Port becoming their base port. This year also saw the launch of *Blue Rover*, the first of one of the RFA's most useful classes, the small fleet replenishment tankers of the Rover-class. Only *Blue Rover* saw service in the Falklands, where, amongst other duties, she was stationed at Cumberland Bay, South Georgia, as station tanker.

It was also a vessel of the Rover-class that was involved in a historic incident in 1971, when a VSTOL (Vertical/Short Take-off and Landing) Harrier landed on *Green Rover* while the latter was anchored in the Thames, paving the way for the use to which the ill-fated *Atlantic Conveyor* was put during the Falklands War.

Malta, Cyprus and the second 'Cod War' with Iceland all saw RFA involvement in the following years.

In 1976 RFA *Tidesurge* was assigned to support Lord Shackleton's Falklands survey. Shackleton's recommendations, basically a cash injection of several million pounds to allow the islanders to continue to live independently, were not well received in Whitehall and sent relations with Argentina, never cordial at the best of times, plummeting. Whitehall had deemed the situation so bad that, earlier in the year, from February to April, RFA *Tidesurge* and HMS *Eskimo* had been deployed to the South Atlantic to discourage any thoughts the Argentineans might have had of military adventures against the Falklands.

A new Commodore was appointed to the service the following year in the person of Captain S C Dunlop MBE RFA, coinciding with the Queen's Silver Jubilee review of the Fleet, which also involved a number of auxiliaries. The RFAs put on a good show, independent observers remarking that the ships and ship's companies had been turned out to Royal Navy standard.

Later in 1977 there was more Falklands involvement, when, following the Argentine occupation of South Thule, a small task force was sent to the area, consisting of a nuclear submarine, two frigates, the tanker RFA *Olwen* and the store ship RFA *Resurgent*. Designated 'Operation Journeyman', the deployment remained a closely-guarded secret, until James Callaghan revealed it, just after the Stanley invasion in 1982.

Two important new additions to the RFA fleet were made in the years following, with RFA *Fort Grange* completing at Scott Lithgow's Cartsburn yard, Greenock, in 1978 and her sister ship RFA *Fort Austin* joining the service the following year. Equipped with modern navigation and communications equipment, both these vessels became an essential part of the Falklands Task Force.

RFA *Fort Austin*, then commanded by Commodore Dunlop, was, in fact, the first British surface ship ordered south, her Master receiving his orders on 26 March 1982, just as the ship and crew were preparing to leave for the UK after six months on the Armilla patrol.

Helicopters have become essential equipment on RFAs in recent years and this was marked in 1978 when 824 NAS became the parent unit for RFA helicopters. Other technological advances for this period included the 1979 fitting of a satellite communications terminal to RFA *Olmeda* and the trialling by RFA *Resource* of the Mk2 RAS rig, which allowed transfer of Sea Wolf missiles to UK warships, these events coinciding with the closure of the base at Malta and the RFA's evacuation of the remaining personnel, which included 41 Commando who came home aboard RFA *Sir Lancelot*.

Royal Navy involvement in the Iran–Iraq conflict began in 1980 with the deployment of a task force to the Mediterranean to assist the US Navy. RFAs were assigned to this task force, which came to be known as the Armilla patrol. A single tanker together with an armaments/stores carrier was the usual deployment, beginning with *Olwen* and *Stromness* from October to December 1980.

Earlier that year, the MOD had bareboat chartered the standard product tanker *Hudson Deep*, which after conversion was renamed RFA *Brambleleaf*. Unlike the store/armament ships and the Tide, Ol and Rover-classes of RFA tanker, the giant Leaf-class support tankers (RFA *Brambleleaf* has a displacement of over 40,000 tons) were all under long-term bareboat charter. That means the ship owner provides only the ship, the charterer being totally responsible for the vessel's operation, such as: appointing the crew, repairs, refits, cargo and, most importantly from the RFA's point of view, running the vessel where they want to within any limits set by the ship owner or Classification Society.

The Navy continued its deployment on the Armilla Patrol in 1981, operating in the Red Sea, Gulf of Oman and Persian Gulf, with continuing RFA support. Fuel, of course, was and is the main part of the RFA's work so most of the support deployment on Armilla and elsewhere consisted of tankers. By 1982, the fleet had the following vessels available:

Five fast fleet tankers
(*Tidespring, Tidepool, Olwen, Olmeda, Olna*)

Five small fleet tankers
(*Blue Rover, Gold Rover, Black Rover, Green Rover* and *Grey Rover*)

Five freighting tankers
(*Pearleaf, Bayleaf, Appleleaf, Plumleaf* and *Brambleleaf*)

Five ammunition and general stores carriers
 (*Fort Austin, Fort Grange, Stromness, Regent* and *Resource*)

Six Landing Ship Logistics
 (*Sir Galahad, Sir Bedivere, Sir Tristram, Sir Percivale, Sir Geraint, Sir Lancelot*)

One helicopter training ship
 (*Engadine*)

This situation was not to last, however, because in May 1981, John Nott, then Minister for Defence in the Thatcher Government, published his long-awaited Defence Review.

In the words of Denis Healey, Labour's shadow defence spokesman, he: '. . . crippled the Royal Navy for the sake of Trident.'

In Nott's view, the job of the Royal Navy was to '. . . provide a strategic nuclear force by the modernisation of the Polaris force with the Trident system,' adding that this was '. . . the United Kingdom's surest way of preserving peace.'

So, in future, warfare was only to be conducted by the superpowers, concentrated in the North Atlantic. Surface ships were to be run down, numbers of Trident-carrying submarines increased. And, of course, in that sort of war, an amphibious capability was unnecessary, so the Marines weren't needed nor were the amphibious landing ships.

The RFA was hit hard. Immediate losses were to be *Tidespring, Tidepool* and *Stromness*, while by the mid-eighties all six LSLs would be sold off as well. Manning levels were to reflect this, with over 1,000 RFA men being made redundant, 420 of those officers: just about a third of the entire workforce.

Most worrying, however, was that it was the future RFA which was being hit as well. With the loss of six ships between 1977 and 1981 and the further proposed losses under Nott's Defence Review, there was what the RFA's Personnel department called a serious surplus of RFA Deck and Engineer Officers at junior level. One result of this was that in 1981, there was no possibility that the service could absorb any of their Deck or Engineering Cadets who had qualified that year. A parent of one of these young men wrote to the relevant Government department about, amongst other things, his concern over Britain's defence capability if the Navy lost the use of the specialist replenishment ships of the RFA.

It may be of interest to quote the relevant paragraph of the Parliamentary Under Secretary of State for Trade's reply: 'Mr— also implies concern about our defence capability in the light of the decline of the fleet. In the event of hostilities, the *merchant fleets of NATO countries* would be pooled and allocated to tasks in the best interests of the alliance.' (Author's italics.)

Even more interesting was the reply from the Minister of State for the Armed Forces, in which after explaining that their priorities had changed due to '. . . rapidly rising cost of some kinds of equipment', by which he presumably meant Trident, he finished by saying: '. . . we shall retain sufficient auxiliaries to meet all foreseen requirements for essential afloat support.'

Comment about what might have happened to the Navy if this scenario, with its pooling the merchant fleets of NATO countries, had been in place during the Falklands War or later Gulf War seems unnecessary.

With the loss of the assault ships HMS *Fearless* and *Intrepid*, both designated for eventual sale, and the disappearance of the LSLs from the RFA fleet, the Navy's ability to stage any sort of small war involving amphibious operations would have disappeared completely.

To his credit, Nott realised this after a visit to HMS *Fearless* in November 1981 and both LPDs were reprieved, although the LSLs were still designated for disposal. Alongside this loss of amphibious capacity, disposal of the two Tide-class fast fleet tankers would also have seriously reduced the Navy's ability to remain at sea for extended periods.

The First Sea Lord, Sir Henry Leach, didn't need this spelling out and he fought an articulate and all but hopeless rearguard action on those very grounds.

Then the Argentineans landed on East Falklands.

And on a final, deliciously ironic note, the first redundancy notices were issued to RFA personnel on 2 April, the day Argentina chose to invade Port Stanley.

Despite this, RFA men rushed back to their ships on receipt of those urgent telephone calls, re-stored and headed south unquestioningly, despite the redundancy notices still decorating mantelpieces or sitting, disregarded, in back pockets.

INDEX

Wilson, Brigadier M J A, OBE, MC –
131, 137
Wimpey Seahorse – 88, 142
Woodward, Rear Admiral Sir John
(Sandy) – 4, 7, 8, 43, 88, 92

Yarmouth, HMS – 49, 102, III, II2, I7I,
I72
Yorkshireman (tug) – 47
Young, Capt (RN) B – 76